NVQ Level 3

Children's Care, Learning and Development

2nd Edition   Candidate Handbook

Miranda Walker

Nelson Thornes

Contents

Mandatory units

Optional units

Published in 2009 by:
Nelson Thornes Ltd
Delta Place
27 Bath Road
CHELTENHAM
GL53 7TH
United Kingdom

9 10 11 12 13 / 10 9 8 7 6 5 4 3 2 1

ISBN: 978 1 4085 0441 3

Cover photograph: Jim Wileman

Illustrations by Jane Bottomley and Angela Lumley and Florence Production Ltd

Page make-up by Florence Production Ltd

Printed and bound in Spain by GraphyCems

Acknowledgements

I would like to thank Nick Walker for his endless support, help, encouragement and enthusiasm. Thanks for support also goes to Rachel Davis, Clive Essame, Lesley Sharp, Susan Holding, Steve Morgan and my family: Gill, Bill and Betty Denner and Hayley and Adam Milton. Lastly, thank you to all the children and families I have worked with – you have been an inspiration. (Miranda Walker)

The author and publisher would like to thank the following for the permission to use or adapt copyright material: Childhood Infections and Sites of Injuries, Bruce and Meggit, Child Care and Education, 1997, published by Hodder & Stoughton, pp46-7, p136; The chain of abuse, Take Ten More for Play Modules, 2002, published by Furzeham Publishing, p143; Example of a long-term planning chart and short-term planning chart, Curriculum Guidance for the Foundation Stage, published by QCA, pp233-4; Example of a completed observation profile and case study on a fruit activity, Foundation Stage Profile Handbook, published by DFEE, pp263-4; Introduction to the birth to three matters framework and headings, An Introduction to the Framework in the Birth to Three Matters Material Pack, published by Sure Start, pp297-9; Weaning plan, Dare and O'Donovan, A Practical Guide to Child Nutrition, published by Nelson Thornes, p321.

Photo Credits: © Bubbles / Angela Hampton, p20; Photodisc 18 (NT), p63 (2nd); © Bubbles / Jennie Woodcock, p63 (4th); Scott Baxter / Photodisc 61 (NT), p64 (4th); Jack Hollingsworth / Photodisc 61 (NT), p68 (3rd); Digital Vision PB (NT), p68 (4th); Martial Colomb / Photodisc 61 (NT), p69 (3rd); Photodisc 79 (NT), p75 (2nd); Photodisc 71 (NT), p.76 (1st); Photodisc 79 (NT), p76 (2nd); © Bubbles / Angela Hampton, p76 (3rd); Brenda Byrne / Digital Vision SD (NT), p98; Image 100 CP (NT), p122; © John Walmsley, p125; © Bubbles / Francis Rombout, p130; Digital Vision 10 (NT), p161; © Sally and Richard Greenhill / Alamy, p173; © Bubbles / Jennie Woodcock, p179; © Bubbles / Jennie Woodcock, p184; © Bubbles / Francis Rombout, p210; Image 100 CP (NT), p261; Photodisc 79 (NT), p281; © Bubbles / Jennie Woodcock, p285; © Bubbles / Jennie Woodcock, p342; Photodisc 24 (NT), p391; © Janine Wiedel Photolibrary / Alamy, p401 81a/ Alamy 173, Adam Borkowski/ Fotolia.com 212, Adams Picture Library t/a apl/ Alamy 14, Charlotte Fenton/ Alamy 182, Chris Baker/ Alamy 33, Christina Kennedy/ Alamy 393, Coka/ Fotolia.com 116, Corbis Super RF/ Alamy 3, 159, 326, Deborah Waters/ Alamy 349, Digital Vision/ Alamy 79, Gareth Byrne/ Alamy 391, Ian Miles/ Alamy 259, Ian Shaw/ Alamy 407, image100/ Alamy 335, JLImages/ Alamy 356, JUPITERIMAGES/ BananaStock/ Alamy 310, JUPITERIMAGES/ Brand X/ Alamy 294, JUPITERIMAGES/ Comstock Images/ Alamy 198, Natrow Images/ Alamy 375, PhotoAlto/ Alamy 342, Photodisc/ Alamy 383, Radius Images/ Alamy 310, 416, Radosław Brzozowski - Fotolia.com 24, Slate River Productions/ Alamy 282, Stockbyte/ Alamy 332, Stuart Monk/ Alamy 308, terry harris just greece photo library/ Alamy 369, Vladimir Mucibabic/ iStock.com 185, wonderlandstock/ Alamy 166, Xavier Gallego/ iStock.com 53.

Many thanks to the parents, children and staff at ABC Day Nursery and Playtime Out of School Club, Cullompton, Devon.

Every effort has been made to contact copyright holders and we apologise if any have been overlooked. Should copyright have been unwittingly infringed in this book, the owners should contact the publishers who will make corrections at reprint.

Children's Care, Learning and Development   NVQ 3

Introduction

This book is a guide to the care, learning and development of children from birth to 16 years. It has been written for practitioners and students who are studying for a **level 3 National Vocational Qualification (NVQ)**, or **Scottish Vocational Qualification (SVQ)** in **Children's Care, Learning and Development**. This book is based on the National Occupational Standards, but it will also be useful to students on a range of other courses that relate to the care and education of children. For childcare settings, it is a valuable reference tool that can be used to support the professional development of both practitioners and students.

Contents of the book

This book is divided into 14 units. Each corresponds to a unit of the level 3 NVQ/SVQ in Children's Care, Learning and Development. Full coverage is given of the five mandatory units (CCLD 301–CCLD 305), and of nine optional units (CCLD 306, CCLD 307, CCLD 309, CCLD 310, CCLD 312, CCLD 314, CCLD 318, CCLD 321, CCLD 337). The titles of the units are shown in the table below.

NVQ unit number	Unit title
CCLD 301	Develop and promote positive relationships
CCLD 302	Develop and maintain a healthy, safe and secure environment for children
CCLD 303	Promote children's development
CCLD 304	Reflect on and develop practice
CCLD 305	Protect and promote children's rights
CCLD 306	Plan and organise environments for children and families
CCLD 307	Promote the health and physical development of children
CCLD 309	Plan and implement curriculum frameworks for early education
CCLD 310	Assess children's progress according to curriculum frameworks for early education
CCLD 312	Plan and implement positive environments for babies and children under three years

CCLD 314	Provide physical care that promotes the health and development of babies and children under three years
CCLD 318	Plan for and support self-directed play
CCLD 321	Support children with disabilities or special educational needs and their families
CCLD 337	Create environments that promote positive behaviour

To gain the level 3 award, you must complete the mandatory units and four optional units. This book covers nine optional units that are likely to be chosen by students or practitioners wishing to work in early years childcare and education. This may be within a variety of settings including nurseries, pre-schools and the home. Coverage of an optional unit suitable for those working within out-of-school clubs has also been included (Unit CCLD 318 Plan for and support self-directed play). There is further information about the structure of the NVQ/SVQ award on page xii.

How to use this book

Principles and values

Three principles and nine values are firmly embedded within the National Occupational Standards. These are outlined on page xii. It is important that you understand the principles and values. You should promote them in your practical work with children, and make reference to them as you work through each unit of your qualification. Your assessor will look for evidence that you are committed to the principles and values, and that you apply them in practice.

Assessment

An explanation of the how the NVQ/SVQ is both structured and assessed is given on page xi.

Units and elements

The level 3 qualification is primarily for those who are working in face-to-face roles with children and families, who may have supervisory responsibilities, specialist roles or work unsupervised.

To gain the NVQ/SVQ award, you must demonstrate that you can carry out practical work with children to the appropriate standard. You must also demonstrate that your practical work is underpinned by the appropriate level of knowledge and understanding.

Each unit of the qualification relates to a different area of working with children. Units are divided into elements, which focus on different aspects of the unit. Each element consists of performance criteria, which tell you what you must do competently in your practical work. The performance criteria are numbered for ease of reference. Each unit also has knowledge criteria. These tell you what you need to know and understand to be competent in the unit. The knowledge criteria are also numbered.

This book provides detailed coverage of the performance and knowledge criteria of the units included. The information in the book is divided into elements that correspond to the elements of the qualification. To help you keep track of what you are learning as you use this book, each element begins with the numbers of the knowledge evidence that is covered. The following example shows how the knowledge criteria is given on yellow stickers within the elements:

K2D48.15
K2D49.12

Throughout this book, the term 'parent' is used to refer to a child's primary carer. The term 'practitioner' is used to refer to anyone working with children within early years, childcare or playwork settings.

Practical examples

This feature of the book gives realistic scenarios to help you to understand how your learning can be used in practice. One or two questions are included. Responding to the questions will help you to develop an understanding of how to apply your knowledge to your practical work. Here is a practical example from Unit CCLD 301.

The invitations

Three-year-old Carly goes to nursery. She is having a birthday party. Her dad asks her key worker, Jodie, to supply him with the addresses of Carly's friends, so that he can send out invitations in the post. Jodie explains that this would break confidentiality, but she offers to take the invitations and give them out by hand at the nursery.

➤ *Why did Jodie do this?* **K3C181, K3C183**

Are you ready for assessment?

At the end of each element, there is a section that gives helpful guidance on preparing for assessment. For example:

Are you ready for assessment?

Communicate with children

You need to show that you can communicate with children competently. To do this you will need to be directly observed by your assessor and present other types of evidence. The amount and type of evidence you need to present will vary. You should plan this with your assessor.

Direct observation by your assessor

Observation and/or expert witness testimony is the required assessment method to be used to evidence some of each element in this unit. If your assessor is unable to observe you, s/he will identify an expert in your workplace who will provide testimony of your work-based performance. Usually your assessor or expert witness will observe you in real work activities and this should provide most of the evidence for the performance criteria for the elements in this unit.

Preparing to be observed

You must show your assessor that you can communicate with children appropriately, listening and responding to them and asking questions effectively. You must also show that you can encourage children to ask questions, offer ideas and make suggestions. You must show that you can recognise when there are communication difficulties and adapt the way you communicate accordingly.

Other types of evidence

You will need to present different types of evidence in order to:

- Cover criteria not observed by your assessor
- Show that you have the required knowledge, understanding and skills.

Such evidence could include:

- Work products such as resources/ materials made for use with children
- Case studies, projects, assignments and reflective accounts of your work
- Confidential records such as notes on individual children's communication needs and how these will be met. These should not be placed in your portfolio – they must remain in their usual location and be referred to in the assessor records in your portfolio.

Check your knowledge

This section appears at the end of each unit. A few questions are provided to test your knowledge and understanding of the information that has been given within the unit. The questions relate directly to the knowledge evidence. The numbers of the knowledge evidence are given as you will see in this example:

Check your knowledge

- What techniques of observation are used in your setting?   **K3D206**
- What is 'emotional intelligence'?   **K3D219, K3D220, K3D221**
- What transitions may occur in children's lives between the ages of 0 and 16 years?   **K3T1111**
- Explain how a current theory of play can inform practice.   **K3D210**

Reflective practice

A key component of professional development is learning from past experience. This is known as 'reflective practice'. You need to demonstrate that you can think about your practice, notice areas for development and plan how to improve your knowledge, understanding and skills, as you work through your qualification. To help you achieve this, a 'reflective practice' section is included at the end of each unit. It provides suggestions to help you focus on relevant aspects of your professional development. For example:

Reflective practice

Consider the way in which you usually make resources available to children. Compare this with the guidelines on pages 156–67. Do you need to introduce any changes to your current practice? Make notes in your reflective journal. Draw up a plan of action if necessary.

You will find further information about how to carry out reflective practice in Unit CCLD 304 Reflect on and develop practice.

Legislation

There are differences in the legislation that applies in England, Northern Ireland, Scotland and Wales. The country in which you work is referred to as your 'home country' throughout this book. You must ensure that you know about and understand the legislation that applies to the care and education of children in your home country. You can ask your assessor and/or workplace supervisor about this.

Principles and values of good practice

The principles and values of good practice underpin the National Occupational Standards, and are firmly embedded within them. The three principles are:

1. The welfare of the child is paramount.

2. Practitioners contribute to children's care, learning and development and this is reflected in every aspect of practice and service provision.

3. Practitioners work with parents and families who are partners in the care, learning and development and are the child's first and most enduring educators.

The nine values are:

1. The needs, rights and views of the child are at the centre of all practice and provision.

2. Individuality, difference and diversity are valued and celebrated.

3. Equality of opportunity and anti-discriminatory practice are actively promoted.

4. Children's health and well-being are actively promoted.

5. Children's personal and physical safety is safeguarded, whilst allowing for risk and challenge as appropriate to the capabilities of the child.

6. Self-esteem, reliance and a positive self-image are recognised as essential to every child's development.

7. Confidentiality and agreements about confidential information are respected as appropriate unless a child's protection and well-being are at stake.

8. Professional knowledge, skills and values are shared appropriately in order to enrich the experience of children more widely.

9. Best practice requires reflection and a continuous search for improvement.

The principles and values of good practice are embedded in the content of this book.

Assessment of National Vocational Qualifications

You need to become familiar with the way in which your qualification is structured, and how the assessment process works.

Starting an NVQ/SVQ

To start an NVQ you must register with an Awarding Body. This can be done by registering with an Assessment Centre that has been approved by an Awarding Body to offer the qualification. Colleges, private training organisations and employers may all be approved Assessment Centres. The Awarding Body will check that the Assessment Centre assesses candidates fairly. This ensures that candidates throughout the UK are working to the same standards, no matter which Assessment Centre they are registered with. This helps to maintain high standards in the childcare sector.

Once registered with an Assessment Centre, you will be fully inducted into the qualification. Everything you need to know about how the qualification works will be explained. You will meet your assessor, and you will have the opportunity to talk about your experience and knowledge of children's care, learning and development. It may be appropriate for you to attend a training course, or you may receive coaching, mentoring or tuition as you work.

The assessment process

The National Occupational Standards for **Children's Care, Learning and Development** are statements of the skills, knowledge and understanding needed in childcare employment at different levels. Awarding bodies (organisations that provide and award qualifications) design qualifications that cover these standards. Your qualification is based on the National Occupational Standards for Children's Care, Learning and Development at level 3.

You must show that you can work competently at the level of these standards in order to achieve your qualification. Your practical work will be assessed against the standards within your workplace. The person who assesses you is referred to as your assessor. Your assessor will carry out a series of observations of your work. He or she will also assess your knowledge of children's care, learning and development, to make sure that you know why are doing the things you do. When your assessor has observed your practical work and checked if you have good background knowledge, they will decide if you are competently meeting the relevant standards. They must also check that there is sufficient evidence to show that you meet the standards consistently. If there is not sufficient evidence that you are consistently meeting a standard, you can carry on working towards achieving it, and you will be assessed against the standard again at a later date. Information about providing evidence of your skills, knowledge and understanding is given on page xiii.

When you are ready to think about assessment, your assessor will make an assessment plan with you. You will agree together what will be assessed, how it will assessed, when it will be assessed and who will be involved in the assessment. You will then begin to collect evidence to be used for assessment. This will be placed in a folder, known as a portfolio. Your assessor will explain how you should organise and number your evidence. Some assessment centres keep evidence on computer. If this is the case, the process will be explained.

Once the evidence has been collected, the assessor will check it to see that:

- The appropriate methods of assessment have been used. If so, the evidence is said to be **valid**
- The work is your own, and that any written testimonies have been completed by appropriate people. The appropriate signatures and dates must be included. If so, the evidence is said to be **authentic**
- The work meets the standards of good practice today, the legislative requirements of the home country and the setting's organisational policies. If so, the evidence is said to be **current**
- There is enough evidence to show that you consistently meet the required standards. You must have covered all the performance and knowledge criteria successfully. If so, the evidence is said to be **sufficient.**

After assessing these things, your assessor will give you feedback to let you know how you have got on. There will be an opportunity to review the progress you are making towards your qualification. Details of the feedback meeting will be recorded. As you work through the award, one of the Assessment Centre's Internal Verifiers will check samples of your evidence and assessment records. This is to ensure that you are being assessed properly. After sampling your work, the Internal Verifier will either agree or disagree with your assessor's decision. They may identify areas that need further work, or ask for further clarification.

The structure of NVQs/SVQs

The qualification is broken down into units. As explained, each unit of the qualification relates to a different area of working with children. Units are divided into elements, which focus on different aspects of the unit. Each element consists of performance criteria, which tell you what you must do competently in your practical work. The performance criteria are numbered for ease of reference. Each unit also has knowledge criteria. These tell you what you need to know and understand to become competent in the unit. The knowledge criteria are also numbered.

There are five mandatory units in your qualification, which you must do. They are: CCLD 301, CCLD 302, CCLD 303, CCLD 304, CCLD 305.

There are 40 optional units. Optional means you can choose which unit you do. You only have to do four optional units out of the 40. The optional units are divided into two option groups. You must choose two optional units from option group one, and two optional units from option group one or two. You must choose optional units that suit where you work. You can, for example, only choose optional units concerned with the care of babies if you work directly with babies. You should discuss your choice of optional units with your assessor before starting your qualification.

The optional units in group one are: CCLD 306–CCLD 313.

The optional units in group two are: CCLD 314–CCLD 346.

Nine of the optional units are covered in this book.

Evidence

You will collect evidence to show that you consistently meet the National Occupational Standards. The types of evidence you may use for each element is given in your candidate handbook. In addition, there are tips on providing evidence at the end of each element in this book.

The following can be used as evidence:

- Observation

   This type of evidence is required for some part of all units, and for some part of most elements. Your assessor will observe you working in a series of observations to check that you are working to the correct standards. A written statement giving the details of the assessment will be produced.

- Expert witness testimony

   Occupational experts within your setting can produce written statements of your practice when they have observed you carrying out a specific activity. The expert must understand their role in your NVQ/SVQ. The expert witness must be known to your assessor.

- Witness testimony

   This is a statement written by someone who is not an occupational expert, but who does have knowledge and experience of your work practice. Your assessor will advise you on the use of witness testimony. People likely to write a witness testimony include co-workers and parents of the children with whom you work.

- Simulation

   Simulation is the process of role-playing a situation. This may be used where it is difficult to obtain evidence from a real work situation. Simulations in Children's Care, Learning and Development are only permitted as evidence in certain circumstances. These are specified in the Assessment Strategy and Unit Evidence Requirements. It is also referred to when relevant in the 'Are you ready for assessment?' feature of this book.

- Work products

   You can show your assessor evidence that is produced as part of your everyday work. This includes items such as forms which you are responsible for completing. They can be included in your portfolio.

- Confidential records

   These are records that you complete that contain confidential information. Examples include individual education plans, and information relating to child protection. Confidential records used as evidence must not be placed in your portfolio. They must be left in their usual location. They will be referred to in the assessment records made by your assessor.

- Reflective accounts, case studies, projects, assignments

   These are written explanations of work you have completed. This type of evidence is often used to cover the knowledge criteria, and also to cover performance criteria that are difficult to observe. They can also be a helpful way of providing evidence of events that do not occur very often.

Questioning

Your assessor may ask you to demonstrate your knowledge and understanding by answering questions. These may be written or oral. A record of the questions and answers will be made and kept in your portfolio.

Once you have been found competent in all elements of a unit, that unit is complete. When you have completed the five mandatory units and the four optional units you have chosen, your qualification will be complete. Your Assessment Centre will then give you a certificate from the Awarding Body.

Conclusion

It does take a little while to get used to the assessment process. You may be confused about the way an NVQ/SVQ works and how to provide evidence at first. But don't give up. Your assessor will help you to understand. You will find the assessment process becomes easier once you have made a start. You will soon become familiar with the units, elements and criteria. If you do experience difficulties, ask your assessor for assistance.

Using this book will help you to approach your qualification with confidence. Remember that being a childcare practitioner is an important, valuable and rewarding job. Good luck with your studies!

Develop and promote positive relationships

THE LIBRARY
NORTH WEST KENT COLLEGE
DERING WAY, GRAVESEND

This unit is about developing and promoting positive relationships with children, communicating with children and adults, and fostering positive relationships between children and with other adults. The unit is appropriate for all children's care, learning and development, childcare and playwork settings and services where children and young people are present.

This unit contains four elements:

⌣ **CCLD 301.1** *Develop relationships with children*

⌣ **CCLD 301.2** *Communicate with children*

⌣ **CCLD 301.3** *Support children in developing relationships*

⌣ **CCLD 301.4** *Communicate with adults*

Introduction

The ability to foster good relationships with others is one of the foundation stones of being a good practitioner. It is essential to master the skills of developing and promoting positive relationships with children and adults; this includes family members, colleagues and other professionals.

301.1 — *Develop relationships with children*

K3C154
K3C155
K3M156
K3D157
K3M158
K3P159
K3C160
K3D161
K3D162
K3D164
K3D165
K3D166

⌣ Good working relationships

Opportunities to form, strengthen and promote positive relationships exist in every practitioner's working day. There are many benefits to be gained by practitioners, other adults and children when these opportunities are taken.

Good relationships between colleagues are important. When practitioners respect one another and enjoy a good rapport, the foundations of a pleasant atmosphere are laid. This is good for everyone involved in the setting – the practitioners, children, parents and carers.

Establishing a good relationship with parents and carers allows trust to develop. It also opens the lines of communication, and paves the way for working in partnership. In addition, it is worth noting that all adults within the setting are role models for the children.

Children may imitate the way in which they see adults relating, whether this is positive or negative.

Relating to and interacting with children

Children's experience of a setting will largely depend on the relationships that they make with practitioners and their peers. There are legal requirements covering the way in which you relate to children and how you interact with them.

The key pieces of legislation are outlined below. Links are given where appropriate to direct you to further information in other units. You are advised to read the further information in conjunction with this unit:

- United Nations Convention on the Rights of the Child (see page 119 Unit CCLD 305 Protect and promote children's rights)
- Human Rights Act 1998 (see page 122 Unit CCLD 305 Protect and promote children's rights)
- Data Protection Act 1998 (see pages 5–6)
- Protection of Children Act 1999 (see pages 132–3 Unit CCLD 305 Protect and promote children's rights)
- Every Child Matters (see pages 225–31Unit CCLD 309 Plan and implement curriculum frameworks for early education).

 Link   **Unit CCLD 305** Protect and promote children's rights

Helping children to feel welcome and valued

Starting at a new setting can be daunting for any child. It can be particularly hard for young children who are not used to being away from their parents or carers. Learning how to interact with children in a way that makes them feel welcomed and valued can make all the difference. We have all been in the position of being 'new' at some time. Even as adults we are likely to feel anxious when we start work at a new setting. We feel relieved when we are made to feel welcome. We start to settle as we get to know people and the new environment. The same is true for children. However, the situation can be made even more difficult for children who are learning English as an additional language. They may not be able to understand instructions, or be able to ask questions. A child could feel excluded without adult support.

The process of introducing new children to a setting is most successful when it is gradual. Ideally, children should accompany parents or carers on their first visit to view the setting. The child's initial response to the setting can then be considered when deciding to register the child. This can be very important for older children, who may ultimately settle more easily if they have been involved in the decision-making process. If a child's family is also learning English as an additional language, the setting can look for an interpreter to help them to communicate with the family at the important initial stage when crucial information is exchanged and people need to get to know each other.

Depending on a child's age, abilities and levels of confidence, children will usually be accompanied by their parent or carer on a second, longer visit. This time, the child should

Key Terms

Key worker

A person appointed to take a special interest in the welfare of a particular child. Most key workers will look after the interests of several children within a setting, taking the main responsibility for liaising with their parents and carers.

be invited to participate in the activities available. The child's key worker should join in sensitively. (A key worker is a practitioner who takes a special interest in the welfare of a particular child and their family, forming an effective bond. This is explained in more detail in Unit CCLD 312 Plan and implement positive environments for babies and children under three years.) Depending on the child, the practitioner may interact directly, or simply play close by to give the child the sense of sharing an experience with the key worker. This may also entice the child to interact with the key worker directly through play. This is a good opportunity for the key worker to get to know parents and carers too. It is reassuring for the child to feel that their primary carer is comfortable with their key worker.

On subsequent visits, the parent or carer should leave the child in the care of the key worker. At first this can be done for just a few minutes. The length of time can then be gradually increased until the child attends a whole session alone. Children will be ready for this at different rates. It is important that parents and carers say goodbye, and it can be helpful to establish a routine. Perhaps a parent will go and hang up their child's coat with them every day, and then say goodbye, waving through the window as they leave. Routines help many children to feel secure.

All children need to feel welcomed and valued every day, even if have they have been attending a setting for some time. The following strategies help:

- Verbally greeting each child by name, with a smile
- Not asking questions if a child prefers not to talk on their arrival. (You can still chat to them using statements, i.e. telling them about the activities planned for the session)
- Sensitively taking care of children who may become upset on arrival
- Designing the layout of the environment so there is an easy, welcoming passage in
- Encouraging children to play together or with you, while remembering that some children may want to watch on the fringes of the group until they settle
- Telling older children which of their friends are expected
- Having familiar/favourite activities or resources easily visible or displayed enticingly
- Having comfortable, quiet areas as well as areas for being busy
- Displaying welcoming signs and/or symbols (pictures of smiling faces near the entrance for example)
- Making families feel welcome too.

It is important to offer children reassurance

Children will unknowingly pick up and absorb numerous subtle signals from the way in which practitioners interact with them. These signals add up, influencing a child's overall sense of whether they are valued within the setting. In turn, this affects children's self-esteem and confidence, as well as how comfortable they feel. Factors that affect a child's sense of being valued include the way in which you:

- Look at children
- Talk and listen with children
- Respond to children
- Show your respect for children
- Meet children's needs
- Use facial expressions
- Use body language.

Think of the ways people interact with you – what makes you feel valued, or otherwise? This links with Element 301.2.

Anti-discriminatory practice

All practitioners must understand the importance of providing equal opportunities and promoting anti-discriminatory practice. This is explained in detail on pages 119–30 of Unit CCLD 305 Protect and promote children's rights, and throughout Unit CCLD 321 Support children with disabilities or special educational needs and their families. You should read this information in conjunction with this unit.

Decision-making and negotiation

As children grow up, they can increasingly be involved in making decisions that affect them and the provision. Learning to negotiate is part of the decision-making process. There is further information in Unit CCLD 306 Plan and organise environments for children and families.

 Link **Unit CCLD 305** Protect and promote children's rights
Unit CCLD 321 Support children with disabilities or special educational needs and their families
Unit CCLD 306 Plan and organise environments for children and families

Confidentiality

Key Terms

Provision
The setting providing childcare. This could be a nursery, out-of-school club, childminder's home, etc.

Early years practitioners are often aware of many personal details about the families that they work with. You may be given confidential information verbally, and you may have access to confidential records, depending on your position. Respecting confidentiality is extremely important. Passing on information when you should not do so can have serious consequences. It can upset people. Trust may be lost, causing damage to working relationships. Your professional reputation can be affected, and disciplinary action may be taken by employers. Make sure that you read and understand your setting's confidentiality policy. It will explain your organisational confidentiality procedures.

You should treat any personal information about the people at your setting as confidential – that includes information relating to children, parents, carers and colleagues. Types of confidential information include:

- Personal details such as those recorded on the registration form, including addresses, telephone numbers and medical information
- Information about children's individual development and individual needs, including the type of information held in development reports and on special educational needs registers
- Details about family or social relationships or circumstances, including things you may know about the current or past relationships within families, or details about people's jobs or events in their lives
- Financial information, including details about how children's places are funded, and how fees are paid
- Information relating to past incidents or experiences of a sensitive nature. For instance, a family may have suffered a traumatic event. Or perhaps you know that social workers, therapists or other professionals are working within a family.

Sensitive information should be made available to practitioners on a 'need-to-know basis'. That means that different practitioners in the same setting will not necessarily have access to the same information. Therefore, you should not discuss confidential matters with colleagues unless you are sure that it is appropriate to do so, and it can be done privately. If you are not sure about any issue of a confidential nature, check with your supervisor before disclosing information to anyone else.

Holly passes on information selectively

Holly works as team leader of the nursery's toddler room. Parent Mr Jacobs confides in Holly. He tells her that he and his wife are spending time apart after some family problems, but that this is not to be made 'common knowledge'. He says that that he and his son Tom are staying with Tom's grandparents. They will be collecting him for a few days. Holly checks the registration form. The grandparents need to be authorised to collect Tom, and so they are added to the form. Holly tells her staff that Tom will be collected by his grandparents, but since there is no need for staff to know the reason why, Holly does not mention the Jacobs' family problems.

➤ *Why does Holly not mention the family problems?* **K3M158**

Sometimes, confidential information needs to be discussed with a parent or carer. In this case, you should arrange to talk privately, ideally in another room. It is your responsibility not to reveal private matters to others who do not need to know. You should also consider whether it is appropriate for the parent's child to hear the discussion.

Confidential information is also contained within the records of a setting. These could be paper based or kept in computer files. This data must be handled with care and stored securely. Do not leave sensitive paperwork or files where people who do not need to know will have access to them. Parents and carers should be aware of, and party to, information held about them and their children.

If a setting stores records on computer, they must be registered on the Data Protection Register according to the Data Protection Act of 1984/1998. To summarise, those registered must only collect information that is:

- Accurate at the time
- Obtained legally and without deceit
- Relevant for its purpose.

Collected information should:

- Only be used for the purpose explained when it was collected
- Be kept confidential from anyone who does not have the right to see it
- Be kept up to date
- Be made available to the person it is about – individuals are entitled to see information held about them
- Be kept securely – there must be security measures in place protecting against unauthorised access
- Only be kept as long as is necessary.

Key Terms

Disclosing
The process of passing on confidential information.

Disclosing information

You must respect confidential information about children, as long as doing so will not affect their welfare. If, for example, you suspected that a child was being abused, you would have a duty to disclose this information, but only to the relevant person or authority – for further details see Unit CCLD 305 Protect and promote children's rights.

Link **Unit CCLD 305** Protect and promote children's rights

Balancing children's needs

Every child is an individual. All children have different, individual needs whatever their age, gender, ethnicity or ability. To thrive within settings, children must receive the care and attention they need from practitioners. All children will need support, encouragement and practical help – but the areas in which they need these things will differ. It all depends on the individual child, and the circumstances they are in.

Treating all children the same is not treating all children fairly, because children have different needs. When working with a group of children, it is the practitioner's aim to meet everyone's needs. This means giving all children the attention that they need and deserve. Practitioners must learn to give attention to individual children in a way that is fair to them but also fair to the rest of the group as a whole.

Children naturally attract the attention of adults when they behave in certain ways. All sorts of behaviour, desirable and undesirable, grabs adult attention. Children who tend to exhibit that behaviour could be given the most attention. For instance, some children frequently approach adults, initiating contact and conversations themselves, while others do not. Infants that cry frequently may be picked up and held more often than quieter babies. Children who are misbehaving are likely to receive plenty of adult time and attention. The following strategies help practitioners to give attention to individual children in a way that is fair to them and the group as a whole:

- Developing an awareness of the attention that is given to individual children
- Developing an awareness of behaviour that attracts attention
- Planning strategies for handling attention seeking
- Considering how the attention given to individuals affects the group as a whole

- Paying attention to those who do not demand it
- Operating a key-worker system, so each child's welfare is given special consideration by one person who knows them well
- Planning time to work on a one-to-one basis with each child
- Avoiding displays of favouritism
- Taking into consideration that some children will want physical contact, while others will want to be more independent.

Are you ready for assessment?

Develop relationships with children

You need to show that you can competently develop relationships with children. To do this you will need to be directly observed by your assessor and present other types of evidence. The amount and type of evidence you need to present will vary. You should plan this with your assessor.

Direct observation by your assessor

Observation and/or expert witness testimony is the required assessment method to be used to evidence some of each element in this unit. If your assessor is unable to observe you, s/he will identify an expert in your workplace who will provide testimony of your work-based performance. Usually your assessor or expert witness will observe you in real work activities and this should provide most of the evidence for the performance criteria for the elements in this unit.

Preparing to be observed

You must show your assessor that you can make children feel welcomed and valued, and that you can negotiate with them about their needs and preferences. You must also show that you can adapt your behaviour to suit individual children, ensuring your behaviour with children is always appropriate, and applying inclusive practice. You must show that you can give attention fairly to all children and respect confidential information about them.

Other types of evidence

You will need to present different types of evidence in order to:

- Cover criteria not observed by your assessor
- Show that you have the required knowledge, understanding and skills.

Such evidence could include:

- Work products such as resources/materials made for use with children
- Case studies, projects, assignments and reflective accounts of your work
- Confidential records such as individual children's participation plans. These should not be placed in your portfolio – they must remain in their usual location and be referred to in the assessor records in your portfolio.

Element 301.2 Communicate with children

Communicating well with children

The way in which you talk with children communicates much more than just the words that you say. By communicating well, you can demonstrate good use of language and show children that you value what they say and feel. It is important to master the basics of communicating effectively with children. All successful practitioners are able to develop good relationships with children. We build relationships through communication and interaction. Children also learn from their conversations with adults.

Considering communication needs and abilities

Practitioners should consider individual children's communication needs and abilities. There are likely to be a range of these within any group. Once you are aware of them, you can select methods of communication that will suit the children. Much will depend on children's age and stage of development, so you will need a sound knowledge of communication development – see Unit CCLD 303 Promote children's development. There is further information in Element 312.2.

Link **Unit CCLD 303** Promote children's development

Communication difficulties

Practitioners should learn to recognise when children have communication difficulties. This is important because the earlier a difficulty can be detected, the earlier a child can get the specialist support that they need. Some children with minor or temporary difficulties progress quickly when they receive the appropriate help. Children may experience difficulties speaking, hearing or understanding, or they may lack a general interest in communicating.

Hearing impairments can be present at birth or they may develop later on. Signs that young children or babies cannot hear properly include:

- Reduced vocal noises

   A lack of babbling and other sounds
- Reduced alertness

   The child is less responsive to external stimulus and sounds. Children may appear to be 'in their own world'
- Difficult to comfort, soothe or distract verbally

   Children are not comforted by the soothing noises made instinctively by adults.

It can be hard to detect when an older child develops a hearing impairment, particularly if the onset is gradual or temporary. Signs include:

- Attention seems to drift/lack of concentration

   A child may be hearing some sounds but not others. Some sounds may seem muffled, distorted or go unheard. This causes children's concentration to lapse.

This may be particularly noticeable at story time or circle time. When children concentrating, they may look intensively at the speaker's face in an effor follow what is said

- Difficulty in following instructions

   Instructions are not fully heard. It may also be difficult to catch a child's attenti because they do not always hear their name called. This can be misconstrued the child simply being very absorbed in their current activity, or not wishing t comply with instructions. Children may find it particularly difficult to fully hea what is said to them when there is background noise – the sound of a group of children at play for instance, or music playing

- Appearing isolated or withdrawn

   A child may appear 'lost in their own world'

- Little interest in activities where careful listening is required

   Listening to the radio, watching television or following story tapes for example

- Difficulties with speech

   Children's speech may be unclear. They may mispronounce familiar words that sound alike.

If you suspect that a child has a communication difficulty, you should tell the appropriate colleague or colleagues at your setting, in line with your setting's policies and procedures. Depending on your own position, this could include the child's key worker, your supervisor and the appointed SENCO (special educational needs co-ordinator). The appropriate person should tell parents or carers about the concerns. It is likely that parents will raise the issue with a doctor or health visitor. The child may then be referred on to a specialist such as a speech therapist or a psychologist.

Practitioners must be sensitive to the communication needs of children. It may be necessary to adapt communication methods to suit children's needs. It is helpful to find out what you can about specific difficulties, and for the setting to liaise with families and other professionals about communication strategies. Children's language and communication difficulties or delays could be affected by the following factors.

Medical and genetic causes

For various reasons a wide range of medical and genetic conditions can lead to communication problems. For example:

- Some conditions, such as those on the autistic spectrum, are synonymous with a lack of interest in communicating with other people
- Others lead to developmental delays, and so communication is also delayed
- Some children are born deaf or with a hearing impairment
- Children with a cleft pallet often have difficulties with pronunciation
- Some medical conditions may only affect communication temporarily – as in the case of children with Bell's palsy for instance, where speech is affected while the condition lasts
- Many children experience a temporary hearing difficulty after a cold as fluid can build up in the ear. Grommets are devices that drain such fluid – children who experience frequent build ups may have a grommet fitted to the ear

Communicating via sign language

- Some children with communication difficulties are taught to use sign language. It is beneficial for all practitioners to learn some key signs. You can take sign language courses and workshops.

Environmental causes

- Some children are not sufficiently exposed to language. If adults do not interact and talk with children regularly, children's communication opportunities are limited. Language may be delayed or limited because children have not had enough experience of using and hearing language. Providing an environment that is rich in language and communication will encourage children's development. Make time to talk with individual children.

- Some children are shy. They may be happy to talk with familiar adults at home, but reluctant to speak in front of people they do not know. They may be nervous of talking within groups of children, preferring to listen quietly. Shy children need understanding and support. Give them plenty of opportunities to communicate – do not just assume that they will not want to talk. However, while gentle encouragement is appropriate, you should not push shy children to speak – avoid situations when the whole group is waiting for them to answer for instance. This may cause a great deal of anxiety, only adding to a child's reluctance to speak, and leading to a desire to avoid group times.

Stuttering and stammering

- Some children start to stutter or stammer early on in their language development. This is reasonably common. It can often be attributed to the fact that children cannot talk as fast as they are able to think, and this causes them to stumble over their words. Adults should give children the time they need to finish their words or sentences. Avoid interrupting children and finishing their sentences for them. It is counterproductive; it encourages children to rush what

they say even more, because they expect not to be given adequate time to sp
slowly *and* finish all they have to say. Childhood stutters and stammers often
away, but they can progress into adulthood too, or develop later on.

There is further relevant information in Unit CCLD 321 Support children with disab
ties or special educational needs and their families, and in Unit CCLD 312 Plan a
implement positive environments for babies and children under three years.

> **Link**
>
> **Unit CCLD 321** Support children with disabilities or special educational needs and
> their families
> **Unit CCLD 312** Plan and implement positive environments for babies and children
> under three years

Learning two or more languages

We live in a culturally diverse society, so it is important for practitioners to recognise
that many children will learn more than one language.

- Children who are learning two or more languages at the same time sometimes
  show a delay in their communication. This is generally put down to the fact that
  they are absorbing two languages – or twice as much. However, with support,
  children's overall communication development need not be affected.

- Some experts believe that children pick up a second language more easily if it is
  introduced to them after they have mastered the basic use of one language.

- Someone who speaks two languages is known as bilingual. Someone who can use
  three or more languages is multilingual.

- Children tend to learn languages best by simply absorbing them naturally. This
  happens when people frequently interact and talk with children in a language.

- Bilingual and multilingual children may confuse languages at times, mixing up
  simple words, sentences or phrases. This might be because they have not yet
  learnt the particular word they want in the language they are currently speaking.
  For instance, if a child usually eats their meals at home where they speak only
  Italian, they may not know 'mealtime' words in English, even though they speak
  English at their pre-school every morning. So when they play with a tea set at
  pre-school, they may introduce some Italian words into their spoken English.
  Word games and activities (such as picture lotto) can help fill children's
  vocabulary gaps.

- It is thought that children learn to separate different languages most easily when
  they clearly identify them with people and places. For instance, if grandparents
  only talk to their grandson in Chinese, he is likely to only communicate back in
  that language. If a child only speaks English at a setting, they are less likely to
  switch between English and their home language when they are there. Difficulties
  are more likely to occur when children hear adults switching in and out of
  languages frequently when they talk.

Key Terms

Bilingual
Someone who speaks
two languages.

Multilingual
Someone who speaks
three or more
languages.

You may speak just one language with a bilingual or multilingual child, but it is
important to recognise that they are developing their communication skills in other
languages too. This achievement should be acknowledged. Bilingual and multilingual
settings should ensure all languages spoken are recognised and valued as part of
children's culture. The languages we speak are part of our identity, and not to value a

child's language is not to value part of that child. By broadly celebrating cultural diversity, settings show that they value different languages. For further information see Unit CCLD 305 Protect and promote children's rights.

Unit CCLD 305 Protect and promote children's rights

Games such as lotto can help to fill gaps in children's vocabulary

Active listening

Listening well is important because it impacts on the quality of the communication between you and the children in your care. It demonstrates that you value what children say and feel. This in turn impacts on children's levels of confidence and self-esteem. Practice active listening by employing the following strategies:

- Let children see you are interested in what they are saying

  Establish eye contact, getting down to the children's level whenever necessary. Smile and nod encouragingly if appropriate

- Give children time

  Children need time to formulate their ideas as they speak. Listen for long enough to let them finish what they have to say, even if they need to pause for thought

- Ask children questions about their topic

  This encourages children to talk further (and to think). They will know you are interested if you are asking for more information

- Clarify and confirm

  You can also ask questions to check you are following what a child is telling you. Making sure you are interpreting correctly is part of listening well. You can repeat the essence of what a child says, asking afterwards, 'Is that right?' Or you can ask clarifying questions, for instance, 'So you borrowed three books from the library on Saturday?'

Key Terms

Active listening

The process of employing techniques to consciously demonstrate that you are listening during conversation.

Showing empathy

An active demonstration by one person, which shows that they identify with the feelings of another person.

- React to what children say

  Show empathy for children's feelings when they are expressed. Be aware of y[our] facial expressions – look happy for children, or concerned, or whatever appropriate

- Respond

  Make sure that you answer children when they talk to you. Even if they have no[t] asked you a direct question, you should still respond appropriately, perhaps just t[o] say, 'That's interesting' or, 'That sounds like fun'. These acknowledgements are important. They let children know that you have received their communication, and that you appreciated their message.

The following types of behaviour could indicate to children that you do not value their ideas and feelings:

- Not really listening
- Not making eye contact
- Looking bored
- Not contributing to the conversation
- Not responding
- Not acknowledging or answering
- Interrupting
- Rushing children to get to the point
- Not acting upon children's ideas
- Not thanking or praising children for their contributions.

Sometimes, particularly in group discussions, children will be keen to share their thoughts and may interrupt one another. Allowing interruptions sends the message that one child's thoughts are more important than another's. When a child interrupts, try acknowledging them, but encouraging them to wait. You might say for instance, 'Hold on to that idea Maria. Let's finish listening to Declan, and then we'll hear from you.'

Asking questions, offering ideas and making suggestions

It is important to encourage children to ask questions. It promotes curiosity and inquisitiveness, which enhances children's thirst for learning. Asking questions is a key way for children to check their understanding and expand their knowledge. It also gets children involved in two-way conversation, encouraging them to practise active listening themselves.

Encouraging children to share their ideas and suggestions has several benefits. Like asking questions, the process requires children to think about, and engage with, the topic or task at hand. This has the potential to deepen children's understanding and learning. Whenever children offer an idea they are actively participating and joining in. When their own suggestions are acted upon, children are likely to feel valued, appreciated and motivated. Children can also be encouraged to suggest ideas and then test them. This promotes the skills of investigation. (Perhaps children have suggested ways of sinking a toy boat in the water tray – they can then try out their ideas and find out what actually sinks the boat.)

You can encourage children to ask questions and to share their ideas and suggestions by:

- Inviting them to

  'Has anyone got a question they'd like to ask?' or, 'Can you suggest some places we could visit on our summer trips?'

- Role modelling

  Let children hear you put forward your own ideas and questions

- Planning questions with children

  For instance, if a visitor is coming to the setting, you can plan questions to ask them beforehand. What do children want to find out?

- Having a suggestion box

  This is popular with older children

- Responding positively when children ask questions or make suggestions

  Answer questions fully. Praise children's efforts, and thank children for their contributions, 'I'm glad you asked me that' or, 'What a good idea!'

- Giving opportunities for children to listen to one another

  Children may be inspired by each other's ideas.

Children
communicating

Increasingly, settings are introducing 'consultation and participation' policies. These set out an organisation's intentions to consult with children by seeking their opinions, ideas and suggestions as a matter of course, and by involving children in the decision-making process. Groups may consult children about many aspects of the provision, including the rules, activities and resources. There is more about this in Unit CCLD 318 Plan for and support self-directed play.

 Link   **Unit CCLD 318** Plan for and support self-directed play

Ravi gets the ideas flowing

Ravi is a playworker at an out-of-school club. He has been asked to plan activities for the coming non-pupil day. The children have voted for a beach theme. Ravi gathers the group in a circle. He sticks a big sheet of paper to the wall. He asks the children for their beach activity ideas, making a couple of suggestions himself to get the ball rolling. He lets the children know that they need lots of ideas to choose from later. Soon the children are calling out suggestions, and Ravi writes them all down, thanking each contributor. At this stage, the group is not worrying about how they would carry out the activities, or if the ideas have merit – they are simply getting them all out in the open. Consequently, the suggestions come thick and fast. At the end of the activity, the group have plenty of ideas to choose from.

➤ *How does Ravi's activity support children effectively?* **K3D164, K3C170, K3C171**

Are you ready for assessment?

Communicate with children

You need to show that you can communicate with children competently. To do this you will need to be directly observed by your assessor and present other types of evidence. The amount and type of evidence you need to present will vary. You should plan this with your assessor.

Direct observation by your assessor

Observation and/or expert witness testimony is the required assessment method to be used to evidence some of each element in this unit. If your assessor is unable to observe you, s/he will identify an expert in your workplace who will provide testimony of your work-based performance. Usually your assessor or expert witness will observe you in real work activities and this should provide most of the evidence for the performance criteria for the elements in this unit.

Preparing to be observed

You must show your assessor that you can communicate with children appropriately, listening and responding to them and asking questions effectively. You must also show that you can encourage children to ask questions, offer ideas and make suggestions. You must show that you can recognise when there are communication difficulties and adapt the way you communicate accordingly.

Other types of evidence

You will need to present different types of evidence in order to:

• Cover criteria not observed by your assessor

• Show that you have the required knowledge, understanding and skills.

Such evidence could include:

• Work products such as resources/ materials made for use with children

• Case studies, projects, assignments and reflective accounts of your work

• Confidential records such as notes on individual children's communication needs and how these will be met. These should not be placed in your portfolio – they must remain in their usual location and be referred to in the assessor records in your portfolio.

Element
301.3

Support children in developing relationships

K3C173
K3D174
K3D175
K3D176
K3D177
K3D178
K3D179
K3C180

Children need to discover how to develop positive relationships with each other, and with adults. Through experience children begin to understand other people's feelings and learn about acceptable ways of behaving. Children will need the support and encouragement of caring adults as they develop their social skills.

Valuing and encouraging positive relationships

It is worth noting that most children display a very strong need to be liked by other people. Children want to be accepted, and they pay attention to messages that tell them what is and is not acceptable to other people. This process is known as 'socialisation'. It takes two distinct forms. Primary socialisation (sometimes called 'initial socialisation') occurs first, as children learn, from their parents or primary carers, how to behave within their family and/or home. Secondary socialisation occurs as children learn, from people outside of their family or home, how to behave in society. In the case of settings this may be from other children, practitioners and other adults, including other children's parents and carers, visitors and outside professionals.

Practitioners are ideally positioned to promote children's secondary socialisation by encouraging and supporting positive relationships between children and adults. At the same time, you can help children to understand the value and importance of developing such relationships. This is worthwhile because it enhances children's motivation to form friendships, to develop rapports and to behave in socially acceptable ways. Remember, actually experiencing the benefits of developing positive relationships with others is by far the best way for children to learn the value of relationships. You can help by:

Key Terms

Primary socialisation

Occurs when children learn, from their parents or primary carers, how to behave within their family and/or home.

Secondary socialisation

Occurs as children learn, from people outside of their family or home, how to behave in society.

- Making all adults aware of the importance of promoting positive relationships between themselves and the children

- Inviting appropriate visitors into the setting to interact with children (under the supervision of staff)

- Introducing children to stories that promote friendship, citizenship and community spirit, featuring characters who celebrate individuality

- Talking with children about how to help people, and how to be a friend

- Giving children the opportunity to undertake a range of activities in pairs, small groups and large groups as appropriate to their age and stage of development

- Introducing older children to teamwork activities, and utilising activities that value individuality

- Giving children opportunities to help

- Praising children when they behave in socially acceptable ways

- Encouraging children to participate in activities that help them to get to know each other better

- Demonstrating that you respect other people's individuality.

Behaviour policies and boundaries

All registered settings are required to have a behaviour policy in place. The purpose of the policy is to identify the types of behaviour that the setting considers to be both appropriate and inappropriate. There should be a statement addressing how the setting encourages appropriate behaviour, and how it deals with inappropriate behaviour when it occurs. It is important that the policy is based on the values of fairness and anti-discriminatory practice. You should familiarise yourself with your setting's policy, and be confident that you fully understand it. This is important as practitioners deal with behaviour constantly. If practitioners do not act consistently on matters of behaviour, children become confused about what is expected of them.

If you consider all of the activities offered, there will be many rules at any setting. Lots of them will be connected with keeping children safe. There may be rules about how many children can play on the climbing frame at once for example, or about removing shoes when visiting a baby room. Over time, children will pick up the cues for how they should behave during different activities.

However, it is usual for settings to draw up a short list of the main rules that underpin the values of the setting, and guide general behaviour. Some settings refer to their list as a 'code of conduct', and others use the term 'boundaries.' This list may be displayed as visual reminder of the boundaries which should apply to everyone within the setting, including all adults. Older children may be able to read the boundaries, but pictures and symbols can also be used in conjunction with words. In any case, it will be essential to discuss the boundaries with children, as appropriate to their age and stage of development.

Playground rules

Older children can be actively involved in devising the boundaries with practitioners. This helps them to think carefully about acceptable and unacceptable behaviour. It also involves them in the decision-making process, and provides opportunity for discussion. There is also the opportunity for negotiation where appropriate. (Some boundaries will not be negotiable – those relating to safety, for instance.) Involving older children in devising the boundaries helps to give them a sense of ownership of their setting, and it shows respect for their opinions. Older children may also be more willing to follow boundaries they have helped to design.

Remember that:

- Children understand boundaries best when they are expressed simply, and there are not too many to keep track of
- Your aim should be to help children not just to know and follow each boundary, but to understand why it exists.

It is good practice to phrase boundaries in a positive way whenever possible. A list of things *not* to do will not tell children what they *should* do. For instance, if you were to say, 'Don't hurt other people', you would be focusing on the inappropriate behaviour that children should avoid. It would be better to say, 'Please be kind and respect other people'. You then focus on the appropriate way to behave, and you can talk about why children should be kind and respectful, and ways in which they can achieve that.

Promoting positive behaviour

Information on how to promote positive behaviour is given on pages 403–10 of Unit CCLD 337 Create environments that promote positive behaviour.

Link   **Unit CCLD 337** Create environments that promote positive behaviour

Challenging behaviour

All adults have felt frustration when it comes to relationships, the behaviour of other people and keeping to rules and regulations. Children are no different. They have even less experience of life to draw on than adults, which is worth noting. While you should have high expectations of children, make sure they are realistic.

All children occasionally display challenging behaviour. Young children learn through repetition, and it is natural for children to test their boundaries as they grow up and enter new stages of development. Practitioners should anticipate this, and have agreed strategies in place to challenge and deal with inappropriate behaviour. It is important to be familiar with some common factors that may affect children's behaviour patterns as this may influence the way in which behaviour is dealt with. Children may be reacting to:

- Tiredness
- A heightened sense of excitement
- Boredom
- Illness
- Hunger or thirst

- Changes at home (living circumstances within the home or moving home)
- Changes in routine (different timings or layout of environment, for instance)
- New children or adults at setting
- Temperature (feeling too hot or cold, or changes in the weather)
- Lack of opportunity for physical play.

More serious factors may lead to prolonged periods of challenging behaviour:

- Bereavement
- The child becoming disabled or seriously/chronically ill
- A close family member becoming disabled or seriously/chronically ill
- Parents' relationship breaking down
- Parents becoming separated or divorced
- Parent/s beginning new serious relationships
- Becoming part of a step family
- Having new carers.

Practitioners who frequently praise children for their positive behaviour are practising the best strategy of all for dealing with inappropriate behaviour – avoidance. The more you reinforce appropriate behaviour, the less challenging behaviour you will have to deal with. There is further information in Unit CCLD 337 Create environments that promote positive behaviour. You should read that unit in conjunction with this chapter.

 Link   **Unit CCLD 337** Create environments that promote positive behaviour

Strategies for managing behaviour

It is essential that you understand what strategies are acceptable and unacceptable when dealing with behaviour, and that you become confident in your ability to handle challenging behaviour appropriately. This is explained in Unit CCLD 337 Create environments that promote positive behaviour. Brief guidelines to appropriate strategies for different types of behaviour are outlined below.

- Attention seeking

  Children may throw tantrums, cry frequently or refuse to settle at activities for long unless an adult is beside them. Children may be hostile or jealous towards another person receiving attention. Children displaying this type of behaviour may be feeling insecure and in need of adult reassurance. However, they may simply be used to lots of adult attention.

  Strategy: Go out of your way to praise positive behaviour, and try to ignore inappropriate behaviour when possible. Otherwise, you reward the inappropriate behaviour with the attention the child is seeking

- Aggressive/destructive behaviour

  Children may hurt others, by hitting or kicking. They may throw or kick over equipment or furniture. Children may be experiencing frustration, and may have been feeling unhappy for some time. This behaviour has often 'built up' with older children, but may be more spontaneous in younger children.

Strategy: Be firm and in control, to stop the child becoming out of control. Calm the child quickly, in a quiet place if possible. Children who have lost control may be quite scared, and eventually tearful. When the child is ready, find out the source of the upset and resolve the issue. Talk with children about the consequences of their behaviour

- Offensive comments

    Children swear or use offensive words or comments that they have heard. They may not understand what they are saying.

    Strategy: Tell children why their words are unacceptable within the setting, making it clear that they cause hurt and upset. This also applies to name calling, which should also be regarded as completely unacceptable and should be taken seriously.

In all cases it is important to encourage children to acknowledge the feelings of other people they may have hurt, and for them to apologise. They can also do what they can to make up for it if appropriate (known as 'making restitution').

Dealing with conflict

When conflict arises between children, it is a good opportunity for practitioners to encourage children to think about the situation carefully, but much depends on the children's age, needs and abilities. With encouragement, older children will often be able to sort out their own conflicts. They will be familiar with finding fair compromises, and can sometimes be quite creative in their approach to resolution.

Younger children will need much more support, and perhaps a practitioner to start them off. Encourage children to identify the problem as they see it, and then help them to hear the other side of the argument, so that they can understand the feelings of other people. Ask children, 'What do you think we can do about it now?' If they cannot think of a solution, you could suggest one or two and help them to consider their options.

Children who are upset will need sensitive comforting – they often begin to feel better if they receive an apology – but they should only get one if it is due to them of course!

Friends are often very good at comforting one another. Most children will show concern if someone else is upset, even toddlers.

Friends are good at comforting one another

Element 301.3

Are you ready for assessment?

Support children in developing relationships

You need to show that you can competently support children in developing relationships. To do this you will need to be directly observed by your assessor and present other types of evidence. The amount and type of evidence you need to present will vary. You should plan this with your assessor.

Direct observation by your assessor

Observation and/or expert witness testimony is the required assessment method to be used to evidence some of each element in this unit. If your assessor is unable to observe you, s/he will identify an expert in your workplace who will provide testimony of your work-based performance. Usually your assessor or expert witness will observe you in real work activities and this should provide most of the evidence for the performance criteria for the elements in this unit.

Preparing to be observed

You must show your assessor that you can support children in developing agreements about ways of behaving and that you can encourage other adults to have positive relationships with children. You must show that you can support children in understanding the feelings of others, and support children who have been upset by others. You must also show that you can effectively encourage children to sort out conflict for themselves.

Other types of evidence

You will need to present different types of evidence in order to:

- Cover criteria not observed by your assessor
- Show that you have the required knowledge and understanding and skills.

Such evidence could include:

- Work products such as resources/materials made for use with children
- Case studies, projects, assignments and reflective accounts of your work
- Confidential records such as details of individual children's behaviour goals and programmes. These should not be placed in your portfolio – they must remain in their usual location and be referred to in the assessor records in your portfolio.

Element 301.4   *Communicate with adults*

K3C181
K3P182
K3C183
K3C184
K3C185
K3C186

Establishing positive relationships with adults

Practitioners must establish positive relationships with other adults within their setting. This includes colleagues, other professionals, parents, carers and other family members. This is important for a number of reasons.

Colleagues and other professionals

Positive working relationships lead to a pleasant, comfortable atmosphere in the working environment. This is beneficial to the staff and also the children because the practitioner's working environment is the child's play and learning space. When positive relationships are formed it is easier for colleagues to give and receive trust, support, help, advice, information and encouragement. It is more likely that any problems arising between colleagues will be positively approached and resolved. It is also more likely that skills and knowledge will be shared. In short, good teamwork depends on positive working relationships.

Parents, carers and other family members

We know that children are generally regarded as very precious by their parents, carers and other family members. It is normal for parents to feel anxious about sharing the care, learning and development of their child with practitioners. But as a positive relationship is established between parents and practitioners over time, trust is built, and parents generally begin to gain confidence in both the practitioner and the setting. Good practitioners work in partnership with parents and carers – but this can only be achieved when a positive relationship has been established.

The relationship between a child's key worker and their parents is therefore particularly important, as the key worker will normally be the parent's chief point of contact with the setting. Parents and practitioners are much more likely to share important information and concerns when a positive relationship exists.

Communicating with respect

You should always communicate politely and courteously with the adults within your setting. This means that you need to address people appropriately. People's names are part of their identity and their individuality, and it is important to respect that. Find out how people would like to be addressed – you should not assume that it is acceptable for you to use a parent's first name, even though it may be given on the registration form. Also, do not make assumptions about people's titles. Not all parents share the same last name as their child, and not all mothers go by the title 'Mrs'. You should not shorten the name of an adult (or a child) unless you are invited to do so.

Remember your manners whenever you are communicating – good manners show respect for other people. More importantly, a lack of manners is often interpreted as a lack of respect for other people. No doubt you can think of a time when you have been offended by someone else's lack of manners. Perhaps someone asked you to do something without saying please, or talked over you when you were speaking, or brushed past you without saying excuse me. Demonstrating good manners plays an important part in establishing and maintaining positive relationships, and it influences the behaviour of children too. You must always remember that you are a role model.

Communicating appropriately

Aim to communicate clearly, in a way that is appropriate for individual adults. To do this, you should consider the methods of communication available to you, what you need to say, and the needs and preferences of the adult. You can then select the method of communication that will most effectively suit the situation.

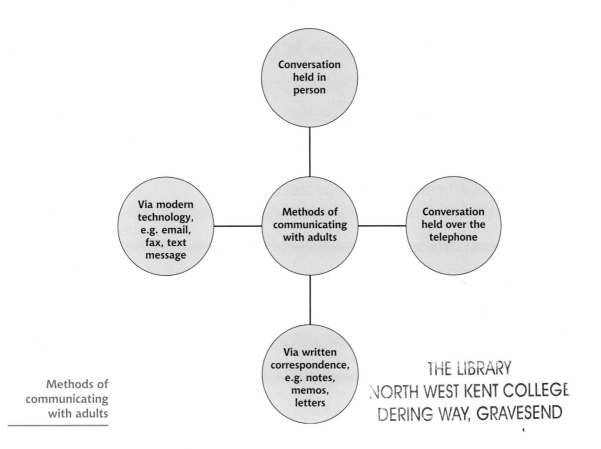

Methods of communicating with adults

THE LIBRARY
NORTH WEST KENT COLLEGE
DERING WAY, GRAVESEND

Before you choose your communication method, there are further factors to consider. For instance, is your communication urgent? If you want to make a parent aware that their child has been coughing on and off throughout the afternoon, it would be appropriate to wait and tell them in person when they collect their child. However, if a child has vomited and they need to be collected, it may be appropriate to telephone a parent straightaway at their workplace.

Remember to give due consideration to the issue of confidentiality, as this will influence how you should communicate. For instance, it may be appropriate to put a general, round-robin note in children's bags for them to take home. But a formal, confidential letter would need to be sealed in an envelope, addressed and marked 'confidential'. It should then be posted, or handed, to the appropriate adult.

Methods of
communicating
with parents

Communication preferences

Most communication between colleagues takes place in conversation. But when practitioners are with the children, it is their duty to focus their attention on the children's care, learning and development. Remember this when you need to talk with other practitioners. Unless there is a reason for urgency, avoid interrupting colleagues when they are working closely with children, or when they need to concentrate fully on the task in hand. If you are unsure about this, you can always ask a colleague if it is a good time to talk. Detailed discussions are best scheduled for non-contact time, when practitioners are not responsible for children's care.

It is important to behave professionally within the setting – practitioners should only have appropriate discussions within earshot of children. Friendly chats about subjects unrelated to the setting should be kept for free time, spent away from the children. Children should not be aware of any conflict between practitioners.

There may be guidelines at your setting about how you should communicate formally, and you should familiarise yourself with these. For instance, there could be set procedures for passing information to practitioners working on a different shift. They may include handing over written reports, or verbally running through a checklist. You may also find that there are systems for leaving messages for staff you will not see, and for making appointments to talk to senior staff.

Communication needs

Adults can experience the same communication difficulties as children. This means that practitioners may need to adapt their communication techniques to meet the needs of other adults. It is important that you are as sensitive to the communication difficulties of adults as you would be to those of children. Otherwise, adults may become isolated or feel excluded within the setting, and may ultimately leave. In the case of parents, if the partnership with practitioners is hampered by communication difficulties, there may be implications for both the adult and their child. Children may even be withdrawn from the setting.

Practitioners can adapt their communications in a number of ways to suit adult's needs, and the circumstances of the communication. Strategies may include:

- Learning some signs (sign language)
- Talking clearly and facing anyone who is lip reading
- Arranging for an interpreter (for adults for whom English/Welsh is an additional language)
- Translating signs, letters and other written communications into the languages required (this can be done via computer)
- Arranging to talk in a quiet area free from background noise
- Taking the time to give key information verbally as well as in writing (for adults who have difficulty reading).

Communicating clearly

It is essential to communicate clearly to ensure that your message is received. Once you have chosen the appropriate communication method for the situation and the individual, you are on the right track. But there is a key question to ask yourself prior to communication – what is your message? Or, in other words – what exactly are you trying to say? You need to be clear about the point of your message before you try to communicate it to someone else. These strategies can help:

- Thinking through/writing down key points in advance

  So that you do not forget anything, and you feel focused

- Practising or seeking advice

  If you are unsure about how to phrase something, practise a few different ways aloud, or in writing, or seek advice from a superior

- Considering whether a certain response or answer is required

  Do you need to wait for a reply, or some information in response?

It is important that you are clear about the communications that you receive too. Whenever you are unsure about any information you are given, or unclear about what is being asked of you, it is vital that you check to avoid making mistakes. Ask questions, and clarify key points to ensure you have understood correctly. This has a second advantage – it demonstrates that you are listening. You should practise the principles of active listening with adults, just as you would when talking with children (see page 12). In addition to asking questions, clarifying and confirming, you should also make eye contact, react and respond.

Key Terms

Times of transition

Times when children are moving onto a new stage in their lives or development. When children leave the baby room or start school, for instance.

Responding to requests for information

At times, all practitioners are asked to supply other adults with information. For instance, colleagues often share information about children, particularly at times of transition, or a parent may ask for further information about a forthcoming event. Whatever the request, practitioners should be clear about what is being asked for and when the information is needed by. They must then be careful to give accurate information within the agreed timescales, as long as doing so will not compromise confidentiality.

The invitations

Three-year-old Carly goes to nursery. She is having a birthday party. Her dad asks her key worker, Jodie, to supply him with the addresses of Carly's friends, so that he can send out invitations in the post. Jodie explains that this would break confidentiality, but she offers to take the invitations and give them out by hand at the nursery.

➤ *Why did Carly do this?*   **K3C181, K3C183**

Conflict with other adults

In all settings there are times when conflict arises between adults. Typical situations that cause conflict include:

- Practitioners feeling that others are not sharing responsibilities or tasks. They may express this by saying that a colleague is not pulling their weight
- People have different ways of doing things, and adults may feel that their way is the right way, or the best way. Consequently, they may be unwilling to compromise
- Change is challenging for many people. Adults may find changes of plan and staff changes unsettling, and they may be reluctant to accept new circumstances
- People making comments that are insensitive, or inappropriate, to or about another person. This can lead to hurt feelings and resentment.

Resolving conflict

It is important to act professionally and deal with conflict effectively. Conflict should normally be worked through in a discussion between the people involved. This should be done at an appropriate time, away from the children. Children should not be aware of conflict between practitioners.

Practitioners should know that if disagreements arise when they are with the children, they can be raised and resolved later on. Generally, they then feel prepared to overcome any negative feelings, and to get on with working professionally. However, you should make sure that you do not leave matters longer than necessary. It is often better to catch conflict early and deal with it before resentment builds up.

There may be exceptional circumstances when you have to speak up right away on a matter of conflict because not to do so might harm a child's safety or welfare, for instance if a colleague was about to do something you considered unsafe.

Techniques for resolving conflict

There are various techniques for resolving conflict. Some settings have set guidelines and procedures to help staff. It can be helpful to review such procedures at times of conflict. Resolution techniques centre on discussion, and will vary according to the situation. They include the following steps, which can be helpful in most circumstances:

- Approaching the resolution process positively

  There may be an issue, but you are going to sort it out calmly – think positively

- Understanding an issue fully

  Identifying what exactly an issue is. If you have an issue, you should think it through carefully before you raise it with someone else. If someone raises an issue with you, make sure you fully understand their source of conflict – repeat it back to them. Check you have understood correctly

- Noticing and identifying feelings

  Take time to notice how you, and other people, are feeling about an issue. Does everyone feel the same? Sometimes simply understanding each other's feelings is enough to resolve conflict

- Looking for solutions

  There may be an outright solution that will work for everyone, or a good compromise. However, compromises may not be possible, not only because they can be difficult to reach, but because it may breach regulations to compromise on certain issues, for instance safety or confidentiality

- Refering to superiors if you need support

  You may want the advice of superiors before dealing with conflict. Or, you may want to refer to a superior if a solution cannot be agreed upon. Sometimes a superior may act as a mediator for adults

- Reviewing

  Set a time to review the situation. Has the solution worked, or do you need to think again?

Key Terms

Mediator
A mediator is someone neutral, who is not directly involved in a matter of conflict. They will help adults to work through their conflicts together by providing encouragement and support and often asking key questions.

Deal with conflict in a mature and positive manner

Element 301.4

Are you ready for assessment?

Communicate with adults

You need to show that you can communicate competently with adults. To do this you will need to be directly observed by your assessor and present other types of evidence. The amount and type of evidence you need to present will vary. You should plan this with your assessor.

Direct observation by your assessor

Observation and/or expert witness testimony is the required assessment method to be used to evidence some of each element in this unit. If your assessor is unable to observe you, s/he will identify an expert in your workplace who will provide testimony of your work-based performance. Usually your assessor or expert witness will observe you in real work activities and this should provide most of the evidence for the performance criteria for the elements in this unit.

Preparing to be observed

You must show your assessor that you can communicate with adults politely and appropriately, showing respect for their individuality and responding to their requests for information as appropriate. You must also show that you can actively listen to adults and handle any disagreements in a way that will maintain a positive relationship. You must show that you can recognise when there are communication needs and adapt the way you communicate accordingly.

Other types of evidence

You will need to present different types of evidence in order to:

- Cover criteria not observed by your assessor
- Show that you have the required knowledge, understanding and skills.

Such evidence could include:

- Work products such as information leaflets or letters for parents and carers, or minutes of meetings with colleagues
- Case studies, projects, assignments and reflective accounts of your work.

Check your knowledge

- What information should be treated as confidential? **K3M158**
- What does anti-discriminatory practice mean? **K3P159**
- Name three ways to make children feel welcomed. **K3D161**
- What does multilingual mean? **K3C168**
- What specific issues may occur in bilingual/multilingual settings? **K3C168**
- Describe three strategies for dealing with challenging behaviour. **K3D178**
- How should you approach conflict with a colleague? **K3C186**

Reflective practice

Imagine that you are unhappy with the way a colleague sometimes deals with children's behaviour. You feel her tone of voice is unnecessarily harsh at times. How could you handle the situation effectively, addressing your concerns while maintaining a positive relationship?

Make notes in your reflective journal.

UNIT 302

Develop and maintain a healthy, safe and secure environment for children

This unit is about the provision of an environment for children that promotes their health, safety and protection. This unit is appropriate for all children's care, learning and development, childcare and playwork settings and services where children and young people are present.

This unit contains three elements:

⌒ **CCLD 302.1** *Establish a healthy, safe and secure environment for children*

⌒ **CCLD 302.2** *Maintain a healthy, safe and secure environment for children*

⌒ **CCLD 302.3** *Supervise procedures for accidents, injuries, illnesses and other emergencies*

Introduction

The safety and well-being of children should be of paramount importance to all practitioners. It is essential for you to learn how to establish and maintain healthy environments for children that are both safe and secure.

Accidents, injuries and illnesses happen to all children occasionally, regardless of the precautions you take. Although this is concerning, it is reassuring for practitioners to know that they have learnt how to respond in an emergency.

When providing environments for children you must comply with the laws and regulations relevant to your home country. All of the laws and regulations referred to in this unit apply in England. However, health and safety legislation is fairly universal. You can find out more about the specifics for your home country online:

- Scotland: www.scotland.gov.uk
- Wales: www.wales.gov.uk
- Northern Ireland: www.deni.gov.uk
- England: www.direct.gov.uk.

This unit links closely with Unit CCLD 306 Plan and organise environments for children and families. You should read pages 151–191 in conjunction with this unit.

 Link **Unit CCLD 306** Plan and organise environments for children and families

Establish a healthy, safe and secure environment for children

Health, safety and security requirements

K3P189
K3H190
K3H193
K3H192
K3H194
K3H246
K3H195

Several regulations and requirements apply to all workplaces in the UK, in addition to those that apply specifically to environments for children. Settings have to comply with these by law. The main regulations and requirements that settings must meet are:

- Health and Safety at Work Act 1974 and 1992
- Health and Safety (First Aid) Regulations 1981
- Food Safety Act 1990 and Food Handling Regulations 1995
- Control of Substances Hazardous to Health Regulations 1994 (COSHH)
- Fire Precautions (Workplace) Regulations 1997
- Reporting of Injuries, Diseases and Dangerous Occurrences Regulations 1995 (RIDDOR)
- Personal Protective Equipment at Work Regulations 1992
- Children Bill 2004
- Protection of Children Act 1999
- Children's Act 1989
- Health and Safety (Young Persons) Regulations 1997
- Every Child Matters
- The Early Years Foundation Stage Welfare Requirements.

In addition, the Childcare Act 2006 was passed to introduce the Early Years Foundation Stage and to support settings in providing high-quality, integrated care and education for children aged from birth to five years. It also gave local authorities the responsibility to improve outcomes for all children under five.

You should note that requirements are updated over time, and it is important that you remain well informed. As part of your study towards this unit, you are advised to visit www.standards.dcsf.gov.uk/eyfs/site/requirements/index.htm. Here, you'll find a list of requirements for settings, which is regularly updated. There are also links to further information.

Policies and procedures

Regulations and requirements tell settings what they must do and what standards they must meet. For instance, the Health and Safety at Work Act 1974 and 1992 says that employers must ensure that the workplace and equipment within it are in a safe condition. But it doesn't tell settings how to achieve this. So that everyone involved knows how to keep the workplace and equipment safe, settings draw up their own policies and procedures explaining what should be done. It is likely that the policy will explain when and how equipment should be cleaned, for instance, and what to do if equipment becomes damaged. Sometimes, extra information is needed to explain how areas of a policy will work in action, so settings may devise additional written procedures that explain what to do in more detail.

Good, clear policies and procedures are important because they communicate how the staff must work. Policies also let other professionals, parents, carers and children know how your setting works. You must make sure that you understand all of your setting's policies, and you must work within them.

Security

Settings must make suitable security arrangements in the interests of the children's safety. There should be clear procedures for children's arrival at the setting, their departure from the setting, and their security when on outings.

Arrivals and departures

All settings must keep a record of the children and adults who are in attendance at each session. This is known as keeping a register. In addition, a record of when children arrive and leave must also be kept. Some settings may keep a 'signing in/out book' for this purpose, while others may include this information on their register document. Whatever the arrangement at your setting, it is essential that children are signed in as soon as they arrive, and marked out as soon as they leave. Try the following visualisation to see why this is so important:

Visualisation

> **Imagine there is a fire. You must evacuate. You take the register or signing in/out book with you. After checking them, you think all of the children have got out safely. But one child was not marked in on his arrival, and so you have not yet noticed that he is missing.**

There could be awful consequences, couldn't there? **Do not forget to mark children in!** In a similar scenario, if a child who has already been collected has not been signed out, fire fighters could end up searching a burning building for a child perceived to be missing. **Do not forget to sign children out!**

For many settings, if a child does not arrive, then it is generally no cause for concern. The child is not the responsibility of the provider until their parent or carer brings them along. However, this is different for after-school clubs. If a child who has been booked in does not turn up, practitioners must quickly find out their whereabouts. It is helpful to bear in mind that a club may be:

- Based within a school or
- Based elsewhere, in which case club escorts will be collecting children from school and then taking them to the club premises. The escorts will need to deal with the situation if children they are expecting to collect do not appear.

Staff should contact the parent or carer to find out if other arrangements have been made for the child's care. Frequently in these events, parents have forgotten to cancel a place that they no longer need. It often helps the situation if a practitioner can talk with the child's teacher to find out if the child was absent from school or if they saw who collected the child. It may be the case that a parent has rung the school to let them know that their child is off sick, but they have forgotten to let the club know. If a child did not attend school and a parent has not

Outings can be
educational
and fun

called either the school or the club, it may mean that the child went missing early in the morning on their way to school, and so contacting parents is still a matter of urgency to confirm the child's whereabouts.

Written procedures for non-arrival are helpful for out-of-school club practitioners to refer to in these often complicated circumstances. It is also important that practitioners at all settings are aware of who is authorised to collect each child. This information must be held on the registration form.

During sessions, practitioners must ensure that children do not leave the setting unattended, and that visitors cannot gain entry without detection. The indoor and outdoor premises must be secure. The way in which this is achieved depends entirely on the building and the age and stage of development of the children. However, fire exits must always be unobstructed, and the method of opening the door to escape must be quick and easy. Many settings fit an alarm to fire doors so that practitioners are alerted immediately if a child should open an outside door. Element 302.3 contains information about procedures when a child is missing.

Outings

On outings, settings need to take extra care with regard to security. It is important to ensure that the staff to child ratio is sufficiently high to enable the increased supervision that is necessary. Take the children's ages, needs and abilities into consideration, as well as regulations. It is usual practice to split the children into small groups or pairs, with each assigned one or more adults to take care of them. This is particularly useful when children are walking around in a public place, from one location to another, even though the whole group may join in activities together on arrival. Whenever you change location, enter a building or get on or off of transport, count the children TWICE, in case of a miscount. It is good practice for more than one practitioner to count, so that you have double-checked that everyone is present before you move off.

Before embarking on a trip, it is wise to talk with children and staff about security. It is reassuring to know that the safety information they need is fresh in their minds. Children may be very excited when they arrive at their destination, so it is best to talk with them before leaving the setting. You do not want to dampen the children's good spirits, but do insist that they listen carefully to all you have to tell them. Reassure the children that the additional rules will help everyone to stay safe and enjoy the day.

Remind children that they must stay in their small groups when asked to do so, and that they must not wander off at any time. Talk through your procedures for crossing roads too if this is applicable. If you will be using transport, remind children about the importance of wearing their seatbelts and not leaving the vehicle until instructed. Tell children what they should do if they do get separated from the group. This will depend largely on where you are going. Let them know that you expect them to pay attention quickly should you need to give the group further instruction while you are out. This is important in case of an emergency. You should plan frequent toilet stops throughout the trip. Staff should always enter public toilets with the children to keep them safe from harm.

Manual handling

There are some risks associated with lifting and carrying children and equipment. Manual-handling courses teach practitioners to employ the correct lifting methods to avoid injury, and you will be given demonstrations. It is recommended that you take such a course. But essentially, you should plant your feet firmly either side of the child/equipment you will be lifting. Bend your knees and keep your back straight. Use your legs to power the lift to avoid straining your back or neck. Do not pick up or carry alone any child/equipment that you find too heavy for you. Seek assistance. Check that equipment is safely positioned after putting it down. It is often possible to help toddlers climb a specially designed slope up to a changing unit to save practitioners from frequently lifting them up and down when changing nappies.

Risk assessment

The process of risk assessment makes settings safer places for children. However, no setting or activity can be completely safe. Children need to be able to take acceptable levels of risk in play, or their development will be stifled. Think of a child who is just starting to walk. They will fall down many times before they master the skill, and they might hurt themselves occasionally. But we would not dream of stopping them from walking. It would be overreacting. The risk of injury from a fall is acceptable when a child is learning to walk. But we may decide to take some steps to reduce the chance of injury – perhaps we will move a rug that they may slip on, and make sure there is plenty of clear floor space. Risk assessment is simply a formal version of this process.

You will need to risk assess premises, both indoors and outdoors, and also activities. If you plan to take children on an outing you must risk assess the trip. This will require a prior visit by a practitioner. You must give due consideration to the movement and transport of children on an outing as well as to the destination itself.

There are six key risk assessment steps to follow:

- Identify hazards

    A HAZARD is the actual item or situation that may cause harm – a stack of chairs for instance

- Decide on the level of risk posed by the hazards – low, medium or high

    The RISK is the likelihood of the hazard causing harm. How risky would you rate the stack of chairs? It would all depend on the circumstances. A stack of chairs in a baby and toddler room would be high risk. It is likely that a child will pull themselves up on the chairs causing them to tumble. A young child could be badly injured

- Evaluate the risks

    What measures, if any, could/should be taken to minimise or remove the risk? Are there any safety precautions already in place? If so, are they adequate? Is the risk acceptable given the ages, needs and abilities of the children? What levels of supervision will be required? Consider the benefits of activities against the potential for harm. Finally, decide if the risk can be taken

- If measures are to be taken to minimise or remove the risk, they should be carried out at this stage

    In our example, we can either remove the chairs from the room altogether, or simply unstack them. The risk is then removed

- Record your assessment

    You should record the whole process, and note your findings. Detail any measures you have taken, and enter the date

- Review the risk assessment at a later date

    How effective have your measures been? Make revisions if necessary.

    You should review assessments periodically as a matter of good practice, in line with your organisational policies. But you must also reassess if there are significant changes to premises or activities that impact on the original assessment. Record, date and sign all reviews.

Considering stages of development

A sound knowledge of child development will help you when you are carrying out risk assessments and planning security arrangements. You will be able to consider how aware children are of danger at various ages, their skill levels, and the things they are likely to do (pulling themselves up on a chair, for example). This links with the development information in Unit CCLD 303 Promote children's development.

 Link   **Unit CCLD 303** Promote children's development

Levels of supervision

Practitioners must supervise children safely at all times and maintain the minimum staff to child ratios. However, many settings aim to exceed these ratios in the interests of quality. In daycare settings in England (without a qualified teacher) the minimum ratios are:

- Children under two years: one adult to three children (1:3)
- Children aged two years: one adult to four children (1:4)
- Children aged three to seven years: one adult to eight children (1:8).

Everyone working with children must be checked by the Criminal Records Bureau. There's more about this in Unit CCLD 305 Protect and promote children's rights. Settings must also be staffed by practitioners with acceptable qualifications, as specified by the Children's Workforce Development Council. You can see a full list of these online at www.cwdcouncil.org.uk/qualifications-list. The list becomes active in September 2009 and replaces the existing Early Years and Playwork Qualifications Database.

 Link   **Unit CCLD 305** Protect and promote children's rights

Health and safety measures in relation to age

Approximate age	Development indicator	Implications for health, safety and security arrangements	Measures to be taken
4–5 months	Baby will roll from their back to their side	Baby may roll when on a high changing unit	Use units with side bars and anticipate that baby may roll
6 months	Baby is fascinated by small toys within reaching distance, grabbing them with the whole hand	The baby will now pick up objects within their reach independently. This could include safety hazards such as sharp objects, unsafe substances and small objects which present a choking hazard	Ensure that nothing unsuitable is left in the vicinity of the baby
9 months	Baby starts to crawl and pull itself up to standing position	Crawling means a baby may independently move anywhere – to the stairs for instance. Standing up gives access to a whole new level – baby may be able to reach heaters.	Install safety equipment such as stair gates, socket covers, cupboard locks and heater guards. Assess safety of the objects now on the baby's new level. Baby may pull objects onto themselves, and push less sturdy items of furniture over
15 months	Child is walking alone. Explores objects using trial and error	Child may want to walk alone instead of riding in a buggy when out and about. May wander off to explore	Use reins for safety. Supervise carefully on the stairs
2 years	Child runs safely. Starting to understand consequences of own behaviour	May disappear from sight quickly	Keep a close eye on child's whereabouts. Be prepared to deal with more minor grazes and bumps
3 years	Child walks upstairs, one foot on each step. Rides tricycle. Children are impulsive. May resent adults limiting their behaviour. Child asks lots of questions	Learning to use stairs without supervision. May suddenly do something dangerous on impulse, like jump from a slide. May be reluctant to heed safety warnings	Ensure that there is a handrail of appropriate height on stairs. Give child safety information as appropriate. Be prepared to be firm on matters of safety. ('No means no')
4 years	Child climbs play equipment. May confuse fantasy and reality	Using bigger, higher equipment. May become engrossed in fantasy play and forget the safety limits of the real world. (We cannot fly, even if we jump from somewhere high)	Ensure safety playground covering is suitable for the higher equipment. Gently remind about safety limits if necessary, but try not to disturb imaginary play unnecessarily

5 years	Child balances on beam. Greater levels of independence achieved	Child will want less adult support	Encourage child to think about their own safety
6–7 years	Child rides a bicycle, makes running jumps. Is increasingly mature	Child is spending more time alone at home, playing in the bedroom or garden perhaps, or riding their bike on their own street if it is in a residential area	Continue to support awareness of safety. Ensure cycle helmet is worn
8–11 years	Child rides scooters, bigger bicycles and skateboards/skates. May play sports. Increasingly independent	Child may ride a bicycle on the road. Goes out to play with friends without adult supervision. Children become more aware of risks, but may misjudge their abilities. May cross local roads alone	Continue to support awareness of safety. Ensure that helmets and padding designed for safety are used with skateboards, etc. Ensure children have access to safe, good-quality sports equipment, and encourage them to warm up/cool down before/after sports. Ensure children learn road safety (and cycle safety if appropriate)
11 onwards	Independence grows as children enter teenage years, and time spent unsupervised by adults increases greatly. Peer pressure may affect young people, and they may experiment with new experiences	Often, young people will not have an accompanying adult to point out risks to them, and they may not have an adult to turn to if they are in an unsafe or difficult situation. Children may try alcohol, drugs (including cigarettes) and engage in sexual behaviour	Ensure children/young people can recognise risks for themselves. Teach them what to do when hazards occur (role plays, quizzes and moral dilemma games can all be used for this purpose). Teach children/young people about the dangers of alcohol and drugs. Support young people who ask questions about relationships and sex (see Unit CCLD 303 Promote children's development)

Link   **Unit CCLD 303** Promote children's development

For safety, the deployment of staff should be considered carefully throughout the session. Generally, the younger children are, or the more challenging an activity, the closer the supervision will need to be. For some activities, it is safe for children to work independently as long as there are adults in the room keeping a general eye on things – children can approach them if they need assistance. Other activities would be unsafe without one-to-one support from an adult, for example when a child is learning to use woodworking tools such as hacksaws. Levels of supervision required can change as problems occur, the mood of children changes, or children master skills. Practitioners learn through experience to adjust the supervision they give.

Vicky steps in

A group of children that would not normally require close supervision during a board game attract the attention of playworker Vicky. The children are squabbling and tempers are becoming frayed. The children temporarily resolve their issue and carry on with the game. However, Vicky notices that one child still looks quite angry. Another looks upset. A third says she no longer wants to play. Vicky goes over to the group and sits with them. 'This game looks like fun,' she says casually. Her presence seems to diffuse the tension. Vicky watches the game with interest and chats to the group for a while. When the children have settled down, Vicky retreats again, keeping an eye on the game from across the room.

➤ *Why was Vicky's strategy effective?*   **K3H194**

Are you ready for assessment?

Establish a healthy, safe and secure environment for children

You need to show that you can competently establish a healthy, safe and secure environment for children. To do this you will need to be directly observed by your assessor and present other types of evidence. The amount and type of evidence you need to present will vary. You should plan this with your assessor.

Direct observation by your assessor

Observation and/or expert witness testimony is the required assessment method to be used to evidence some of each element in this unit. If your assessor is unable to observe you, s/he will identify an expert in your workplace who will provide testimony of your work-based performance. Usually your assessor or expert witness will observe you in real work activities and this should provide most of the evidence for the performance criteria for the elements in this unit.

Preparing to be observed

You must show your assessor that you can carry out risk assessment and ensure that you, the children and adults have relevant up-to-date health, safety and security information. You must also show you can conduct health, safety and security reviews.

Other types of evidence

You will need to present different types of evidence in order to:

- Cover criteria not observed by your assessor
- Show that you have the required knowledge, understanding and skills.

Such evidence could include:

- Work products such as risk assessments and checklists
- Case studies, projects, assignments and reflective accounts of your work.

Maintain a healthy, safe and secure environment for children

Element 302.2

**K3H191
K3H192**

Even when risk assessments are in place, it is necessary for practitioners to make daily checks to ensure that good standards of health, safety and security are maintained. The following must be checked:

- The setting
- Each activity.

Many settings design their own daily checklist to ensure that the setting is fully assessed indoors and outdoors, and nothing is forgotten. One person will usually take responsibility for completing the checklist before each session starts. During the session, all practitioners share responsibility for keeping the setting to the appropriate standards. At the end of the session, the setting should be checked again to ensure that it is left in good order. It is worth noting that many organisations do not have sole occupancy of their premises. Other community groups may use the space before the next childcare session. These groups may well have different standards to your own – the premises may need attention before your session begins.

Your complete check will depend on your individual setting. But as part of your initial daily checks, you should consider the following.

The outside area:

- Are gates locked and boundary fences secure?
- Can strangers come into contact with the children?
- Are their any problems caused by weather – slippery surfaces, water-logged areas? Is there adequate shelter from the sun? Will children need their sun protection?
- Are their any other risks from water?
- If there are litter bins, are they covered and secure?
- Is the area free of litter, glass, poisonous plants and animal faeces? (Cats in particular are attracted to sand trays – keep them covered when not in use. Even if poisonous plants are not grown, birds sometimes drop berries, or plant matter can be scattered on the wind.)
- Have any items or equipment that could cause harm been left out?
- Is play equipment assembled safely and is it in good order?
- Is play safety flooring in good order? If mats are needed, are they present?

The inside area:

- Are all doors (that should be locked) secured?
- Are all fire exits unobstructed?
- Are all fire doors closed?
- Is fire-fighting equipment in place and intact?
- Are windows intact and safe?
- Are all safety equipment items in place? (Socket covers, cupboard catches, radiator covers, and so on)

- Is the first-aid kit present?
- Are safety notices and all documentation required under legislation fully displayed?
- Is the setting the correct temperature?
- Are the premises clean and hygienic?
- Are the kitchen and bathroom areas scrupulously clean?
- Is there a sufficient supply of consumables such as toilet rolls, tissues, soap, disposable towels, wet wipes, nappy bags and antibacterial cleaning sprays?
- Are equipment and resources safe, clean and assembled correctly?
- Has equipment in storage been put away safely, so that it will not fall or otherwise cause harm?
- Are activities planned and prepared in line with risk assessments?

During the session

During the session, all staff should share responsibility for keeping the setting and activities safe, although the person in charge of the room will usually oversee this. It is important to check that:

- The appropriate levels of supervision intended are maintained
- The intended levels of supervision are adequate for children's ages, needs and abilities
- When equipment and resources are packed away, they are stored safely
- When new equipment and resources are introduced during the session, they too are assessed as before. Are equipment and resources safe, clean and assembled correctly?
- The activities are being carried out in line with risk assessments, and that measures taken to reduce or remove risk are working effectively
- The activities are given sufficient space
- No one obstructs the fire exits
- Toilet and kitchen areas are kept hygienically clean throughout
- Any documentation necessary is carried out – marking the register for example, filling in medication logs, accident or incident books
- The movement of children is safely supervised. For instance, before children go outside, a practitioner should check that no one entering or leaving the setting has left the gate open. There should be room to move safely between activities. Toys should not be allowed to litter the entire floor space, impeding safe passage. Consider the needs of disabled children and adults with regard to moving freely around the setting.

Children's role in safety

Children will not always be under the close supervision of adults, and as they grow older they will become entirely independent. So it is essential that children learn to recognise and manage risk for themselves. Experience of doing this should increase as children mature. Involve children in thinking about safety, and encourage them to tell an adult if they see something unsafe.

Older children may help adults to check appropriate parts of the premises for safety and assist in carrying out risk assessment informally. 'Moral dilemma' games and role-plays can also be an effective way to encourage older children to think about how they should handle potentially dangerous situations. For instance, what should they do if their lift home from a disco does not turn up? Or if someone should offer them alcohol or drugs?

There is more information about safety on outings in element 302.1.

Are you ready for assessment?

Maintain a healthy, safe and secure environment for children

You need to show that you can competently maintain a healthy, safe and secure environment for children. To do this you will need to be directly observed by your assessor and present other types of evidence. The amount and type of evidence you need to present will vary. You should plan this with your assessor.

Direct observation by your assessor

Observation and/or expert witness testimony is the required assessment method to be used to evidence some of each element in this unit. If your assessor is unable to observe you, s/he will identify an expert in your workplace who will provide testimony of your work-based performance. Usually your assessor or expert witness will observe you in real work activities and this should provide most of the evidence for the performance criteria for the elements in this unit.

Preparing to be observed

You must show your assessor that you can assess the health, safety and security of the setting, follow relevant procedures yourself and ensure that other adults and children do the same. You must show that you can encourage children to be aware of safety and to manage risk, and also that you can contribute to safety on outings. Make sure that you understand your setting's policies and procedures and that you can explain them.

Other types of evidence

You will need to present different types of evidence in order to:

- Cover criteria not observed by your assessor
- Show that you have the required knowledge, understanding and skills.

Such evidence could include:

- Work products such as checklists and resources/materials devised for use with children
- Case studies, projects, assignments and reflective accounts of your work.

Element 302.3

Supervise procedures for accidents, injuries, illnesses and other emergencies

K3H196
K3H197
K3H199
K3H200
K3H201
K3H46
K3H198

It is worthwhile spending plenty of time familiarising yourself with emergency procedures, as this will help you to remember how to respond should an emergency occur.

Evacuation procedures

It may be necessary to evacuate a setting for a number of reasons, including:

- Fire
- Flood
- Gas leak
- Identification of a dangerous substance.

To ensure that premises can be evacuated effectively in an emergency, it is essential that:

- All staff know how to raise the alarm, where the exit points are, and where the assembly point is
- All staff are aware of their individual roles

  Such as taking the register, dialling 999, checking that rooms are empty
- There are regular opportunities to practice evacuation drills

  These should be taken seriously, and any difficulties should be resolved.

  The sound of the alarm may upset some children, so be sensitive, and help children to settle after the drill
- Evacuation drill notices should be displayed for visitors to refer to

  These should give details of where the fire-extinguishing equipment is kept
- Fire alarms, smoke detectors and emergency lighting should be checked regularly and maintained, and staff should be trained in their use

  Details of checks should be recorded in a log book
- Emergency exits must not be obstructed.

One person often takes responsibility for overseeing evacuation procedures and fire safety.

Missing child procedures

All registered settings must have written procedures addressing what practitioners would do if it was discovered that a child was missing. You should know and understand these procedures, as in such an emergency it will be important to act quickly. In most situations it would be appropriate to organise a full initial search of the setting, including outdoor areas, and to check when the child was last seen. If the child cannot be found, the search should be widened to the local area. The person in charge should raise the alarm, contacting police and the missing child's parents or carers. Later, Ofsted should also be informed (In England). Sufficient staff must stay on the premises

**Fire-fighting
equipment**

to care for the remaining children, but surplus staff may join the search. Police will take charge of the search when they arrive. Practitioners should log events in the incident book while they are fresh in their mind. There will need to be an urgent review of the setting's security.

Common childhood illnesses

All children experience illness from time to time. It is important that you learn to recognise the signs and symptoms of illness in a child. When you notice that a child is feeling unwell, you should promptly take the appropriate action in line with your setting's policies and procedures. It is a legal requirement that all registered settings have written guidelines for the management of illness within the setting.

It is not the job of childcarers to diagnose diseases or illnesses – that is the role of health professionals such as doctors. It is also not your job to care for sick children, and children who are ill should not attend the setting. However, there will be times when a child's illness develops whilst they are in your care. It is your job to:

- Recognise promptly when a child is ill

  See the diagram on page 45

- Respond to symptoms, if appropriate, in line with policies

  Cooling down a child with a temperature for instance, or administering a child's asthma inhaler

- Monitor a child's condition

  In case it becomes worse. Record appropriate details such as temperature readings or inhalers given

- Arrange for children to be collected as soon as possible in the case of minor illness

The child's parent, carer or alternative contact person (as stated on the registration form) should be called. Be calm and supply the facts. A parent may initially become very anxious about their child, even if symptoms seem minor. If symptoms are more serious, a parent may understandably panic. You must stay in control. Sometimes a parent may need to call you back to confirm collection arrangements as they may need a few minutes to organise things, such as leaving work, or seeing if an alternate contact person is free to come in their place. Parents or carers may ask you what they should do for their child. You are not a doctor, and so you should simply advise them to seek medical attention if they are unsure what to do or if they are worried by any symptoms

- Get emergency assistance urgently if necessary, and know which signs and symptoms indicate that immediate medical help is needed

Do not wait for parents or carers if it is an emergency. Dial 999 and request an ambulance. If the child needs to go to hospital before a parent or carer arrives, a practitioner should accompany the child and meet parents at the hospital

- Do all you can to make a child comfortable until they leave your care

Children who are ill may be upset or embarrassed. Be sensitive and caring to soothe them. Stay with a child in a quiet area, and carry out a quiet activity, such as sharing a book, if the child is interested

- Record the illness

See 'Record keeping' on page 48

- Do what you can to stop the spread of infection

See 'Good hygiene practices' on page 54.

Signs and symptoms of illness

Children who become ill at the setting may display the following common signs and symptoms of illness.

The following signs and symptoms of illness indicate that you may need to call for urgent medical attention:

- Breathing difficulties
- Convulsions
- Child seems to be in significant pain
- Child cannot easily or fully be roused from sleep or a state of drowsiness
- Baby becomes unresponsive and/or their body seems to be floppy
- Severe headache which may be accompanied by a stiff neck or a dislike of light
- Rash that remains (does not fade) when pressed with a glass
- Vomiting that persists for more than 24 hours
- Unusual, high-pitched crying in babies
- High temperature that cannot be lowered
- Child will not drink fluids – this is most worrying in babies.

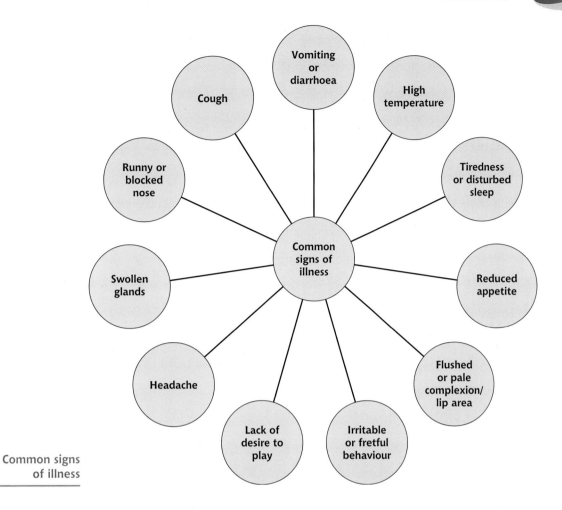

Common signs
of illness

High temperatures

The normal temperature reading for a child is between 36.5 °C and 37.4 °C. Children may have a higher temperature when they are ill, or after physical activity such as running around, or after they have taken hot food or fluids.

Taking a child's temperature with a thermometer helps you to monitor their illness. Most settings will use a fever scan thermometer (placed on a child's forehead) or a digital thermometer (either placed in the mouth or the ear). These come with directions for use. They are safer than clinical thermometers, which are made of glass and contain mercury.

You should take steps to lower a child's temperature by:

- Seeing that warm clothing is removed so that the child wears just a cool layer
- Providing a cool drink either of water or diluted by water
- Cooling the environment (opening windows, turning off heat sources, using a fan)
- Providing a cool wipe for the face and forehead.

Childhood infections

Disease and cause	Spread	Incubation	Signs and symptoms	Rash or specific sign	Treatment*	Complications
Common Cold (coryza) Virus	Airborne/droplet, hand-to-hand contact	1–3 days	Sneezing, sore throat, running nose, headache, slight fever, irritable, partial deafness		Treat symptoms. Vaseline to nostrils	Bronchitis, sinusitis, laryngitis
Chickenpox (varicella) Virus	Airborne/droplet, direct contact	10–14 days	Slight fever, itchy rash, mild onset, child feels ill, often with severe headache	Red spots with white centre on trunk and limbs at first; blisters and pustules	Rest, fluids, calamine to rash, cut child's nails to prevent secondary infection	Impetigo, scarring, secondary infection from scratching
Dysentery Bacillus or amoeba	Indirect: flies, infected food; poor hygiene	1–7 days	Vomiting, diarrhoea, blood mucus in stool, abdominal pain, fever, headache		Replace fluids, rest, medical aid, strict hygiene measures	Dehydration from loss of body salts, shock; can be fatal
Food poisoning Bacteria or virus	Indirect: infected food or drink	½ hour to 36 hours	Vomiting, diarrhoea, abdominal pain		Fluids only for 24 hours; medical aid if no better	Dehydration – can be fatal
Gastro-enteritis Bacteria or virus	Direct contact. Indirect: infected food/drink	Bacterial: 7–14 days Viral: ½ hr–36 hrs	Vomiting, diarrhoea, signs of dehydration		Replace fluids – water or Dioralyte; medical aid urgently	Dehydration, weight loss – death
Measles (morbilli) Virus	Airborne/droplet	7–15 days	High fever; fretful, heavy cold – running nose and discharge from eyes; later cough	Day 1: Koplik's spots, white inside mouth. Day 4: blotchy rash starts on face and spreads down to body	Rest, fluids, tepid sponging. Shade room if photophobic	Otitis media, eye infection, pneumonia, encephalitis (rare)

Disease / Cause	How spread	Incubation period	Symptoms	Signs	Treatment	Possible complications
Meningitis (inflammation of meninges which cover the brain) Bacteria or virus	Airborne/droplet	Variable – usually 2–10 days	Fever; headache, drowsiness, confusion, photophobia, arching of neck	Can have small red spots or bruises	Take to hospital, antibiotics and observation	Deafness, brain damage, death
Mumps (epidemic parotitis) Virus	Airborne/droplet	14–21 days	Pain, swelling of jaw in front of ears, fever; eating and drinking painful	Swollen face	Fluids: give via straw, hot compresses, oral hygiene	Meningitis (1 in 400), orchitis (infection of testes) in *young* men
Pertussis (Whooping cough) Bacteria	Airborne/droplet direct contact	7–21 days	Starts with a snuffly cold, slight cough, mild fever	Spasmodic cough with whoop sound, vomiting	Rest and assurance; feed after coughing attack; support during attack; inhalations	Convulsions, pneumonia, brain damage, hernia, debility
Rubella (German measles) Virus	Airborne/droplet;	14–21 days	Slight cold, sore throat, mild fever, swollen glands behind ears, pain in small joints	Slight pink rash starts behind ears and on forehead. Not itchy	Rest if necessary. Treat symptoms	Only if contracted by woman in first 3 months of pregnancy – can cause serious defects in unborn baby
Scarlet fever (or Scarlatina) Bacteria	Droplet	2–4 days	Sudden fever, loss of appetite, sore throat, pallor around mouth, 'strawberry' tongue	Bright red pinpoint rash over face and body – may peel	Rest, fluids, observe for complications, antibiotics	Kidney infection, otitis media, rheumatic fever (rare)
Tonsillitis Bacteria or virus	Direct infection, droplet		Very sore throat, fever; headache, pain on swallowing, aches and pains in back and limbs		Rest, fluids, medical aid – antibiotics, iced drinks relieve pain	Quinsy (abscess on tonsils), otitis media, kidney infection, temporary deafness

*This column gives an overview of treatment that may be advised by medical professionals. It does not replace the need for medical advice or diagnosis.

Some children may be given paracetamol syrup by parents or carers, or with parental consent, but this depends on the circumstances and the policy of the setting. For instance, a child may be prone to febrile convulsions brought on by a high temperature. Parents may therefore bring paracetamol syrup to the setting, giving written permission for it to be administered if their child runs a temperature, in the hope that convulsions may be avoided.

Medication

Some children may take medication regularly to treat conditions that they suffer from. For instance, a child with asthma may use inhalers, and a child with attention deficit hyperactivity disorder (ADHD) may take tablets, or a child with eczema may use creams. Other children may need to take medication that was prescribed to treat an illness from which they have since recovered. For instance, a child may have been ill for several days, and absent from the setting, but when they are well enough to return they may still need to finish a course of antibiotics.

Parents need to give written consent for their child's medication to be administered by the setting. The dosage, when medication should be given and by whom, should all be recorded. The medication should be labelled clearly with the child's name, and it should be kept in a safe, appropriate place. Some medicine needs to be kept in a refrigerator. Settings will have strict, but differing policies about the way in which medicine is stored and administered, and these must be followed. You should be shown how to administer medication such as inhalers. Make sure you are confident about how to administer the particular type of medication. Rather than make an error, ask for help or clarification if you are in any doubt at all. In some settings, older children may keep their own inhalers close at hand – this will depend on the policy of individual settings.

Record keeping

In addition to keeping a medication log that includes written parental permission to administer medication, settings should log the details of when medication has been given, and the practitioner should sign the record. Parents and carers should also be asked to sign the log at the end of the session.

When a child becomes ill at a setting, the practitioner should record the time and date, and describe the signs and symptoms of illness. They should record their response to the child's condition, making a note of details such as temperature readings if appropriate. The parent or carer should be asked to sign the record.

If an injury or accident occurs, practitioners should record the time, date, location and circumstances of the incident. You should record the detail of any injuries and any action taken, including first-aid treatment. The log must be signed by the parent or carer and the practitioner who dealt with the incident.

Your setting may have additional procedures for reporting to superiors any illnesses, accidents and injuries – you should follow organisational policies.

First-aid kits

Every setting must have a first-aid kit. They now come with a list of contents, often on a sticker inside the lid. The illustration below shows the contents of a first-aid kit. Kits should be stored somewhere accessible for staff, but out of the reach of children, in a dry place so that items do not perish. It is crucial that as items are used, the box is replenished. Systems should be devised to ensure that is the case. Often, one person takes responsibility for overseeing the first-aid kit.

It is good practice to keep 'guidance cards' within a first-aid kit. These contain brief notes (reminders) on how to carry out life-saving procedures – many kits now come with cards.

It is good practice to wear gloves when carrying out first-aid procedures in order to protect yourself and the casualty from cross-infection. Gloves should be kept in the first-aid kit.

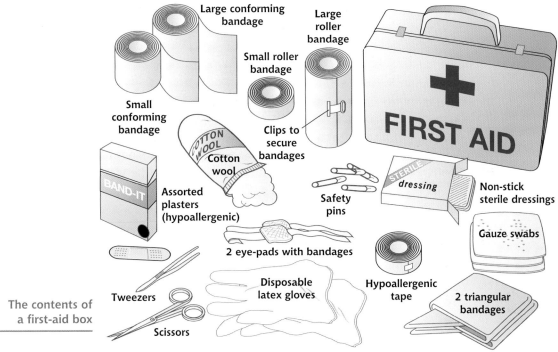

The contents of a first-aid box

First aid in emergencies

Accidents will happen however carefully you carry out risk assessment and supervise children. That is why it is recommended that practitioners take a first-aid course. There has to be at least one first-aider present at all registered settings. The aims of first aid are often remembered as 'the three p's', that is to:

- Preserve life
- Prevent the condition worsening
- Promote recovery.

Sometimes first aid is all that is necessary – for instance, common minor injuries such as grazes can be treated sufficiently. However, it is important to recognise when medical assistance is required urgently. Whenever you are dealing with an accident, incident or illness you must stay calm. You should reassure casualties, and children who are bystanders, as they may be very frightened. You should ensure that you and others are not put at unnecessary risk. OFTEN, THE MOST QUALIFIED PERSON AT THE SETTING WILL TAKE RESPONSIBILITY FOR ADMINISTERING FIRST AID, SO YOU MAY JUST BE REQUIRED TO INFORM THEM, DEPENDING ON THE CIRCUMSTANCES. Think through your actions carefully, and make safety your priority. When you first respond to a first-aid emergency, you should do the following.

A first-aid course will teach you how to examine a casualty. But essentially, you should:

- Check for a response – call the child's name, pinch their skin
- Open the airway and check for breathing
- Check the pulse.

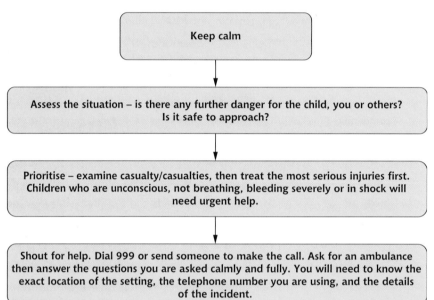

Keep calm

↓

Assess the situation – is there any further danger for the child, you or others? Is it safe to approach?

↓

Prioritise – examine casualty/casualties, then treat the most serious injuries first. Children who are unconscious, not breathing, bleeding severely or in shock will need urgent help.

↓

Shout for help. Dial 999 or send someone to make the call. Ask for an ambulance then answer the questions you are asked calmly and fully. You will need to know the exact location of the setting, the telephone number you are using, and the details of the incident.

Responding to an emergency

Managing an unconscious child who is breathing

An unconscious child who is breathing and has a pulse should be put into the recovery position. This will keep the airway clear. Keep checking the airway and pulse until help arrives. If you are trained, send someone to dial 999 for an ambulance while you begin CPR.

How to manage an unconscious child who is breathing

How to recognise and deal with emergencies

Type of emergency	Response required
Anaphylactic shock A severe allergic reaction which can be fatal. Blood pressure falls and breathing is impaired. Tongue and throat may swell	Dial 999 – the casualty needs to be given an adrenaline injection. A child with a known allergy may have adrenaline to be administered. A sitting position helps breathing. Watch for shock, lie casualty down and raise legs if you suspect it. The casualty may need to be resuscitated if they become unconscious
Asthma The airways go into spasm making breathing difficult. This may occur after contact with allergens such as dust, pollen or pet hair. Severity of attacks vary, but they can be serious. Severe attacks are frightening for the child concerned and can also frighten children witnessing the attack. The child wheezes and becomes breathless. Prompt action is needed	Reassure. Give bronchodilator inhaler as instructed if child is a known asthmatic. These inhalers should always be immediately available – they deliver medication to the lungs to relieve affected airways. Children may also have another type of inhaler used to prevent attacks. Make sure you know which to use in an emergency, particularly if older children generally use their inhalers themselves. Sit child upright and leaning forwards in comfortable position. Stay with them. If this is the first attack or the condition persists or worsens call for an ambulance
Electric shock	Do not touch casualty while he/she is in contact with an electrical current as he/she will be 'live' and you may be electrocuted. Break the electrical contact by turning off the power supply if possible or pulling out the plug or wrenching the cable free. If you cannot reach these, stand on dry insulating material (such as a telephone directory) and use something made of wood (such as a broom handle) to push the appliance aside. You can then check the casualty. They may need to be resuscitated. Dial 999
Bleeding: 1. Minor cuts and grazes 2. Severe 3. Severe with an object embedded in wound (e.g. glass)	1. Clean with water and apply a clean dressing 2. Lay casualty down and cover the wound with a dressing. Apply direct pressure with your hand. If a limb is bleeding, raise and support it. Raise and support legs if you suspect shock may develop. Dial 999 3. As before, but apply direct pressure to either side of the wound. Build padding up around the object, then bandage over the top of it without pressing on the object
Burns and scalds	Cool immediately with cold water. Place body part under running tap, if possible, for at least 10 minutes. Otherwise, lie casualty down and douse the injury, through any clothes, by pouring on cold water if possible, or applying wet cloths. Remove any restricting clothes or jewellery as long as clothes are not stuck to the burn. Cover with a clean, non-fluffy dressing. Watch for shock, and raise and support legs if you suspect it. Dial 999, take or send to hospital, depending on severity Do not cover burns to the face – you could block an airway or cause distress. Do not over-cool or the body temperature may lower dangerously – this applies particularly to babies
Suspected fractures	Keep the casualty as still as possible. Immobilise the affected part of the body and support it. If possible, bandage it to an unaffected part of the body (e.g. bandage a fractured leg to the unaffected leg for support). Depending on the circumstances, take or remove to hospital or dial 999

Neck and back injuries	Steady and support the head, and tell the casualty to keep still, with head, neck and back in alignment. Keep holding the head, but get a helper to place rolled up towels or other padding either side of the neck and shoulders. Send the helper to dial 999, and remain holding the head until help arrives
Poisoning – swallowed poisons (e.g. tablets, chemicals, berries)	Dial 999. Take a sample of poison to hospital for analysis if possible. If the child is sick, keep a sample, but never try to make a child sick intentionally. Watch for signs of unconsciousness
Bites and stings – minor 1. General, insect For allergic reactions to bites and stings, see Anaphylactic shock 2. To mouth and throat	1. Brush sting away with fingernail if it is visible. Do not use tweezers (if tweezers do need to be used, it is a job for a health professional and medical help should be sought). Raise the affected part and apply an ice-pack or cold compress. The casualty should see a doctor if the pain and swelling persist 2. Give the casualty an ice cube to suck or a cold drink. If swelling starts, dial 999
Effects of extreme heat and cold: 1. Heatstroke Body becomes dangerously overheated, generally due to high fever or overexposure to heat. There may be dizziness, headache, restlessness, hot flushed skin and rapid deterioration in casualty's level of response. Can cause unconsciousness 2. Hypothermia in infants May develop over several days in poorly heated homes or be due to prolonged exposure to the cold outdoors. Babies are particularly vulnerable. Signs are shivering; cold, pale skin; body may feel limp or there may be impaired consciousness; slow, shallow breathing; slow, weak pulse; refusal to feed; unusually quiet	1. Remove casualty to a cool place and remove as much clothing as possible. Dial 999. Wrap the casualty in a cold, wet sheet. Keep the sheet wet until temperature falls to below 38 °C. Then replace the sheet with a dry one. Watch for signs of unconsciousness 2. Re-warm the baby gradually by warming the room and wrapping the infant in blankets. You should call a doctor or take or send a baby to hospital if you suspect hypothermia
Meningitis 1. In children: There may be high temperature or fever, vomiting, severe headache, stiff neck, drowsiness, confusion, dislike of brightlight, seizures, skin rash of red/purple 'pin prick' spots. If the spots spread they may resemble fresh bruising, but this is difficult to see on black skin. The rash does not fade when the side of a glass is pressed against it 2. In babies: There may also be restlessness and high-pitched crying or screaming, a limp or floppy body, swelling of the soft fontanelle area of the skull, and refusal to feed	For children and babies: If a doctor cannot be contacted or will be delayed, dial 999. Do not wait for all of the signs and symptoms to appear. If a casualty has already seen a doctor but is becoming worse, seek urgent medical attention again. Reassure the child and keep them cool until help arrives

Foreign bodies stuck (not penetrating) in the: 1. Eyes 2. Ears 3. Nose This may cause swelling and breathing difficulties	1. Sit the casualty down, facing the light, and tip their head back. Stand behind them, and open their eye with your finger and thumb. Pour clean water from a glass gently into the inner corner of the eye. The water will run out of the outer corner of the eye, hopefully flushing the eye clean. If this does not work, take or send to the doctors/hospital 2. Sit the casualty down and have them tip their head to the side. Pour clean water into the ear gently, hopefully flushing the ear clean. If this does not work, take or send to the doctor/hospital 3. Do not try to remove the object, even if you can see it. Take or send to hospital. Watch for breathing difficulties
Choking: 1. Children 2. Babies	1. If the child is conscious, encourage them to cough. If this does not work, bend the child forwards and give up to five back slaps between the shoulder blades with the heel of your hand. Check the mouth. If this has failed, try five chest thrusts, one every three seconds – stand behind the child and make a fist against the lower breastbone. Grasp the fist with your other hand. Pull sharply inwards and upwards. If this does not work, dial 999. Continue alternating between back slaps and thrusts until help arrives or the child becomes unconscious 2. Lay the baby along your forearm, with its head low, supporting the head and back. Give five back slaps. If this fails, do chest thrusts. Turn the baby on its back. Using two fingers push upwards and inwards towards the baby's breastbone (towards the head). This is one finger's width below the nipple line. Dial 999 and continue until help arrives or the infant becomes unconscious
Febrile convulsions May be due to epilepsy or a high temperature. Violent muscle twitching, clenched fists, arched back. May lead to unconsciousness	Do not try to restrain the child. Instead, clear the immediate area and surround the child with pillows or padding for protection. Cool the environment and the child gradually (as for a temperature), sponging skin if necessary. When seizure stops, place child in recovery position. Dial 999
Head injuries There may be dizziness, disorientation, headache, vomiting. May lead to unconsciousness	Treat any bleeding by covering with a dressing and applying direct pressure. Take or send to hospital. If injury is severe, dial 999

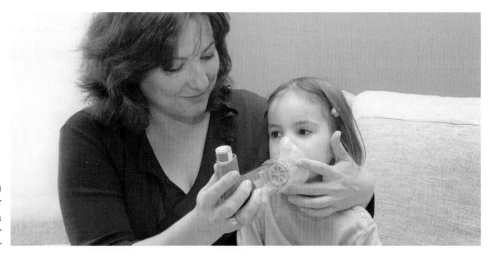

Young children often take their asthma inhaler via a spacer

Managing an unconscious child who is not breathing

If a child is unconscious and not breathing, the heartbeat will slow down and eventually stop. You will need to breathe for them. You will need to have done a registered first-aid course in order to do this. If you are not trained to do this, you must get help as quickly as possible.

Summary

You will learn how to recognise and deal with various illnesses and accidents on a first-aid course, but a brief overview of key conditions is given in the table on pages 51–3.

Dealing with bleeding

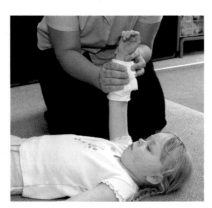

1 Apply pressure to the wound and raise the injured part

2 Lay the child down, while continuing to apply pressure and keep the injured part raised.

3 Keeping the injured part raised cover the wound with a firm, sterile dressing and bandage.

Good hygiene practices

Good standards of hygiene are the key to preventing disease and the spread of infection. Cross-infection occurs when germs are passed from one affected person or material to another, previously unaffected person or material. Settings should have written guidelines covering the prevention of cross-infection through the safe handling of body fluids (blood, urine, faeces and saliva) and other waste. This is necessary because waste products are a source of germs. An example of this is the risk of infection from blood-borne viruses. This includes hepatitis B, hepatitis C and HIV (human immunodeficiency virus). It is recommended that all practitioners become immunised against hepatitis B. This entails three injections given in the arm. There is currently no vaccine against HIV or hepatitis C. However, the viruses can only be transmitted through an exchange of body fluids. Such an exchange could happen within a setting – if an affected person's blood made contact with a practitioner's blood through a cut or graze on the practitioner's hand, for example. But if you follow good practice guidelines and take sensible precautions, you will not need to be overly anxious.

Handling waste

When dealing with waste you should ensure that:

- There are designated areas for covered bins
- There are covered bins kept specifically for different types of waste, including waste items containing body fluids and domestic waste

- Items containing body waste, such as nappies, dressings and used gloves, are disposed of in a sealed bag, which is placed into a sealed bin for disposal
- Bins are emptied daily
- You always put on disposable latex gloves before dealing with any body fluids and before you begin first-aid treatment. You may also wear a disposable apron. Wash your hands well with antiseptic soap afterwards (and before you approach a first-aid casualty if possible)
- Cover any cuts or grazes on your hands with a waterproof dressing
- Cover blood with a 1% hypochlorite solution before wiping it up
- Teach children good hygiene procedures – make sure they wash their hands after going to the toilet and before eating or preparing food. Teach them to cover their mouths and noses when they cough or sneeze, and make sure they dispose of tissues in the bin. Adults must do these things too! Make sure you wash your hands with antiseptic soap after wiping a child's nose.

Food hygiene

Food hygiene is essential for the prevention of food poisoning. Those handling or preparing food should attend a course about food hygiene, gaining a Basic Food Hygiene certificate. Essentially, you should ensure that food is stored safely, prepared and cooked safely, and that food areas are kept hygienically. You should wash your hands with antiseptic soap before and after handling food.

Food storage guidelines include:

- Keep the fridge and freezer cold enough. Use a thermometer to check. Fridges should be below 4°C, and freezers –18°C maximum. They must be cleaned/defrosted regularly
- Cool food quickly before placing in the fridge
- Cover food stored, or wrap with cling-film
- Label items with a correct use-by date if necessary
- Separate raw and cooked food – store raw food at the bottom of the fridge, and cooked food higher up, so that raw juices (should they spill) will not contaminate cooked food
- If food has started to thaw, never refreeze it
- Ensure food is fully thawed before cooking.

Food preparation guidelines include:

- Use waterproof dressings to cover any cuts or grazes on hands
- Do not cough or sneeze over food
- Wear protective clothing (such as an apron) that is only used for food preparation
- Cook food thoroughly – cook eggs until firm and cook meat all the way through
- Test chicken to check it is cooked properly
- Do not reheat food.

Food preparation area guidelines include:

- Keep all areas of the kitchen scrupulously clean. Use a bin with a lid and empty it daily. Keep bins away from food. Disinfect them regularly

- Keep all kitchen appliances and utensils scrupulously clean, including ovens and microwaves
- Keep kitchen cloths and other cloths separate, and keep them scrupulously clean
- Tea towels, cloths and oven gloves must be washed/boiled frequently
- Disposable towels should be used to clear up spills and to dry hands
- Keep insects and pets out of the kitchen
- Do not allow anyone who is unwell to prepare food or enter food preparation areas. This is particularly hazardous when someone has had diarrhoea or vomiting.

Element 302.3

Are you ready for assessment?

Supervise procedures for accidents, injuries, illnesses and other emergencies

You need to show that you can competently supervise procedures for accidents, injuries, illnesses and other emergencies. To do this you will need to be directly observed by your assessor and present other types of evidence. The amount and type of evidence you need to present will vary. You should plan this with your assessor.

Direct observation by your assessor

Observation and/or expert witness testimony is the required assessment method to be used to evidence some of each element in this unit. If your assessor is unable to observe you, s/he will identify an expert in your workplace who will provide testimony of your work-based performance. Usually your assessor or expert witness will observe you in real work activities and this should provide most of the evidence for the performance criteria for the elements in this unit.

Preparing to be observed

You must show your assessor that you can identify signs of accidents and illness and follow procedures to deal with emergencies safely, providing appropriate first aid and medication when necessary. You must show that you can comfort those involved, ensure that your and others are not put at unnecessary risk, and that you can follow

recording procedures correctly. Make sure you are familiar with the signs and symptoms of accidents, illness and other emergencies, and that you know how to deal with them. Simulation is permitted in this element – your assessor may arrange to observe you responding to simulated emergencies.

Other types of evidence

You will need to present different types of evidence in order to:

- Cover criteria not observed by your assessor
- Show that you have the required knowledge, understanding and skills.

Such evidence could include:

- Work products such as records of times you have dealt with illness or accident
- Case studies, projects, assignments and reflective accounts of your work.

Check your knowledge

- Why should you learn about manual handling? **K3P189**
- Why must you always mark the register as soon as children arrive or depart? **K3H192**
- What are the six steps of risk assessment? **K3H194**
- Who should sign a medication record and accident record? **K3H193, K3H196**
- When is it important to wear latex gloves to prevent cross-infection? **K3H200**
- What would you do if you discovered a child was missing from the setting? **K3H201**

Reflective practice

Obtain copies of the health and safety documents used within your setting, including the health and safety policy, accident forms and risk assessments. Look through them carefully. Do you fully understand the purpose and content of each document? Make notes in your reflective journal. Ask your workplace supervisor to explain anything you're unsure about.

UNIT 303

Promote children's development

*T*his unit includes the observation and assessment of children and young people's development and planning to promote development. It is a unit that requires knowledge and understanding of children's development from 0 to 16 years and the ability to demonstrate competence with the children you are working with. The unit covers observing children, recording observational findings, assessing development and planning to promote development.

This unit contains four elements:

⌣ **CCLD 303.1** *Observe development*

⌣ **CCLD 303.2** *Assess development and reflect upon implications for practice*

⌣ **CCLD 303.3** *Plan provision to promote development*

⌣ **CCLD 303.4** *Implement and evaluate plans to promote development*

Introduction

This is a key unit in your qualification. In order to work successfully with children, you need to understand how they develop in all areas. Observing the children that you work with and making careful assessments of their development will enable you to understand a child's achievements and needs, and to plan for them.

This unit on promoting children's development covers:

● Understanding the principles of children's development with charts that show developmental sequences for physical, emotional, social and behavioural development and for communication and intellectual development

● Promoting children's development using observation as a starting point for planning. The principles and practice of observation, assessment, planning, and implementation and evaluation of plans are also considered

● The role of planning and assessment in children's transitions, creative development and emotional intelligence.

This unit is fundamental to your whole qualification because it underpins your work with children and their families. It is impossible to separate the performance criteria and knowledge for this unit from the other units in this book. It is most likely that your assessor will help you to gather evidence for this unit as you work on other units in this qualification. For example, when you are observed communicating with children for

Unit CCLD 301 Develop and promote positive relationships, you will probably be gathering evidence for this unit too. For this reason, you will only find one 'Are you ready for assessment?' section, at the end of this unit. Your assessor will help you to identify how your knowledge and performance can be demonstrated as you work through all of the other units.

Element 303.1

Observe development

K3M202
K3MD211
K3D209
K3D212
K3D214
K3D215
K3D216
K3D217

Key aspects of understanding child development

Children's development is holistic. In other words, although we refer to different areas of children's learning for convenience, in practice children do not learn in a compartmentalised way. There is information about adopting an integrated, holistic approach to providing activities to stimulate children's learning and development in Unit CCLD 309 Plan and implement curriculum frameworks for early education, and in Unit CCLD 312 Plan and implement positive environments for babies and children under three years.

Link | **Unit CCLD 309** Plan and implement curriculum frameworks for early education
Unit CCLD 312 Plan and implement positive environments for babies and children under three years

Tables within this unit give an approximate guide as to when babies, children and young people are likely to achieve certain milestones in their development (such as learning to walk). These are the accepted expected development rates or developmental norms. But it is important to understand that children develop at different rates – this is entirely normal and should be expected. Remember that the guides are *approximate.* Children of the same age will not reach all of the milestones at the same time – some children will achieve milestones earlier than the accepted rates of development and some will achieve them later. The same child may well be ahead of suggested norms in some areas and behind them in other areas. For example, a child may crawl and walk early but begin to talk a little late.

Children generally develop in broadly the same sequence – babies will learn to roll over before they sit up for example, and children will say single words before they string two or three together in early sentences.

Practitioners must have a good understanding of the child development norms so that:

- They can carry out observation and assessment effectively

  Practitioners must evaluate individual children's development by making comparisons between a child's actual developmental stage and the expected development rates

- They can offer appropriate activities and experiences for individual children

  This will be informed by observation and assessment of individual children

- They can anticipate the next stage of a child's development

  This allows the practitioner to provide activities and experiences that will challenge and interest children, stimulating their development
- They notice when children are not progressing as expected

  Although children develop at different rates, significant delays or many delays in several areas, can be an indication that children need intervention and extra support.

There are two key factors that influence how development occurs:

- Nature

  Development occurs in response to the way children are genetically programmed from birth to be able to do certain things at certain times. This is referred to as 'nature'
- Nurture

  Development occurs in response to the experiences that individual children have from the time they are born onwards. This is referred to as 'nurture'.

It is generally accepted that individual children develop as they do because of a combination of the two factors – nature and nurture. Language is a good example of this. Studies have shown that babies all over the world make coos, gurgles and other sounds that are very similar. The potential to speak and a common ability to make similar pre-language sounds would seem to be down to nature. But children learn to speak the language they are exposed to – this is down to nurture.

This means that practitioners must understand that individual children's development and levels of maturity will depend in part on the experiences they have had (or the way they have been nurtured). To have realistic expectations about children's development and maturity, practitioners must take into account that:

- Children develop within unique families. Different families influence children in widely different ways

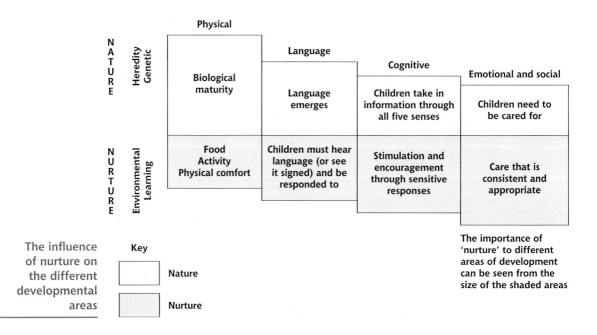

The influence of nurture on the different developmental areas

Families exist within a social and cultural system. Social and cultural systems interact with and influence the family, and therefore the child's development.

Children have different experiences at different times and so they develop at different rates. Children cannot be expected to achieve aspects of development that are largely attributed to nurture if they have not yet been exposed to experiences that encourage this development. Practitioners must keep this in mind. The diagram on page 60 shows how nature and nurture influence aspects of children's development.

You need to have detailed knowledge about the expected development rates for babies, children and young people. There are many books available dedicated solely to the topic of child development. It is advisable for practitioners to read widely about the subject. The tables on pages 63–76 give an overview of the expected rates of development from the age of 0–16 years, in the followings areas:

- Physical development
- Communication, intellectual development and learning
- Social, emotional and behavioural development.

When discussing development, the term 'neonate' is used to refer to a newly born baby. 'Prone' is the term used to describe the position of a baby lying on her front. 'Supine' is the term used to describe the position of a baby lying on her back.

Key Terms

Neonate
newly born baby

Prone
position of a baby lying on her front

Supine
position of a baby lying on her back

Gross motor skills

Gross motor skills are an aspect of physical development. The term 'gross motor skills' is used to refer to whole-body movements such as sitting up, crawling and walking. These skills develop rapidly during a child's first five years.

Crawling

Sitting from lying down

Bear-walking

Walking with two hands held

Walking with one hand held

Walking alone

Gross motor skills involved in the development of walking

Fine motor skills

Fine motor skills are also an aspect of physical development. The term 'fine motor skills' is used to refer to the delicate, manipulative movements that are made with the fingers. Fine motor skills and the development of vision are linked. This is often referred to as 'hand/eye co-ordination'. Fine motor skills and hand/eye co-ordination are used when a child is threading cotton reels for example – the child will look carefully at the position of the hole in the reel, and manipulate the string accordingly.

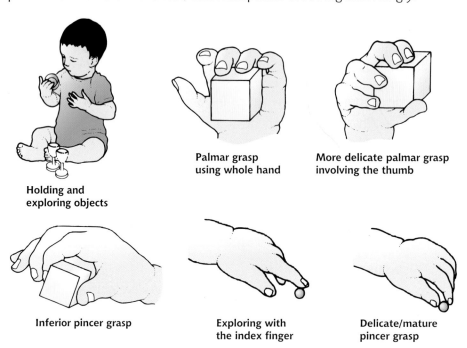

Holding and
exploring objects

Palmar grasp
using whole hand

More delicate palmar grasp
involving the thumb

Fine motor skills
involved in the
development of
manipulation

Inferior pincer grasp

Exploring with
the index finger

Delicate/mature
pincer grasp

Physical development

The neonate (newly born baby) has reflexes. These are physical movements or reactions that they make without consciously intending to do so. For example, the neonate will move her head in search of the mother's nipple or the teat of a bottle when her lips or cheek are touched (known as rooting), and she will also suck and swallow milk. These reflexes help the baby to feed, and therefore survive. You may have experienced the grasp reflex – a baby will clasp their fingers around yours if you touch their palm. You will have probably seen the startle reflex too – a startled baby will make a fist and their arms will move away from their body. This can often be seen if there is a loud noise, or if the baby wakes suddenly.

Newly born
babies usually
have their fists
clenched

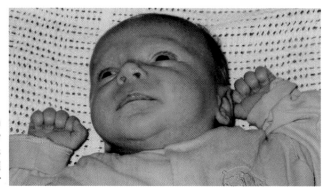

Rates of development for 1 month

Physical development – gross motor skills

In supine: head is on one side

In prone: head is on one side, can be lifted

When sitting: head falls forwards (known as head lag), and the back curves

Head will turn towards light and noise

Hands are closed tighlty

Reflexes help a baby to survive

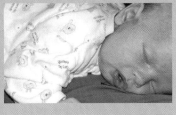

Physical development – fine motor skills

Gazes attentively at faces, particularly when fed and talked to

Social and emotional development

Totally dependent on others

Smiles from about 5 weeks

Senses are used for exploration

Begins to respond to sounds heard in the environment by making own sounds

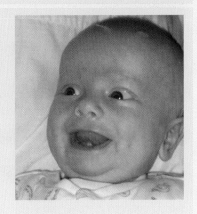

Communication and intellectual development

Communicates needs through sounds

Communicates needs through crying

Communication occurs through the physical closeness

Begins to coo and gurgle in response to interaction from carers

Rates of development for 3 months

Physical development – gross motor skills

Turns from side to back

In supine: head in central position

In prone: head and chest can be lifted from the floor, supported by the forearms

When sitting: little head lag remains, back is straighter

Arms can be waved and brought together

Legs can be kicked separately and together

Physical development – fine motor skills

Alert, the baby moves her head to watch others

Engages in hand and finger play

Holds rattle briefly before dropping

Social and emotional development

Through use of senses, a baby begins to understand she is a separate person

Baby begins to discover what she can do, and this creates a sense of self

May cry if a primary carer leaves the room, not yet understanding that they still exist and will return

Shows feelings such as excitement and fear

Reacts positively when a carer is caring, kind and soothing. If a carer does not respond to a baby, she may stop trying to interact

Communication and intellectual development

Recognises and links familiar sounds such as the face and voice of a carer

Will hold 'conversations' with carer when talked to, making sounds and waiting for a response

Can imitate high and low sounds

Rates of development for 6 months

Physical development – gross motor skills

Turns from front to back, and may do the reverse

In supine: head can be lifted and controlled when pulled to sitting position

In prone: head and chest can be fully extended supported by arms, with the hands flat on the floor

Sits unsupported for some time, with back straight, and plays in this position

Uses hands to play with feet, and may take them to the mouth

Weight-bears when held in standing position

Physical development – fine motor skills

Interested in bright, shiny objects

Watches events keenly

Uses palmar grasp to pick up objects. Takes them to the mouth for exploration

Passes objects from hand to hand

Social and emotional development

Shows a wider range of feelings more clearly and vocally. May laugh and screech with delight, but cry with fear at the sight of a stranger

Clearly tells people apart, showing a preference for primary carers/siblings

Reaches out to be held, and may stop crying when talked to

Enjoys looking at self in the mirror

Enjoys attention and being with others

Communication and intellectual development

Sounds are used intentionally to call for a carer's attention

Babbling is frequent. The baby plays tunefully with the sounds they can make

Rhythm and volume are explored vocally

Enjoys rhymes and accompanying actions

Rates of development for 9 months

Physical development – gross motor skills

Sits unsupported on the floor

Will go on hands and knees, and may crawl

Pulls self to standing position using furniture for support

Cruises around the room (side-stepping, holding furniture for support)

Takes steps if both hands are held by carer

Physical development – fine motor skills

Uses an inferior pincer grasp to pick up objects

Explores objects with the eyes

Points to and pokes at objects of interest with index finger

Social and emotional development

Enjoys playing with carers, e.g. peek-a-boo games and pat-a-cake.

Offers objects, but does not yet let go

Increasing mobility allows baby to approach people

Begins to feed self with support

Communication and intellectual development

Initiates a wider range of sounds, and recognises a few familiar words. Understands 'no', and knows own name

Greatly enjoys playing with carers and holding conversations

Makes longer strings of babbling sounds

Intentionally uses volume vocally

Rates of development for 12 months

Physical development – gross motor skills

Sits down from standing position

Stands alone briefly and may walk a few steps alone

Throws toys intentionally

Physical development – fine motor skills

Clasps hands together

Uses sophisticated pincer grasp, and releases hold intentionally

Looks for objects that fall out of sight, understanding they still exist although they can't be seen

Feeds self with spoon and finger foods

Social and emotional development

The sense of self identity increases, as self-esteem and self-confidence develop

Waves goodbye, when prompted at first, and then spontaneously

Content to play alone or alongside other children for increasing periods of time

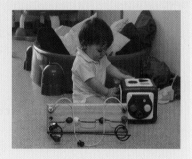

Communication and intellectual development

Increasingly understands the basic messages communicated by carers and older siblings

Can respond to basic instructions

Babbling sounds increasingly like speech, and leads to the first single words being spoken

Shows understanding that particular words are associated with people and objects, by using a few single words in context

Rates of development for 15 months

Physical development – gross motor skills

Walks independently

Crawls upstairs. Crawls downstairs feet first

Sits in a child-sized chair independently

Physical development – fine motor skills

Tries to turn the pages of a book

Makes a tower of two blocks

Makes marks on paper with crayons

Holds own cup when drinking

Social and emotional development

Curious. Wants to explore the world, as long as carers are close by

May show signs of separation anxiety (i.e. upset when left at nursery)

May 'show off' to entertain carers

Shows a keener interest in the activities of peers

Can be jealous of the attention/toys given to another child

Changeable emotionally. Quickly alternates between wanting to
do things alone and being dependent on carers

Communication and intellectual development

Will put away/look for very familiar objects in the right place

Uses toys for their purpose, e.g. puts a doll in a pram

Understands the concepts of labels such as 'you', 'me', 'mine', 'yours'

The use of single words increases, and more words are learnt

Behavioural development

May respond with anger when told off or thwarted. May throw toys
or have a tantrum

Can be distracted from inappropriate behaviour

Possessive of toys and carers. Reluctant to share

Child 'is busy' or 'into everything'

Rates of development for 18 months

Physical development – gross motor skills

Walks confidently. Attempts to run

Walks up and down stairs if hand is held by carer

Bends from the waist without falling forwards

Balances in the squatting position

Pushes and pulls wheeled toys

Rolls and throws balls, attempts to kick them

Physical development – fine motor skills

Uses delicate pincer grasp to thread cotton reels

Makes a tower of three blocks

Makes large scribbles with crayons

Can use door handles

Social and emotional development

Has a better understanding of being an individual

Very curious, and more confident to explore

Becomes frustrated easily if incapable of doing something

Follows carers, keen to join in with their activities

Plays alongside peers more often (parallel play), and may imitate them

Still very changeable emotionally

May show sympathy for others (e.g. putting their arm around a crying child)

Communication and intellectual development

Understands a great deal of what carers say

More words spoken. Uses people's names

Uses trial and error in exploration (tries to post several shapes in the hole of a shape sorter)

Behavioural development

Can be restless and very determined, quickly growing irritated or angry

May assert will strongly, showing angry defiance and resistance to adults

Can still be distracted from inappropriate behaviour

Rates of development for 2 years

Physical development – gross motor skills

Runs confidently

Walks up and down stairs alone holding hand rail

Rides large wheeled toys (without peddles)

Kicks stationary balls

Physical development – fine motor skills

Makes a tower of six blocks

Joins and separates interlocking toys

Draws circles, lines and dots with a pencil

Puts on shoes

Social and emotional development

Beginning to understand own feelings. Identifies sad and happy faces

Experiences a range of changeable feelings which are expressed in behaviour

More responsive to the feelings of others

Often responds to carers lovingly, and may initiate loving gestures (a cuddle)

Communication and intellectual development

Completes simple jigsaw puzzles (or 'play-trays')

Understands that actions have consequences

Will often name objects on sight (e.g. may point and say 'chair' or 'dog')

Vocabulary increases. Joins two words together, e.g. 'shoes on'

Short sentences are used by 30 months. Some words are used incorrectly, e.g. 'I *goed* in'

Behavioural development

May use growing language ability to protest verbally

May get angry with peers, and lash out on occasion (e.g. pushing or even biting them)

Rates of development for 3 years

Physical development – gross motor skills

Walks and runs on tip-toes

Walks up and downstairs confidently

Rides large wheeled toys using peddles and steering

Kicks moving balls forwards

Enjoys climbing and sliding on small apparatus

Physical development – fine motor skills

Makes a tower of nine blocks

Turns the pages of a book reliably

Draws a face with a pencil, using the preferred hand. Attempts to write letters

Puts on and removes coat. Fastens large, easy zippers

Social and emotional development

Child can tell carers how she is feeling. Empathises with the feelings of others

Uses the toilet and washes own hands. Can put on clothes

Imaginary and creative play is enjoyed

Enjoys company of peers and makes friends. Wants adult approval. Is affected by mood of carers/peers

Communication and intellectual development

Child is enquiring. Frequently asks 'what' and 'why' questions

Use of language for thinking and reporting. Enjoys stories and rhymes

Vocabulary increases quickly. Use of plurals, pronouns, adjectives, possessives and tenses

Longer sentences are used. By 42 months, most language is used correctly

Can name colours. Can match and sort items into simple sets (e.g. colour sets)

Can count to ten by rote. Can only count out three or four objects

Begins to recognise own name on sight

Behavioural development

Increasingly able to understand consequence of behaviour and the concept of 'getting in trouble'

Understands the concept of saying sorry and 'making up'

Less rebellious. Less likely to physically express anger as words can be used

Rates of development for 4 years

Physical development – gross motor skills

Changes direction while running

Walks in a straight line successfully

Confidently climbs and slides on apparatus

Hops safely

Can bounce and catch balls, and take aim

Physical development – fine motor skills

Makes a tower of ten blocks

Learning to fasten most buttons and zips

Learning to use scissors. Cuts out basic shapes

Draws people with heads, bodies and limbs. Writes names and letters in play as the awareness that print carries meaning develops

Social and emotional development

May be confident socially. Self-esteem is apparent. Awareness of gender roles

Friendship with peers is increasingly valued. Enjoys playing with groups of children

Control over emotions increases. Can wait to have needs met by carers

As imagination increases child may become fearful (e.g. of the dark or monsters)

Communication and intellectual development

Completes puzzles of 12 pieces

Memory develops. Child recalls many songs and stories. Fantasy and reality may be confused

Problem solves (I wonder what will happen if), and makes hypothesis (I think this will happen if)

Sorts objects into more complex sets. Number correspondence improves

As an understanding of language increases so does enjoyment of rhymes, stories and nonsense

Behavioural development

If exposed to swearing child is likely to use these words in her own language

Learning to negotiate and get along with others through experimenting with behaviour

Experiences being in/out of control, feeling power, having quarrels with peers, being blamed, blaming

Has a good understanding of familiar, basic rules

Distraction works less often, but child increasingly understands reasoning

Rates of development for 5 years

Physical development – gross motor skills

Controls ball well. Plays ball games with rules

Rides bike with stabilisers

Balance is good, uses low stilts confidently

Sense of rhythm has developed. Enjoys dance and movement activities

Physical development – fine motor skills

Controls mark making materials well (e.g. pencils). Writing more legible

Writes letters and short, familiar words

Learns to sew

Social and emotional development

Child will have started school. This transition may be unsettling

Enjoys group play and co-operative activities

Increasingly understands rules of social conduct and rules of games, but may have difficulty accepting losing

Increasing sense of own personality and gender

Keen to 'fit in' with others. Approval from adults and peers desired

Friends are important. Many are made at school

Many children will have new experiences out of school (e.g. play clubs, friends coming for tea)

Increasingly independent, undertaking most physical care needs for themselves

Communication and intellectual development

Options/knowledge of subjects are shared using language for thinking

Enjoys books. Learning to read. Recognises some words

Thinking skills and memory increase as vocabulary grows

Spends longer periods at activities when engaged. Shows persistence

Children learn from new experiences at school. Learning style preferences may become apparent

Behavioural development

Feels shame/guilt when adults disapprove of behaviour

May seek attention, 'showing off' in front of peers

Keen to win and be 'right'. Adults need to meditate in squabbles

Often responds to 'time out' method of managing behaviour

Rates of development for 6–7 years

Physical development – gross motor skills

Can hop on either leg, skip and play hopscotch

Rides bicycle without stabilisers

Confidently climbs and slides on larger apparatus in school and in parks

Physical development – fine motor skills

Can catch a ball with one hand only

Writing is legible

Sews confidently and may tie shoe laces

Social and emotional development

Enjoys team games and activities

Towards age 7, a child may doubt their learning ability ('I can't do it')

May be reluctant to try or persevere, becoming frustrated easily

Personality is established. Attitudes to life are developed

Solid friendships are formed. The relationship with 'best friends' is important

More susceptible to peer pressure. Cultural identity also established

Has learnt how to behave in various settings and social situations (e.g. at school, play club, a friend's house)

Communication and intellectual development

Imagination skills are developed. Fantasy games are complex and dramatic

Language refined and more adult-like. Enjoys jokes and word play

Many children read and write basic text by age 7, but this varies widely

Ability to predict and to plan ahead has developed. Understands cause and effect well

Can conserve number. Does simple calculations. Understands measurement and weighing

Behavioural development

May sulk or be miserable at times (when under pressure or when conflict arises)

May be over-excitable at times, leading to 'silly' behaviour

May still rebel, but more capable of intentionally choosing behavioural response to conflict

Increasingly able to settle minor disputes and conflict independently

May argue over carrying out tasks (e.g. tidying up or doing homework)

Has a strong sense of right and wrong. May tell adults when another child has broken a rule

Rates of development for 8–12 years

Physical development – gross motor skills

Physical growth slows at first, so there are fewer physical milestones reached

Puberty generally begins between 11–13 years (see 13–16 years table)

Co-ordination and speed of movement develops

Muscles and bones develop. Has more physical strength

Begins to run around less in play

Interest in TV, computers, console games, DVDs may mean child is less active. A balanced, active lifestyle should be encouraged

Physical development – fine motor skills

Does joined-up writing, which becomes increasingly adult-like

Has computer skills. May type well and control the mouse as an adult would

Can sew well, and may be adept at delicate craft activities such as braiding threads

Social and emotional development

May feel unsettled when making the transition from primary school to secondary school, and as puberty approaches

Stable friendships are relied upon. These are generally same-sex, although children play in mixed groups/teams

May be reluctant to go to a play club or event unless a friend will be there too

More independent. Makes more decisions. May play unsupervised at times. May travel to school alone by end of age band

Communication and intellectual development

May read for enjoyment in leisure time

Can make-up and tell stories that have been plotted out

Verbal and written communication is fluent, often with correct grammar usage. Enjoys chatting to friends/adults

Range of new subjects may be learnt at secondary school

Child may follow their interests, learning outside of school

Sense of logic develops. Thinking in abstract by 10 (can consider beliefs, morals and world events)

Behavioural development

Mood swings may be experienced during puberty (see 13–16 years table)

Conflict with parents due to desire for increasing independence ('Why can't I stay home alone?')

May feel rules are unfair ('But all my friends are allowed to do it!')

May refuse to go along with some decisions made by parents (e.g. refusing to wear certain clothes purchased for them)

Rates of development for 13–16 years

Physical development – gross motor skills

The bodies of both boys and girls change throughout puberty. There is variation in the age at which this occurs

Girls generally enter puberty by 13 years, becoming women physically by 16 years

Boys generally enter puberty by 14 years, becoming men physically by 16 or 17 years

Sporting talents may become apparent

Physical development – fine motor skills

May learn/refine new manipulative skills (such as drawing, stitching, carpentry, woodwork, playing an instrument)

Talent in arts or crafts may become apparent

Social and emotional development

Desire to express individuality, but also a strong desire to fit in with peers

Becomes interested in own sexuality, and feels attracted to others

May express self creatively through art/music/dance or creative writing

May worry about aspects of physical appearance

May express self/experiment with identity through appearance (e.g. dress, hairstyles, piercings)

Pressure at school mounts as exam curriculum is followed

Young people may feel overwhelmed or anxious

A balance of school work/leisure time is important, especially if young people take on part-time jobs

Developing own morals, beliefs and values outside of parents' influence

Likely to communicate innermost thoughts and feelings more frequently to friends than to adults

May prefer to spend more time with friends than with family. May stay in bedroom more at home

Communication and intellectual development

Academic knowledge increases as exam curriculum is followed

Towards age 16, decisions are made about the future (college course/career)

Young people may be reluctant to directly ask adults for the advice or information they need. They may prefer to access it anonymously

Behavioural development

May swing between acting maturely, and saying/doing 'childish' things (e.g. may watch a young children's TV programme, or sit on a swing in the park)

May experiment with smoking, alcohol, drugs or early promiscuity. This behaviour is linked with low-self esteem

May experience mood swings. Tense atmospheres are lightened when adults remain in good humour

May disregard the opinions/values of parents if they conflict with those of the peer group

Acting on own values may cause conflict at home (e.g becoming a vegetarian)

Confidentiality

Practitioners must handle sensitive information about children and families with confidentiality and care. Further information about confidentiality, security and data protection can be found on pages 4–6 of Unit CCLD 301 Develop and promote positive relationships.

Link   **Unit CCLD 301** Develop and promote positive relationships

Observation

K3D303
K3D204
K3D205
K3D206
K3D207
K3D208
K3D215

Observation is a tool used by practitioners. It requires practitioners to temporarily distance themselves from the children they work with in order to be objective about their behaviour and development. Through observation, practitioners can evaluate all areas of the progress and development of children.

Observation is carried out in a cycle. Firstly, baseline information is collected which tells practitioners about a child's current stage of development (see below). Later, observations are carried out. These help practitioners to monitor the progress made since the baseline assessment information was collected. Regular observations continue, and an ongoing record of children's development is built up. Observations are then used to inform the planning.

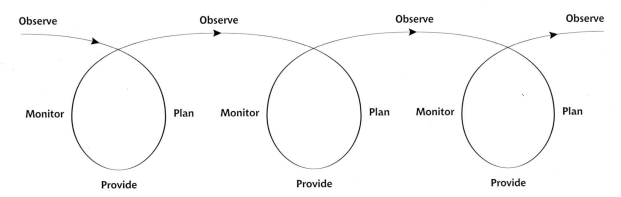

The planning cycle

There is further information about summative and formative assessment in Unit CCLD 310 Assess children's progress according to curriculum frameworks for early education.

Link   **Unit CCLD 309** Plan and implement curriculum frameworks for early education

Sometimes practitioners will carry out general, broad observations of whatever children happen to be doing. But other observations are focused. For instance, a practitioner may decide to observe a child playing outside with his peers because they are particularly interested in observing the child's gross motor skills and his social skills. This is referred to as the 'objective' of the observation. Settings will have their own policies and procedures about the way in which observations are carried out. Practitioners must work in line with them at all times.

In addition to monitoring general developmental progress, observation is particularly helpful for building up a picture of the social relationships and bonds children are making with their peers and with adults. It can also reveal whether children are provided with a stimulating environment, interesting activities and appropriate routines.

Regular observations can also help to highlight changes in children's behaviour patterns. This can be very helpful if a child has become quiet and withdrawn, or perhaps unsettled or angry, as there is a record of the change to refer to. Records are also helpful for reporting to parents, carers and other professionals if appropriate.

Methods of observation

There are several methods of recording observations. It is good practice for you to become familiar with all of the methods over time. However, you should select the most appropriate method to suit your objective and purpose, and work in line with the requirements of your setting.

During observations the behaviour of children can change. If they are aware of being watched, some children may feel anxious or excited, or they may try harder than usual. To counteract this, the practitioner may decide to be a 'non-participant observer'. This means that the practitioner will be unobtrusive – they will settle themselves somewhere suitable to watch the child without alerting them to the fact they are being observed. The practitioner will not interact with the children during this time. They will not speak and so there will be no need to make a record of their own actions or words during the observation.

It is easier to be objective and to record what is happening when you are not involved in events. However, it can be hard to find somewhere unobtrusive that still allows you to see and hear everything that occurs. Although you can use any method of observation as a non-participant observer, if you are looking to observe certain aspects of development or behaviour, you may not see them if you do not encourage children to carry out particular activities or tasks. However, this technique is well suited to the 'free-description' and 'target child' methods of observation, which are explained on page 79 and pages 81–2.

Alternatively, the practitioner can be a 'participant observer'. The participant observer can directly ask or encourage children to do things. This technique works well with the 'checklist method' of observation described on page 80, which is often used with babies and young children. Participant observers can ask questions to find out the reason for a child's behaviour – 'Why are you doing that?'

Practitioners must plan their observation time with colleagues to ensure that it fits in with the overall plans of the setting. Sometimes practitioners find it necessary to abandon an observation, for example if they see something unsafe about to happen or if a child in search of assistance cannot be redirected to another adult.

Whatever method of observation is used, the following key pieces of information are always needed:

- The name of child (or alternate method of identifying them – initials perhaps)
- Date and timing of the observation
- Where the observation was carried out
- Name of the observer

A practitioner observing

- Activity observed/objective of observation
- Other children present
- Other adults present.

THE LIBRARY
NORTH WEST KENT COLLEG.
DERING WAY, GRAVESEND

The presentation of observations differs from setting to setting. However, this key information is often recorded on a separate piece of paper which accompanies the observation itself.

The key methods of observation are outlined below.

Free description (also known as written or narrative description)

The observer focuses on the activity of the child, writing down everything seen during the allotted time. Free description observations are generally short, lasting for perhaps five minutes or less. They are helpful for focusing on areas of difficulty for children, for instance working out exactly what is happening when a child struggles to feed herself. These observations are often recorded in a notebook and written up afterwards.

You will need:

- A notepad
- A pen.

What to do

Write a detailed description of how the child carries out the activity being observed. Note their actions and behaviour, including their facial expressions. Record what the child says and any non-verbal communication such as gestures. This is intensive work, which is why this type of observation is usually used for just a few minutes. Observations are usually recorded in the present tense.

Example

Ben is sitting at the painting table next to Jessica. He picks up his paintbrush and looks at her. She looks back. He smiles and holds his brush out to her. Jessica takes it and smiles back. Ben says, 'Thank you'.

Checklists (also known as tick lists)

A form prompts the observer to look for particular skills or reflexes that a child has. The observer ticks them off as they are seen. This method is frequently used for assessing a child's stage of development. It is well suited to the observation of babies, whose physical development will typically progress rapidly. The observations may be done over time or babies and children may be asked to carry out specific tasks.

You will need:

- A prepared checklist (these can be purchased or developed by practitioners)
- A pen.

What to do

The checklist tells you what to observe and record. As a participant observer, encourage children to carry out the necessary tasks, ticking the relevant boxes to record the child's response – generally whether they could carry out the task competently. As a non-participant observer, tick the boxes as you see evidence of children's competence naturally occurring.

Example

Activity	Yes	No	Date	Observer's comments
Rolls from back to front				
Rolls from front to back				

Time samples

The observer decides on a period of time for the observation, perhaps two hours or the length of a session. The child's activity is recorded on a form at set intervals – perhaps every 10 or 15 minutes. This tracks the child's activity over the period of time. However, significant behaviours may occur between the intervals and these will not be recorded.

You will need:

- A prepared form giving the times for the observations
- A pen
- A watch.

What to do

Keep an eye on the time to ensure you observe at regular intervals. At each allotted time, observe the child and record their activity in the same way as in the 'free description' method.

Example

10.00 a.m.

Ben is sitting at the painting table next to Jessica. He picks up his paintbrush and looks at her. She looks back. He smiles and holds his brush out to her. Jessica takes it and smiles back. Ben says, 'Thank you'.

10.15 a.m.

Ben gets down from the table. He goes to the nursery nurse. He looks at her and says, 'Wash hands'.

Event samples

This method is used when practitioners have reason to record how often an aspect of a child's behaviour or development occurs. A form is prepared identifying the aspect being tracked. Each time the behaviour or development occurs a note of the time and circumstance is recorded. Samples may take place over a session, a week or in some circumstances longer. Practitioners may want to observe how frequently a child is physically aggressive for instance.

You will need:

- A prepared form adapted for the objective of the observation
- A pen.

What to do

Watch a child, and each time the aspect of behaviour or development being observed occurs, record the circumstances along with the time.

Example

Event no.	Time	Event	Circumstances
1	2.30 p.m.	Joshua pushed Daisy over	Joshua had left his teddy on the floor. He saw Daisy pick it up. He went over to Daisy and tried to take the teddy. She did not let go. Joshua pushed her over. Daisy gave Joshua the toy and started to cry. Joshua walked away quickly with the teddy

Target child

The observer will record a child's activity over a long period of time, but unlike the time sample method, the aim is not to have any gaps in the duration of the observation. To achieve this the observer uses a range of codes to record, in shorthand on a ready-prepared form, what is happening.

You will need:

- A prepared form with a key to the abbreviations that will be used
- A pen
- A watch.

What to do

With this type of observation the observer has to make decisions about which things are significant and should be recorded because it is impossible to record every detail over a long period. (It is interesting for two people to observe the same target child over the same period and then compare their forms. They are likely to have recorded different things.) Language and activity are recorded in separate columns for ease. It takes practice to get used to using the codes.

Example

Time	Activity	Language	Social grouping	Involvement level
11.30	TC goes to the box of blocks. Uses both hands to tip the box up and get the blocks out	_TC_ 'Out'	SOL	1
11.31	TC sits down. Using right hand he places one block on top of another. He repeats this, building a tower of four blocks		SOL	1

Key:

TC = target child
_TC_ = target child talking to self
SOL = solitary grouping
1 = target child absorbed in their activity

Additional codes will be used. Codes vary within settings. Refer to your organisational procedures. Further information is given in *A Practical Guide to Observation and Assessment* (Hobart, C. and Frankel, J. (1999) Nelson Thornes Ltd, Cheltenham)

Reliability and validity

When practitioners carry out observation, they aim to be objective. In other words, they aim to record exactly what is happening without interpreting events from their own point of view. Because we all use our past experience and knowledge to process what we see happening in the world, there is a danger that we will interpret events from our point of view. But when you are observing, you should only record what you see. Otherwise the observation is not valid.

Practitioners may sometimes be tempted to record that a child can do something, perhaps because the child can *nearly* do it, and the practitioner wants them to have a favourable outcome. Or, perhaps the practitioner thinks they have seen the child do something before, and so they want to give them the benefit of the doubt. However, once again the practitioner must only record what they see.

Sometimes there are factors outside of the practitioner's control that may affect the reliability or outcome of an observation. If it is a very hot and sticky day for example, children may be feeling fractious and irritable and they may behave differently than they usually do. This means that an observation may not give a reliable picture of the children's general behaviour. Alternatively children may be excited, or they may be feeling a little unsettled as they get to know a new child or adult who has joined the setting. If you identify a factor that is likely to affect the reliability of the observation, you should record it on the observation record. Failing to do so could make the observation misleading as adults reading it may believe the behaviour recorded is representative of the way in which a child generally behaves. The outcome would then be compromised.

Baseline information

Before practitioners can evaluate the progress that children are making they must get a picture of their current level of development. This is known as 'baseline information'. It is the information on which future observation is based and so it must be documented carefully. Baseline information also informs the way in which practitioners approach their work with individual children. This is because the activities that practitioners offer, and the way in which they will relate with children, will depend on individual children's abilities.

Baseline information can be collected from several sources including:

- Discussions with parents and carers
- Records that parents may have if their child has been to another setting previously
- Information from assessments made by other professionals, such as health visitors, GPs or speech therapists
- Baseline assessment carried out by the practitioner.

Although information will be gathered from the sources above, practitioners often conduct their own baseline observations to fill in the gaps. For instance, parents may not know if their child can stack bricks or sort shapes because they may not have the relevant resources at home. So the practitioner will observe the child playing with these resources at the setting in order to inform the baseline assessment.

Parental permission

As the primary carers and guardians of their children, parents have the right to decide what personal information is collected and recorded about their child. It is essential that practitioners obtain written permission from parents authorising them to carry out observations and to keep relevant documentation on record. Many settings ask for parental permission on the registration form that parents complete prior to their child attending the setting. This must be signed and dated. The details of observation should be kept confidential unless withholding information would affect the well-being of the child.

It is essential that students also gain permission from workplace supervisors *before* carrying out observations. Supervisors will probably ask to see your completed observation and the child's family may also want to have a copy.

Theories of play, learning and development

K3D210
K3D213

You can read about the key theories of learning and development and how they may influence practice in Unit CCLD 309 Plan and implement curriculum frameworks for early education. There are also further details later in this unit. Information about theories of play can be found in Unit CCLD 318 Plan for and support self-directed play.

 Link   **Unit CCLD 309** Plan and implement curriculum frameworks for early education
Unit CCLD 318 Plan for and support self-directed play.

Element 303.2
Assess development and reflect upon implications for practice

Assessing and evaluating observations

K3D204
K3D206
K3D207
K3D208
K3D216

Once an observation (or series of observations) has been completed, a practitioner will consider the observation carefully and then draw conclusions. The consideration aspect is known as 'assessment', and the conclusions drawn are known as the 'evaluation' or the 'outcome'. Some people refer to the whole process of assessing and evaluating as the 'interpretation'.

Settings will have developed their own techniques for interpretation and for the way in which the interpretation is presented in written format. You should follow your setting's guidelines. However, generally speaking practitioners will follow an assessment procedure similar to the one outlined below:

> Go through the observation, noting sections that seem significant in terms of behaviour or development. Significant events could reflect achievement, progress, difficulty or the child's feelings. Unusual behaviour will also be of interest

> Reflect on the significant events, considering what conclusions can be drawn. For example, if a two-year-old has been observed getting out a box of blocks for himself, you may conclude that a level of independence has been achieved in selecting and accessing materials

> Consider if the behaviour observed is consistent with what you know about the child development norms. Although it is not required by most settings, your assessor may ask you to make reference to the child development theories on which you are basing your conclusions. This demonstrates that you have a sound knowledge base from which to make assessments

> Consider what you already know about the individual child from baseline assessment and prior observations. Are they making progress? If so, how is this evident? If not, is this currently a cause for concern?

> Once these assessments are finalised, practitioners will write up their evaluations, generally in a free-flowing style. It is essential to ensure that the final evaluation:
> • Is firmly based on what was recorded at the time of observation
> • Makes links between the development norms and the child's actual stage of development

Observation

> The last stage is to use the information gathered to inform the setting's planning

⟨ Sharing information

It is appropriate to share information gained through observation with colleagues who work directly with the child in question, and with senior staff (in a group setting). Discussion between practitioners can help to build up a well-rounded picture of a child. It is good practice for more than one practitioner to carry out observations on children as this helps to ensure validity.

It is good practice to share with parents or carers information about the development and progress of children. This should be done in an open, positive way – key workers often arrange a meeting with families for this purpose. The information given by the practitioners should be used a starting point for discussion. It is important to remember that the parents are generally a child's primary carer and that they know their child best. Families have much to contribute to a discussion about the progress of their child and this information should be valued. It can also be recorded in the child's records.

If you become concerned about a child following observation, it is important that you do not delay in reporting your concerns in line with your setting's policies and procedures. This means that children can get the help and support they may need as soon as possible. Early intervention can often make a difference to how a child continues to progress in their development. There is more information about reporting concerns to senior staff, SENCOs, families and outside professionals on pages 304–5 of Unit CCLD 321 Support children with disabilities or special educational needs and their families. In that unit there are also details about involving families in observations.

Link   **Unit CCLD 321** Support children with disabilities or special educational needs and their families

Information about observing, assessing and recording can be found throughout Unit CCLD 310 Assess children's progress according to curriculum frameworks for early education, and in Element 312.1 of Unit CCLD 312 Plan and implement positive environments for babies and children under three years. In Unit CCLD 321 Support children with disabilities or special educational needs and their families, there is additional information about involving families in observations.

Link   **Unit CCLD 310** Assess children's progress according to curriculum frameworks for early education
Unit CCLD 312 Plan and implement positive environments for babies and children under three years
Unit CCLD 321 Support children with disabilities or special educational needs and their families

Element 303.3   *Plan provision to promote development*

K3D218
K3D219
K3D220
K3D221

What practitioners plan and provide for children to promote their development should be based on what is known about them, and so observations of children inform the planning of provision. Practitioners' reflections on their practice should also inform the planning. There is more about this in Unit CCLD 304 Reflect on and develop practice.

Link   **Unit CCLD 304** Reflect on and develop practice

Different settings will have their own methods of recording, reviewing and updating plans. It is important that you understand your setting's methods and work in line with them. Practitioners must also take into consideration curriculum frameworks that apply within the setting. Information on the Birth to Three Matters Framework can be found in Unit CCLD 312 Plan and implement positive environments for babies and children under three years. Information on the Foundation Stage can be found in Unit CCLD 309 Plan and implement curriculum frameworks for early education.

 Link   **Unit CCLD 312** Plan and implement positive environments for babies and children under three years
Unit CCLD 309 Plan and implement curriculum frameworks for early education

Selecting knowledge evidence in this unit

You must select from ONE of the four age ranges that covers the age range you currently work with and provide knowledge evidence for the points listed. The options are:

- 0–3 years (K3D218)
- 3–7 years (K3D219)
- 7–12 years (K3D220)
- 12–16 years (K3D221).

K3D218

If you are currently working with the 0–3 age range you must provide knowledge evidence for the 25 points listed in the National Occupational Standards. The following table shows how to find relevant information in this book.

Chapter links for K3D218

K3D218	Chapter links for knowledge evidence
1	Unit CCLD 301 Develop and promote positive relationships Unit CCLD 302 Develop and maintain a healthy, safe and secure environment for children Unit CCLD 306 Plan and organise environments for children and families Unit CCLD 312 Plan and implement positive environments for babies and children under three years
2	Unit CCLD 301 Develop and promote positive relationships Unit CCLD 305 Protect and promote children's rights Unit CCLD 306 Plan and organise environments for children and families Unit CCLD 321 Support children with disabilities or special educational needs and their families
3	Unit CCLD 302 Develop and maintain a healthy, safe and secure environment for children Unit CCLD 305 Protect and promote children's rights Unit CCLD 312 Plan and implement positive environments for babies and children under three years Unit CCLD 321 Support children with disabilities or special educational needs and their families

4	Unit CCLD 305 Protect and promote children's rights Unit CCLD 321 Support children with disabilities or special educational needs and their families
5	Unit CCLD 301 Develop and promote positive relationships Unit CCLD 312 Plan and implement positive environments for babies and children under three years Unit CCLD 314 Provide physical care that promotes the health and development of babies and children under three years
6	Unit CCLD 301 Develop and promote positive relationships Unit CCLD 303 Promote children's development (this unit) Unit CCLD 306 Plan and organise environments for children and families Unit CCLD 312 Plan and implement positive environments for babies and children under three years Unit CCLD 314 Provide physical care that promotes the health and development of babies and children under three years
7	Unit CCLD 301 Develop and promote positive relationships Unit CCLD 306 Plan and organise environments for children and families Unit CCLD 312 Plan and implement positive environments for babies and children under three years Unit CCLD 314 Provide physical care that promotes the health and development of babies and children under three years
8	Unit CCLD 301 Develop and promote positive relationships Unit CCLD 302 Develop and maintain a healthy, safe and secure environment for children Unit CCLD 306 Plan and organise environments for children and families Unit CCLD 314 Provide physical care that promotes the health and development of babies and children under three years
9	Unit CCLD 301 Develop and promote positive relationships Unit CCLD 312 Plan and implement positive environments for babies and children under three years Unit CCLD 314 Provide physical care that promotes the health and development of babies and children under three years
10	Unit CCLD 301 Develop and promote positive relationships Unit CCLD 314 Provide physical care that promotes the health and development of babies and children under three years Unit CCLD 337 Create environments that promote positive behaviour
11	Unit CCLD 306 Plan and organise environments for children and families
12	Unit CCLD 312 Plan and implement positive environments for babies and children under three years Unit CCLD 314 Provide physical care that promotes the health and development of babies and children under three years
13	Unit CCLD 307 Promote the health and physical development of children Unit CCLD 312 Plan and implement positive environments for babies and children under three years Unit CCLD 314 Provide physical care that promotes the health and development of babies and children under three years

14	Unit CCLD 306 Plan and organise environments for children and families Unit CCLD 312 Plan and implement positive environments for babies and children under three years Unit CCLD 314 Provide physical care that promotes the health and development of babies and children under three years
15	Unit CCLD 312 Plan and implement positive environments for babies and children under three years Unit CCLD 314 Provide physical care that promotes the health and development of babies and children under three years
16	Unit CCLD 305 Protect and promote children's rights Unit CCLD 321 Support children with disabilities or special educational needs and their families Unit CCLD 306 Plan and organise environments for children and families Unit CCLD 309 Plan and implement curriculum frameworks for early education Unit CCLD 312 Plan and implement positive environments for babies and children under three years Unit CCLD 314 Provide physical care that promotes the health and development of babies and children under three years
17	Unit CCLD 309 Plan and implement curriculum frameworks for early education
18	Unit CCLD 312 Plan and implement positive environments for babies and children under three years
19	Unit CCLD 301 Develop and promote positive relationships Unit CCLD 312 Plan and implement positive environments for babies and children under three years
20	Unit CCLD 301 Develop and promote positive relationships Unit CCLD 312 Plan and implement positive environments for babies and children under three years
21	Unit CCLD 301 Develop and promote positive relationships Unit CCLD 305 Protect and promote children's rights Unit CCLD 312 Plan and implement positive environments for babies and children under three years Unit CCLD 321 Support children with disabilities or special educational needs and their families
22	Unit CCLD 301 Develop and promote positive relationships Unit CCLD 312 Plan and implement positive environments for babies and children under three years
23	Unit CCLD 302 Develop and maintain a healthy, safe and secure environment for children Unit CCLD 307 Promote the health and physical development of children Unit CCLD 314 Provide physical care that promotes the health and development of babies and children under three years
24	Unit CCLD 307 Promote the health and physical development of children Unit CCLD 312 Plan and implement positive environments for babies and children under three years Unit CCLD 314 Provide physical care that promotes the health and development of babies and children under three years
25	Unit CCLD 302 Develop and maintain a healthy, safe and secure environment for children Unit CCLD 307 Promote the health and physical development of children Unit CCLD 312 Plan and implement positive environments for babies and children under three years

K3D219

If you are currently working with the 3–7 age range you must provide knowledge evidence for the 20 points listed in the National Occupational Standards. The following table shows how to find relevant information in this book.

Chapter links for K3D219

K3D219	Chapter links for knowledge evidence
1	Unit CCLD 301 Develop and promote positive relationships Unit CCLD 302 Develop and maintain a healthy, safe and secure environment for children Unit CCLD 306 Plan and organise environments for children and families
2	Unit CCLD 301 Develop and promote positive relationships Unit CCLD 305 Protect and promote children's rights Unit CCLD 306 Plan and organise environments for children and families Unit CCLD 321 Support children with disabilities or special educational needs and their families
3	Unit CCLD 302 Develop and maintain a healthy, safe and secure environment for children Unit CCLD 305 Protect and promote children's rights Unit CCLD 321 Support children with disabilities or special educational needs and their families
4	Unit CCLD 305 Protect and promote children's rights Unit CCLD 309 Plan and implement curriculum frameworks for early education Unit CCLD 321 Support children with disabilities of special educational needs and their families
5	Unit CCLD 301 Develop and promote positive relationships Unit CCLD 309 Plan and implement curriculum frameworks for early education
6	Unit CCLD 301 Develop and promote positive relationships Unit CCLD 306 Plan and organise environments for children and families
7	Unit CCLD 301 Develop and promote positive relationships Unit CCLD 306 Plan and organise environments for children and families
8	Unit CCLD 301 Develop and promote positive relationships Unit CCLD 337 Create environments that promote positive behaviour
9	Unit CCLD 302 Develop and maintain a healthy, safe and secure environment for children Unit CCLD 307 Promote the health and physical development of children
10	Unit CCLD 301 Develop and promote positive relationships Unit CCLD 302 Develop and maintain a healthy, safe and secure environment for children Unit CCLD 306 Plan and organise environments for children and families Unit CCLD 309 Plan and implement curriculum frameworks for early education
11	Unit CCLD 305 Protect and promote children's rights Unit CCLD 321 Support children with disabilities or special educational needs and their families Unit CCLD 306 Plan and organise environments for children and families Unit CCLD 309 Plan and implement curriculum frameworks for early education

12	Unit CCLD 303 Promote children's development (this unit) Unit CCLD 309 Plan and implement curriculum frameworks for early education
13	Unit CCLD 301 Develop and promote positive relationships
14	Unit CCLD 301 Develop and promote positive relationships Unit CCLD 305 Protect and promote children's rights Unit CCLD 321 Support children with disabilities or special educational needs and their families
15	Unit CCLD 301 Develop and promote positive relationships
16	Unit CCLD 303 Promote children's development (this unit) Unit CCLD 309 Plan and implement curriculum frameworks for early education
17	Unit CCLD 301 Develop and promote positive relationships Unit CCLD 306 Plan and organise environments for children and families Unit CCLD 307 Promote the health and physical development of children Unit CCLD 309 Plan and implement curriculum frameworks for early education Unit CCLD 318 Plan for and support self-directed play
18	Unit CCLD 302 Develop and maintain a healthy, safe and secure environment for children Unit CCLD 307 Promote the health and physical development of children
19	Unit CCLD 307 Promote the health and physical development of children Unit CCLD 309 Plan and implement curriculum frameworks for early education
20	Unit CCLD 302 Develop and maintain a healthy, safe and secure environment for children Unit CCLD 307 Promote the health and physical development of children Unit CCLD 309 Plan and implement curriculum frameworks for early education

K3D220

If you are currently working with the 7–12 age range you must provide knowledge evidence for the 16 points listed in the National Occupational Standards. The following table shows how to find relevant information in this book.

Chapter links for K3D220

K3D220	Chapter links for knowledge evidence
1	Unit CCLD 302 Develop and maintain a healthy, safe and secure environment for children Unit CCLD 306 Plan and organise environments for children and families
2	Unit CCLD 301 Develop and promote positive relationships Unit CCLD 305 Protect and promote children's rights Unit CCLD 306 Plan and organise environments for children and families Unit CCLD 321 Support children with disabilities or special educational needs and their families

3	Unit CCLD 302 Develop and maintain a healthy, safe and secure environment for children
	Unit CCLD 305 Protect and promote children's rights
	Unit CCLD 321 Support children with disabilities or special educational needs and their families
4	Unit CCLD 305 Protect and promote children's rights
	Unit CCLD 309 Plan and implement curriculum frameworks for early education
	Unit CCLD 321 Support children with disabilities or special educational needs and their families
5	Unit CCLD 301 Develop and promote positive relationships
	Unit CCLD 306 Plan and organise environments for children and families
6	Unit CCLD 301 Develop and promote positive relationships
	Unit CCLD 306 Plan and organise environments for children and families
	Unit CCLD 337 Create environments that promote positive behaviour
7	Unit CCLD 303 Promote children's development (this unit)
8	Unit CCLD 318 Plan for and support self-directed play
9	Unit CCLD 302 Develop and maintain a healthy, safe and secure environment for children
	Unit CCLD 306 Plan and organise environments for children and families
10	Unit CCLD 301 Develop and promote positive relationships
11	Unit CCLD 301 Develop and promote positive relationships
12	Unit CCLD 301 Develop and promote positive relationships
13	Unit CCLD 302 Develop and maintain a healthy, safe and secure environment for children
	Unit CCLD 307 Promote the health and physical development of children
14	Unit CCLD 302 Develop and maintain a healthy, safe and secure environment for children
	Unit CCLD 307 Promote the health and physical development of children
15	Unit CCLD 302 Develop and maintain a healthy, safe and secure environment for children
	Unit CCLD 307 Promote the health and physical development of children
16	Unit CCLD 301 Develop and promote positive relationships

K3D221

If you are currently working with the 12–16 age range you must provide knowledge evidence for the 17 points listed in the National Occupational Standards. The following table shows how to find relevant information in this book.

Chapter links for K3D221

K3D221	Chapter links for knowledge evidence
1	Unit CCLD 301 Develop and promote positive relationships Unit CCLD 302 Develop and maintain a healthy, safe and secure environment for children Unit CCLD 306 Plan and organise environments for children and families
2	Unit CCLD 301 Develop and promote positive relationships Unit CCLD 305 Protect and promote children's rights Unit CCLD 306 Plan and organise environments for children and families Unit CCLD 321 Support children with disabilities or special educational needs and their families
3	Unit CCLD 302 Develop and maintain a healthy, safe and secure environment for children Unit CCLD 305 Protect and promote children's rights Unit CCLD 321 Support children with disabilities or special educational needs and their families
4	Unit CCLD 305 Protect and promote children's rights Unit CCLD 309 Plan and implement curriculum frameworks for early education Unit CCLD 321 Support children with disabilities or special educational needs and their families
5	Unit CCLD 301 Develop and promote positive relationships Unit CCLD 306 Plan and organise environments for children and families Unit CCLD 337 Create environments that promote positive behaviour
6	Unit CCLD 303 Promote children's development (this unit)
7	Unit CCLD 302 Develop and maintain a healthy, safe and secure environment for children Unit CCLD 306 Plan and organise environments for children and families
8	Unit CCLD 301 Develop and promote positive relationships Unit CCLD 306 Plan and organise environments for children and families Unit CCLD 337 Create environments that promote positive behaviour
9	Unit CCLD 303 Promote children's development (this unit)
10	Unit CCLD 301 Develop and promote positive relationships
11	Unit CCLD 301 Develop and promote positive relationships
12	Unit CCLD 301 Develop and promote positive relationships
13	Unit CCLD 302 Develop and maintain a healthy, safe and secure environment for children Unit CCLD 307 Promote the health and physical development of children
14	Unit CCLD 302 Develop and maintain a healthy, safe and secure environment for children Unit CCLD 307 Promote the health and physical development of children
15	Unit CCLD 303 Promote children's development (this unit)
16	Unit CCLD 302 Develop and maintain a healthy, safe and secure environment for children Unit CCLD 307 Promote the health and physical development of children
17	Unit CCLD 303 Promote children's development (this unit) Unit CCLD 307 Promote the health and physical development of children

Supporting literacy

In addition to the information in Unit CCLD 309 Plan and implement curriculum frameworks for early education, the following table gives details of how children's literacy can be supported at various stages of their development.

Literacy

Aspect of literacy development	Key concepts
Mark making	Plenty of early opportunities to make marks in a range of ways – with pencils, pens, felt tips, paint and brushes, printing, finger painting, chalking, tracing marks in the sand, etc. – all help children to learn how to make and control the arm and hand movements necessary for writing, and can help them to learn how to hold mark-making tools. It is helpful to encourage children to make patterns, perhaps by sitting at the painting table and making some yourself.
	This also helps children to understand that marks can be used to communicate with other people. Practitioners can comment on children's pictures and patterns to demonstrate this.
	Children can make marks from the time they are babies
Understanding that letters and words carry meaning	Sharing stories, books and giving children plenty of opportunities to see adults reading and writing for real purposes, helps children to understand that print carries meaning. For instance, this can be demonstrated by making a list of the drinks that children would like at snack time and giving it to the practitioner who will fetch the drinks. When sharing books on a one-to-one with children, practitioners can run their finger along the sentences as they read, demonstrating that they are following text. In settings that do this, children may be observed 'playing reading', copying the technique when 'reading' to a doll or teddy
Recognising letters and words	Children usually recognise their own name first. You can help by providing children with plenty of opportunities to see and look for their name. For instance, you may have names displayed above the coat pegs or have names written on pieces of paper for the children to find at craft time. You can also provide labels on familiar objects (on your boxes of resources for instance) or in familiar places (such as the book corner). Help children to learn both the names of letters and the sound that they make. This aids learning to read phonetically
Emergent writing	When children first attempt to write, they tend to draw rows of patterns and shapes that look similar to letters. They will eventually include some letters amongst the patterns and shapes, although they may be muddled – perhaps back to front. Children benefit from lots of practice at emergent writing, and this can be effectively provided as children play. You can supply envelopes and paper (a good use for junk mail) and encourage children to write 'letters' and post them in an imaginary post office area for instance. You can provide a notepad when the imaginary area is turned into a restaurant, and encourage children to take orders.
	Give children opportunities to see words and letters in the areas in which they mark make so that they can try to copy them. For instance, you may place children's name cards on the drawing table and invite children to find their seat. They may then attempt copy their name since all the materials will be at hand.
	When children can write their name and some letters, they can begin copying simple words. Many children learn to do this by writing simple captions for their art work, e.g. a cat, my doll

Communication and language	Communication and language are inseparably linked to literacy; children cannot progress with reading and writing unless they are progressing in terms of their understanding and use of communication and language
The Foundation Stage: Communication, language and literacy	By the end of the Foundation Stage, in the area of Communication, language and literacy, most children should be able to: ● Use language to imagine and recreate roles and experiences ● Use talk to organise, sequence and clarify thinking, ideas, feelings and events ● Hear and say initial and final sounds in words, and short vowel sounds within words ● Link sounds to letters, naming and sounding the letters of the alphabet ● Use their phonic knowledge to write simple regular words and make phonetically plausible attempts at more complex words ● Explore and experiment with sounds, words and text ● Retell narratives in the correct sequence, drawing on language patterns of stories ● Read a range of familiar and common words and simple sentences independently ● Know that print carries meaning and, in English, is read from left to right and top to bottom ● Show an understanding of the elements of stories, such as main character, sequence of events and openings, and how information can be found in non-fiction text to answer questions about where, who, why and how ● Use their phonic knowledge to write simple regular words and make phonetically plausible attempts at more complex words ● Attempt writing for different purposes, using features of different forms such as lists, stories and instructions ● Write their own names and other things such as labels and captions and begin to form simple sentences, sometimes using punctuation ● Use a pencil and hold it effectively to form recognisable letters, most of which are correctly formed.
Ongoing progress	Children may begin to read independently around the age of seven, although there is a wide variation in this. As time progresses, most children will go on to read and write and understand more complex words and text

Supporting mathematical development

In addition to the information in Unit CCLD 309 Plan and implement curriculum frameworks for early education, the following table gives details of how children's mathematical development can be supported at various stages.

Mathematical development

Aspect of mathematical development	Key concepts
Counting	Often, children's first experience of mathematics is counting. This introduces them to numbers. Young children will count by rote (they will recite numbers as they would a nursery rhyme), but at this stage they do not really understand the meaning of numbers or counting. By encouraging children to touch objects as they count you can help them to understand the concept (meaning) of counting and numbers – this understanding is called 'one-to-one correspondence'. Children will muddle or miss out numbers at first – you can help by counting along with them and giving them plenty of opportunities to count, e.g. together you can count out the cups at snack time or use counting songs and rhymes and count the steps to the slide when going up them. When children have a secure understanding of the concept of number, they can begin to learn simple number operations, e.g. adding one or taking one away.
Matching	Matching requires children to look carefully, comparing two or more objects – they must decide if the features of the objects are the same. Learning to do this lays the foundations for mathematical learning which will come later, e.g. children will need to learn what values are equal to each other when doing sums (=). You can help by giving children opportunities to match, e.g. lotto games, card games such as snap and pairs, colour-matching games, finding the socks that match into pairs from a selection.
Sorting	Once children can match, they can begin to learn how to sort. Sorting is the process of comparing objects and deciding what features make them the same or different (or what links and separates them). Children can sort according to shape, colour, size, type and so on. They can sort with many resources including beads, buttons, toys, etc. Sorting at tidying up time is an example of a naturally occurring everyday activity.
Recognising and writing numbers	Children who have a good understanding of the concept of number will find it easier to learn to recognise written numbers because the number symbols that we use will have meaning to them. Children learn to recognise numbers when they see them frequently in their environment and come across them in their play. They can see numbers on wall displays and on calendars, on board games and in imaginary areas (prices on food in the 'shop' perhaps). As adults refer to these numbers, children begin to remember them. Children often learn to recognise numbers with personal meaning first – the number on their front door, or their age. You can help by making number cards and asking children to match the written number with a number of objects (such as the number of toy cars you have set out). Introduce one or two numbers at a time. Learning the symbols is difficult for children. Children can practise writing numbers informally, e.g. provide stickers and pencils in the imaginary shop area and let children price some items themselves, or draw out numbered stepping stones for children to follow outside, providing chalk so they can draw and number their own too.
Measuring	Measuring refers to the measurement of weight, length, volume and capacity. Before children can effectively learn about the formal measurement of these using numbers, they need to learn about the concept of measurement. Weight measurement using simple balancing scales helps children to understand the concepts of heavier, lighter, heaviest, lightest. Allowing children to feel the weights themselves reinforces the concept and helps children to learn to predict weight. Children can be introduced to concepts such as long, short, longest, shortest and distance in simple ways. They can see how far they can all jump and record this with a line, comparing the distance. They can use string to measure the height of a plant as it grows – they can display each length of string to show the growth.

Volume and capacity	These are difficult concepts to understand. However, young children can make informal discoveries about volume and capacity. You can help by providing vessels of different sizes for children to play with in the sand and water trays. They may discover that a bucket holds five beakers full of water for instance. Children can also learn about volume and capacity when tidying up, e.g. the large box will hold all the wooden blocks, but they will not all fit in the small box.
Shape	Shapes are often one of the first sets children are able to sort by. Children usually learn the basic shapes first – circle, square, rectangle and triangle. Children generally draw shapes and patterns before they learn to write numbers. You can help children to learn shapes by encouraging them to recognise shapes when they come across them ('what shape is the window in the picture?'), referring to them ('let's sit at the square table'), using shape sorters, shape board games and jigsaw puzzles (which encourage shape and spatial awareness).
Time	Most children do not fully understand the abstract concept of time until they are in at least their seventh year. However, young children can be encouraged to recognise the time through a routine, e.g. after snack time it is story time. Children can also be encouraged to understand what is meant by today, yesterday and tomorrow by talking about past events and planning. The more distant past can also be referred to. Most four-year-olds will recall their last birthday for instance, or a festival significant to their family, such as Christmas.
The Foundation Stage	By the end of the Foundation Stage, most children should be able to: • Say and use number names in order in familiar contexts • Count reliably up to ten everyday objects • Recognise numerals 1–9 • Use developing mathematical ideas and methods to solve practical problems • In practical activities and discussion begin to use the vocabulary involved in adding and subtracting • Use language such as 'more' or 'less' to compare two numbers • Find one more or one less than a number from 1–10. • Begin to relate addition to combining two groups of objects and subtraction to taking away.
Ongoing progress	Children will move on to more complex number operations as they progress at school.

Support children through transitions

K3T1111

In childcare terms, a transition occurs when a child moves from one care situation to another. Children of all ages experience transitions. For example, transitions occur when:

- Children attend a setting for the first time – a nursery, pre-school, crèche, childminder's home, primary school, out-of-school club or secondary school
- Children move within a setting – from the baby room to the toddler room, or from class to class
- Children have new living arrangements (this includes young people who are preparing to leave home or children preparing for a stay in hospital)
- Young people leave school and prepare for work/college.

Transitions are periods of change which generally involve a loss of familiar people in a child's life. As an adult you may be familiar with feeling unsettled and under pressure at a time of transition – perhaps when starting a new job or living somewhere new. Children experience the same feelings and they may find them hard to cope with. Different children respond differently to transitions. Their response will be influenced by their previous experience of change, their age, ability and their personality.

Practitioners can assist children in their care by helping them to prepare for the transitions ahead of them. The value of preparing children for transitions is now widely accepted. Some transitions are predictable – for instance, children will start school by the statutory age of five – this is known to all involved with supporting a child early on. So schools and early years settings now routinely prepare children for this known transition. Policies and procedures are generally in place to outline how this will be done. In many cases the early years setting, school and family will work together to prepare a child, as in the practical example on page 98.

The following strategies can be used to prepare children for a variety of transitions:

- Communicating with children about the transition. Talking about what will happen as well as listening to children's concerns. It is important for practitioners to be honest and open as well as reassuring. It can be helpful to teach children strategies to deal with their biggest concerns. For instance, if a child is worried about getting lost at secondary school you can talk to the child about what they should do if they actually become lost.

- Arranging visits to a new setting prior to the transition. Depending on the child's age this may be in the company of parents or carers or with a current practitioner. For example, young children will generally visit a nursery school with their families. Children in their last year of primary school will often spend a day at secondary school escorted by their current teachers.

- Books, leaflets/brochures, stories, watching videos/DVDs or CD-ROMs that deal with the subject of their future transition all help children to become more familiar with the process of change ahead of them. This helps to minimise a fear of the unknown.

- Allowing plenty of opportunities for children to express their feelings through conversations, imaginative and expressive play.

- Giving children and young people opportunities to experience increasing independence in line with their needs and abilities.

- Ensuring that all documentation about a child is organised and ready to be passed on to parents/carers or other professionals as appropriate to the situation.

There is further information about transitions for children aged 0–3 in Unit CCLD 312 Plan and implement positive environments for babies and children under three years.

 Link **Unit CCLD 312** Plan and implement positive environments for babies and children under three

Practical Example

Jamal prepares for school

Four-year-old Jamal will be leaving pre-school in July and starting primary school in September. His future teacher, Mr Evans, has been invited to attend the pre-school during May to read stories to the children. In the same month, Jamal's dad will attend a meeting for new parents at the school. He has already been sent a booklet called 'Starting School: A Parent's Guide'.

In June Mr Evans will visit Jamal and his family at home. In July the pre-school children are going on two visits to the school to join in with music activities. Jamal will also attend a story session at the school with his dad. In September Jamal will only attend school in the morning for the first week. From the second week onwards he will attend full time.

➤ *What benefit will each activity have?*   **K3T1111**

Pre-school children visiting a school

The following guidelines can help practitioners to offer support to children experiencing a transition (on their first days at a new setting, for example):

- Ensure all registration information has been received before the child attends, so that practitioners are prepared to meet the child's needs
- Have a key worker allocated to the child
- If appropriate, allow children to adjust to the session slowly through a combination of visits with parents/carers and one or more short stays alone before the child attends for a longer period
- Tell children and adults that the new child is coming and encourage them to make the child welcome. Tell them the child's preferred name – Nicholas may prefer to be called Nick, for example
- Give the child a warm welcome – the key worker should ideally be available to receive the child

- Encourage children and parents/carers to say goodbye to one another (if parents are present). Provide honest reassurance for children – never lie about when they will be reunited with their family. When appropriate, families should ideally have access to children. If children are away from home overnight (perhaps during a stay in hospital), personal reminders of families, such as photographs, are helpful. Regular communication can also be established in the form of telephone calls, letters, text messages and emails, as appropriate to the child and family

- If children have comfort objects brought from home, ensure the child has easy access to them

- Take the child to hang up their outside clothes and to store their personal belongings. If possible, provide children with their own pegs, drawers and/or lockers. Younger children can have a picture/word label to help them recognise their own space

- Show children around so that the environment becomes familiar. Help children to understand routines and/or timetables

- Provide interesting activities, appropriate to the child's age, needs and abilities. In the case of younger children, it is helpful to include an activity they specifically enjoy – building with bricks, for example. The provision of imaginative/creative activities can encourage children to express their feelings

- Provide positive images of people. Reminders of the child's home culture should also be promoted

- Remain supportive while allowing children time to adjust to their new situation. Make sure children know who they can go to if they need help. Even if there is a key worker designated, children should know who to go to if the key worker is not available

- Advise families that children may experience unsettled feelings while they adjust to the transition. This may include temporary regressive behaviour (when children go back to an earlier stage of development for comfort, for example a three-year-old may want to be fed)

- Provide ways to involve families in the child's experience, to assist the transition from the setting to home. This is as important for children starting nursery or school as it is for children away from home for longer periods. Daily reports or home-to-setting diaries are helpful.

Children often have common anxieties about transitions, as outlined in the diagrams on pages 100–1. It is helpful for practitioners to anticipate these and to help children to prepare for them. For instance, the diagram on page 101 shows that young people preparing to leave home may be anxious about looking after themselves in terms of shopping, cooking and laundry. By encouraging young people to take some responsibility for these things prior to leaving home, families and practitioners can help them to feel more confident and better prepared.

Young people also need plenty of information and support as they make career, further education (FE) and training choices. Appointments to see careers advisers can be made. Careers advisers have access to a range of information about careers, FE and training. Many colleges and training centres provide taster days when young people can visit, meet key staff and find out more about courses and training. Some young people will need basic skills support. Careers advisers, colleges and training centres are used to meeting people's basic skills needs. Practitioners can assist by providing information about a young person's needs where appropriate, and by ensuring the young person has support in handling information given to them in the form of brochures, leaflets and so on.

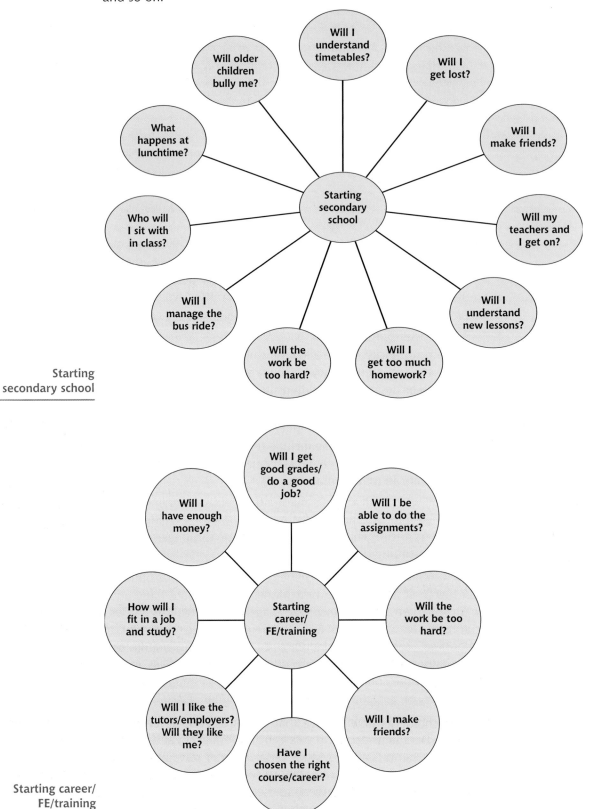

Starting secondary school

Starting career/ FE/training

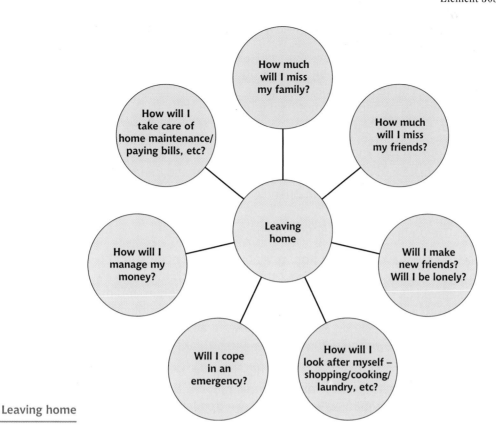

Leaving home

Some children experience multiple transitions. This may be due to frequent family breakdowns or perhaps the nature of a parent's work. In these circumstances, children sometimes become accustomed to change, but they may find it difficult to relate closely with carers and peers. They may become distrustful of adults. Practitioners should persevere and allow a relationship to form gradually with such children, taking care not to overwhelm them. Social Services recognises the problems of multiple transitions – social workers try to make long-term or permanent plans for looked-after children whenever possible.

Emotional Intelligence

A relatively new theory from psychologists promotes the idea that there is a type of intelligence related to social and emotional development, known as Emotional Intelligence. It is proposed that this is quite separate from intelligence related to intellectual development. The psychologist Howard Gardner was one of the first to discuss this theory, and further studies have been conducted by others including E.L. Thorndike, Peter Salovey, Professor William Damon and L.E. Shapiro.

Many psychologists now believe that having a good level of Emotional Intelligence Quotient (EQ – the measure of emotional intelligence) is at least as important as having a good level of Intelligence Quotient (IQ – the measure of intellect) in the case of both adults and children. It is believed that children with good emotional intelligence skills are happier, more confident and more successful in school, and that they are likely to grow into responsible, caring and productive adults. It is interesting to note that it is entirely possible to have a high level of EQ and a much lower level of IQ, and vice versa.

Psychologist Daniel Goleman wrote a book about this, published by Bantam Books in 1995. It is entitled *Emotional Intelligence: Why it can matter more than IQ*. He identifies five principles of building emotional intelligence skills:

- Be aware of your own feelings and those of others
- Show empathy and understand others' point of view
- Regulate and cope positively with emotional and behavioural impulses
- Be positive goal and plan orientated (i.e. motivated by goals and plans that are optimistic)
- Use positive social skills in handling relationships.

The theories have stemmed from psychologists and neuroscientists (i.e. brain scientists) making discoveries together about the way in which the brain controls human beings. The amygdala is situated in the limbic system of the brain. It is our emotional centre. It is able to instantly affect our thoughts, feelings, physiology (body responses) and subsequently our actions. If it senses that we are being challenged or threatened, it can instantly shut down the part of our brain that thinks rationally (the cortex).

Goleman refers to the 'emotional hijacking of the brain' – he suggests that the amygdala can temporarily rob us of our rational thinking, causing us to take action from a state of emotion, which may be regretted later when the rational brain has been released. This line of thinking could be applied to a child who hits out at someone in anger but regrets their actions later when they have calmed down.

It is believed that human beings learn their beliefs, habits and much of their behaviour, although some of these things are put down to nature. Humans are driven by their emotions and feelings, whether they are positive or negative. It is thought that positive-thinking habits and other EQ skills can be developed and improved at any stage of life, from childhood to adulthood – since they are *learnt*, they can be *taught*. It is generally agreed that the best way to help children to develop high EQ levels is for adults to model and demonstrate them routinely.

Emotional Intelligence skills can be broken down into six key areas, as follows.

Moral behaviour

Damon suggests that children should understand what distinguishes acceptable behaviour from the unacceptable. They should then get into the habit of behaving in ways they perceive to be acceptable. They should develop concern, regard and a sense of responsibility to others. This might be expressed in acts of caring, kindness or mercy.

Thinking

Shapiro believes that EQ includes 'realistic thinking skills'. Realistic thinking is the ability to see the world as it is and respond to it with appropriate behaviours and decisions. She says the opposite of realistic thinking is self-deception. She believes adults should sensitively tell children the truth in difficult situations, as this helps them to develop the emotional strength they will draw on as adults. She suggests that trying to protect children from the truth (perhaps by covering up the death of a pet) is acting from self-deception.

Problem solving

Shapiro believes that problem-solving skills are essential to EQ. She says that children like solving problems. She suggests that giving children opportunities to solve problems allows them to build up facts and experiences that can be drawn on later to solve future problems. She believes in developing an atmosphere of positive problem solving around children, e.g. by having family meetings where adults can work alongside children, modelling how to solve real-life problems.

Social interaction

Shapiro believes that the ability to get along with other people is the skill that contributes most to a human being's sense of success and satisfaction in life. Building good communication skills is seen as important as they are at the heart of social interaction. She believes that humour is another important social skill since it aids social relationships and helps individuals to cope with life's problems, stresses and strains. She suggests that plenty of adult time spent talking, playing and joking with children is essential to the development of strong social interaction skills.

Academic and work success

Shapiro believes that motivation leads to success in education and the workforce. She believes that babies and children are naturally motivated to learn until the age of seven or eight. At this age school work may become taxing and the eagerness to discover may fade. Other researchers have suggested principles of how to promote development of self-motivation in children which include:

- Encouraging children to be optimistic
- Encouraging children to value persistent effort and to expect success when they try
- Teaching children the value of overcoming failure
- Encouraging children to follow their interests and to develop hobbies
- Encouraging children to celebrate and enjoy achievement
- Giving children opportunities to 'master their world' (to be successful at things within their lives)
- Making learning relevant to the individual child's interest
- Teaching children in ways that appeal to their styles of learning.

Emotions

It is believed to be important for children to learn how to feel about themselves and how other people react to their feelings. They should also learn how to understand and express their emotions, including their hopes and fears. They should learn the value of being optimistic. Studies of successful parent–child interactions have shown that children are happier when parents:

- Are aware of the children's emotions
- Empathise, soothe and guide children's emotions, listening to children with empathy to validate their feelings
- Help children to label with words the emotion they are experiencing

- Set limits on behaviour while exploring strategies to solve problems with the child
- Recognise emotions as opportunities for learning and personal growth for the child.

Practitioners now routinely work in ways that encourage children to develop emotional intelligence skills. This also links to the provision of creative activities.

Supporting creativity

Creative play can extend children's imaginations and promote intellectual development. It can also help children to express themselves and their feelings. Many people find creative pursuits enjoyable and relaxing – think how many adults take up creative activities as hobbies, for example.

Creativity should be encouraged throughout childhood, starting when children are babies. There are many creative possibilities, giving practitioners plenty of opportunity to provide a range of experiences suited to children's ages, abilities and interests. For example, babies can participate in finger painting and crayoning, while young people may enjoy experimenting with oil paints and charcoals. Three- and four-year-olds can retell familiar stories, while eight- and nine-year-olds may enjoy designing a comic strip. Young people may enjoy writing a script or short story.

It is important that practitioners value the PROCESS of creative activity, rather than simply the PRODUCT. There is further information about this in Unit CCLD 306 Plan and organise environments for children and families.

Link   **Unit CCLD 306** Plan and organise environments for children and families

Creative activities include:

- Imaginary play

    Such as play with puppets, dolls, small-world resources such as farmyards, imaginary areas such as home corners, imaginary games (such as playing 'families', charades or moral dilemmas), drama, performing on stage

- Art and crafts

    Including drawing, painting, colouring, recycled modelling, sculpture, woodwork, metalwork, fashion design

- Music, singing and dance

    Including group sing-along sessions, karaoke, playing percussion instruments, learning to play musical instruments, writing songs/music, performing on stage, impromptu discos, dance lessons such as ballet, tap, modern and jazz

- Story telling

    Including retelling familiar stories, making up stories and telling them, creative writing

- Creative thinking

    Coming up with new, original ideas, creating solutions to problems/issues – team games, brainteasers to solve, group thought-storming sessions.

Implement and evaluate plans to promote development

Implementing plans flexibly

It is good practice to implement (i.e. carry out) plans flexibly. This will allow you to respond to changes in circumstances and take advantage of naturally occurring opportunities to promote children's development. There is more information about this in Unit CCLD 309 Plan and implement curriculum frameworks for early education.

Link | **Unit CCLD 309** Plan and implement curriculum frameworks for early education

Evaluating plans

Evaluating how well plans have been implemented helps practitioners to develop their practice. Practitioners can identify what worked well in practice – these aspects of the implementation can be repeated or built upon. Practitioners can also identify weaknesses in the implementation – these aspects can then be improved.

An important indicator of how effectively plans have been implemented is the developmental progress made by individual children and the group as a whole. For example, regular reviews of observations and assessments will reveal how children are learning and developing. Practitioners can compare this with the learning and development outcomes identified in the planning to see if the outcomes are being successfully met – in other words, are the children generally learning and developing as intended? The learning and progress made (or the lack of it) reflects on the planning and implementation of provision.

Settings have their own methods of evaluating plans. Some settings leave space directly on the plans for notes to be made about the implementation shortly after a planned activity. This often works well as events are fresh in the mind of the practitioner.

There is further information in Unit CCLD 304 Reflect on and develop practice, Unit CCLD 309 Plan and implement curriculum frameworks for early education and Unit CCLD 312 Plan and implement positive environments for babies and children under three years.

Link | **Unit CCLD 304** Reflect on and develop practice
Unit CCLD 309 Plan and implement curriculum frameworks for early education
Unit CCLD 312 Plan and implement positive environments for babies and children under three years

Unit CCLD 303

Are you ready for assessment?

Promote children's development

Throughout this qualification you will need to show how you competently promote the physical, emotional, social, communication and intellectual development of the children with whom you work. To do this, in this unit you will be observing children's current skills and abilities, recording observational findings, assessing development and planning to promote development. You will need to demonstrate a detailed understanding of child and young person development across the whole range of 0–16 years.

The amount and type of evidence you will need to present will vary. You should plan this with your assessor.

Direct observation by your assessor

Observation and/or expert witness testimony is the required assessment method to be used to evidence some of each element in this unit. If your assessor is unable to observe you, s/he will identify an expert in your workplace who will provide testimony of your work-based performance. Usually your assessor or expert witness will observe you in real work activities and this should provide most of the evidence for the performance criteria for the elements in this unit.

Preparing to be observed

Plan carefully with your assessor to make sure you are able to demonstrate the national standard required. Think about how you will observe and record children's development, how you will plan provision to promote development and how you will implement and evaluate your plans. Plan for your assessor to observe you undertaking these tasks.

Other types of evidence

You will need to present different types of evidence in order to:

- Cover criteria not observed by your assessor
- Show that you have the required knowledge, understanding and skills.

Such evidence could include:

- Work products such as curriculum plans
- Confidential records such as child observations. These should not be placed in your portfolio – they must remain in their usual location and be referred to in the assessor records in your portfolio
- Case studies, projects, assignments and reflective accounts of your work
- Original certificates/attendance records and other evidence of prior experience and learning that matches the requirements of the standards.

Check your knowledge

- What techniques of observation are used in your setting?   **K3D206**
- What is 'emotional intelligence'?   **K3D219, K3D220, K3D221**
- What transitions may occur in children's lives between the ages of 0 and16 years?   **K3T1111**
- Explain how a current theory of play can inform practice.   **K3D210**

Reflective practice

Reflect on the way in which you currently manage your own feelings and emotions within the setting. Considering the information on pages 101–4, do you think you are promoting good emotional intelligence skills in your position as a role model for children? You may wish to read more widely on the topic of emotional intelligence. There are many books aimed at adults who wish to raise their own EQ.

UNIT 304

Reflect on and develop practice

*T*his unit is about the competence you need to reflect on your practice. Reflecting on practice is a tool for self-evaluation and will enable you to develop and learn from assessing your own practice. The unit also includes taking part in continuous professional development and how this is used to develop your practice.

This unit contains two elements:

⌣ **CCLD 304.1** *Reflect on practice*

⌣ **CCLD 304.2** *Take part in continuing professional development*

Introduction

It is important that practitioners continue to develop their skills and professional knowledge throughout their career. This promotes improvement in practice, and positively impacts on the quality of children's care, learning and development. A key component of professional development is learning from past experience – practitioners think about their practice, notice areas for development and plan how to improve their knowledge, understanding and skills.

Element 304.1 *Reflect on practice*

⌣ ### Reflective practice

K3P222
K3P226
K3P228
K3D223
K3D224
K3D225
K3D227

Reflecting on how you do things, what you do and what you achieve (known as your processes, practices and outcomes) effectively helps you to see how well you are working in practice. Reflective practitioners regularly:

- Think about their practice
- Analyse their actions
- Evaluate their personal effectiveness
- Record their reflections, perhaps in a journal
- Discuss their reflections with others
- Use feedback from others to improve their own evaluations.

Key Terms

This helps them to:

- Identify their strengths

    Practitioners may ask themselves: 'What do I do well or to a high standard?'

- Identify their weaknesses

    'What don't I do all that well? What don't I feel confident doing?'

- Notice their achievements

    'Where have I made progress? What targets or goals have I reached?'

- Identify their development needs

    'Which areas of my work or knowledge should be developed? What new information and/or skills should I learn? How can I address my weaknesses?'

    (All practitioners benefit from continuing professional development in the form of ongoing learning and professional updating)

- Solve problems

    'What problems do I currently have, and how can I tackle them?'

- Improve practice

    'What can I do to improve my practical work with the children, parents, carers, my colleagues?'

A practitioner writing in a reflective journal

Key Terms

Reflection also helps you to see which of your practical strategies and techniques are successful, and where a fresh approach would be beneficial. This increases your professional knowledge, understanding and skills. With the benefit of hindsight you can take time to think through an event or an issue, gaining deeper insight or a clearer idea of the impact of your actions. You can share your reflections with others, using their feedback to further inform your evaluation. In the interests of high quality, you should measure how well you are doing by the best-practice benchmarks not by the minimum standards.

Techniques of reflective analysis

Several techniques can be used to analyse past practice:

- Questioning what, why and how

  Imagine a practitioner has experienced previous difficulty keeping children seated at story time. Today, one child got up and took another's cushion, causing them to cry. The practitioner may question, 'What actually happened, and why did the event occur? How did I respond and why?'

- Seeking alternatives

  'How else could I have handled things?'

- Keeping an open mind

  'There could be a better way to handle or prevent such situations'

- Viewing from different perspectives

  'How might colleagues have responded? How were the children involved feeling at the time?'

- Asking 'what if?'

  'What if I'd given children more time to settle in their seats?'

- Thinking about consequences

  'A colleague came to deal with the situation while I tried to carry on with the story. But what would have happened if I'd stopped reading the story to the rest of the group until the situation was resolved?'

- Testing ideas through comparing and contrasting

  'What similar events have I experienced, and were they handled effectively? Could techniques used then work in this situation? Did my actions compare or contrast with the policies and values of my setting?'

- Synthesising ideas

  'I've thought about the issue myself, and discussed it with a colleague. I remember reading that it is good to take time to settle children at story time. It can help them to concentrate and feel engaged during the session.'

- Seeking, identifying and resolving problems

  'On reflection, I think the problem was that the children had not settled before I started reading. Next time I will try giving them more time, and I will ask if they are comfortable and can see the book.'

Key Terms

Synthesising ideas
The process of gathering different ideas from different sources. These are reflected upon, and in a considered way they are blended or joined together to form a new idea.

Good reflective practitioners learn to use all of these techniques, applying one or more of them to each situation or issue they reflect on. They keep a record of their processes and outcomes.

Reflection as a tool for comparing and challenging practice

Reflection is an effective tool for comparing and contrasting what we say we do and what we actually do. It is important to think about this periodically, since although principles, values and policies may be known and understood, there can be times when practice does not promote them. Reflection allows practitioners to identify this, and indicates when it may be necessary for them to challenge their own practice. This can be difficult to do. It can be hard to admit that personal beliefs, values or feelings may be prejudiced or otherwise negative in some way, and that personal development is necessary. However, in order to address weaknesses and improve practice, honest reflection is required. Remember that everyone has room for improvement and the capacity for continuing professional development.

Focusing on strengths and achievements can increase confidence and self-esteem.

The identification of weaknesses is also a positive thing, since informed practitioners can take steps to develop their practice. They can feel good about improving their work performance.

Naomi has reason for reflection

Naomi understands her nursery's policies and values. She would say that she always treats the children fairly and consistently in line with them.

Yesterday, four-year-old Joe deliberately poured a jug of water from the water tray onto the floor. The day before, Naomi saw him deliberately throw his drink to the ground. Today she notices a lot of water on the floor with a jug next to it. Joe is at the water tray with several other children. Naomi heads towards the water tray to remind Joe once again how dangerous it is to pour liquid on the floor, and to see that Joe cleans up the water himself. However, Naomi's colleague reaches the water tray first. He saw the whole incident – another child had in fact accidentally dropped the jug, and Joe had told her to tell a grown up, since someone could slip up.

Having realised she was about to jump to the wrong conclusion and take inappropriate action, Naomi resolves to reflect on the incident later.

➤ *Which technique/techniques of reflection would be appropriate in this instance?* **K3D225**

➤ *How can the process of reflection help Naomi to both challenge and improve her future practice?* **K3D223, K3D227**

Element 304.1

Are you ready for assessment?

Reflect on practice

You need to show that you can competently use and share reflection. You must also show that you can monitor the processes, practices and outcomes from your work, and evaluate your own performance. To do this you will need to be directly observed by your assessor and present other types of evidence. The amount and type of evidence you need to present will vary. You should plan this with your assessor.

Direct observation by your assessor

Observation and/or expert witness testimony is the required assessment method to be used to evidence some of each element in this unit. If your assessor is unable to observe you, s/he will identify an expert in your workplace who will provide testimony of your work-based performance. Usually your assessor or expert witness will observe you in real work activities and this should provide most of the evidence for the performance criteria for the elements in this unit.

Preparing to be observed

You must show your assessor that you can solve problems and improve practice by reflecting on and discussing with colleagues the processes, practices and outcomes from your work. You also need to show that you can evaluate your own performance and reflect on interactions with others.

Observation for this element could be carried out during a supervision session (with the prior agreement of your workplace supervisor).

You should plan with your supervisor to discuss:

- How you have monitored processes, practices and outcomes from your work
- How you have evaluated you own performance using best-practice benchmarks
- How you have reflected on your interactions with others
- How you have shared your reflections with others and used their feedback to improve your own evaluation
- How you have used reflection to solve problems and improve practice.

Other types of evidence

You will need to present different types of evidence in order to:

- Cover criteria not observed by your assessor
- Show that you have the required knowledge, understanding and skills.

Such evidence could include:

- Notes from reflective analysis, evaluations, self-appraisals, staff appraisals, journal entries
- Notes/minutes from meetings with colleagues.

Take part in continuing professional development

Planning

K3P229
K3P230
K3P231
K3M232

Personal development should be continuous, and practitioners should plan regular non-contact time for reflection. This ensures the process is not forgotten and that you have the time to think. Records kept, perhaps in a reflective diary or journal, will build into a helpful account of your development. Reflection may also be planned in response to:

● A naturally occurring event

   When a practitioner has come across a new situation, or when they feel something has gone particularly well or badly

● Feedback received

   This may come from a number of sources, including colleagues, supervisors, assessors, parents, carers or children. It may be given formally or informally. For instance, an assessor will give formal feedback during an assessment, while a parent may make an informal passing comment about their child's care

● Emerging new best practice/changes to regulations

   As new discoveries are made and new theories are developed, what we consider to be best practice changes and evolves. You may be able to see how this has happened in your life time – think back to how you learnt and played in various settings when you were a child, and compare this with how children are encouraged to learn and play now. Regulations are often changed to reflect what is newly considered to be best practice. Practitioners must adapt and develop their own practice in accordance with regulations. This may mean that they need to learn new information or skills which they will integrate into their practice. (See 'Policy/procedure reviews' below)

● Annual appraisals

   Many settings have an appraisal system. Generally, senior staff will make an appointment to talk with each worker individually. The staff member's work performance will be jointly discussed. Strengths and weaknesses will be considered, and a training/development plan will be agreed. Workers get the most out of an appraisal when they reflect on their own strengths, weaknesses and development needs prior to the meeting, and contribute their own thoughts during the meeting

● Policy/procedure reviews

   Most settings review their policies and procedures annually. Staff members consider how effective the policies are. They also evaluate how well their practice promotes the policies. It may be decided to develop a policy or an aspect of practice in the interests of improvement. Alternatively, if regulations alter, it may be essential to change policies and practice to stay in line with them. (See 'Emerging new best practice/changes to regulations' above.) This may also mean that practitioners need to learn and integrate new information or skills.

● Organisational evaluations

Settings may regularly review a number of aspects of their provision, such as the success of activities, or the partnership with parents and carers. Staff, children, parents, carers and outside agencies may all be involved in the evaluation process

● Taking part in quality assurance

Ofsted inspects daycare settings to ensure that their quality of care meets the minimum acceptable standards. But settings may also elect to undertake a quality assurance scheme.

Quality assurance schemes state the best-practice benchmarks for settings to aim towards. When undertaking quality assurance, settings are generally required to compile a portfolio of evidence. When the setting is ready, the portfolio will be assessed by a representative of the scheme, and an observation visit will be made to the setting. Gaining accreditation for their quality assurance is an achievement for settings. It demonstrates that the setting provides a service that is better than the minimum standard legally required. Many organisations have their own schemes available, including the National Day Nurseries Association and the Pre-School Learning Alliance. Your local Early Years Development and Childcare Partnership or Sure Start will hold details of all schemes. Many settings find it necessary for staff to undertake and integrate new learning during the quality assurance process.

Key Terms

To integrate new learning

The process of taking information and/or skills that have been newly learnt, and incorporating them into existing knowledge and/or practice. This updates/improves a practitioner's prior knowledge and practice, and makes active use of the new learning.

An appraisal meeting

When it is clear that further personal development is required, it is important to make a written plan of action. Progress made should be monitored against the plan. Plans should include clear objectives that are SMART (see opposite).

There will be times when you need to identify and seek out further learning opportunities as part of your continuing professional development. There is a range of ways to learn. For example, you can access distance learning via mail, email or the internet wherever you live. You can conduct your own research, or you can attend

SMART objectives

Specific	State exactly what you are planning to achieve and how you will achieve it so that you can focus clearly on your objective
Measurable	Decide in advance how you will know when you are on the way to meeting your objective. How will you know when you have achieved it?
Achievable	Make sure your objective is achievable. Large goals are sometimes best broken down into several achievable objectives. The task then feels more manageable and you can see that you are making progress
Realistic	Worthwhile objectives can be challenging, but be realistic about how and when you can achieve things or you may become disheartened and discouraged
Time-bound	Timescales help you to get on with working towards your objectives, and can motivate you effectively. Set dates for when each objective should be met and monitor your progress

seminars, tutored courses or workshops. You can find out about the options and access learning by:

- Enquiring about in-house learning opportunities at work, and letting your workplace know the type of development opportunities you are looking for. It is good practice to negotiate a learning plan with your workplace

- Contacting the local Early Years Development and Childcare Partnership (EYDCP) or Sure Start. They may also have details of funding for learning

- Requesting details of learning opportunities from colleges, other training organisations and membership associations. Specific enquiries can also be made to Learn Direct – advisers will help you to find appropriate local learning opportunities

- Reading about and researching up-to-date developments and thinking in the field, making use of resources such as the internet, the public library and your workplace reference information. When undertaking web-based research, the sites of national organisations are often a good starting point. Ofsted, National Day Nurseries Association, Pre-School Learning Alliance, National Child Minding Association and 4Children all have websites, and useful links are provided to further informative sites.

Practical Example

Sophia gets SMART

After reflecting on her practice, Sophia feels that she could improve her communication with adults. She sets the following SMART objective:

'My objective is to improve my communication with adults because I often feel nervous when I'm interacting with them. I will attend a communication skills training course, and read about the subject. I will use the techniques I learn to help me feel more confident, particularly when I am interacting with senior colleagues, parents and carers. I will know I am on my way to achieving the objective when I have done some reading and found a course. I will be closer to achieving it when I have completed the course and learnt some communication techniques. I will have achieved my goal when I feel more confident when I am communicating with adults.

Timescale:
Locate an appropriate course and book a place – by 1 March
Use the library and internet to research communication skills – by 14 March
Attend course and use communication techniques – date to be set by 1 March as it depends on the length of the course.'

➤ *Why is it important that Sophia's objectives are specific, measurable, achievable, realistic and with timescales?*   **K3P230**

➤ *How can Sophia find a communication course in her local area?*
   K3P231

Integrating new information and learning

It is important to keep up with new information and to integrate your learning in order to meet current best practice, regulatory requirements (regulations) and quality assurance schemes. These constantly evolve. Those who do not integrate will soon be left behind, and this will impact on the quality of their practice.

A training session

Element 304.2

Are you ready for assessment?

Take part in continuing professional development

You will need to show that you can use continuing professional development to improve your practice. You will need to identify areas for development in your skills, knowledge and understanding, and compile a plan for your own development. To do this you will need to be directly observed by your assessor and present other types of evidence. The amount and type of evidence you need to present will vary. You should plan this with your assessor.

Direct observation by your assessor

Observation and/or expert witness testimony is the required assessment method to be used to evidence some of each element in this unit. If your assessor is unable to observe you, s/he will identify an expert in your workplace who will provide testimony of your work-based performance. Usually your assessor or expert witness will observe you in real work activities and this should provide most of the evidence for the performance criteria for the elements in this unit.

Preparing to be observed

You must show your assessor that you have identified areas within your knowledge, understanding and skills which you can develop further. You must also show your assessor that you have negotiated a plan for this development which includes seeking out and accessing opportunities for continuing professional development. You must demonstrate your ability to use professional development to improve your practice.

Observation for this element could be carried out during a supervision session (with the prior agreement of your workplace supervisor).

You should plan with your supervisor to discuss:

- The areas you have identified for further development in your knowledge, understanding and skills
- The details of the plan you have devised for this development that includes seeking out and accessing opportunities for continuing professional development. This should be negotiated with your supervisor
- How you are using continuing professional development to improve your practice.

Other types of evidence

You will need to present different types of evidence in order to:

- Cover criteria not observed by your assessor
- Show that you have the required knowledge, understanding and skills.

Such evidence could include:

- Notes from reflective analysis, self-appraisals, journal entries, professional development plans
- Certificates/attendance records from professional development courses undertaken.

Check your knowledge

- Why is it so important to reflect on your practice and assess your personal effectiveness? **K3P222**
- Describe three techniques of reflective analysis. **K3D225**
- Thinking about continuous professional development, how can you make effective use of resources such as the internet, libraries and journals? **K3P229**
- What are 'SMART' objectives? **K3P230**
- How can reflection be used as a tool for contrasting what practitioners do and what they say they do? **K3P226**
- Why is it important to integrate new information and/or learning with existing practice? **K3M232**

Reflective practice

Revisiting reflective notes after a period of time can help practitioners to gain further insight into a situation or an aspect of their practice.

Go back to an entry you have made in your journal after two weeks have passed. Consider your notes again. Have you any new insights, ideas or thoughts? If so, note them in your journal and plan how to act on them if appropriate. Remember that you can use this technique at any time.

Protect and promote children's rights

*T*his unit is about ensuring and protecting the rights of children and the importance of promoting children's welfare. It includes the child's right to have a voice and to be protected and safeguarded.

This unit contains three elements:

⌒ **CCLD 305.1** *Support equality of access*

⌒ **CCLD 305.2** *Implement strategies, policies, procedures and practice for inclusion*

⌒ **CCLD 305.3** *Maintain and follow policies and procedures for protecting and safeguarding children*

Introduction

Equality and child protection are both extremely important issues. The effects of discrimination and child abuse are serious and far reaching – once experienced, children may suffer the impact of them throughout their lives.

Practitioners have a key role to play in safeguarding children and promoting good self-esteem and confidence levels with all the children they work with.

Support equality of access

K3P233
K3P234
K3P235
K3P236
K3D237
K3C238
K3D239
K3D240

There is legislation in place covering children's rights, equality and inclusion. Your setting will have its own Equal Opportunities policy in place, which must be in line with the relevant requirements of your home country. You must know and understand these, and work in accordance with them. An outline is given here.

⌒ UN Convention on the Rights of the Child

The UK Government made this convention law in 1991. It contains Articles that refer to the rights and needs of children. These acknowledgements include:

● Children have the right to non-discrimination – all the rights within the Convention apply equally to all children regardless of their race, sex, religion, disability or family background

Key Terms

Home country
The country in which you work. Each home country will have set out national guidelines, recommendations and legislation relating to the care of children. Your setting will have drawn up organisational policies and procedures that interpret these. The policies and procedures explain how you must approach your work within the setting. You must ensure you understand and work in line with both national and organisational requirements at all times.

Children also have a right to be aware of their rights. You should let children know (within the context of your setting) that they have equal rights, and will be accepted for who they are, and respected when they are there. They also have the responsibility to respect other children and adults within the environment. This will be communicated by your actions and attitudes towards young children, but it is appropriate to be more direct as children mature

- Children have the right to rest, play and leisure, and opportunities to join in with activities including those that are cultural and artistic

  Practitioners should ensure that disabled children have full opportunities to join in, since they may experience inequality in this area. A range of different cultural activities should be provided for all children, whatever their own culture

- Children have the right to freedom from exploitation

  Practitioners must ensure children are not abused, bullied or used. See Element 305.2

- Children have the right to a cultural identity

  Settings should recognise, respect and value the cultural identity of individual families, and celebrate diversity throughout the group

- Disabled children have the right to live as independently as possible, and to take a full and active part in everyday life

  Practitioners must consult with families to support disabled children's independence in the most effective way

- Parents and guardians have the right to support in carrying out their parental responsibilities

  Practitioners must work in partnership with all families

- Children have the right to have their views heard

  Practitioners should consult with children, particularly about decisions affecting them, and take notice of what they say. They should seek out and respect the views and preferences of children. This may be achieved through discussion, 'All About Me' theme work, or even through artwork. Practice should be adapted to suit the child's age, needs and abilities

- Children need a strong self-image and self-esteem

  Children should feel valued and accepted for who they are within the setting. This is achieved through showing children respect. There is more information in Element 305.3.

Every Child Matters

Every Child Matters: Change for Children aims to improve outcomes for all children and young people. As many disabled children's needs are complex and cross traditional service boundaries, they are one of the groups who stand to gain the most from this programme of change. *Every Child Matters* is supported by a number of policies and strategies that should work together to improve outcomes for disabled children, young people and their families. There is a dedicated website at www.everychildmatters.gov.uk. See also page 000 of Unit CCLD 306 and Element CCLD 309.01 for information on how the Early Years Foundation Stage aims to help young children achieve the five outcomes specified in *Every Child Matters.*

Unit CCLD 306 Plan and organise environments for children and families
Unit CCLD 309 Plan and implement curriculum frameworks for early education

The Disability Discrimination Act 1995

The Disability Discrimination Act 1995 (DDA 1995) was devised to support the rights of disabled people (adults and children) to take a full and active part in society. It gives them equality of access; in other words, the same opportunities to participate in society as non-disabled people have. This important piece of legislation gives disabled people rights regarding the way in which they receive services, facilities or goods. This includes education, care and play services.

The DDA 1995 was introduced in three stages:

- In 1996, it became illegal for service providers to discriminate against disabled people by treating them less favourably than non-disabled people.
- In 1999, service providers became required by law to make reasonable adjustments for disabled people, such as providing extra assistance.
- In 2004, service providers became required by law to make reasonable adjustments to their premises. This means that it must not be unreasonably difficult for disabled people to access the provision because of physical barriers, such as narrow doorways or steps. If a premise's physical features cause a barrier for a disabled person, that feature may be removed or altered. Or a service may provide a reasonable way of avoiding the feature or may make its service available in a different way: for example, a pre-school may replace steps into the front of its building with a ramp; or it may open a fire door at the side of the building to let a wheelchair user in.

A disabled person is defined in the DDA 1995 as someone who has a physical or mental impairment that adversely affects their ability to carry out normal day-to-day activities. This will be long-term – the impairment will have lasted for 12 months or be likely to last for more than 12 months. This includes some chronic illnesses, such as ME, which affect some people's ability to carry out normal day-to-day activities. See also Element CCLD 321.1 for details of the Special Educational Needs Code of Practice.

Unit CCLD 321 Support children with didabilities or special educational needs and their families

The Human Rights Act 1998

This Act was brought into force in 2000. It allows people in the UK to enforce rights given under previous laws in the British courts. Before the Act it was necessary to take cases to the European Court in Strasburg, which incurred time, expense and inconvenience.

The previous laws are the European Convention on Human Rights, which was ratified by the UK in 1951. It guarantees rights and freedoms for all as identified in the United Nations Declaration on Human Rights.

Race Relations Act 1976

This Act states that racial discriminatory practice is unaccepted, and defines in law what that means. The Act was introduced to make discriminatory practice illegal in the UK due to substantial ingrained discrimination within our society.

Children Act 1989

This Act requires all settings to have an equal opportunities policy that is regularly reviewed and to take account of children's:

- Religion
- Racial origin
- Cultural background
- Linguistic background.

Discrimination

Discrimination occurs when people are treated unfairly because of stereotypical views held about a group they belong to or are perceived to belong to. There are all kinds of

All children are equal and important

stereotypes, and people treat others unfairly based on a broad range of them. However, discrimination is commonly based on:

- Disability
- Ethnicity
- Culture
- Race
- Religion
- Gender

    (Evidence shows women are still discriminated against)

- Age
- Sexuality
- Low socio-economic group.

Inequalities are embedded in our society, in all geographical areas. It is not possible to identify where within the home countries certain prejudices or stereotypical beliefs are held because they are widespread and complex. Assumptions that this is not the case may in fact be based on stereotypes.

However, we have more equal opportunities legislation and awareness now than ever before, and children are growing up in settings that are required to promote equal opportunities. Your setting's equal opportunity policy is a public declaration of commitment to equality. However, practitioners can provide additional information about this on the advertisements and leaflets that feature the service, so that families and communities can easily see your values.

It is also good practice to implement 'transparent procedures' about admissions. This means making it clear how places are given to families, demonstrating that this is done fairly. Many settings have admissions policies stating that places are allocated on a first-come-first-served basis.

Types of discrimination

There are four types of discrimination:

- Direct discrimination

    This occurs when obvious action is carried out to the detriment of a person, because of their age, sex, race, religion, ethnicity or disability. For instance, if a setting were to refuse a child admission because they are Asian

- Indirect discrimination

    This occurs when a condition is applied that will favour one group over another unfairly. For instance, a multilingual setting offering extra places to parents on completion of forms, but only supplying the forms in English

- Segregation

    This is when people are unfairly separated when there is no reason for this. For instance, a setting with a separate area set aside for disabled children to eat in

- Victimisation

    This occurs when people are intentionally treated unfairly after complaining about previous discrimination. For instance, a parent complains that they were not given a chance to book an extra place because they could not understand the form. As a result the practitioner says there has been a double booking, and their child will not be able to come at all.

If discrimination occurs because an organisation will not meet the needs of someone, or because workers are jointly discriminating, the term 'institutionalised discrimination' may be used.

Effects of discrimination and inequality

Within families that experience it, discrimination can lead to:

- Missed opportunities that may affect a child's experiences and therefore impact on development
- Low self-esteem
- Low confidence
- Little sense of self-worth or self-value
- Confused identity
- Fear of rejection.

Inequality has a negative effect on all children, even if they have not been the target of discrimination. If one child is stopped from participating within a group, then the rights of all the children to participate equally, alongside one another, are affected. Children should not be exposed to inequality, regardless of whether they are the target of it. They should not be introduced to discrimination – this is introducing children to what is, after all, criminal behaviour.

Tara discriminates

Practitioner Tara thinks it will be too much trouble to have disabled children in the setting. Whenever a parent or carer of a disabled child enquires about a place, she lies and says the setting is full.

Tara is directly discriminating against the disabled children and their families. But this inequality affects the children who do attend too. She is not allowing them to play and make friends with disabled children. She is keeping them segregated from disabled children. This is unacceptable.

➤ *What effects may Tara's discrimination have?*   **K3D237**

Barriers to participation

Barriers to participation are factors that can cause difficulties for families and children who experience discrimination, preventing them from accessing services. Practitioners must welcome children from all backgrounds, ensuring barriers to participation are identified and removed. Barriers fall into three categories:

- Environmental
- Attitudinal
- Institutional.

Attitudinal and institutional barriers are often based on practitioners' worries and anxiety. They may be concerned that they will not adequately be able to meet the needs of a disabled child, or that they will not understand how to give the right cultural respect to a family. These things can be overcome with equality training and support.

All children should be allowed to participate in activities

There is no place in early years for attitudinal or institutional barriers based on prejudice to go unchallenged. If you come across them, you should follow your settings equal opportunities policy and report your concerns as soon as possible.

Environmental barriers can be identified and removed with procedures and practices to overcome the negative effects. Examples include:

- Steps – A parent who uses a wheelchair cannot get into the setting

  A ramp could be built from concrete, or a free-standing ramp could be used

- Poor lighting – A child with a visual impairment is experiencing more difficulty than usual due to inadequate light

  In consultation with the family, practitioners can find out what lighting works effectively for the child and introduce it

- Lack of space – A setting does not have enough space for a child who uses crutches to manoeuvre between activities

  The furniture can be altered to a better position. It may be necessary to put out fewer activities at one time, but change them more frequently

- Language – A child and her family speak so little of the setting's home language that practitioners cannot explain the admissions procedure clearly

  Find out the family's home language and translate documents, while arranging an interpreter.

An effective way to break down barriers is to find appropriate ways to reach families that have found services hard to access, and provide them with information about your setting and the equality of access that you offer. Your local EYDCP or Sure Start will have information to help you target appropriately within your area. They will also hold details of community resources and support that are available within your locality to assist with equality of access. This may include funding in some circumstances. This may be valuable to you, and it is helpful to have this information at hand for families who may need it. There may also be scope for referral if necessary.

It is also valuable to involve all relevant community groups in your setting or service. If you have a committee, 'friends', 'supporters' or 'partners' scheme, you can invite appropriate groups to link up with you by joining. This adds to the diversity of your group, and helps to ensure that your practices and activities are appropriate and accessible to everyone in the community. You can also provide information on local community groups to the families at your setting, perhaps via posters and leaflets.

Are you ready for assessment?

Support equality of access

You need to show that you can competently support equality of access. To do this you will need to be directly observed by your assessor and present other types of evidence. The amount and type of evidence you need to present will vary. You should plan this with your assessor.

Direct observation by your assessor

Observation and/or expert witness testimony is the required assessment method to be used to evidence some of each element in this unit. If your assessor is unable to observe you, s/he will identify an expert in your workplace who will provide testimony of your work-based performance. Usually your assessor or expert witness will observe you in real work activities and this should provide most of the evidence for the performance criteria for the elements in this unit.

Preparing to be observed

You must show your assessor that you can provide relevant people with information that promotes participation and equality of access, including information about children's rights and responsibilities. You must also show that you can implement transparent procedures, and welcome children from all backgrounds, identifying and removing barriers to participation. You must show that you can seek and respect the views and preferences of all children, and that you can involve all relevant local community groups in the setting. You may like to plan to be observed

when you are consulting with children and/or liaising with community groups.

Other types of evidence

You will need to present different types of evidence in order to:

- Cover criteria not observed by your assessor
- Show that you have the required knowledge and understanding and skills.

Such evidence could include:

- Work products such as leaflets for families explaining the setting's equal opportunity policies and procedures, or information translated into another language
- Case studies, projects, assignments and reflective accounts of your work
- Confidential records such as notes from meetings held to discuss barriers to participation that exist for individual children. These should not be placed in your portfolio – they must remain in their usual location and be referred to in the assessor records in your portfolio.

Implement strategies, policies, procedures and practice for inclusion

K3P241
K3D242
K3D243
K3P244
K3P245

Meeting relevant guidance

It is the responsibility of settings to ensure that they meet the current guidance for implementing inclusion and anti-discriminatory practice. Details of this are included in Element 305.1, which refers to legislation and organisational policy.

Policies should be reviewed regularly – this is a requirement of the Children Act 1989. When reviews take place, usually annually, practitioners should invite those involved in the setting to participate. This includes families, outside professionals and perhaps members of local community groups. Discussions should take place about the effectiveness of the policy. Does it meet the needs of the setting's users? Checks should be made to ensure that it remains in line with legislation, which does evolve over time. Any changes decided on should be implemented and then monitored to see if they are effective.

Assessing children's needs

All children have a right to high-quality childcare provision that meets their individual needs. So it is essential that practitioners undertake assessment of children's needs when they begin at the setting. This will require particular focus if a child has individual needs. The child's appointed key worker and the setting's appointed person taking responsibility for inclusion are likely to work together on this. (The appointed person is generally known as the SENCO or Special Educational Needs Co-ordinator.) Where appropriate, there must be regard to the Special Educational Needs Code of Practice 1994 and Assessment of Special Educational Needs. Practitioners may also contact outside professionals for support, and/or draw down resources available locally to help them meet children's needs – this may include funding.

Talking with parents and carers should be the first step. The child's family will know them better than anyone, and parents and carers are generally very pleased when practitioners show commitment to finding out how best to support their child. This sets the tone for working in partnership together from the outset, which is valuable for practitioners and families. Practitioners will want to discuss the following, recording notes on the registration documents:

- The detail of a child's individual needs
- How the needs impact on the child
- What strategies the child/family currently uses to meet the child's needs
- If there are any potential barriers within the setting (see Element 305.1)
- How barriers should be overcome. An action plan and a date of completion should then be drawn up by practitioners and acted upon
- What support the child may need on a daily basis and how this will be facilitated. The information may be quite detailed depending on the needs of the child. It is important to get everything down so that needs are not overlooked. If the child will need personal assistance that is not usually consistent with their age, practitioners must arrange for this to be done with regard to the child's right

to privacy. Details of any special equipment, extra staffing and so on should be recorded, and practitioners must action this accordingly

- Where appropriate and depending on the regulations within your home country, practitioners may also work with parents to activate Early Years Action or Early Years Action Plus. This is explained in Unit CCLD 321 Support children with disabilities or special educational needs and their families.

It is good practice to monitor the plans made in case adaptations are required.

It is important that confidentiality and privacy are always maintained unless the child's welfare is at stake, in line with the setting's confidentiality policy. Parents and carers should be reassured about this.

 Link   **Unit CCLD 321** Support children with disabilities or special educational needs and their families

Organising the provision

Once the needs of a child have been assessed, practitioners need to follow up by completing the action points that were identified. This may entail making physical changes to the premises, such as moving furniture to ensure a wheelchair user can manoeuvre with ease. Practitioners will also want to check the setting's future activity plans, some of which are likely to have been drawn up already. The purpose is to identify any adaptations or support that will be necessary to ensure the child can fully participate in all of the activities and experiences on offer, as is their entitlement.

Positive images

Within the setting practitioners should promote positive images of all people, reflecting the wider society. That is, they should seek to show, through the way they portray people, that all different kinds of people are valued positively in the setting. This can be done by ensuring that the pictures children see in books, displays, on puzzles, etc., show males and females, people of all sizes, ethnicities and cultures, and people who have impairments.

A stair lift that can be folded down into position when needed

Positive images should also be reflected in the toys that you choose whenever these represent people. For instance, within the setting's collection of baby dolls you may include dolls of different ethnicities, and within your puppets you may have different ages represented. Your doll's house may feature a ramp and a doll with a wheelchair, or perhaps crutches, or a hearing aid. The purpose is to represent society's diversity overall. It would be unrealistic to attempt to cover every eventuality in each collection of resources.

You should also ensure that people are shown in a positive light. Strong images of those people who may be discriminated against are particularly important. Some examples of strong image resources on the market are:

- A set of jigsaw puzzles that each show a family of a different culture eating a meal together
- A poster on the theme of celebrations, that shows six families of different religions celebrating
- A set of picture postcards showing athletes competing in the Paralympics
- A set of doll's house dolls, featuring four elderly couples of different ethnicities
- A set of puppets with the theme of 'People who help us' – including a female police officer and an Asian doctor
- A set of jigsaw puzzles showing children helping, which includes a child with special educational needs washing a car
- Stories that are not about a child's disability, but the lead character just happens to be disabled.

Be wary of images that are not positive – in a story or picture disabled people are sometimes shown as being dependant on non-disabled people for instance, perhaps by being cared for or pushed in a wheelchair. Similarly, females may be shown as the underdogs to male characters.

To weave the thread of diversity throughout your setting, you should extend this further wherever you have the opportunity. For instance, you can ensure that different styles of clothing are represented in the dressing-up clothes, and that cooking utensils and food in the home corner (an area that mimics the children's home environment) are also representative of the wider world. You can purchase crayons in a range of flesh tones for art activities. There are many possibilities.

Practical Example

Nina's choice

Nina is planning to buy some toys to promote positive images. She comes across a doll's house doll that she initially likes the look of. It is a woman sitting in a wheelchair. It is made of one piece of plastic.

It occurs to Nina that this may be a problem. The woman cannot be taken out of her wheelchair. The wheels of the chair do not go around. Nina wonders if this toy promotes positive images, and if it would give good play value.

➤ *What do you think? Should Nina buy the toy with the money earmarked for promoting positive images? Why?* **K3D239**

Toys that promote positive images

Monitoring data

You can make use of data available to you to monitor how effectively your provision is implementing inclusive practice. You can do this by selecting a period of time, perhaps the last six months. You should then:

- Collect data

  Compile information about the children who have attended the provision. Take care to be accurate

- Analyse the data

  Organise the data so it becomes meaningful information. Count up the number of children attending from groups likely to be discriminated against. Work out how many of each attended. For instance, how many children with special educational needs came? How many disabled children came? How long did children attend for? You can work this out as a percentage of the number of children attending overall

- Evaluate the data

  What conclusions can you draw? Does the information reveal that you are implementing inclusive practice well – perhaps because the number of children coming from groups likely to be discriminated against has risen? Or do figures show that children did not stay for long, so perhaps their needs were not met effectively? Look to see where change can be implemented to improve the service you are currently offering.

You can also collect other information – qualitative data rather than quantitative data. That is, information about quality rather than statistics. You could do this by compiling a questionnaire for children and families, asking how they feel about the inclusive service you aim to provide.

Element 305.2

Are you ready for assessment?

Implement strategies, policies, procedures and practice for inclusion

You need to show that you can competently implement strategies, policies, procedures and practice for inclusion. To do this you will need to be directly observed by your assessor and present other types of evidence. The amount and type of evidence you need to present will vary. You should plan this with your assessor.

Direct observation by your assessor

Observation and/or expert witness testimony is the required assessment method to be used to evidence some of each element in this unit. If your assessor is unable to observe you, s/he will identify an expert in your workplace who will provide testimony of your work-based performance. Usually your assessor or expert witness will observe you in real work activities and this should provide most of the evidence for the performance criteria for the elements in this unit.

Preparing to be observed

You must also show your assessor that you can use inclusive and anti-discriminative practice in the planning and delivery of your provision, assessing and contributing to the meeting of children's individual needs. You must show that you can facilitate access for disabled children and children with special educational needs, promote entitlement to a full range of activities, and promote positive images of children. You must also show that you can collect and evaluate relevant data and ensure confidentiality and privacy where appropriate.

You may like to arrange to be observed at a time when you will be working with children of diverse needs and abilities.

Other types of evidence

You will need to present different types of evidence in order to:

- Cover criteria not observed by your assessor
- Show that you have the required knowledge, understanding and skills.

Such evidence could include:

- Work products such as plans for activities and experiences that are accessible to all, resources or materials made to promote positive images of people
- Case studies, projects, assignments and reflective accounts of your work
- Confidential records such as notes from meetings held to discuss barriers to participation that exist for individual children. These should not be placed in your portfolio – they must remain in their usual location and be referred to in the assessor records in your portfolio.

Maintain and follow policies and procedures for protecting and safeguarding children

Element
305.3

K3P1121
K3P247
K3S249
K3S250
K3S251
K3S252
K3S253
K3D248
K3D254
K3M333

Safeguarding and protecting children

Everyone who works with children has a duty to keep them safe from abuse. This is known as 'child protection'. There are laws, regulations and codes of practice in place that make this a legal requirement. You must know and understand those relevant to your home country.

Legislation, regulations and codes of practice

Children Act 1989

When it was introduced in 1989 this law enforced a big change in the way parents' roles are regarded. The emphasis is now on parents having a responsibility to their children, rather than rights over them. It recognises that children themselves have rights, and that they should be treated with respect. Under the Act children have rights to:

- Be protected from harm
- Discuss their concerns
- Be listened to
- Be told what their rights are
- Have their wishes considered when decisions that affect them are being made
- Have details about their age, culture, race and gender considered when decisions are made
- Be told about the decisions that are made
- Have a right to be heard if they are involved in a court case, and to have their own solicitor to represent them
- Refuse a medical examination if they understand what that entails and do not want to have it done.

The table on page 133 provides further details.

Protection of Children Act 1999

This Act includes clauses that set out the child protection duties of local authorities. It also defines the term 'significant harm'. A summary of the relevant points is given in the table opposite.

UN Convention on the Rights of the Child

The UK Government ratified this convention in 1991. It contains Articles that refer to the rights and needs of children. These acknowledgements include:

- Children have the right to protection
- Children have the right to a family life

Significant harm

Legislation says ...

There must be **provision of services for children and their families**. Every local authority has a duty to safeguard and promote the welfare of children within their area who are in need. They should promote the upbringing of such children by their families by providing services appropriate to those children's needs

Local authorities have a **duty to investigate** if they are informed that a child who lives, or is found, in their area:
- Is the subject of an emergency protection order
- Is in police protection.

They must also investigate if there is reasonable cause to suspect that a child who lives, or is found, in their area is suffering, or is likely to suffer, significant harm. Enquiries must be undertaken to enable the authority to decide whether they should take any action to safeguard or promote the child's welfare

'Harm' is defined as **ill treatment or the impairment of health or development**
- 'Ill treatment' includes physical abuse, sexual abuse and forms of abuse that are non-physical, such as emotional abuse
- 'Health' means mental health and physical health
- 'Development' means social, physical, intellectual or behavioural development

- Parents and guardians have the right to support in carrying out their parental responsibilities
- Children have the right to have their views listened to
- Children's views should be given due consideration
- Children need to receive good physical care
- Children need to be shown love
- Children need to feel secure
- Children need a strong self-image and self-esteem.

Children Bill 2004

Prior to this bill, there had been concerns that children's services were not working together effectively to protect vulnerable children from abuse. This was highlighted by an independent inquiry into the death of Victoria Climbié, who died tragically at the hands of her carers. This led to *Every Child Matters* (a green paper) and then to the introduction of the Children Bill. (This applies in England. Equivalent legislation was also established in the other home countries). The bill was passed to improve child protection for children and to ensure better co-ordination of services. This included the introduction of a tracking system to record information on all children, including whether they are known to the police or the social, welfare or education services; the appointment of national children's commissioners who must protect the rights of all children; and the appointment of lead councillors for children's services who have local political child welfare responsibilities.

Safe working practices

The term 'safe working practices' refers to the way practitioners work to protect children and to protect themselves from allegations of abuse. Your organisation's guidelines will be included within the Child Protection policy, and based on the requirements of your home country. You must ensure you know and understand these, and always work in accordance with them.

It is the role of the person in charge to check that the safe practices are adhered to, and to monitor their effectiveness. Regulative bodies, such as Ofsted, will also want to be satisfied that these practices are observed. Practitioners need to be open and accepting about being accountable to children, parents, families and other agencies.

The following are typically included within 'safe working practice' guidance.

- All adults working/volunteering/living on the premises of the setting must undergo a Criminal Records Bureau (CRB) check, known as a CRB Disclosure Standard or Enhanced (different levels of check apply to different peoples' roles) to see if they are regarded as fit to work/live on premises with children. Any prior convictions must be disclosed on the relevant form – none are considered spent in this case.

- Adults in group settings who have not yet received their check or disclosure may not be left alone with any children, or carry out personal assistance such as toileting or changing nappies.

- At least two adults must always be present at a setting, however many children are there. This applies even if there is one child left who is late being collected – at least two staff must stay. If the parents/carers/alternative adults authorised to collect the child have not contacted you, and cannot be contacted, you may need to take action. After an hour or more has elapsed since the setting officially closed, practitioners should ring the Duty Social Worker (listed under Social Services in the telephone directory) for support. A practitioner must not take the child to the child's home or to their own home. Practitioners have a duty to stay with the child until the situation is resolved, only passing the child on to a person authorised to collect them, a police officer or a social worker.

- Adults should not invite children into their homes, or in the case of childminders, they should not do so out of the normal childminding hours arranged with parents or carers.

- Adults should not offer children lifts in their car, or take them anywhere if they should accidentally meet them outside of the setting.

- Adults must record and report any incidents when they have had no choice but to restrain a child, for instance to protect them from seriously harming themselves or others (see Unit CCLD 337 Create environments that promote positive behaviour).

- Adults must record and report all accidents, injuries and incidents. A child being bullied is an example of an incident. (See Unit CCLD 302 Develop and maintain a healthy, safe and secure environment for children).

- There are guidelines in place about what should happen if an allegation of abuse is made about a member of staff.

Link   **Unit CCLD 337** Create environments that promote positive behaviour.
Unit CCLD 302 Develop and maintain a healthy, safe and secure environment for children

Indicators of abuse

For children's welfare, it is important that you learn how to recognise the signs and symptoms of abuse. Practitioners learn this so that if they come across them they will realise that abuse could be taking place, and they will take the appropriate action. Experts sometimes use more categories to describe the specifics of abuse, but essentially there are four main types:

- Physical abuse
- Emotional abuse
- Sexual abuse
- Neglect.

Physical abuse

Physical abuse occurs when someone deliberately causes physical harm to a child. It includes the actions of hitting, kicking, shaking, biting, squeezing, burning, scalding, throwing, attempting suffocation or drowning, giving children poisonous substances or inappropriate drugs or alcohol.

Signs

Signs of physical abuse include bruises, cuts and abrasions. Since children frequently have minor accidents and therefore have bumps and bruises, it is important to take into account where on the body bruising or marking occurs – see the diagram on page 136 for parts of the body that are likely to become bruised or marked when abuse is taking place. (This is called a 'body map'.)

In addition, consider how often a child has bruises and marks. If frequency is a concern you can keep a dated record of the marks you observe, to see if a pattern emerges. Bruises made by abuse may be in the shape of hands, fingers or other implements. A torn frenulum (web of skin inside the upper lip) is often a sign of abuse. The injury may occur if a child has something forced into their mouth, for instance if they are forcibly fed with a bottle or spoon. Injuries to this area rarely occur accidentally.

Blank body maps are often used to record the marks actually seen on a child. Remember that physical signs are not always left by physical abuse.

Common sites for bruising that occurs as a result of play and/or accident include marks to the legs and arms, particularly below the knees and elbows. Mongolian spots (or blue spots) are birthmarks that may occur on the lower spine or buttocks of children of southern European, African or Asian descent. They are smooth, with the bluish grey tone of a bruise, and can be quite large. They should not be confused with a bruise or a sign of abuse.

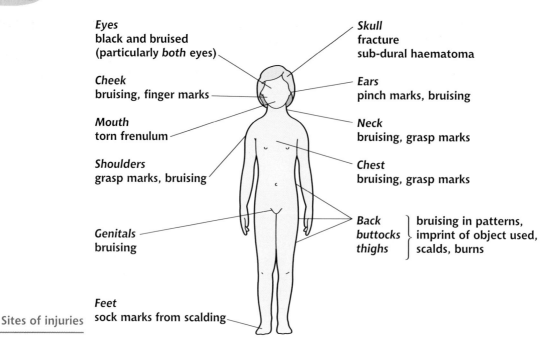

Eyes
black and bruised
(particularly *both* eyes)

Cheek
bruising, finger marks

Mouth
torn frenulum

Shoulders
grasp marks, bruising

Genitals
bruising

Feet
sock marks from scalding

Skull
fracture
sub-dural haematoma

Ears
pinch marks, bruising

Neck
bruising, grasp marks

Chest
bruising, grasp marks

Back
buttocks } bruising in patterns,
thighs   imprint of object used,
              scalds, burns

Sites of injuries

Behavioural/emotional signs

Children who are being physically abused may show signs of changed behaviour in addition to physical signs or in the absence of physical signs. They may include:

- Being withdrawn
- Avoiding physical contact
- Lack of trust
- Afraid to go home or go with abuser
- Aggressive behaviour
- Acting out aggression in play
- Signs of stress such as bedwetting
- Seeming sad/preoccupied/unable to have fun
- Lack of confidence
- Watches others carefully but does not participate (sometimes called 'frozen watchfulness').

Emotional abuse

Emotional abuse occurs when children are harmed emotionally. When children's emotional needs, which include love and affection, are not met, then children's development is seriously damaged. They are likely to experience difficulties with social and emotional development, finding it particularly hard to relate to adults and to make friends with children. This can have the effect of putting a child at further risk of bullying. Children often have low self-esteem, and may develop poor emotional health (mental health). Children who are emotionally abused may live with constant threats, shouting, ridiculing, criticism, taunting and repeated rejection.

The signs of emotional abuse are listed below. However, when children experience an emotional upheaval in their life, such as bereavement, divorce or a new baby in the family, they can also show some of those signs of stress for a period of time. Record instances and share the information with parents and carers. You will have notes in case the signs persist.

Signs

Children who are being emotionally abused may show signs of changed behaviour. They may include:

- Low self-esteem and lack of confidence
- Difficulty making friends
- Being very wary of their parent's mood
- Behaviour difficulties – aggression (may be towards self, e.g. head banging, biting), attention seeking, demanding, stealing, lying, tantrums (in children over five)
- Indiscriminately affectionate – may cuddle or sit on lap of any adult, even if they do not know them
- Poor concentration leading to learning difficulties
- Inability to have fun
- Toileting problems after previously being dry
- Overly upset by making a mistake
- Behaviour associated with comfort seeking in children over five – sucking thumb, rocking, masturbation.

Sexual abuse

Sexual abuse is defined as the involvement of dependant and developmentally immature children in sexual activities. It also includes behaviour that may not involve any physical contact – exposing children to pornography via any media, for instance photographs, videos, DVDs and the internet, or having them witness the sexual acts of others.

Sexual abuse happens to both girls and boys, and to babies. Both men and women sexually abuse children. The majority of children who are sexually abused are abused by someone they know who is in a position of trust, such as a family member or family friend. A *minority* of sexually abused children go on to become abusers. Sexual abuse frequently causes lifelong emotional damage and serious difficulties in forming relationships. Sometimes children do not show signs of abuse until much later, when they have reached puberty for instance. It may be that the child had not previously realised that what was happening to them was wrong and abusive.

Signs

There are few physical signs that are likely to be noticed after a child is independent in terms of caring for their own body, so the behaviour signs are particularly important. Over-sexualised behaviour (also called pseudo-sexual) is when children act in sexual ways that are inappropriate for their age – they may say or know things you would not expect, or role play or act out sexual situations.

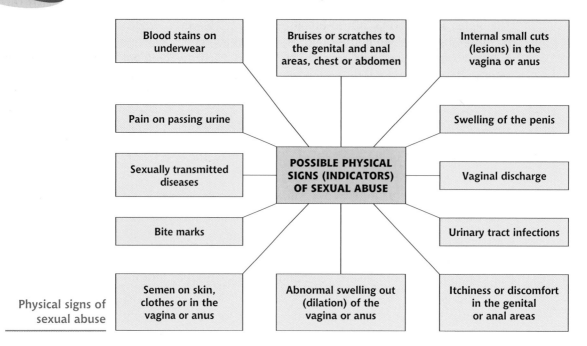

Physical signs of
sexual abuse

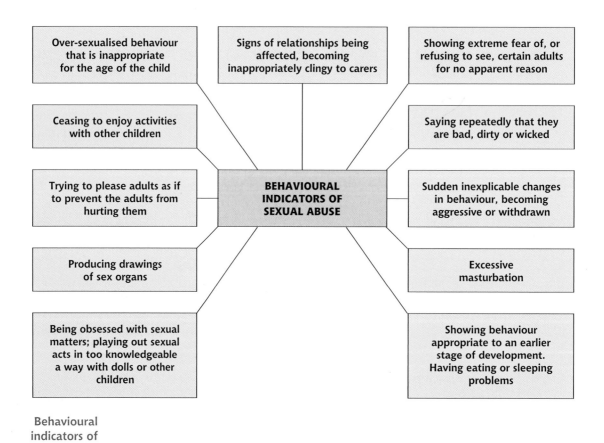

Behavioural
indicators of
sexual abuse

Neglect

Neglect occurs when a family does not provide for a child's basic, everyday, essential needs. This can include a lack of supervision (such as leaving the child alone inappropriately), supervising a child whilst the adult is under the influence of alcohol or drugs, not protecting a child from danger and not providing stimulation. Children who have been neglected are often said to be 'failing to thrive'. Because of a lack of care and attention to their most basic needs, they may not be able to grow and develop as they should. These children are deprived.

Signs

Signs may include:

- Lack of food, or lack of healthy food leading to malnourishment, obesity (being overweight), hunger
- Clothes uncared for, may be dirty, smelly, worn, may have clothes that are not suitable for the weather. This can lead to bullying. (In addition there may not be adequate heating at home)
- Child may not be cared for hygienically. They may be dirty and they may smell. They may have skin infections and infestation which go untreated (such as head lice). This is also likely to lead to bullying. The child may live in an unhygienic environment and frequently be unwell. Food poisoning is common
- Inadequate supervision and lack of safety features at home may lead to frequent accidents, the child having too much freedom (they may be out alone in the street or garden late at night for instance, or a younger child may be out unsupervised). The child may be truant from school, leading to a lack of stimulation and education. There may not be a child's safety seat in the car
- Poor medical care. Illnesses and injuries may go untreated; impairments may go unchecked; developmental check ups, immunisations and dental appointments may be missed, possibly leading to serious or prolonged health problems and disability
- Lack of love, care, affection and moral guidance leading to isolation and possible early smoking, drinking and substance abuse.

Children may appear to be:

- Nervous, attention seeking or clingy
- Sad, unpopular with peers
- Caring for siblings or other family members, including parents
- Angry, and may tell lies
- Streetwise – they look after themselves.

Disclosure

'Disclosure' is the term that is used to refer to a child revealing to an adult that they have been abused. This may be in the form of:

- A full disclosure

  When the child says who has abused them, and goes into the history and nature of the abuse

- A partial disclosure

  A child may begin to tell of abuse, and then shy away and not continue. Or they may reveal only some details, leaving out what exactly has happened, or the name of the abuser

- An indirect disclosure

  This occurs when a child indicates abuse indirectly, through their play (often in a role-play or imaginary situation), their artwork or, in the case of older children, through letters, stories or school work. Children may choose to disclose in this way if they are too afraid to tell directly, too embarrassed or ashamed, or if they find it too painful to discuss. They may fear that they will not be believed, or fear they will be punished or sent away from home. They may not know the right words to explain what has happened to them. Children sometimes disclose in this way unintentionally – they may not be aware that what is happening to them is wrong, or they may have tried to block out or disguise the abuse, but have inadvertently revealed it in their play or conversation.

When a child discloses abuse, it can be quite a shocking experience for a practitioner. However, your response is very important in terms of the welfare of the child, so you must stay calm, let the child see you are in control of yourself, and follow these guidelines for dealing with the situation.

When the child is disclosing

- Look at the child, maintaining eye contact if the child is choosing to look directly at you. Aim to be on the same level as the child (or lower) so that you do not appear intimidating. Do not look away from the child – this can be interpreted by them as disapproval. Do not show any signs of disgust on your face, whatever the child says, or they are likely to feel that they disgust you because they were involved in the abuse.
- Let the child do the talking, allow them to tell you spontaneously and in their own way.
- Listen and follow carefully. Try to remember exactly what the child is saying and the language they are using, rather than interpreting what it all means.
- Do not ask the child questions or prompt them for more information. This may lead to confused information. It is not helpful for the child to have been 'led' should evidence be needed legally later on. If appropriate, a trained specialist will interview the child at another time.

What to say to the child

- Let the child know that telling you was the right thing to do

  ('I'm so glad you've told me.')
- Tell them the abuse was not their fault
- Praise them for having told you, and for surviving their ordeal
- If the child asks if you believe them, say yes

  All allegations of abuse must be reported and taken seriously. It has been shown that children do not often lie about abuse. Even if the story seems confused or improbable, you must let the child see that you accept it. Your role is not to investigate, but to record and report. Never ask questions such as, 'Are you telling me the truth?' or, 'Are you sure that's what happened?'

- If the child asks you to comment on the abuser, tread carefully. You should not be judgemental. Remember the child may love the abuser. It is acceptable to say that the abuser was wrong to do the things they have done

- If a child asks you what will happen to the abuser, say they will need some help

- Tell them you have to tell someone else. You should never promise not to tell. It is your duty to report suspicions and disclosures of abuse, and the child will lose their trust in you when you do report it if you have not explained this

- Tell them what you are going to do next

- Say you will talk to them again to let them know what has happened

- Reassure them that they can speak to you again about the abuse if they want to talk about it.

You should record and report a disclosure as soon as possible. See below.

Recognising and recording signs and symptoms

You should read this section in conjunction with information on avoiding premature judgements on page 143.

By recognising signs of abuse, practitioners can take the first steps that may ultimately stop the abuse happening to a child. It is very important to learn the signs and symptoms. Having a good knowledge of children's expected development and behaviour is key, since you will then be more likely to spot behaviour that is inappropriate for a child's age – tantrums or wetting themselves in children generally too old for this, or streetwise or overtly sexual behaviour in children generally too young.

This is informed by the regular observations and assessment that practitioners make on children in their care. Observations can reveal and record how the child forms relationships, how their behaviour or mood may change over time, and reccurring themes in their play or conversation. Always date your observations. This is good practice in any case, but it is also important if the information is required as evidence. See Unit CCLD 303 Promote children's development.

Link   **Unit CCLD 303** Promote children's development

If you suspect a child may be being abused you should write down all the information as soon as you can, while it is still fresh in your mind. It is easy to forget details later, particularly those that do not seem to have much significance at the time but may prove to be important. You must record your observations, and you must inform your supervisor of your concerns, following your setting's procedures and the requirements of your home country. Make sure you know and understand these. Your setting will have a Child Protection policy that sets out how you should report concerns, and what will happen next. But broadly, you will need to include the following information:

- The date the report is made

- Child's name, address and date of birth

- Name of the child's parents or carers

Practitioners can observe any major changes in a child's behaviour or physical appearance

- Your name and job title
- Whether you are reporting your own concerns or those which have been reported to you by someone else
- Concise description of your concerns
- Incidents leading to your concerns, if applicable (for instance, you may have noticed a behaviour or bruising before, but did not record it until now because you were not concerned before a repetition of the behaviour or bruising occurred)
- Accurate description of physical signs, if applicable, recorded on a body map. Do not make assumptions about the cause of the signs, just record facts
- Accurate description of behaviour signs if applicable. Again, only record facts
- If concern has been caused by something a child has said, or if disclosure has taken place, again record only facts, using their exact words as much as possible, not your interpretation of them. You must also record what you said to the child, even if you are concerned that you may not have handled the situation effectively. It is important detail
- If a parent or carer has given you any explanations for the signs or symptoms you are concerned about, record the facts, again using their exact words as much as you can
- Sign the record and store it safely and confidentially in a locked filing cabinet or cupboard to which only appropriate staff members have access. Only those who need to know, that is your superiors and those who work closely with the child, should be able to access such files. Under the Data Protection Act 1998, parents and carers have a right to see records kept about them and their children if they ask to do so.

Procedures

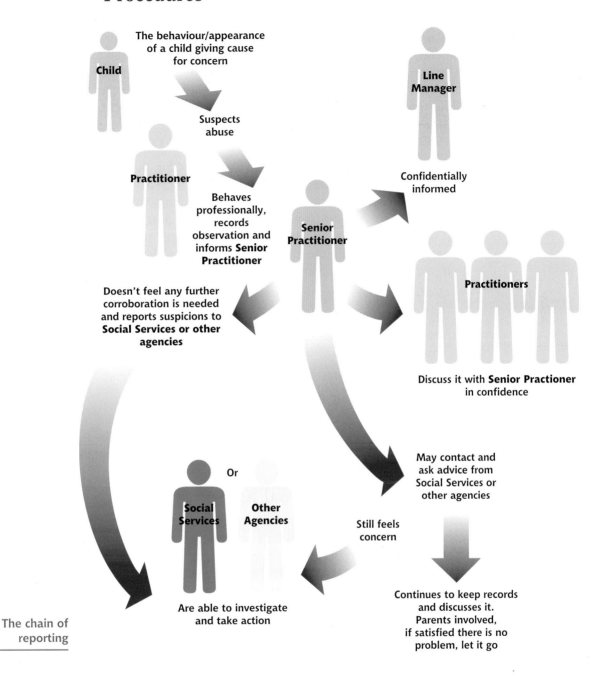

Child

The behaviour/appearance of a child giving cause for concern

Suspects abuse

Practitioner

Behaves professionally, records observation and informs **Senior Practitioner**

Senior Practitioner

Line Manager

Confidentially informed

Doesn't feel any further corroboration is needed and reports suspicions to **Social Services or other agencies**

Practitioners

Discuss it with **Senior Practioner** in confidence

Or

Social Services   **Other Agencies**

Are able to investigate and take action

May contact and ask advice from Social Services or other agencies

Still feels concern

Continues to keep records and discusses it. Parents involved, if satisfied there is no problem, let it go

The chain of reporting

⤷ Avoiding premature judgements

If you notice signs and symptoms that cause you to suspect abuse, it is very important that you remain objective. You must follow procedures closely without making judgements. Remember that there could be other reasons for the child's behaviour or physical signs. You must ask parents or carers if they have noticed the signs and symptoms, and ask them why they think they have occurred. There may be a simple explanation, and you should note what you are told.

You must not make judgements even if actual abuse is confirmed. In the case of either suspected or actual abuse, it can be hard for a practitioner who cares about children not to become upset and/or feel angry. However, as a professional you will want to help the child by doing what is best for them. In the past, children who were being abused were frequently removed from their families. However, it has been found that this is often not the best thing for the child. Some children who were removed have felt that they were being sent away as punishment for 'telling on' their families. The threat that children will be sent away if they tell is often used by abusers – it is often an effective threat because children may desperately want to stay within their family. The Children Act 1989 says that what is best for children should be paramount.

The modern approach is often to keep children within the family, whilst helping them by preventing further abuse. Families need support if this is to happen, and that requires a multi-professional, multi-agency approach, which includes practitioners. You must continue to treat the parent as you would any other, and work in partnership with them. If parents feel as though they are being judged or treated differently, they may ultimately stop bringing the child, which would be detrimental to the child and the family. Partnerships with parents and families can be developed and supported by:

- Making sure the key worker has opportunities to get to know the family

  Be available at dropping off and collection times, and be sure to greet adults and make general conversation. This need only be brief but regular for parents to see that you are approachable, and to feel that you are not judging them

- Regularly sharing information about the child's progress and achievements
- Asking the family to share information about the child's progress and activities at home
- Encouraging parents to get involved with their child and the setting, by bringing resources such as empty boxes for making models, for example.

A multi-professional approach

A multi-professional approach is recognised as the best way for children to be supported where there are concerns of abuse or actual abuse. Traditionally, this has described the way in which adults who perform different job roles within different organisations work together regionally, adopting a joint, multi-agency approach. Early years workers, other childcarers and teachers may be involved in maximising the child's learning and experiences through their settings, while outside professionals work on providing support in other areas (see diagram). This approach draws on the professionals within local communities, while accessing external expertise.

New organisations, known as 'Children's Trusts', are now bringing together services for children and families:

- Health services – including health visitors, speech and language therapists and educational psychologists
- Early years provision – integrated child care and early education
- Social services – including social workers, family support workers and child protection teams.

At present, the scope of individual Trusts varies. Some already employ a wide range of professionals and handle all children's services. They may also incorporate local Sure

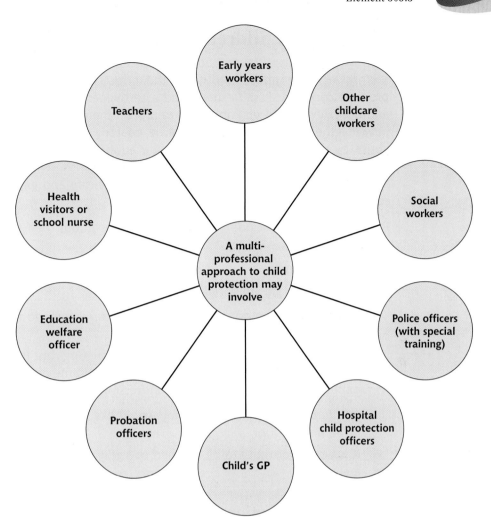

A multi-professional approach to child protection

Start programmes and work in partnership with independent sector organisations, including voluntary organisations such as the National Society for the Prevention of Cruelty to Children (NSPCC) and a range of community sector organisations such as housing services and leisure services. Other Trusts are working towards this. Some Trusts may focus on the provision of services for vulnerable children, for example disabled children, those 'looked after' by their local authority (including children living in residential care homes and with foster parents) and children in need of child protection services.

Professionals are also there to support you. If you are feeling distressed after or during involvement in a case of suspected or actual abuse, you will need the opportunity to talk through your feelings. But because of strict confidentiality, you must not talk to anyone who does not 'need to know'. However, it is appropriate for you to talk to your supervisor, or to ask your supervisor for the name of the outside professional you should contact to talk things over. This is generally a social worker or a worker from the NSPCC.

Helping children to protect themselves from abuse

Empowerment, confidence and resilience are factors that help children to protect themselves from abuse and from the effects of abuse. General activities that promote confidence, self-esteem and assertiveness are beneficial to all children. In addition, when children know how to protect themselves, and are aware of the way in which they should and should not be treated, they are empowered to act to stop abuse by disclosing it to an appropriate adult. You can help children by teaching them about their rights in respect of their bodies, what to do in emergency situations when they are vulnerable, how to identify and express their feelings and what to do if they are bullied.

Practitioners should support children in learning about the following.

Children's bodies

- Their bodies are their own.
- They do not have do show physical affection if they do not want to, including kissing, hugging or sitting on people's laps.
- They can have help if they need it when toileting, but they have a right to privacy if they want it. For older children the same applies to bathing/showering and dressing/undressing.

  Adults should ask children if they would like some help before opening a toilet or bathroom door.
- It is wrong for them to be touched in a way that hurts them, frightens them or feels rude.

Emergency situations

- What to do if they are lost.

  Stop, look around carefully for the adult they were with. If they cannot see them, approach a safe person – a police officer, crossing-patrol guard (lollipop person), cashier at a till in a shop, or lastly a parent with children. They should wait outside until their adult, their parent or a police officer comes to look after them. They should not go anywhere with strangers, not to a phone, workplace or to a house.
- Who to go home with – when at a setting, both the child and practitioners should know who the child is allowed to leave with.
- They should never answer the door unless an adult is with them (in the case of younger children).
- The child should know their personal details: full name, address and telephone number.
- Stranger Danger – who strangers are, what to do if approached.

  If an unknown person talks to them, they need not be rude – they can pretend they have not heard and walk away quickly, telling an adult if they feel worried. But if a stranger asks or invites the child to go with them, they should run away and tell a safe adult immediately. They must learn to 'Say no and never go!' If children are touched, grabbed or feel otherwise frightened or worried they might be in danger, it is alright to break the usual behaviour rules. They should attract attention by shouting and screaming, and punch, kick, etc. if they feel they need to.

Police officers often visit settings to talk to children about being lost and stranger danger, which helps to establish them as a safe person in the minds of children.

Identifying and expressing feelings

- They can express their feelings, including worry and fear, knowing they will be taken seriously, and not dismissed or ridiculed.

  Children learn this through experience of being respected.

  General activities that encourage naming, thinking about and expressing feelings are good for all children.

- They do not have to keep secrets unless they want to, even if it is an adult's secret.

  Using the word 'surprise' is often better than using the word 'secret' with young children. Surprises are usually thought of as pleasant things that are only secret for a little while before everyone finds out about them – birthday presents and treats are good examples of this. Older children can learn that they should not keep 'bad' secrets. A touch, kiss, etc. should never be a secret.

If they are bullied

- They should know who to tell, and tell them immediately.

  Most settings and all schools have anti-bullying policies.

- At the time, they should resist, saying firmly or shouting 'NO!' Friends should stick together as there is safety in numbers.

  The charity Kidscape have devised the 'Keepsafe Code' suitable for children over five. It is especially helpful for children who have experienced bullying and
  may be afraid of it happening again. You can find further details online at www.kidscape.org.uk. Kidscape's telephone number is 020 7730 3300.

Vulnerability

Abuse occurs in all cultures and socio-economic groups. It happens to boys, girls and babies from families of different kinds within different communities. It is not exclusive to particular types of families. Abusers can be men or woman. Children are most likely to know their abuser, and they are likely to be in a position of trust – they may be a family member or a family friend. Some children are made a scapegoat; they are abused within a family, whilst other children are not. This child may be chosen because of their personality – they may be naturally reserved for instance. Children can also be vulnerable because of the following factors:

- Disability
- Being a loner

- Being the result of an unwanted pregnancy
- Being the opposite gender to the one a parent wanted
- Being the eldest child
- Being a step-child
- Being a child who does not feed well or does not like eating (particularly as a baby).

Children are also more likely to be abused if they do not meet a parent's expectations – this can be for a range of reasons. Statistics have shown that a child who has been abused is more likely to be abused again, even at the hands of a different person.

Social factors

Social factors can also lead to abuse. If parents or carers are abusing substances, the focus of their life may shift. Someone who is addicted to alcohol or drugs may not notice the needs of their child, or be aware that they are being abusive. People dealing with addiction may find that it takes over their lives, frequently or at times leaving them unable to deal with other things. It is hard for someone whose own needs are not being met to meet the needs of someone else.

In order to feed their addiction, those who are addicted may frequent places that are inappropriate for young children. They may take a child with them, or leave them at home inappropriately while they purchase alcohol or drugs. Alternatively, they may use substances at home, around or in front of their child, alone or in company. It can be very frightening for a child to see their parent or carer under the influence of these substances. If drugs or alcohol are kept in the home, young children may ingest them accidentally or as a result of copying a parent.

Whistle blowing

Whistle blowing is the term used to describe when a practitioner alerts superiors or outside professionals to their concerns relating to their own setting. All those within the sector have a duty to safeguard children, and as such they must take action to blow the whistle if necessary, even though it may be uncomfortable.

You must report concerns about colleagues to superiors if you suspect them of abuse.

If you have reported to superiors any concerns about abuse but you feel they have not acted appropriately by taking your concerns seriously or by taking the appropriate action, you should report this to Social Services. (This relates to suspicions you may have about children being abused outside of the setting as well as concerns you have about colleagues.)

Are you ready for assessment?

Maintain and follow policies and procedures for protecting and safeguarding children

You need to show that you can competently maintain and follow policies and procedures for protecting and safeguarding children. To do this you will need to be directly observed by your assessor and present other types of evidence. The amount and type of evidence you need to present will vary. You should plan this with your assessor.

Direct observation by your assessor

Observation and/or expert witness testimony is the required assessment method to be used to evidence some of each element in this unit. If your assessor is unable to observe you, s/he will identify an expert in your workplace who will provide testimony of your work-based performance. Usually your assessor or expert witness will observe you in real work activities and this should provide most of the evidence for the performance criteria for the elements in this unit.

Preparing to be observed

You must show your assessor that you can maintain and follow procedures and safe working practice to safeguard and protect children and practitioners. You must also show that you can help children to protect themselves from abuse and promote an environment of openness and trust. You must show that you can recognise indicators of abuse and that you can respond sensitively to a disclosure.

You may like to arrange to be observed at a time when you working with children on keeping themselves safe.

Other types of evidence

You will need to present different types of evidence in order to:

- Cover criteria not observed by your assessor
- Show that you have the required knowledge, understanding and skills

Such evidence could include:

- Work products such as plans for activities, or guides to safe working practices for colleagues or volunteers
- Case studies, projects, assignments and reflective accounts of your work
- Confidential records. These should not be placed in your portfolio – they must remain in their usual location and be referred to in the assessor records in your portfolio.

Check your knowledge

- What are the four forms of discrimination? **K3P235**
- What is meant by 'barriers to participation'? **K3D239**
- How should you assess and plan for a child's needs? **K3D242**
- What should you do if you suspect abuse? **K3P1121, K3S249, K3S252**
- What are 'safe working practices'? **K3S253**
- Why is it that practitioners must not be judgemental in cases of suspected or actual abuse? **K3D248, K3S249**

Reflective practice

Try the following exercise.

Do you feel confident that you would react in the appropriate way if a child made a disclosure to you? Imagine a child disclosed to you right now. What are the things you would need to remember to say? What would you not say?

Now, turn back to pages 139–41. Read them again and compare your answers. Notice any errors you may have made. Make a note in your journal to remind you to try this exercise again in a few months time. You will not be able to look up the answers if you are ever in the difficult position of handling a disclosure – it is best to be sure you know.

Plan and organise environments for children and families

*T*his unit is about the planning and organisation of environments for children and families.

The unit contains four elements:

- **CCLD 306.1** *Plan and provide an enabling physical environment for children*
- **CCLD 306.2** *Organise space and resources to meet children's needs*
- **CCLD 306.3** *Provide a caring, nurturing and responsive environment*
- **CCLD 306.4** *Facilitate children's personal care*

Introduction

When providing environments for children you must comply with the laws and regulations relevant to your home country. All the laws and regulations referred to in this unit apply in England. However, health and safety legislation is fairly universal. You can find out more about the specifics for your home country online:

- Scotland
  www.scotland.gov.uk
- Wales
  www.wales.gov.uk
- Northern Ireland
  www.deni.gov.uk
- England
  www.direct.gov.uk.

Element 306.1

Plan and provide an enabling physical environment for children

K3D255
K3D264
K3D265
K3D266
K3H256
K3H257

Legislation and regulations

There are many laws and regulations covering the provision of environments for children. The key ones are outlined below. (Many of these are covered in more detail in other units. Links are given where appropriate.)

K3H258
K3H259
K3H260
K3H261
K3H262
K3H263

The Children's Act 1989

This law covers equality of access and opportunity for all children, in addition to health and safety. It also addresses child protection which links with Element 306.4. Further details are included in Unit CCLD 305 Protect and promote children's rights, and Unit CCLD 302 Develop and maintain a healthy, safe and secure environment for children.

Link **Unit CCLD 305** Protect and promote children's rights
Unit CCLD 302 Develop and maintain a healthy, safe and secure environment for children

Every Child Matters

Every Child Matters contains the government agenda which sets out five major outcomes for all children:

- Being healthy
- Staying safe
- Enjoying and achieving
- Making a positive contribution
- Economic well-being.

Turn to Element CCLD Element 309.1 to read about how the Early Years Foundation Stage (EYFS) aims to meet the *Every Child Matters* outcomes by providing equality of opportunity and anti-discriminatory practice.

Link **Unit CCLD 309** Plan and implement curriculum frameworks for early education

The Early Years Foundation Stage welfare requirements

Settings to which the Early Years Foundation Stage applies must meet the EYFS welfare requirements. These fall into the following five categories:

- Safeguarding and promoting children's welfare

  The provider must take necessary steps to safeguard and promote the welfare of children.

  The provider must promote the good health of the children, take necessary steps to prevent the spread of infection, and take appropriate action when they are ill.

  Children's behaviour must be managed effectively and in a manner appropriate for their stage of development and particular individual needs.

- Suitable people

  Providers must ensure that adults looking after children, or having unsupervised access to them, are suitable to do so.

  Adults looking after children must have appropriate qualifications, training, skills and knowledge.

  Staffing arrangements must be organised to ensure safety and to meet the needs of the children.

- Suitable premises, environment and equipment

    Outdoor and indoor spaces, furniture, equipment and toys must be safe and suitable for their purpose.

- Organisation

    Providers must plan and organise their systems to ensure that every child receives an enjoyable and challenging learning and development experience that is tailored to meet their individual needs.

- Documentation

    Providers must maintain records, policies and procedures required for the safe and efficient management of the settings and to meet the needs of the children.

 Unit CCLD 309 Plan and implement curriculum frameworks for early education

Personal Protective Equipment at Work Regulations

Under these regulations, employers must provide all protective equipment that their employees need to do their job safely. For instance, settings will provide disposable gloves and aprons to be used when dealing with bodily fluids and waste.

Health and Safety (Young Persons) Regulations

These regulations require employers to conduct special risk assessments for employees or volunteers under the age of 18, as they may be less aware of health and safety issues than more experienced workers.

Health and Safety at Work Act 1974 and 1992

This Act is relevant to all places of employment, not just children's settings. Employers must ensure that the workplace and equipment within it are in a safe condition that does not pose a risk to health. Employees (and volunteers) have a responsibility to take care of themselves and others in co-operation with the employer. The Act also requires employers to use the basic principles of risk management, which are risk assessment, balanced control measures and training. Further details are included in Unit CCLD 302 Develop and maintain a healthy, safe and secure environment for children.

 Unit CCLD 302 Develop and maintain a healthy, safe and secure environment for children

Health and Safety (First Aid) Regulations 1981

While most childcare settings will have several members of staff qualified to carry out first aid (and must have at least one trained first-aider), these regulations set a minimum standard that applies to all workplaces. Under them, employers must appoint at least one person to be a designated first-aider, responsible for first aid if an accident occurs. Employers must also keep a stocked first-aid box.

Key health and safety issues covered in a health and safety policy

Issue	General details likely to be given
Registration	Registration forms That all families must complete forms, giving children's personal and medical details, before children can attend the setting Daily registers That all children and adults attending a session must be registered on arrival and signed out on their departure
Safeguarding procedures	What the setting does to safeguard children. For instance, the use of safety equipment such as high-chair harnesses and procedures for ensuring young children cannot wander off the premises/older children cannot leave undetected
Risk assessment	When risk assessment will be carried out and how often assessments will be reviewed. What staff training is given on risk assessment
Emergency procedures	Drills Where the details of drills are displayed on the premises (who does what, where the meeting points are, who will call 999, etc.), and how often drills are carried out Maintenance of equipment When equipment such as fire extinguishers and alarms are tested, and who by. Where records/certificates of testing are displayed First aid Who the qualified first aider is, how they were trained and where their certificate is displayed. How first-aid supplies are checked and replenished. The procedures for calling an ambulance and the family should a child need medical treatment urgently Care of sick children How sick children cannot be cared for at a group setting. How arrangements will be made for the collection of sick children. The procedure for calling an ambulance and the family should a child need medical treatment urgently
Substances harmful to health	How the setting will identify substances harmful to health and ensure their safe use and storage
Food and drink	Drinking water How the setting makes water constantly available to children Dietary requirements How children's dietary requirements are met with regard to families' beliefs/religions/preferences, and regard to individual children's allergies or medical requirements Healthy foods How the setting will provide healthy meals and/or snacks for children Hygiene How hygiene will be ensured with regard to food and drink preparation areas. How staff preparing food will have a Food Hygiene Certificate
Hygiene	Cleaning arrangements How the setting will be kept clean and hygienic. Procedures for each room and the outdoor space may be referenced Waste disposal How all waste is handled and disposed of safely
Child protection	Settings will have a separate Child Protection Policy, but it may be referenced in the Health and Safety Policy

Disability Discrimination Act 1995

This law covers equality of access and opportunity for disabled people (adults and children) including those with special educational needs. Further details are included in Unit CCLD 321 Support children with disabilities or special educational needs and their families.

 Link   **Unit CCLD 321** Support children with disabilities or special educational needs and their families

Children Bill 2004 and Protection of Children Act 1999

These laws cover child protection, which links with Element 306.4. Further details are included in Unit CCLD 305 Protect and promote children's rights.

Link   **Unit CCLD 305** Protect and promote children's rights

Race Relations Act 1975

This law covers equality of access and opportunity by legislating against racial discrimination. Further details are included in Unit CCLD 305 Protect and promote children's rights.

Link   **Unit CCLD 305** Protect and promote children's rights

Human Rights Act 1998

This Act allows people in the UK to enforce in the British courts rights given under previous laws. Further details are included in Unit CCLD 305 Protect and promote children's rights.

Link   **Unit CCLD 305** Protect and promote children's rights

Food Safety Act 1990, and regulations of 1995

This Act and the regulations cover how food should be prepared and stored, how food areas must be maintained, and how staff who prepare food must be trained. The guidance given in the food hygiene section of Unit CCLD 302, Develop and maintain healthy, safe and secure environments for children, is in line with the Food Safety Act 1990.

Link   **Unit CCLD 302** Develop and maintain healthy, safe and secure environments for children

The Control of Substances Hazardous to Health Regulations 1994

Under these regulations, settings must assess which substances used on the premises are potentially hazardous to health. Practices to manage and store these safely must be devised and recorded. See page 161 for further details.

Fire Precautions (Workplace) Regulations 1997

These regulations apply to all workplaces. Under these regulations, settings must carry out a fire risk assessment addressing seven key areas:

- Fire ignition sources and risk from the spread of fire
- Escape routes and exits
- Fire detection and early warning of fire
- Fire-fighting equipment
- Fire routine training for staff
- Emergency plans and arrangements for calling the fire service
- General maintenance and testing of fire protection equipment.

Reporting of Injuries, Diseases and Dangerous Occurrences Regulations 1995 (RIDDOR)

Under RIDDOR regulations, workplaces must have an accident book. All accidents that occur at the workplace should be recorded in the book. In addition, some types of accidents that occur at work – essentially serious ones, or those that result in an employee being absent from work for more than three days – must be reported to the Health and Safety Executive. Some diseases that may be contracted by employees must also be reported. Most settings keep one accident book for employees, and another for children.

In addition, settings should have:

- Public liability insurance covering the children, families and visitors (a necessity for registered settings)
- Employer's liability insurance, covering employees (compulsory under the Employer's Liability Act 1969 if there are paid staff).

You can see that there are pieces of legislation that cover not only children, but families, visitors and staff.

Policy and procedure arrangements within settings

Legislation and regulations tell practitioners what they must and must not do. But generally they are not *prescriptive* – they do not tell practitioners how things should be done. So settings must interpret the law and the regulations that apply to them. Settings do this by devising policies that explain how the setting will work in line with the law and the regulations.

Good, clear policies and procedures are important because they communicate to practitioners how the setting, and how practitioners, must work. Policies also let other professionals, parents, carers and children know how your setting works. You must make sure that you understand all of your setting's policies, and you must work within them.

Sometimes, extra, specific information is needed to explain how areas of a policy will work in action. To address this, settings may also devise additional written procedures which explain what to do in more detail.

The following table shows some of the key issues that will be covered within a setting's health and safety policy. General details about each issue are included.

To make sure that policies and procedures are effective, it is good practice for settings to review them regularly – at least once a year. Practitioners should check that their policies and procedures still reflect current legislation and regulations, since these are updated from time to time. Practitioners should consider whether the ways of working outlined in the policies and procedures have been followed effectively. If so, these ways of working have proved successful. This should be done in consultation with colleagues and, when appropriate, parents, carers, children and outside professionals.

It is important to make sure that practice reflects the policy – there is no benefit in having good policies and procedures if they are not followed. Sometimes, practice and policy do not match up because practice has evolved over time. In this case it will be appropriate to change policy/procedures to reflect the new ways of working. However, if it is the practitioners' work that is not up to appropriate standards, further explanation of the policy/procedures and perhaps further training will be necessary.

The date and outcome of reviews should be documented, and policies/procedures should be amended in writing if they are changed. It is good practice to plan the next review date and make a note in the setting's diary so that it is not forgotten. Some settings review one or more policies at meetings that they hold monthly, or perhaps quarterly, so that the task of reviewing all of them is spread throughout the year.

Settings will have cause to review policies/procedures before the next set review date if:

- Practitioners become aware of a change in law or regulations
- It becomes apparent that an aspect of a policy/procedure is not being followed
- It becomes apparent that an aspect of a policy/procedure is not working effectively
- A suggestion for improvement is made, which practitioners would like to implement as soon as possible.

Settings must legally develop and maintain systems and procedures for risk assessment. Details of risk assessment can be found in Unit CCLD 302 Develop and maintain a healthy, safe and secure environment for children.

Link   **Unit CCLD 302** Develop and maintain a healthy, safe and secure environment for children

Stars Out-of-School Club interprets legislation

Stars Out-of-School Club mentions in its health and safety policy that suitable toys are sterilised once a month. This is one of the ways in which the club complies with legislation about health and hygiene.

A separate set of procedures gives practitioners a four-week timetable of sterilising – some of the toys get sterilised each week. The practical steps of sterilising are explained, including where to carry out the task and how to make up the sterilising solution.

➤ *Why is it important for settings to interpret legislation and regulations in written policies and procedures?*   **K3H256**

Selecting equipment and materials safely

Before buying toys or equipment, practitioners must check that the items carry a recognised safety mark (see opposite). Safety marks give assurance that products are safe for use as directed by the manufacturer. So it is important that you only use toys and equipment in line with manufacturers' instructions. You should ensure all items are assembled according to the directions, and you should follow age guidelines specified – these will appear on boxes and other packaging. For example, you may find the following statement on the box of a toy car: 'Not suitable for use by children under 36 months due to small parts'.

Safety marks

However, sometimes it is necessary to exercise extra caution. For instance, imagine that you are working with a child who is five years old. He has a substantial developmental delay. He still takes toys to his mouth in the manner of a much younger child. You need to think carefully about the toys that can be given to him safely. The toy car mentioned above would not be suitable for him because, despite his age, he has not yet reached suitable maturity in terms of his stage of development to enable him to play safely with small parts. You must always consider the needs and abilities of children when selecting toys, equipment and materials. For information on adapting resources, see Unit CCLD 321 Support children with disabilities or special educational needs and their families.

> **Link**   **Unit CCLD 321** Support children with disabilities or special educational needs and their families

Selecting good-quality items that are durable (made to last) is practical, since they are most likely to stand up well to group use. This means there is less chance of the items being broken, and therefore becoming potentially dangerous, during play. It is also important to ensure that consumable materials are suitable, particularly those that may be collected and brought in by families. Items such as 'junk' (household items, for example cereal boxes and yoghurt pots, brought in for making recycled models) should be clean, free of sharp edges and should not have contained anything unsuitable, such as medication or cleaning products.

All settings benefit from a good range of materials and equipment (including ICT (information and communication technology), that can be used to promote play and development. This enables staff to offer a range of activities and experiences to maximise learning and development. The activities should support a planned curriculum where this applies – see Unit CCLD 309 Plan and implement curriculum frameworks for early education.

Link **Unit CCLD 309** Plan and implement curriculum frameworks for early education

The range of resources, activities and experiences available should support all types of children's play and areas of their development. They should be appropriate to the ages, needs and abilities of the children attending. For further information see Unit CCLD 318 Plan for and support self-directed play, and Unit CCLD 303 Promote children's development.

Link **Unit CCLD 318** Plan for and support self-directed play
Unit CCLD 303 Promote children's development

The list of possibilities is extensive, but here are some examples of relevant resources, activities and experiences that can be offered across the age range:

SPICE

SOCIAL DEVELOPMENT
- Story time – for sharing the experience of sitting and listening together
- Board games and playground games – for experience of taking turns, sharing, following rules, winning and losing
- Team games or events such as treasure hunts or quizzes – for working together for a common purpose, and supporting one another.

PHYSICAL DEVELOPMENT
- Baby gyms – for reaching, grasping and hand/eye co-ordination
- Large wheeled toys to push, pull and ride – for large motor skills, co-ordination and spatial awareness
- Electronic dance mats – for co-ordination, large/small motor skills and fitness.

INTELLECTUAL DEVELOPMENT
- Board books – for learning about how books work, turning pages, looking at pictures, seeing words
- Sand (wet and dry), water and toys – for learning about capacity, volume, similarities, differences and change
- Games of chess, draughts, battleships and noughts and crosses – for developing strategy and concentration.

CREATIVE DEVELOPMENT
- Paint and paper – for exploration of colour and texture through finger painting
- Musical instruments – for exploring sound, music, rhythm and beat
- Clay and tools – for creative personal expression in 3D.

EMOTIONAL DEVELOPMENT
- Dolls and soft toys – to identify with and care for
- Art and craft resources – for making face masks that show feelings through facial expression
- Writing a play and acting it out – for expressing ideas, thoughts and exploring emotions.

It is important that the layout of the environment supports planning for learning and play. Practitioners should consider this when they are preparing for a session.

Positive, enabling environments

Key Terms

Positive environment

An 'emotional' environment where children are treated sensitively and with regard to equal opportunities. Children's individuality is respected, and their emotional needs are met.

Enabling environment

An 'emotional' environment where children are supported sensitively by staff. The staff work to facilitate children's participation, enabling them to play and learn, and to experience independence where appropriate.

Practitioners want to help children to develop and progress. We have seen how providing the right resources, activities and experiences helps children's development.

However, there is more that can be done. Practitioners can support children further by providing an environment that is both positive and enabling.

You can contribute to the provision of a positive and enabling environment by:

- Ensuring that you respect every child you work with

  Helping children to develop a sense of self-worth and self-respect

- Removing barriers to participation

  Helping children to learn and experience that everyone can join in together, and that individuality is valued

- Encouraging children to try new things

  Helping children to develop confidence and self-esteem

- Encouraging children to be independent when appropriate

  Helping children to develop self-reliance and confidence

- Ensuring that resources are accessible

  Helping children to be independent and resourceful

- Acknowledging individual children's contributions

  Helping children to develop confidence and self-esteem. Also helping them to value other people's contributions

- Acknowledging individual children's achievements

  Helping children to develop confidence and self-esteem, and fostering a love of learning.

Many children will be able to dress and undress themselves

Routine maintenance of equipment and materials

You should carefully check the condition of materials and equipment as you set it out and as it is tidied away. Worn or broken equipment or materials can pose a hazard to safety. When plastic breaks there may be sharp edges, or wood may splinter. Remove any worn or broken items from the play space. Report the condition to the appropriate person within your setting. Some equipment or materials can be safely mended, such as a broken zip on an item of dressing-up clothes. But sometimes it is necessary to dispose of an item and replace it because it would not be safe to attempt to mend the item. For instance, it is doubtful that a broken plastic fence from the farmyard could be mended safely, because glue strong enough to hold the fence together would not be safe to use on an object that young children will play with.

You should also check that resources are in a hygienic condition. Settings will have established a schedule for washing or sterilising appropriate materials and equipment. However, you may notice that resources need cleaning in between times. (Feeding equipment, nappy-changing equipment and baby toys will need cleaning every time they are used.) The process of cleaning gives practitioners a further opportunity to check that equipment is in a safe condition.

Remember to check the condition of large pieces of equipment (which may stay in one place) and furniture too, such as chairs, tables, swings, slides, bookcases and cots.

Control of substances harmful to health

The management of hazardous materials must comply with the Control of Substances Hazardous to Health Regulations 1994 (known as COSHH). These regulations require practitioners to identify any potentially hazardous substances within the setting. Ways to handle and/or store the substances safely must then be devised. For instance, cleaning materials are a potentially hazardous substance. They could cause injury if put in the mouth, on the skin or in the eyes. These may be stored in a room inaccessible to children, or perhaps in a securely locked cupboard.

Bodily waste is also a potentially harmful substance since infections such as HIV and hepatitis could be passed on. Settings will have procedures in place for handling used nappies, vomit and blood and for clearing up after toileting accidents. These will include wearing disposable gloves and using designated disposal bins. See Unit CCLD 302 Develop and maintain a healthy, safe and secure environment for children.

Link Unit CCLD 302 Develop and maintain a healthy, safe and secure environment for children

Layout and organisation of play spaces

Most settings will vary the use of their premises throughout sessions, as explained in Unit CCLD 302 Develop and maintain a healthy, safe and secure environment for children. Other pieces of furniture such as storage units may be rarely moved. The selection of furniture and equipment, and its position, contributes greatly to the overall effect of the environment.

Link Unit CCLD 302 Develop and maintain a healthy, safe and secure environment for children

Some key issues practitioners should consider when selecting furniture and equipment are shown below:

- Is the furniture/equipment appropriate for the children's age and stage of development?

  If not, it could be unsafe. Look for the manufacturer's guidance and the safety marks. Chairs and tables should be of the correct height for the children. Weight restrictions may be given for furniture such as high chairs or babies' floor seats. Sometimes, settings may need to consult specialists, parents and carers if a piece of equipment/furniture must meet the needs of a child with disabilities and/or special educational needs.

- What size is the furniture/equipment?

  It is best to measure accurately to be sure that equipment/furniture is the right size for the setting.

- How will the furniture/equipment be used?

  Because both space and money is limited, many settings try to purchase furniture/equipment that can be used in various different ways or for a number of different activities. For instance, a storage unit may have a work surface. A bookcase may have a cork board attached.

- Where will equipment/furniture be stored?

  If it will not be in use all the time, you will need somewhere suitable to store the furniture/equipment. Depending on your setting, you may need to think about transporting equipment too. This is sometimes the case for after-school clubs in particular, who may hire a room in a local school but have little, if any, on-site storage.

- Is the furniture/equipment durable and easy to clean?

  Choosing equipment that does not withstand group use and frequent cleaning is rarely good value for money in the long run.

When deciding on the layout of the environment, it is important to:

- Provide comfortable, quiet areas for rest

Child-sized tables and chairs

This may be achieved through the provision of large floor cushions/children's beanbags/upholstered children's furniture such as sofas. The area should be away from noisy, busy activities. Screens may be used to give the area a feeling of separateness. In the case of settings caring for young children, this area will be in addition to the sleeping area, which will feature cots/beds

- Provide areas for physical activity and exercise

Physical exercise is essential to children's health and their development. Settings should ensure children have regular opportunities and enough space for physical activities. While it is preferable to have an outdoor area of a good size, it is important to remember that outdoors should not be regarded as simply for physical activities – see Unit CCLD 302 Develop and maintain a healthy, safe and secure environment for children. Also, opportunities for physical exercise can be successfully offered inside. In practice, most settings will use a combination of approaches, e.g. playground games and riding tricycles and bikes may take place outside, whilst dancing and music and movement may take place inside

- Ensure that thought is given to hygiene and cleanliness

Set up messy activities in areas that have furniture and flooring which can be cleaned easily. Make sure there is easy access to sinks for hand-washing too – you do not want children trailing paint over carpeted areas on their way to the bathroom

- Choose the location of each activity carefully

Locate quiet pursuits away from noisy or busy ones. This ensures that children neither disturb each other nor have to be told to keep the noise down needlessly. Give activities the space they need. Overcrowded areas or equipment can be dangerous and/or difficult to supervise – restrict the number of children permitted in an area/at equipment at one time if necessary. Consider safety, for instance by putting the slide on even ground and using safety matting. Ensure that resources do not obstruct fire exits at any time

Considering the needs of all the children, leave sufficient room for children to move around the play space between the activities, furniture and equipment. Also ensure that activities, furniture and equipment are accessible – see Unit CCLD 321 Support children with disabilities or special educational needs and their families

- Ensure a balanced layout

Children need opportunities to engage in different types of play, and the layout of the environment (and the activities offered) should enable this. For example, children need opportunities for imaginative play as well physical play. Children also need opportunities for rest as well as for exercise. There is more information about this in Unit CCLD 318 Plan for and support self-directed play. Practitioners need to ensure that the environment supports planning for children's play and learning, and supports the curriculum if one applies to the setting. There are further details in Unit CCLD 309 Plan and implement curriculum frameworks for early education.

 Link

Unit CCLD 302 Develop and maintain a healthy, safe and secure environment for children
Unit CCLD 321 Support children with disabilities or special educational needs and their families
Unit CCLD 318 Plan for and support self-directed play
Unit CCLD 309 Plan and implement curriculum frameworks for early education

Adapting the environment

It is important that the environment meets the needs of all children, whatever their age, gender, individual needs and abilities. You must ensure that you identify and address barriers to participation within the environment, as mentioned above. See Unit CCLD 321 Support children with disabilities or special educational needs and their families.

Link **Unit CCLD 321** Support children with disabilities or special educational needs and their families

The use of safety equipment

There are various pieces of safety equipment available. Using such equipment can effectively minimise the risk of accident or injury to children. You must always ensure that equipment is in good working order, and that it is used according to the manufacturer's instructions. Always check for a safety mark when purchasing safety equipment. The table on page 35 explains why common pieces of safety equipment are used.

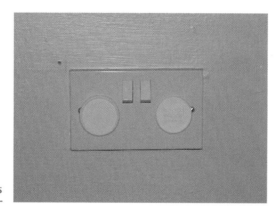

Socket covers

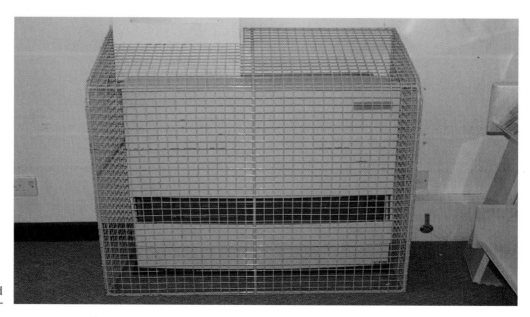

Fireguard

Safety outdoors

While many of the safety requirements of the indoor play space also apply to outdoors (such as the safe positioning of equipment), there are also some particular considerations. It is important to address safety in respect of:

- External security
- Weather
- Animals
- Plants
- Sand pits
- Water.

There is an outdoor safety checklist in Unit CCLD 302 Develop and maintain a healthy, safe and secure environment for children. In addition, settings that keep pets must ensure that:

- Children wash their hands well after touching animals
- Animals are not permitted near the kitchen, eating areas, sleeping areas or anywhere that food is stored
- Items used for feeding pets or for play with pets are only used for that purpose
- Animals' cages, hutches or living environments are cleaned well and regularly
- Animals are kept healthy – follow the advice of a vet regarding worming, vaccinations and so on.

 Link   **Unit CCLD 302** Develop and maintain a healthy, safe and secure environment for children

Sensory experiences

Sensory experiences are those that stimulate children's senses (i.e. their sight, hearing, touch, smell and taste). Sensory experiences are valuable for all children as part of the general learning and play that is offered within a setting. However, they may also be used in specific ways to stimulate the senses of some children who are disabled and/or have special educational needs. Practitioners must consider the needs of all children in their care when planning sensory experiences, making adaptations where necessary. There is more information on making adaptations in Unit CCLD 321 Support children with disabilities or special educational needs and their families.

Examples of sensory experiences include:

- Feely bags

  Practitioners hide items of different textures inside a drawstring bag. Without looking inside, children take turns to delve their hands in. They describe the item they can feel. Older children may enjoy playing this game in teams, scoring points when they can guess the identity of an item

- Tasting fruit

  Children have the opportunity to taste a range of different fruits, from sour lemon to sweet pineapple. They can compare the different tastes, textures and the visual appearance of the fruit

- Sound lotto

  This game is played similarly to ordinary lotto, but instead of matching picture cards to their playing boards, children listen to familiar sounds on a compact disc or audio tape, matching the sounds to the pictures on their boards

- Many everyday toys that have sensory features

  Including rattles, teething rings, battery operated toys such as cars with lights and sirens, play telephones, hand-held electronic games and game consoles (popular with older children), textured play mats and so on.

 Link Unit CCLD 321 Support children with disabilities or special educational needs and their families

Displays

Displays are also a good way of providing children with sensory experiences. Displays tend to fall into three categories:

- Paper-based artwork or writing that is displayed on the wall

  Such as:
  - individual pictures showing various methods of painting that children have used
  - a large group picture that may be related to a theme, e.g. a seasonal scene showing Father Christmas in his sleigh

- Craftwork displayed on shelves or tables or other suitable areas

  Such as:
  - recycled models made from junk
  - mobiles hung from the ceiling

- Interest tables displaying three-dimensional objects, linked together by type or a common theme

  Such as:
  - an autumn table, featuring leaves of different colours, conkers and acorns
  - a shape table, featuring solid objects of different shapes, including a ball, a dice and a brick.

Displays can have features that are:

- Visual
- Tactile
- Auditory.

Using a combination of features can stimulate more than one sense. It also helps practitioners to appeal to different styles of learners through their displays (see Unit CCLD 309 Plan and implement curriculum frameworks for early education). You should ensure that the range of displays available meets the sensory needs and abilities of all the children that attend the setting.

 Link Unit CCLD 309 Plan and implement curriculum frameworks for early education

There are many ways to include visual, tactile and auditory features in displays. For example you can:

- Use fabrics and materials of various textures – smooth, rough, hard and soft
- Use bold or contrasting colours – canary yellow, burnt orange, black and white
- Use bells (e.g. tied onto mobiles), or materials that crunch, rustle or hiss.

With a bit of creativity, practitioners and children can come up with many alternatives. It is important to remember that displays should attract children and stimulate their curiosity, so that they are drawn to explore them. Involving children in the design and construction of displays gives them the chance to be creative while interacting with the materials. Older children may enjoy labelling parts of their display, and devising questions to encourage others to come and explore it. For instance, a label may read, 'What noise do the leaves make when you touch them?' or 'How many different shapes can you find on the table?'

Children should be drawn to explore objects on the interest table

Whilst practitioners should plan some sensory activities, it is important not to forget that children will constantly have sensory experiences during everyday play and learning opportunities. It is good practice to consider how children's senses will be stimulated. You can then maximise the experiences through careful organisation and structuring of the environment. For instance:

- During free-play, to avoid distraction place quiet activities such as looking at picture books (a visual experience) away from noisier or busier activities (such as physically active pursuits)
- Play activities such as karaoke sing-alongs (popular with older children) or sound lotto (audio experiences) at a set time. Then everyone can join in. (Quiet alternatives can be offered to children who do not want to participate.) This allows the audio experience to be absorbed without distraction, which is difficult to achieve during a busy free-play session

● If you have used lots of tactile materials to make a display, mount it low down (with regard to safety), so that children can experience touching it.

Displaying children's work

When children's work is displayed within settings it can:

● Add colour, vibrancy and texture to the environment

● Help give children a sense of ownership of the setting (which is particularly important for older children)

● Give families and visitors a flavour of the activities that children undertake at the setting

● Remind children of past experiences and learning

● Encourage children to feel pride for their work, fuelling self-esteem.

In order to promote children's self-esteem, practitioners need to monitor the work that is chosen for display. It is important to value the PROCESS of being creative, rather than the end PRODUCT. Practitioners should not display just the neatest artwork or the tidiest handwriting. Over time, all children should experience having their work on display, because it is the PROCESS of producing it that should be recognised, not just the quality of the end PRODUCT.

Displaying children's work will encourage their interest and creativity

Are you ready for assessment?

Plan and provide an enabling physical environment for children

You need to show that you can competently plan and provide an enabling physical environment for children. To do this you will need to be directly observed by your assessor and present other types of evidence. The amount and type of evidence you need to present will vary. You should plan this with your assessor.

Direct observation by your assessor

Observation and/or expert witness testimony is the required assessment method to be used to evidence some of each element in this unit. If your assessor is unable to observe you, s/he will identify an expert in your workplace who will provide testimony of your work-based performance. Usually your assessor or expert witness will observe you in real work activities and this should provide most of the evidence for the performance criteria for the elements in this unit.

Preparing to be observed

You must show your assessor that you can ensure the environment meets relevant requirements, and that you can adapt it to meet children's needs, ensuring participation barriers are addressed. You must also show that you can ensure the environment supports children's play and learning, gives opportunities for physical play and exercise, and that you can maximise sensory, play and learning opportunities. You must show that

you can organise displays of children's work appropriately and arrange effective visual and tactile displays.

Other types of evidence

You will need to present different types of evidence in order to:

- Cover criteria not observed by your assessor
- Show that you have the required knowledge, understanding and skills.

Such evidence could include:

- Work products such as displays of children's work, interest tables or activity plans
- Case studies, projects, assignments and reflective accounts of your work
- Confidential records such as children's individual plans. These should not be placed in your portfolio – they must remain in their usual location and be referred to in the assessor records in your portfolio.

Organise space and resources to meet children's needs

Materials and equipment to promote play and development

K3D264
K3D265
K3D268

The list of materials and equipment that can be used to support children's play and development is extensive. Element 309.1 of Unit CCLD 309 Plan and implement curriculum frameworks for early education contains details of resources that can be used to support the curriculum. However, these details are equally relevant to settings without a curriculum, since all the resources mentioned are play materials (see pages 248–9). There are also details about using ICT with children, which can be found on page 253 of the unit.

Link **Unit CCLD 309** Plan and implement curriculum frameworks for early education

ICT can help children to investigate further

Use of physical space

As discussed in Element 306.1, practitioners must ensure that a setting's physical space is:

- Comfortable for children, with some areas of privacy
- Stimulating for children
- Safe for children
- Suitable for children's ages, needs and abilities
- Easy to move around in.

There are further details about the importance of privacy in Element 306.4. There is more information about providing a stimulating environment on page 259 of Unit

CCLD 309 Plan and implement curriculum frameworks for early education. Details of how to change and adapt environments are also included. Further information about adaptations can be found in Unit CCLD 321 Support children with disabilities or special educational needs and their families.

Link **Unit CCLD 309** Plan and implement curriculum frameworks for early education
Unit CCLD 321 Support children with disabilities or special educational needs and their families

Promoting choice and independence in the provision of resources

It is good practice to allow children plenty of choice in the resources they use. Ideally play materials should be stored safely, somewhere that children can easily access them. This allows children to be independent in selecting and fetching resources. Children can also be independent in tidying away resources after use.

Most settings will put out some activities and play materials before the children arrive. This is good because it makes the environment immediately welcoming and stimulating. It allows children to come in and settle down to the business of play right away. However, if practitioners only allow children to play with the items they have chosen for the group, they are not promoting true free-play since the children are not exercising free choice.

When encouraging children to select and access materials independently, consider the following:

- Labelling containers of resources with words and/or pictures for easy selection
- Using low, child-sized furniture for storage
- Making art and craft resources freely available as well as toys and equipment
- Encouraging children to put away the resources as they finish with them. This avoids the setting becoming cluttered. It may sometimes be necessary to ask children to wait until some resources are finished with before any more are set out
- Ensuring resources that are too heavy/awkward/big for children to manage are still accessed by adults – let children know they can ask for these things. Adults should also be responsible for assembling equipment that must be put together carefully for safety reasons
- Ensuring resources that require close supervision (such as woodwork tools) are not freely accessible
- Ensuring children only have free access to materials suitable for their age, needs and abilities.

Involving children in decisions about their environment

Children generally enjoy being involved in decisions about their environment. This helps them to have a feeling of ownership of their setting, giving them a sense of belonging. It also gives them opportunities to organise and to problem solve. This is particularly important as children grow up.

Young children may be involved in making small decisions at first. For instance, a practitioner may ask whether the group would like to have story time inside or outside today. Or perhaps they will be asked where they would prefer the book corner to be set up – two or three choices could be given.

However, older children will be able to take much more responsibility – see Unit CCLD 318 Plan for and support self-directed play. They will be able to make plans for the environment ahead of time.

For instance, children organising a rainforest theme may plan to make props to decorate their play space. This could include tall 3D palm trees, with monkeys hanging from the branches. There could be an interest area with leaves scattered on the floor and artefacts on show, with soaring tropical birds suspended from the ceiling. They may also plan a research area with books about the rainforest, and a computer. There could be an animal make-and-play zone, featuring paper animals to make and play with. There could be many decisions to make.

Link Unit **CCLD 318** Plan for and support self-directed play

Kyle consults

Kyle is a playworker at a primary-school holiday club. A group of children are helping him to plan activities for the summer holidays. They remember how much they enjoyed making dens in the playground at half term. They would like to do the activity again.

Six-year-old Dan suggests making dens inside this time. Eight-year-old Alicia thinks that the dens might take up too much room – there might not be enough space for everything else the children like to have out for free-play. Kyle asks the children if they can think of a solution (he is thinking that den making could be offered at a separate time to free-play – but he waits for the children's response).

Dan suddenly has an idea – he suggests making dens that will 'house' all the activities – the children can go inside the dens to participate. The other children are enthusiastic, and soon there are plans for a craft den, a book den, a refreshment den and an imaginary play den. Kyle does not mention his own idea.

➤ *What benefits were there to Kyle keeping his own idea to himself?*

➤ *How will the children benefit from planning the layout of their own environment?*

Are you ready for assessment?

Organise space and resources to meet children's needs

You need to show that you can competently organise space and resources to meet children's needs. To do this you will need to be directly observed by your assessor and present other types of evidence. The amount and type of evidence you need to present will vary. You should plan this with your assessor.

Direct observation by your assessor

Observation and/or expert witness testimony is the required assessment method to be used to evidence some of each element in this unit. If your assessor is unable to observe you, s/he will identify an expert in your workplace who will provide testimony of your work-based performance. Usually your assessor or expert witness will observe you in real work activities and this should provide most of the evidence for the performance criteria for the elements in this unit.

Preparing to be observed

You must show your assessor that you can plan and organise for appropriate use of physical space, organising furniture and equipment appropriately and making resources accessible to children. You must also show that you can adapt the environment to ensure accessibility for all children, encourage children to be involved in decisions about their environment, and ensure there are areas for quiet and privacy. You must show that you can use ICT to support play and learning.

You may like to arrange for an observation to take place on a session when you have planned the layout of the room and set up some of the activities yourself.

Other types of evidence

You will need to present different types of evidence in order to:

- Cover criteria not observed by your assessor
- Show that you have the required knowledge, understanding and skills.

Such evidence could include:

- Work products such as layout plans of the environment, activity plans and records of consultation with children
- Case studies, projects, assignments and reflective accounts of your work.

Provide a caring, nurturing and responsive environment

Element 306.3

Valuing and respecting children and families

K3D266
K3D267
K3D269
K3D270
K3D272
K3C271

Practitioners must show that they value and respect all children and their families. This includes demonstrating respect for the following:

- Culture
- Ethnicity
- Faith
- Language
- Background.

Always behaving professionally and treating people equally contributes greatly to this. You can read more about showing value and respect for children in Unit CCLD 301 Develop and promote positive relationships. Pages 22–3 of that unit gives information about showing value and respect for adults. For further general information see Unit CCLD 305 Protect and promote children's rights. Element 306.4 explains how practitioners must respect children's individual and cultural care needs.

Link **Unit CCLD 301** Develop and promote positive relationships
Unit CCLD 305 Protect and promote children's rights

Helping children to be positive about their culture

Practitioners have an important role to play in helping children to feel positive about their own cultural background, which is part of their identity. Providing strong positive images of others with the same cultural background is a key strategy. You can read

Celebrating Diwali

about this in Unit CCLD 305 Protect and promote children's rights. Practitioners can also:

- Take time to find out about important cultural events for children (for instance, their bar mitzvah). These can then be acknowledged within the setting
- Show interest in children's conversation about their culture
- Plan to celebrate key festivals.

Encouraging families to participate within the setting

The act of encouraging families to participate within a setting is another way to demonstrate that families are valued and respected. It also strengthens the partnership between practitioners, parents and carers, which is good for everyone concerned. There are many ways to encourage families to participate, including:

- Invitations to social activities, such as fundraising events or coffee mornings
- Invitations to join the setting's committee
- Invitations to annual general meetings, perhaps with a crèche facility to enable their attendance
- Running family sessions, where adults can attend with their child and the child's siblings
- Having training or information evenings on topics of interest, such as first aid, or baby massage
- Organising family trips out
- Organising family festival celebrations, a Christmas party for instance
- Inviting family members to volunteer during sessions, or to help by using their skills, e.g. making dressing-up clothes or story sacks, or demonstrating to the children how to cook a particular dish, or how to do woodwork
- Holding exhibitions of children's art and craft work
- Holding open days
- Organising children's concerts or plays
- Holding a toy library or book exchange.

Some settings may also offer a parents group, which may organise their own events, including some of those mentioned above. A parents room may also be provided within the setting. Newsletters and notice boards help families to feel involved and up to date with activities within the setting.

Consistency and stability

Children tend to feel more settled and secure when they have consistency and stability in their lives. Settled and secure children are more likely to be happy and to learn and play well. The following can contribute to consistency and stability:

- A settled home life, with good, ongoing relationships with family members
- Familiar adults that children know well, providing good care in group situations (nurseries, pre-school, clubs and so on)
- Routines at home (at mealtimes and bedtime, for instance)

- Routines in care environments (such as circle time and story time)
- Regular attendance at nurseries/pre-schools/clubs and so on.

Children tend to need less structure as they grow up, but things like a consistent home life and good relationships with practitioners remain important for all children. Many settings use a key-worker system because of this. See Unit CCLD 312, Plan and implement positive environments for babies and children under three years, for information about the role of the key worker, and pages 96–101 for details about supporting children who are new to the setting and their families.

Link Unit CCLD 312 Plan and implement positive environments for babies and children under three years
Unit CCLD 303 Promote children's development

It is particularly important for babies and young children to develop a bond with consistent carers. Older children with disabilities and/or special educational needs may require a key worker (or 'personal assistant') to help them with tasks such as dressing, toileting and feeding. There is more information about this in Element 306.4. It is important for practitioners to be aware of the differing levels of support required by children of different ages, needs and abilities.

Practitioners should make themselves available to children and families who wish to communicate with them. It might be necessary to schedule a suitable time to talk with families. Arrange somewhere private to talk about matters of a confidential nature.

Flexible routines and changes to environments

While routines are good, they do need to be flexible in order to support children's well-being. For instance, some children may need to eat before the setting's usual lunchtime, perhaps because they get up and eat breakfast very early, or because of a condition such as diabetes.

It will also be necessary to adapt routines sometimes to meet children's changing needs and circumstances. Practitioners must be sensitive to this. For instance, the needs of all babies change as they grow and develop, e.g. during weaning. Also, whether children need to sleep during their time at a setting may depend on the amount of sleep they had the previous night.

Sometimes unforeseeable changes occur within children's environments. Some emergency maintenance work is required to a room of a setting's premises, for instance. In such cases, practitioners should explain them clearly to children and families, as they can be unsettling. Practitioners should also be sensitive to the fact that young children in particular may require reassurance and comfort when unforeseeable changes occur.

Supporting positive behaviour

Practitioners strive to create a good atmosphere within their setting, making it a pleasant place for children, families and practitioners. You can contribute to a happy, settled environment by using techniques that encourage positive behaviour.

Children enjoy adults praising and acknowledging their efforts and achievements. It makes them feel good about themselves and encourages them to repeat their positive behaviour. There is more information about this and other techniques to encourage positive behaviour in Unit CCLD 337 Create environments that promote positive behaviour. There is also information about taking a fair and consistent approach to the way you deal with children's behaviour.

Link Unit **CCLD 337** Create environments that promote positive behaviour

Dealing positively with conflict

There is information on how to deal positively with conflict between children in Unit CCLD 337 Create environments that promote positive behaviour. Pages 26–7 of Unit CCLD 301 Develop and promote positive relationships explains how to handle conflict between adults.

Link Unit **CCLD 337** Create environments that promote positive behaviour
Unit **CCLD 301** Develop and promote positive relationships

Encouraging independence

It should be the aim of every practitioner to encourage the children in their care to develop independence. This is essential for children's well-being and self-esteem. Children gradually learn to take more responsibility for themselves and others as they mature. It is the job of practitioners to allow children levels of independence appropriate to the individual according to children's ages, needs and abilities. This must of course be in line with legislation, the setting's procedures and families' preferences.

Independence affects children's self-esteem and confidence. Children feel good about being self-reliant, and gain personal satisfaction when they are able to do things for themselves. Gently encourage children to try new things, and praise their attempts. Acknowledge and celebrate children's achievements when they master new skills.

Claire receives encouragement

Play leader Jed has noticed that when the children get ready to play outside, play worker Molly automatically goes to fasten five-year-old Claire's coat for her, without the child asking for her help.

Jed asks Molly about this later. Molly says that Claire cannot do it herself. Jed explains that Claire will only learn to do up her coat by trying.

They resolve to give Claire time to attempt the task on her own from now on. If she does not try before asking for help, the staff will encourage her to attempt the task before they assist her. They will praise her for trying, even if she does not succeed.

➤ *Why is Jed keen for Claire to learn to do up her own coat?*   **K3D266**

Element 306.3

Are you ready for assessment?

Provide a caring, nurturing and responsive environment

You need to show that you can competently provide a caring, nurturing and responsive environment. To do this you will need to be directly observed by your assessor and present other types of evidence. The amount and type of evidence you need to present will vary. You should plan this with your assessor.

Direct observation by your assessor

Observation and/or expert witness testimony is the required assessment method to be used to evidence some of each element in this unit. If your assessor is unable to observe you, s/he will identify an expert in your workplace who will provide testimony of your work-based performance. Usually your assessor or expert witness will observe you in real work activities and this should provide most of the evidence for the performance criteria for the elements in this unit.

Preparing to be observed

You must show your assessor that you can value all children and families, help children to be positive about their cultural backgrounds, and be available to those who wish to communicate with you. You must also show that you can be fair and consistent in dealing with behaviour, giving praise and acknowledgement when appropriate, and that you can deal with conflicts that may arise between those involved with the setting. You must show that you can provide consistent care and stability effectively, and work flexibly in the range of appropriate circumstances.

Other types of evidence

You will need to present different types of evidence in order to:

- Cover criteria not observed by your assessor
- Show that you have the required knowledge, understanding and skills.

Such evidence could include:

- Work products such as activity plans or resource/materials developed for use with children
- Case studies, projects, assignments and reflective accounts of your work
- Confidential records such as information gathered about individual families. These should not be placed in your portfolio – they must remain in their usual location and be referred to in the assessor records in your portfolio.

Facilitate children's personal care

⌣ Safe working practices

It is essential that settings adopt 'safe working practices', i.e. procedures to ensure that:

- Children are protected from abuse during care routines (such as toileting and nappy changing)
- Children are not subject to abuse or exploitation at any time they are present in the setting
- The adults who work with children are suitable according to regulatory requirements
- The adults who work with children and who may become vulnerable to accusations of improper behaviour are protected.

There is more information about this in Unit CCLD 305 Protect and promote children's rights.

Link   **Unit CCLD 305** Protect and promote children's rights

⌣ Encouraging children to care for themselves

As children grow up they can begin to care more for their own physical care needs such as:

- Toileting
- Washing
- Bathing
- Washing hair
- Cutting nails
- Applying sun screen/lotions/oils.

It is good to encourage children to care for themselves because:

- It promotes independence
- It promotes self-reliance and confidence
- It promotes a positive self-image and self-esteem
- It also helps to protect children from abuse or exploitation. Children are vulnerable when someone else cares for physical needs such as toileting or washing their bodies.

So, personal care routines not only support children's care, they also inform children's learning and development. However, it is important to stress that children should not be rushed into doing these things until they are ready. Individual children will be ready at different times. Children's ages, needs and abilities must all be taken into account.

Looking after their own physical care needs

Nutritional needs of children

The Government has issued guidelines on healthy eating and nutrition for children. It is important to children's welfare that these are followed by practitioners. The Government published the White Paper 'Our Healthier Nation' in 1999. It aims to improve the health of the nation and to reduce the gap between the health of the most wealthy and the least wealthy in our society. A good diet containing plenty of fruit and vegetables is identified as essential for the good health of adults and children.

The 'Healthy Schools Initiative' is outlined in the White Paper. The purpose of the initiative is to raise the awareness of healthy living amongst practitioners, children and families. It is also to make practitioners, children and families aware of healthy food choices that can be made in settings, schools and at home. This is important, as the foundations for good adult health are laid in childhood. Practitioners should ensure that their setting's policies on child nutrition and infant feeding are in line with current best practice and government guidelines.

In recent years there have been a number of health education campaigns relevant to children's nutrition, notably the following:

- The '5-A-DAY' programme

   This promotes eating five pieces of fresh fruit and vegetables each day. Thanks to the School Fruit and Vegetable Scheme, all children aged four to six years who attend an LEA-maintained school are entitled to receive one free piece of fruit or vegetable each day they attend

- The Water is Cool in School campaign

  This has been introduced to improve the access to fresh drinking water in all schools
- The *Birth to Five* guide

  This free booklet is given to new parents. It introduces child health, safety and nutrition in the early years
- The Change4Life Campaign

  This campaign encourages and supports families in making small changes towards eating well, moving more and living longer. Families can join at www.nhs.uk/Change4Life. They will then receive a welcome pack.

The government's nutrition site (www.eatwell.gov.uk) also gives regularly updated advice on all aspects of nutrition for everyone, from babies to adults.

Further nutritional information can be found in Element 307.2 of Unit CCLD 307 Promote the health and physical development of children, and in Element 314.2 of Unit 314 Provide physical care that promotes the health and development of babies and children under three years.

It is important that practitioners meet children's nutritional needs whilst they are at the setting, in line with the setting's policies and procedures. Depending on the setting, this may involve the provision of all or some of the following:

- Breakfast
- Mid-morning snack
- Lunch
- Mid-afternoon snack
- Dinner.

Some settings may provide food, whilst at others children may eat packed meals brought in from home. In addition, children may occasionally eat food that they have prepared themselves as part of an activity.

Pages 217–8 of Unit CCLD 307 Promote the health and physical development of children explains how and why practitioners must act upon information from families in cases where the children have food allergies. This is of key importance. Children's health – and even their lives – may depend on it.

 Link   **Unit CCLD 307** Promote the health and physical development of children

Provision of drinking water

Drinking plenty of water is good for the human body. Many experts agree that not only is it essential to health, but it can also improve the function of the brain, aiding concentration. It is good practice to offer children drinks regularly. However, children should not be deprived of their right to drink when they are thirsty, and requests for drinks outside of meal or snack times should be met.

Many settings now make drinking water available to children throughout their sessions. This may be done through the provision of a water cooler, or perhaps jugs of water (with lids). If this applies to your setting, you must follow your organisation's guidelines for ensuring that the water is fresh and that clean cups are available.

Physical exercise and activity

Physical exercise and activity is essential for children's physical and mental health. Details of this are in Unit CCLD 307 Promote the health and physical development of children.

Link   **Unit CCLD 307** Promote the health and physical development of children

Attending to care needs

It is important to ensure that all children are allowed their dignity whilst care needs are attended to. Children should also be allowed their privacy when appropriate. You must always remain professional when carrying out care needs, and you should be sensitive to children's preferences, which will vary, partly in relation to their age and stage of development.

For instance, some young children may prefer privacy when they are undressing, for sports or to go swimming, whilst others may be happy to get changed alongside their peers in a communal room. Older children with disabilities and/or special educational needs may require personal assistance for toileting, dressing or washing. They may still use nappies. Practitioners should attend to these needs in private to protect the child's dignity.

Families may have preferences about how their children's care needs are met. These may be based on cultural or religious practices. Care needs should be met in a way that reflects the requirements of individual children, as long this does not compromise the welfare of children. For example:

- Muslim children and some Hindu and Sikh children may to be taught to use the right hand for eating and the left hand for matters of personal hygiene. They may also learn to wash their hands before prayer
- Some Jewish boys may wear a skull cap (known as a kippah)
- Muslim girls may be required to keep their heads, hair and legs covered
- Rastafarian girls may wear a headscarf, and boys may wear a hat (a tam) over dreadlocks
- Some Jewish and Christian groups require girls to wear headscarves
- Sikh boys may not have their hair cut when they are young, but have it plaited around their head. Next they may put their hair in a jura (similar to a bun) covered by cloth. When they become teenagers they may wear a turban.

Skin and hair care

Children's skin and hair needs to be kept clean to prevent disease and the spread of infection. If they are not washed regularly, dead skin cells and bacteria on sweat cause an unpleasant smell, and sore areas develop on the skin and scalp. As mentioned above, children should be encouraged to become increasingly independent in caring for themselves, and children's individual care needs should be addressed. Good hygiene practices include:

- A daily bath or shower. If this is not possible, a thorough wash instead. Care should be taken to ensure that children are properly washed and dried in their skin creases and between their toes (to prevent dryness and skin cracks). Children must learn to wash their bottoms last for hygiene reasons. For younger children, these showers/baths/washes should ideally be taken at the end of the day, as children become dirty during play. The skin should be observed for soreness/rashes

- Washing hair two or three times a week or more frequently if families prefer. Shampoo should be thoroughly rinsed out with clean water, until the water runs clear. Wet hair should be combed not brushed, to prevent hair shafts from breaking

- Hands and face should be washed each morning

- Hands should be washed after toileting, after messy play and before eating, drinking or touching food

- Nails should be kept short by cutting straight across. This should be done as necessary to stop dirt from accumulating beneath the nails

- Sun block or high-factor sunscreen should be applied to skin (according to the directions) when necessary. Children should also wear a hat – legionnaire style caps cover the neck as well as the head. Sun damage can cause the skin to

Sun protection is essential

become painful, to peel and blister. It can also make children feel unwell. These symptoms occur soon after the exposure to the sun. But long-term damage to health may also occur. Some skin cancers that develop in later life are believed to be caused by sun damage in childhood. In addition, sun damage can cause skin to age prematurely.

It is important for practitioners to be aware of children's individual care needs. Children will require different care depending on their skin colour or type and the type and texture of their hair. For instance:

- It is important to note that all skin types need to be protected from the sun. It is sometimes thought that black skin does not need protection – but this is *not* the case
- Dry skin needs to be moisturised with lotions or oils. These may be massaged in or added to bath water. Black skin may have a tendency to be dry
- Very curly hair or thick hair that is difficult to comb out may need to be treated with conditioners after shampooing. A wide-toothed comb with rounded ends should be used for combing out
- Curly black hair may need to be treated daily with oil that is massaged in. This prevents dryness and reduces breakage of the hair shafts. A wide-toothed comb with rounded ends should be used for combing out. This type of hair can have a tendency to pull out from the root. Care must be taken when combing or when styling the hair into braids, bunches and so on.

Bathing and washing babies

Parents and carers will have differing preferences about the way their babies are bathed. Some families will give their baby a bath each day. Others may bath their baby less often, but 'top and tail' the baby daily. This term describes the process of washing a baby's face, neck, hands and bottom without putting them in a bath of water. Some families make bath-time part of the getting ready for bed routine. Others prefer to wash babies in the morning so that they start the day feeling fresh.

There are also choices to be made about the type of bath. Some families or carers may use a baby bath that fits over a normal bath tub, a baby bath on a stand, a baby bath on the floor, or even a large sink. Older babies may go in a normal bath that has a safety mat fitted to the bottom of the tub and a rubber ring for them to sit in. Whatever bath is chosen, it is important that it is securely placed on a flat surface. The toiletries used must be suitable for the individual baby, and they must be selected in line with the parent and carer's wishes.

How to bath a baby

In a daycare setting, it is unlikely that you will be required to bath a baby. However, childminders and nannies working in the home may carry out this task more frequently. Before bathing a baby alone, you should ideally watch an experienced practitioner so that you can see at first hand the correct way to securely hold a slippery baby. It is necessary to adjust the way you support babies according to their age. You must NEVER LEAVE A BABY UNATTENDED IN OR NEAR WATER, and you must NEVER LOOK AWAY, EVEN FOR A SECOND. If you do have to leave the bathing area YOU MUST TAKE THE BABY WITH YOU.

Basic guidelines for bathing a baby of approximately five to seven weeks are given below:

1. Make preparations – gather together all the equipment you will need – bath, changing mat, nappy changing equipment, clean clothes, baby toiletries, such as bathing lotion and other lotions/oils if necessary, cotton wool, a soft warm towel and blunt-ended nail scissors. Close windows and doors to ensure there isn't a draught, and ensure the room is sufficiently warm, as babies loose heat quickly. Consider and remove any risks – taps that are hot to the touch can be covered by a cold wet flannel for instance, and soap should be placed out of reach. Wash your hands thoroughly, and ensure your nails are clean and not too long, or they may dig into the baby. It is advisable to remove jewellery on your hands and wrists and any jewellery that may dangle down, it is also helpful to tie long hair back if appropriate. Wear protective clothing such as an apron and latex gloves. You should also wear flat shoes as the floor may become slippery.

2. Using a bath thermometer, fill the bath with water of the correct temperature – approximately 38°C. Mix the water with your hand to ensure there are no 'hot spots'. You should also prepare a small bowl of boiled warm water to be used for the baby's face.

3. Undress the baby, but leave the nappy on for the time being. Wrap the baby securely in a warm towel (from below the neck) and lay her on the mat.

Bathing a baby

4. Wash the baby's face first, using cooled boiled water to dampen cotton wool. Using a different piece of cotton wool for each eye, gently wipe across each eye in one movement, beginning at the inside corner and moving to the outside edge (nose to ear). The cotton wool should only be used once for hygiene reasons. Use more dampened cotton wool to wipe around the rest of the baby's face and ears. Avoiding the eye area, dry carefully with clean cotton wool.

5. Check the baby's nails are short. Long or jagged nails can be cut carefully straight across with blunt-ended nail scissors.

6. Wash the baby's hair by leaning her over the bath, still wrapped in the towel. To do this you need to use one hand to hold the baby, and the other for washing the hair. Support the baby's head and shoulders in your hand, tucking their legs securely under your arm. Using your other hand, gently cup water over the head – you do not generally need shampoo for young babies. Dry the head gently by patting with a towel. A baby's head must not be left wet as the baby will quickly become cold. Place the baby back on the mat.

7. Remove the towel and the nappy. Clean the nappy area as you usually would when changing a nappy, and dispose of the nappy and soiled toiletries as usual. Lay a towel out ready for after the bath.

8. Lay the baby in the crook of your arm so that the head and neck are supported. Use your hand to hold the arm and shoulder furthest from you. Use your other hand to support the baby's bottom as you lower her into the bath. You can then let go of the bottom half of the baby – you now have a hand free for washing. Ensure you still have a secure grasp with your remaining hand.

9. Gently cup water over the baby with your hand, using stroking movements to massage the skin clean. You may gently use a flannel or sponge, but avoid rubbing. Ensure you pay close attention to skin creases in the thighs, neck, arms and under arms that can trap sweat and bacteria leading to soreness.

10. Some babies enjoy bathing more than others. If a baby is happy, it is good practice to allow them to splash and kick for a short while before ending the bath. However, young babies get cold quickly, so do not prolong this.

11. Support the bottom half of the baby as before. Ensure you have a secure hold as the baby will be slippery. Lift the baby out and lay them on the mat. Wrap them in a warm towel without delay.

12. You must pat the baby's delicate skin dry (don't rub), paying close attention to the skin creases as before.

13. Apply any lotions necessary and put on a clean nappy. Dress the baby and gently brush the hair with a baby brush if appropriate (use a wide toothed comb for African Caribbean hair). Settle the baby somewhere safe before cleaning up.

14. Put everything away. Drain the water away first, as this can be hazardous. You should clean the baby bath out, ready for the next use. Put clothes in the appropriate place ready to be laundered. Wash your hands, even if you have been wearing gloves.

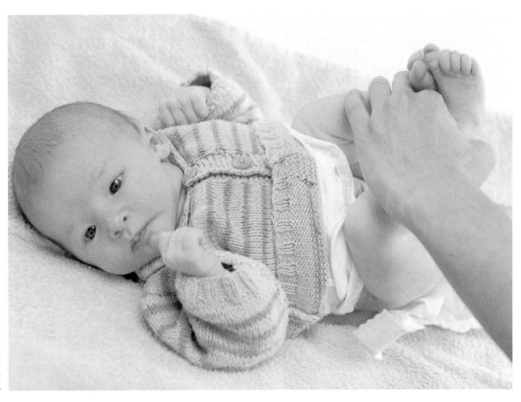

Topping and
tailing

Topping and tailing

As with bathing a baby, you should ideally watch an experienced practitioner top and tail a baby before you carry out the task yourself. The process of topping and tailing requires the same skills as bathing a baby, but you do not need to follow all of the same steps. Basic guidelines are given below.

- Make preparations following steps 1 and 2 of how to bath a baby. Prepare the equipment, the room and yourself.
- Undress the baby and clean her eyes, face and ears, following steps 3 and 4.
- Use additional dampened cotton wool to wash the baby's hands, cleaning in between the fingers. Pat the hands dry gently with a towel. Check the baby's nails, following step 5.
- Following step 7, remove the baby's nappy and clean the nappy area.
- Follow step 13, putting on a clean nappy, dressing the baby, brushing her hair and settling her safely elsewhere.
- Clear up and wash your hands, following step 14.

⤺ Toiletries

Each child needs to have their own flannel and toothbrush and a clean towel. When it comes to using soaps, lotions, oils, toothpaste, sun screens and so on, it is important to ensure that the products selected meet children's individual needs. Practitioners can check this with parents and carers. Failing to check may mean that practitioners use the wrong product for a child's skin or hair type, or use something that they are allergic to. There are products designed specifically for the delicate skin and hair of babies, including soft, baby hairbrushes and toothbrushes.

Oral hygiene

Good oral hygiene is essential for healthy teeth and gums. See pages 212–14 of Unit CCLD 307 Promote the health and physical development of children.

Link | **Unit CCLD 307** Promote the health and physical development of children

Medicines, inhalers and drugs for long-term conditions

Practitioners need to know how to administer medication in different circumstances. You can read more about this in Element 302.3 of Unit CCLD 302 Develop and maintain a healthy, safe and secure environment for children.

Link | **Unit CCLD 302** Develop and maintain a healthy, safe and secure environment for children

Toilet training

Children can only become clean and dry, or 'toilet trained', when they have control over their bowels and bladder. There is no point in trying to toilet train a child until this time. Babies have no bowel or bladder control – they will often wet or dirty their nappy soon after feeding, but they may also do so at any other time.

Bowel and bladder control develops at different times in different children. It often occurs between the age of about 18 months and three years. Most children are dry and clean during the daytime by the time they are three. Frequent accidents can be expected at first as children may not notice until the last minute that they need to go to the toilet. Or children may wait too long to go, particularly if they are absorbed in an activity. Initially adults generally need to remind children to go to the toilet.

Night-time control takes longer to develop. Many children still have accidents at night until the age of six or seven, and some beyond this age. Some disabled children or those with special educational needs may develop bowel and bladder control much later and may continue to use nappies. Some may never develop control.

It is important that toilet training does not become an issue of conflict between children and adults. To avoid conflict and stress, it is best to take a relaxed approach, waiting until the individual child is showing definite signs of being ready for training before attempting the process. Although children may have control as early as 18 months, many children will be into their second year before they show signs of readiness. Some will be older. The signs include:

- Children saying they are about to soil or wet their nappy
- Children telling a carer that their nappy needs changing
- Children showing interest in the toilet or potty, or in other children's use of them
- Children showing reluctance to wear a nappy
- Children saying they want to wear pants
- Children being able to tell adults that they need to use the toilet, verbally or with signs.

It is good practice to ensure that you have the right equipment for toilet training, including:

- A child-sized toilet or potty, or a child's toilet seat that fits inside a normal toilet seat

  It is advisable to introduce children to these prior to training, so have them in the bathroom. Children who already use the toilet or potty can be good role models, helping other children to understand their use
- Soft toilet paper
- Plenty of spare clothes

  Children may wet through everything they are wearing, including socks and shoes
- Materials for cleaning up both children and the environment after accidents.

Good-practice guidelines for toilet training are:

- Plan your approach to training in consultation with parents and carers. Some may ask your advice but others may be clear about the approach they would like to take
- Be relaxed about training, and do not rush children. Otherwise children may become anxious or toilet training may become a battle. Praise children for using the toilet or potty. Deal with any accidents without fuss, and in private, getting children into clean clothes as soon as possible. Do not make children feel bad or embarrassed about having accidents by showing disapproval
- Most libraries stock children's books that show characters using the toilet or potty. There are several that show children learning the skill and being praised. These can be useful to read with children who are toilet training, particularly if they do not have another child as a role model.

Good hygiene practices

Practitioners must always promote good hygiene practices. It is important for you to understand:

- The principles of cross-infection
- How to dispose of different types of waste safely
- How to handle food safely
- How to handle body fluids safely
- The issues concerning the spread of blood-borne viruses such as hepatitis, HIV and AIDS.

You can read more about this on pages 54–5 of Unit CCLD 302 Develop and maintain a healthy, safe and secure environment for children.

 Link   **Unit CCLD 302** Develop and maintain a healthy, safe and secure environment for children

Element 306.4

Are you ready for assessment?

Facilitate children's personal care

You need to show that you can competently facilitate children's personal care. To do this you will need to be directly observed by your assessor and present other types of evidence. The amount and type of evidence you need to present will vary. You should plan this with your assessor.

Direct observation by your assessor

Observation and/or expert witness testimony is the required assessment method to be used to evidence some of each element in this unit. If your assessor is unable to observe you, s/he will identify an expert in your workplace who will provide testimony of your work-based performance. Usually your assessor or expert witness will observe you in real work activities and this should provide most of the evidence for the performance criteria for the elements in this unit.

Preparing to be observed

You must show your assessor that you can meet children's physical care needs appropriately, ensuring that care routines protect children and practitioners, and encouraging children to care for themselves as appropriate. You must also show that you can meet children's nutritional needs for food and water, set up systems to deal with waste, and deal with medicines or medical requirements of children.

Other types of evidence

You will need to present different types of evidence in order to:

- Cover criteria not observed by your assessor
- Show that you have the required knowledge, understanding and skills.

Such evidence could include:

- Work products such as resources/ materials developed for use with children, information posters/leaflets or organisational policies/procedures you have contributed to
- Case studies, projects, assignments and reflective accounts of your work.

Check your knowledge

- What must you do to ensure hazardous materials are stored safely? **K3H260**
- How can you use IT to promote play and development? **K3D264**
- How can you support children and families who are new to the setting? **K3D267**
- Why is physical exercise important for children? **K3D281**
- How can you support children who are toilet training? **K3D285**

Reflective practice

Consider the way in which you usually make resources available to children. Compare this with the guidelines on pages 156–67. Do you need to introduce any changes to your current practice? Make notes in your reflective journal. Draw up a plan of action if necessary.

UNIT 307

Promote the health and physical development of children

This unit is concerned with promoting the health and physical development of children.

The unit contains three elements:

○ **CCLD 307.1** *Plan and implement physical activities and routines for children to meet their physical development needs*

○ **CCLD 307.2** *Plan and provide food and drink to meet the nutritional needs of children*

○ **CCLD 307.3** *Promote children's healthy physical development*

Introduction

Children's health is essential to their overall well-being. Practitioners have an important role to play in encouraging children to be aware of fitness, nutrition and health. They must also meet children's nutritional and health needs whilst caring for them. In addition, practitioners can be instrumental in providing good opportunities for children to undertake physical activities and master physical skills.

Plan and implement physical activities and routines for children to meet their physical development needs

Element 307.1

○ ### The health and physical development needs of children

K3D287
K3D288
K3D289
K3H290
K3D291
K3D292
K3D293
K3D294

Being physically active helps children to be physically fit. There is much concern that children in developed countries are not as active as they ought to be, perhaps because it is considered unsafe in the modern world for children to spend long periods of time outside playing unsupervised, as many children did in previous generations. Studies have shown that many modern children spend long periods each week at inactive pursuits such as watching television, using computers and playing console games. These periods are often not balanced out by enough activity. As a result more children are becoming unfit, which can lead to serious health problems including obesity (being considerably overweight), heart disease and respiratory difficulties.

So for the good of their health, children need opportunities to be active, perhaps more so now than in the past. Practitioners have an important role to play in giving children those opportunities and in promoting a healthy lifestyle that includes regular exercise.

Children also need good opportunities to learn and practice physical movements and skills, which enables them to progress in their physical development. Unit CCLD 303, Promote children's development, contains information about how children are likely to develop in terms of skills and growth. It is important to be aware of this information, as you will read below.

 Link **Unit CCLD 303** Promote children's development

Planning indoor and outdoor physical activities

When you are planning physical activities for children, consider the use of both indoor and outdoor spaces. While physically active pursuits are often suited to outside, it may be appropriate during times of extreme weather (if the playground is icy, for instance) to clear adequate space inside so that activities can still go ahead. Similarly, many traditionally 'indoor' activities can be brought outside. It can help to think of the outdoor space as an additional room that can be used flexibly for all sorts of activities.

The details of your physical activities should be recorded on your plans, showing what skills children should practise and develop competence in, and what support they will need. Always be clear about what resources and equipment will be used. Decisions about what size of ball to use, or whether to use beanbags, impact on the movements that are required of children and alter the experience considerably. You will need to make use of a wide range of small and large resources to effectively promote all-round physical development.

Ensure that your plans are in line with the overall plan for the setting, making sure that the outside play area and pieces of equipment are available when you want them, and that activities such as going to the park generally fit in to the schedule. Thought also needs to be given to the activities that follow physical activity, since children will need an opportunity to rest and recover (see page 204). If you follow an early years education framework, you must ensure that your plans also meet the requirements of the relevant inspectorate for your home country (see Unit CCLD 309 Plan and implement curriculum frameworks for early education).

Link **Unit CCLD 309** Plan and implement curriculum frameworks for early education

When planning physical activities indoors and outdoors, you should consider the following:
- How you will implement warm-up and wind-down exercises
- Promoting a full range of large motor skills
- Promoting a full range of fine motor skills

Tunnels can be used outside

- Promoting a full range of hand/eye co-ordination skills
- How you will extend the range and level of children's skill
- How you will balance challenge and risk
- How you will consider safety
- How you will take into consideration children's stages of development and growth
- How you will encourage co-operation, sharing and turn taking
- How you will ensure inclusive opportunities.

Clothing, warming up and winding down

It is important that you ensure children are properly prepared for physically active play, just as you would prepare yourself for exercise. Ensure children have:

- Safe, supportive, flat footwear
- Layered clothing – it is advisable for children to dress in layers that can be removed when they get warm (from exercise or due to the weather) or added if it is cold outside. Encourage children to think about how warm or cold they are, and encourage them to take the appropriate action
- Comfortable clothing – that is not restrictive, in order that they can easily make a full range of movements
- Safety clothing if appropriate for the activity – such as cycle helmets, or knee/elbow pads for older children who may undertake activities such as skateboarding
- Sun protection – hats, high-factor sun lotion/block.

Children also need opportunities to warm up before physically active play and the chance to wind down afterwards. It is best for the body when the pulse rate and respiration levels are increased slowly at the beginning of exercise and decreased slowly afterwards.

Warming up muscles gently minimises the risk of children straining or otherwise hurting themselves, since the movements help the heart to pump blood carrying oxygen to the muscles. When the body is warm, movement and flexibility are improved.

The following activities are good for warming up children:

- Walking on the spot, slowly at first, just gently flexing the ankles and swinging the arms. Slowly encourage children to pick up the pace, gradually bringing the knees up higher and swinging the arms more vigorously, until eventually children are marching at pace
- Side stepping to the right with the right leg, then bringing the left leg over so that they are standing with feet together. Repeat to the left and bring the right leg over. Start slowly then build up the pace until it seems like a dance movement
- Gently rotating the shoulders around, a few times forward, then a few times backwards
- Clutching hands together in front of their chest, fingers interlocked and arms straight. Slowly raising the arms above the head, then slowly bringing them back to chest level. Repeat a few times
- Bending down slowly to touch the floor, then slowly coming back up, bringing the arms up until fully extended above the head. Repeat a few times.

To wind down with children, repeat the activities above, but this time reverse the speed of first two, so that children begin at pace, and slow down as they progress with the movements. You should do the first two active movements first, while children's heartbeats are raised and their muscles are warm.

Large motor skills

The term 'large motor skills' (sometimes called 'gross motor skills') refers to movements that involve the whole body, such as walking and running, or movements that involve one or more limbs, such as kicking a ball. As children master co-ordination of large muscles, their physical skill levels improve. For instance, when children first attempt to kick a stationary large ball, they sometimes miss it entirely, and when they do kick it they have no control over the direction of the ball. As co-ordination and skill develop, children can learn not only to control the direction of a stationary ball, but to achieve

Gross motor development includes the development of head control

complex movements such as receiving a ball during a football game and turning to score a goal – this is the skill of striking.

'Locomotion' is the term that describes the physical activity that takes place when the whole body moves along. Babies achieve locomotion by crawling, shuffling and eventually walking. Older children run, jump, hop, skip, bunny-hop, swim and dive.

The term 'balance' describes the process by which people are able to hold an upright position overcoming the force of gravity. This requires control of muscles throughout the body. Children first achieve control of their heads and their arms – think of a baby who cannot yet sit up but can lift her head and move her arms to play with a baby gym frame. Next, control of the trunk is achieved, and this is co-ordinated with the movement of arms – a baby learns to roll over. Lastly comes control of the legs – babies learn to crawl. But it is not until they have achieved and practised control of the muscles in all of these parts of their body that they are able to balance and stand alone, and eventually walk. Children's balancing skills improve over time – they can eventually manoeuvre on balancing beams and stilts.

Practitioners should provide plenty of opportunities for children to practise and develop their balance, skill and the co-ordination of large muscles. The key skills to master are as follows.

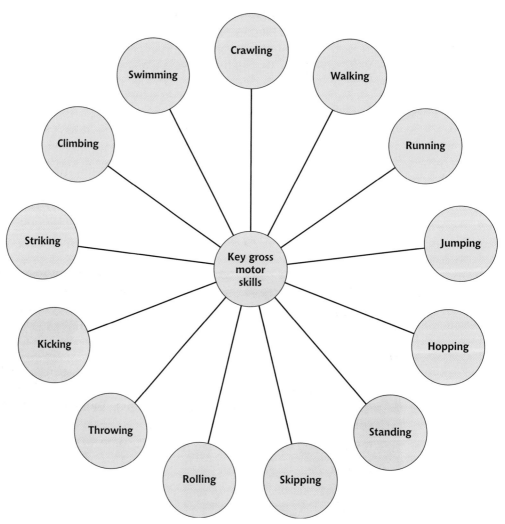

Gross motor key skills

There are many activities and resources that will help to promote these skills. Just a few are suggested here.

For 0–12 months:

- Rolling balls for children to crawl after
- Holding children upright so they can begin to take their weight on their legs
- Baby bouncers (must be CLOSELY supervised at all times; these are generally considered most appropriate in the home)
- Trolleys for standing and walking whilst pushing for balance.

12 months to 2 years:

- Throwing and rolling large balls – simple catch games, skittles
- Kicking with large balls – simple kicking and receiving games
- Walking, and climbing with supervision – up and down steps, on low climbing cubes
- Push and pull toys – such as carts and prams, providing toys to take in and out and transport
- Ride-on toys without peddles (large wheeled toys)
- Swinging and sliding on small items of playground equipment
- Using low stilts
- Splashing around in water – in a bath, paddling pool or swimming pool. Must be CLOSELY supervised at all times.

2–4 years:

- Ball games involving the passing and receiving of balls of varying sizes through catching, bouncing, rolling and kicking
- Hoopla with rings, and other target games – throwing beanbags into hoops
- Walking along broad balancing beams
- Jumping across stepping stones drawn on the playground with chalk
- Crawling and wriggling through tunnels
- Going for walks
- Running games such as catch, and 'traffic lights' for starting and stopping and changing pace (call out colours: amber = walk, green = go, red = stop)
- Swinging and sliding on medium sized items of playground equipment
- Jumping, hopping, skipping, changing-direction games (You can play while singing the following rhyme: 'I went to school one morning and I hopped like this, I hopped like this, I hopped like this, I went to school one morning and I hopped like this, all on my way to school!' Children do the hopping action throughout, then choose a new one, jumping perhaps, and so the rhyme continues)
- Circle games – The Farmer's in his Den, Here We Go Round the Mulberry Bush
- Ride-on toys with peddles, including tricycles
- Twirling streamers
- Learning to swim

5–8 years:

- Trampolines – with CLOSE supervision, and only one child on the trampoline at a time.
- Running races
- Bat and ball games – with various types of bats and rackets – tennis, cricket, rounders, swing ball, paddle ball
- Ball games – football, basketball, netball, volleyball
- Hoops for spinning around the waist
- Walking on stilts
- Twirling batons
- Frisbee games
- A range of playground games with running, chasing, dodging
- Skipping-rope group games and skipping alone
- Riding bicycles
- Skating on roller-skates, skateboards
- There will be PE lessons at school, and children may be taken to lessons such as dance, swimming, horse riding, football, martial arts training
- Climbing, sliding and swinging on large equipment.

Wheeled toys need plenty of space

Fine motor skills and hand/eye co-ordination

Fine motor skills are the delicate, small movements that need control of small muscles, particularly the hands. As this develops, children are effectively able to manipulate objects such as tools, making very fine movements with their fingers. Hand/eye co-ordination is involved in using fine motor skills as children need to see an item and co-ordinate their hand movements to pick it up or manipulate it – threading a needle is a good example of this skill.

Children practise and develop these skills over time. Children's first hand grasps are not very sophisticated – they use their whole hand when attempting to pick things up (see Unit CCLD 303 Promote children's development). But by about one year of age they start to pick things up using their forefinger and thumb – this is called the pincer grasp. By the age of eight children can master skills such as sewing.

 Link **Unit CCLD 303** Promote children's development

There are many activities and resources that will help to promote these skills. Just a few are suggested here.

For 12–15 months:

- Interesting objects such as rattles that children want to pick up, hold and explore
- Different textures to grasp – hard plastic objects and soft toys or soft balls
- Putting objects in and out of a simple posting box
- Stacking cups, blocks of different textures – plastic, wood, soft, hard.

For 15–24 months:

- Building towers with blocks and the largest size of interlocking bricks (with rounded corners)
- Joining large pop-together beads
- Holding own cup when drinking, using both hands
- Starting to assist with feeding self
- Turn pages of board books, fabric books and bath books
- Making marks with broad crayons and very large paintbrushes
- Taking off shoes and socks
- Pressing buttons and sliding levers on pop-up toys.

For two-year-olds:

- Threading with large beads
- Drawing large patterns including circles, starting to show a hand preference
- Feeding independently with a spoon
- Building towers independently
- Using a shape sorter
- Fitting puzzle pieces into a play tray
- Beginning to turn paper pages in books
- Pulling on shoes and beginning to fasten Velcro
- Painting with broad paintbrushes.

For three-year-olds:

- Turning book pages independently whilst holding the book
- Beginning to cut with scissors
- Reliably holding a beaker with one hand
- Reliably feeding themselves with a spoon
- Making simple puzzles
- Putting on and taking off clothes, doing up simple zips and buttons
- Independently washing hands
- Stirring reliably when cooking
- Digging in sand
- Basic pouring in water play
- Making collages by sticking a range of fine items with glue – wool, string, tissue
- Drawing simple pictures with pencils and felt-tips with preferred hand

Fine motor skills develop gradually over time

- Painting with medium-sized brush, beginning to experiment with other painting resources such as rollers
- Building with interlocking bricks and other construction resources
- Manipulating a train around the track
- Manipulating play dough and other malleable materials.

For four-year-olds:
- Fastening zips and buttons
- Using knife and fork
- Cutting out along lines and around large shapes
- Using computer mouse and keyboard
- Putting together puzzles of approximately 12–20 pieces
- Reliably using tools with dough for rolling, cutting and shaping
- More sophisticated sand play and water play – sandcastles and water pumps
- Painting in a variety of ways – stamping, rollering, printing
- Drawing more sophisticated and recognisable pictures and patterns
- Practising early literacy skills through playful activities such as role play – emergent writing that resembles letters and some real letters
- Creating with fine resources such as sequins and confetti.

For five-year-olds:
- Colouring in own pictures
- Using simple stencils and templates

- Cutting items such as thread, and cutting out pictures from magazines
- Completing puzzles of over 20 pieces
- Spreading bread with butter and other spreads such as jam
- Manipulating buttons on small hand-held electronic toys
- Clapping games.

6–8-year-olds:

- Making a sandwich and cutting it in half
- Using paper clips
- Sewing with basic stitches – running stitch, cross stitch
- Using increasingly fine tools with more independence – clay tools, scrapers, woodwork tools
- Braiding and weaving with strips of crêpe paper, wool, ribbon
- Making paper aeroplanes
- Tying and untying shoelaces
- Fastening and unfastening watch straps
- Cats cradle finger-play game.

Extending range and level of skill and experience

It is the job of practitioners to encourage all children (including babies) to increase their range and level of skill and experience. This can be partly achieved by providing a diverse range of activities that are likely to appeal widely to children who will have different preferences, and encouraging children's participation. This can be achieved by:

- Adults joining in alongside children, particularly those who are apprehensive. Many children may feel scared when first attempting a new physical skill – climbing on the climbing frame, for instance. Some children do not like balls because they fear being hit. It is important to gently encourage children and praise them for trying – if you push them they may completely avoid the activity or resource in the future, and trust you less as a result
- Avoiding too much competition. Although children will enjoy the odd race, and competition can have the effect of improving children's performance, make sure that children do not feel as though they are in competition too often. This puts off many children, including some who would enjoy activities such as running or completing an obstacle course for fun
- Ensuring that the activities are inclusive (see page 202).

In addition:

- You can demonstrate new skills
- When children have achieved one skill you can introduce them to a new one, in order of the sequence children's development is likely to follow (see Unit CCLD 303 Promote children's development). For instance, once they can jump and stand on one leg, encourage them to try hopping
- Reward children's efforts, which will encourage them to keep trying. Praise, smiles and clapping are all effective

- Involve children in celebrating their achievements when they have mastered a new skill, perhaps by marking it together on their assessment record documents, or by displaying a photograph of them in action with a caption. (Seek parental permission before taking photographs of children)

- Let children's families know about their success when they are collected, that way they are likely to receive more praise and positive attention at home.

Link   **Unit CCLD 303** Promote children's development

Challenge and development

Encouraging children to increase their range and level of skill and experience is connected to providing them with adequate challenge, so that they have the best opportunities to move on in terms of their development. Practitioners must have a good knowledge of expected child development 'norms' in order to challenge children effectively (see Unit CCLD 303 Promote children's development). You cannot provide appropriate challenge if you do not know what children should master next, as we have discussed. It would be inappropriate, unfair and perhaps even unsafe to challenge children with activities that are too far beyond their capabilities. A child who has not yet mastered a tricycle would be unsafe on a bicycle, for instance.

Link   **Unit CCLD 303** Promote children's development

You must also be aware of the stage of physical development of the individual children you are working with, because every child develops at their own unique pace. You should consider their levels of confidence too. For instance, a child may have physically mastered the skills of climbing up steps and sliding down a slide, but they may not have the confidence yet to take a turn on the tallest slide in the park – even though the skills required remain the same, they are not yet ready for the challenging height.

Challenge and risk

Part of providing children with adequate challenge is permitting them to take appropriate risks. With physically active play there is always a risk of children getting hurt – most setting's accident books are likely to show regular minor playground injuries such as grazed knees and hands from children's falls when running. However, it would be inappropriate of practitioners not to allow children to run in case they fell and hurt themselves. In fact *not* running *would* potentially harm children, affecting their physical development, fitness, confidence and general well-being. In this case, the benefits justify the risk – and the risk is not significant – there may be a high incidence of playground injuries, but they are generally only very minor.

However, it is sensible to minimise risk by making sure children have sufficient space to run around without bumping into each other, for instance. The use of apparatus such as climbing frames is another good example of activities that have an element of risk. But practitioners take a number of steps to minimise the risk by, for example, providing a safety surface underneath and around the apparatus, and restricting the number of children permitted on it at any one time.

The risks that are appropriate for children to take increase in intensity as children develop and grow up, and practitioners must allow for that. Remember, if children are not allowed to take appropriate risks, they will not be sufficiently challenged.

Sometimes children may want to take risks that are inappropriate for safety reasons, or inappropriate for their personal stage of development. Practitioners should not allow children to do things that are dangerous and likely to hurt them. There is a difference between allowing children to take appropriate risks that are worthwhile in terms of development when compared to the likelihood of injury, and allowing children to do things that are likely to seriously hurt them or injure them without a justifiable developmental gain or experience. Sometimes there is a much safer way to give children a similar experience.

To decide what risks are acceptable and unacceptable, and to see what can be done to minimise risk, practitioners should carry out risk assessments (see Unit CCLD 302 Develop and maintain a healthy, safe and secure environment for children). It is important that you know and understand your own setting's policies and procedures for risk assessment and that you follow them closely. Guidelines are generally included within the health and safety policy.

It is helpful if organisations also include information about risk and challenge in their health and safety policy. This is an opportunity to clearly agree and communicate the setting's approach to risk and challenge, which will benefit practitioners, families and children.

 Link   **Unit CCLD 302** Develop and maintain a healthy, safe and secure environment for children

Co-operation, sharing and turn taking

Activities that promote physical skills can also be useful for promoting the social skills of co-operation, sharing and turn taking. You can encourage children to co-operate by introducing them to activities that require collaboration including:

- Playing catch with balls (or bouncing/kicking balls to one another)
- Playing bat and ball games
- Playing playground games such as 'What's the time Mr Wolf?'
- Team games and sports such as volleyball
- Making dens together
- Parachute games
- Using large pieces of equipment that require all children playing on them to co-operate, e.g. climbing frames.

Methods of promoting sharing and turn taking include:

- Not having enough of a resource for everyone (ride-on toys, for instance), and asking children, in advance of the activity, what you can do to make things fair
- Playing games such as skittles and hoopla that require children to take turns
- Providing large pieces of equipment, such as slides, which must be used one at a time

It is important to make sure there are enough resources so that all children can participate fully

- Craft activities that require certain resources to be shared, e.g. sequins, beads, craft feathers.

Rest and recovery

Adults need time to rest and recover after exercise, and children are just the same. They need to catch their breath, slow their heart rates, rest their muscles and generally recharge their batteries. After physical activity ensure children have opportunities to:

- Do wind-down exercises
- Have a drink
- Sit or lie down somewhere comfortable
- Take part in a restful activity that is not demanding either physically or in terms of concentration, for instance looking at books together.

Inclusive opportunities

We have already mentioned the importance of practitioners having a good knowledge of a child's developmental stage. You must ensure that you provide physical opportunities that meet the development needs of all the children, taking into account age, gender, ethnicities, individual needs and abilities. You should consider:

- If children are permitted to wear the clothes you recommend for exercise. For example, some cultures would not permit girls to wear shorts for PE or to get changed in a classroom. Others may not permit the removal of headwear that has religious significance
- If children need games or activities to be adapted so that they can fully participate. For instance, an older child who uses a wheelchair could join in with parachute games if other children kneel down to play them instead of standing

- If children need any adaptations made to equipment, or the introduction of particular resources. For instance, a ball with a bell inside could be purchased for a child with a visual impairment. Or a small ball with a tail could be introduced for an older child who finds catching a tennis ball difficult

- If children would benefit from sensitive grouping. It can be difficult to meet the needs of all children within a group that has wide age ranges, and there may also be safety concerns. Younger children may be unsteady while running around the garden or using ride-on toys, and their sense of space, themselves and others will just be developing. They can easily be knocked over by older children rushing by on foot or on tricycles and bikes. Rather than risk the safety (and confidence) of the younger children or restrict the play of the older children, it would be beneficial to split the group and take the younger children out separately.

You should change and adapt your plans and routines as necessary to fully promote inclusion. Changing routines may also be necessary if weather delays your planned activities or if you arrange a different activity, such as going for a walk or a trip to the park.

Are you ready for assessment?

Plan and implement physical activities and routines for children to meet their physical development needs

You need to show that you can competently plan and implement physical activities and routines for children to meet their physical development needs. To do this you will need to be directly observed by your assessor and present other types of evidence. The amount and type of evidence you need to present will vary. You should plan this with your assessor.

Direct observation by your assessor

Observation and/or expert witness testimony is the required assessment method to be used to evidence some of each element in this unit. If your assessor is unable to observe you, s/he will identify an expert in your workplace who will provide testimony of your work-based performance. Usually your assessor or expert witness will observe you in real work activities and this should provide most of the evidence for the performance criteria for the elements in this unit.

Preparing to be observed

You must show your assessor that you can plan indoor and outdoor activities providing opportunities for children to develop physical skills, balance and large motor skills, hand/eye co-ordination skills and co-operation skills. You must also show that you can ensure children warm up and wind down, and that you can plan routines that allow children to rest and recover from exercise. You must show that you can plan activities that are inclusive and in line with overall setting plans, and you must show that you can encourage children to extend their levels of skill. ➤

You will need to arrange to be assessed at a time when children will be practising physical skills.

Other types of evidence

You will need to present different types of evidence in order to:

- Cover criteria not observed by your assessor
- Show that you have the required knowledge, understanding and skills.

Such evidence could include:

- Work products such as activity plans and indoor/outdoor layout plans
- Case studies, projects, assignments and reflective accounts of your work
- Confidential records such as individual children's observation/assessment records. These should not be placed in your portfolio – they must remain in their usual location and be referred to in the assessor records in your portfolio.

Element **307.2**

Plan and provide food and drink to meet the nutritional needs of children

Healthy eating and nutrition guidelines

K3H295
K3H296
K3H297
K3S298
K3H299
K3H300
K3H301
K3H302

Food and water is the body's fuel. Without it, humans literally cannot keep going – they die. The body must have a combination of different nutrients to be healthy. This is especially important during childhood when the body is growing and developing. Large quantities of the four nutrients listed below are found in our food and drink:

- Protein
- Fat
- Carbohydrates
- Water.

However, only small quantities of the following are present:

- Vitamins
- Minerals
- Fibre.

Consequently, it is most common for vitamins, minerals and fibre to be missing from children's diets. Vitamins and minerals are needed for healthy growth, development and normal functioning of the body. Water contains some minerals, but primarily it maintains fluid in the cells of the body and in the bloodstream. Fibre adds roughage to food. This encourages the body to pass out the waste products of food after it has been digested, by stimulating the bowel muscles.

The charts and tables on pages 205–6 explain the sources and functions of nutrients.

Proteins provide material for:

- growth of the body
- repair of the body.

Types of proteins:

- **Animal** – first-class or complete proteins, supply all ten of the essential amino acids
- **Vegetable** – second-class or incomplete proteins, supply some of the ten essential amino acids.

FOODS CONTAINING PROTEINS

Examples of protein foods include:

- **Animal proteins** – meat, fish, chicken, eggs, dairy foods
- **Vegetable proteins** – nuts, seeds pulses, cereals.

Protein foods are made up of amino acids. There are ten essential amino acids.

Foods containing protein

Carbohydrates provide:

- energy
- warmth.

Types of carbohydrates:

- sugars
- starches.

FOODS CONTAINING CARBOHYDRATES

Examples of carbohydrate foods include:

- **Sugars** – fruit, honey, sweets, beet sugar, cane sugar
- **Starches** – potatoes, cereals, beans, pasta.

Carbohydrates are broken down into glucose before the body can use them. **Sugars** are quickly converted and are a quick source of energy. **Starches** take longer to convert so they provide a longer-lasting supply of energy.

Foods containing carbohydrates

Fats:
- provide energy and warmth
- store fat-soluble vitamins
- make food pleasant to eat.

Types of fats:
- saturated
- unsaturated
- polyunsaturates.

Examples of foods containing fat include:
- **Saturated fat** – butter, cheese, meat, palm oil
- **Unsaturated** – olive oil, peanut oil
- **Polyunsaturated** – oily fish, corn oil, sunflower oil.

FOODS CONTAINING FAT

Saturated fats are solid at room temperature and come mainly from animal fats. **Unsaturated and polyunsaturated fats** are liquid at room temperature and come mainly from vegetable and fish oils.

Foods containing fat

A regular supply of water-soluble vitamins is needed as these cannot be stored in the body. Fat soluble vitamins can be stored in the body, but intake should still be regular.

The main vitamins

Vitamin	Purpose	Foods
A Fat-soluble Pregnant woman must avoid too much vitamin A	Maintenance of good vision and healthy skin. Promotes normal growth and development. Deficiency may lead to skin and vision problems	Carrots, tomatoes, eggs, butter, cheese
B Water-soluble. Very regular intake required	Promotes healthy functioning of the nerves and the muscles. Deficiency may lead to anaemia and wasting of the muscles	Meat, fish, green vegetables. Some breakfast cereals are fortified with vitamin B (it is added to them)
C Water-soluble Daily intake required	Maintenance of healthy tissue and skin. Deficiency leads to a decreased resistance to infection, and can result in scurvy	Fruit. Oranges and blackcurrants have a high vitamin C content
D Fat-soluble	Maintenance of bones and teeth. Assists body growth. Deficiency in children may lead to bones which do not harden sufficiently (skeletal condition known as rickets). Also leads to tooth decay	Oily fish and fish oil, egg yolk. Milk and margarines are fortified with vitamin D. Sunlight on the skin can cause the body to produce vitamin D
E Fat-soluble	Promotes blood clotting, healing and metabolism. Deficiency may result in delayed blood clotting	Cereals, egg yolk, seeds, nuts, vegetable oils
K Fat-soluble	Promotes healing. Necessary for blood clotting. Deficiency may lead to excessive bleeding due to delayed blood clotting. Vitamin K is normally given to babies after birth as deficiency is sometimes seen in newborns, although rare in adults	Whole grains, green vegetables, liver

The main minerals

Mineral	Purpose	Foods
Calcium	Required for growth of teeth and bones. Also necessary for nerve and muscle function. Works with vitamin D. Deficiency may lead to rickets and tooth decay	Milk, cheese, eggs, fish, pulses, whole grain cereals. White and brown flour are fortified with calcium
Fluoride	Maintenance of healthy bones and protection from tooth decay	Present in water in varying quantities. May be added to water. Many toothpastes contain fluoride
Iodine	Used to make the thyroid hormone. Also required for normal neurological development. Deficiency may lead to thyroid problems	Dairy products, sea-foods, vegetables, water. Salt is fortified with iodine
Iron	Essential for the formation of haemoglobin in the red blood cells, which transport oxygen around the body. Deficiency may lead to anaemia. Vitamin C helps the absorption of iron	Meat, eggs, green vegetables, dried fruits
Phosphorus Babies must not have a high intake as can be harmful	Promotes the formation of teeth and bones	Meat, fish, vegetables, eggs, fruit
Potassium	Essential for water balance in the body. Also promotes functioning of cells, including the nerves	A wide range of foods
Sodium chloride Salt must not be added to food for babies or young children during food preparation or at the table	Essential for water balance in the body. Involved in energy utilisation and nerve function	Salt, meat, fish, bread, processed food

Too much salt can be bad for children. Practitioners must not add salt to children's food before, during or after preparation. Nuts are considered a choking hazard for young children, and they are a common cause of food allergy. Consequently, many settings have introduced a 'no nut policy'. They do not use nuts or nut products, and children may not bring them in even for their own consumption.

The Government has produced guidelines on healthy eating and nutrition for children. Further details are supplied in Unit CCLD 314 Provide physical care that promotes the health and development of babies and children under three years, and in Unit CCLD 306 Plan and organise environments for children and families.

 Link **Unit CCLD 314** Provide physical care that promotes the health and development of babies and children under three years
Unit CCLD 306 Plan and organise environments for children and families

Specific dietary requirements and allergies

When a child is registered with a setting it is important for practitioners to find out if the child has any specific dietary requirements so that they can meet the child's needs whilst still promoting a healthy diet.

Food has a spiritual significance within some cultures, religions and ethnic groups, which may mean that certain foods cannot be eaten or that food should be prepared in a particular way. Others make decisions about food based on personal beliefs. It is important that practitioners respect and comply with parental wishes. Individual people vary in terms of the dietary codes or restrictions that they follow. You should never assume that you will be able to tell what a child may or may not eat from their religion – always find out directly from the family. However, in general terms, the table below gives some helpful guidance.

Cultural food

Group	Principles
Christians	May give up certain foods for Lent
Jews	May not eat pork or shellfish. May not cook or eat milk and meat products together. May use different sets of crockery and cutlery for milk products and meat products. May only eat meat and poultry prepared by a kosher butcher. May fast for Yom Kippur (Day of Atonement)
Rastafarians	May be vegetarian. May not eat food from the vine. May only eat 'Ital' foods – those in a whole and natural state. May not eat processed or preserved foods
Muslims	May not eat pork or pork products. Children may be breast-fed until the age of two years. Families may fast between sunrise and sunset during Ramadan, so they may rise early to eat at these times. Children under 12 do not generally fast. May drink no alcohol
Sikhs	May be vegetarian or eat only chicken, lamb and fish. May fast regularly or just on the first day of Punjabi month
Hindus	May eat no beef or be vegetarian. During festivals may eat only pure foods such as fruit and yoghurt. May drink no alcohol

Vegetarian diets:

- The lacto-ovo-vegetarian diet excludes meat but includes milk, milk products and eggs. The lacto-vegetarian diet also excludes eggs. The semi-vegetarian diet eliminates some meat, often red meat, but may include poultry and fish.

Vegan diets:

- These generally exclude all foods of animal origin including meat, milk and milk products, honey, and additives made from animal products, such as gelatine.

Some children have food allergies, intolerances or medical conditions that mean their diets have to be restricted. This can be caused by an allergic response, diabetes or an enzyme deficiency. Common allergens include nuts and milk.

Some children may need to eat at certain times of the day. They might take medication daily or they may have medication to take if they show symptoms of their condition or if you become aware that they have eaten, or in the case of some children even touched, a food they should not have. (The issues relating to this and your setting's policy for administering medication should have been discussed at the time of the child's enrolment.) Often, time is of the essence in these situations. Practitioners must ensure they are absolutely clear about what to do for the individual child, and they must know how to recognise their symptoms. The following guidance applies to all dietary requirements, but in the case of children with allergies and illnesses it can save a life.

It is VERY IMPORTANT to ensure you fully understand children's dietary requirements so that you efficiently meet their needs without error. Practitioners should ensure that full details are recorded on the registration form. They must communicate children's requirements to everyone involved in caring for the child. A list of requirements should be displayed in the kitchen and eating area to remind all staff. These lists must be updated regularly so that they can be safely relied upon. *Never give a child food or drink without checking*. This also applies to raw cooking ingredients or food used in play that is not intended for consumption.

Encouraging healthy eating

It is good practice to make children aware of healthy foods and how good they are for their bodies. This establishes the link between food and health. It is generally considered appropriate to make children aware that no foods are completely unacceptable, but that sugary foods (such as sweets and many drinks) and those which are high in saturated fats (such as cakes) should be regarded as occasional treats.

The following diagram shows how you can encourage children of various ages to eat healthily.

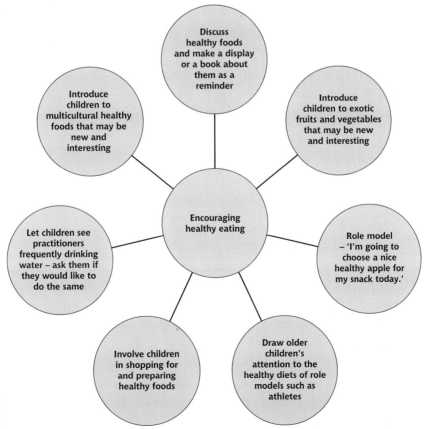

Encouraging
healthy eating

Encourage children to eat independently

Planning menus

When planning menus, including snacks and drinks, it is important to consider:

- The nutritional balance needed by children for a healthy diet – what have children eaten for their previous meal/snack, and what will they have next?
- The current government guidelines
- The time of day the food will be consumed
- Children's individual dietary requirements and allergies
- Children's preferences
- Variety
- Offering children new and interesting foods to try
- Involving children (see opposite)
- How food will be presented to add interest
- How families can be consulted.

If children are reluctant to try something new, or they do not like new food, practitioners are advised to simply remove it and offer an alternative. However, do present the food again on another occasion – some children change their mind once a food is familiar to them. If not, once again, do not make a fuss. Our tastes for food change throughout our lives – we go off things, or suddenly start to enjoy a taste. The child may enjoy the food at some point in the future.

Not making a fuss about food is a good general rule – battling with children over food is unproductive, and the child may come to dread mealtimes, which is not a very positive sign. If children regularly refuse food, not offering food outside of mealtimes can be the solution. If you are concerned about a child's eating habits, talk to their parents or carers to agree a way forward. Dieticians will advise if necessary.

Presenting food attractively

In group settings, mealtimes can feel hectic unless practitioners plan well. It is good practice to present food attractively to children and this can be achieved by setting the table set pleasantly, having all of the right utensils in place, and a creating a calm atmosphere – quiet, gentle music playing in the background can help to settle children at lunchtime after a busy morning.

Consider how much food you put on children's plates. You do not want children to go hungry, but too much food can be overwhelming and put a child off.

Consider how the food looks. Sometimes reluctant eaters can be intrigued if you present their food in a new creative way. For instance, there is nothing wrong with standing carrot batons up in mashed potato or making a tower out of sliced carrot – especially if it means the carrots are eaten!

Involving children in the planning and preparation of food

Involving children in the planning and preparation of food is a good way to ensure you are providing things they like and it is a good opportunity to discuss healthy foods. Children are often much keener to eat food they have helped to prepare. Children are even more eager when they have grown vegetables themselves. Even settings without access to a garden can grow herbs and cress in pots.

Children can help in many ways depending on their age, including:

- Washing fruit
- Scrubbing vegetables
- Cutting fruit (soft fruits such as bananas can be easily cut or mashed with children's knives)
- Putting spread on bread or toast
- Making sandwiches
- Preparing salad
- Growing vegetables
- Harvesting vegetables
- Mixing drinks
- Pouring out drinks
- Sharing out food
- Setting the table
- Washing the dishes.

Encouraging independence in feeding

From birth to three months, babies are fed entirely on milk. Somewhere between three and six months babies are gradually introduced to pureed, smooth foods. This process is called weaning. There are further details in Unit CCLD 314 Provide physical care that promotes the health and development of babies and children under three years.

By nine months most babies are able to sit up straight in a high chair. From about 12 months most children are eating a normal diet rather than baby food. By two years old most children can eat within a social group at the table since they are fairly independent and proficient with a spoon and beaker. Now is the time to introduce a fork and, when that is mastered, a knife. Most children can use a knife and fork by the time they are four, developing the proficiency to cut most food themselves at five.

You must ensure that you only encourage a child's independence in feeding themselves in accordance with the wishes of their family. For instance, there are some cultural practices associated with feeding that differ from the process described above.

Link **Unit CCLD 314** Provide physical care that promotes the health and development of babies and children under three years

Allow children to eat independently

Good oral hygiene

A child's first set of teeth, known as milk teeth, usually start to appear during the first year, but some children do not cut their first tooth until they are two years old. Most children have all 20 of their milk teeth by the time they are three.

From the age of five or six, children's milk teeth begin to fall out as their permanent teeth grow from inside the gum and eventually push them out. Thirty-two permanent teeth are expected in all. As the name suggests, these teeth should be kept as long as possible – hopefully a lifetime – so it is very important to look after them from the outset.

Cleaning the teeth should become a habit from the time a baby has their very first tooth. Even before then you can introduce babies to a baby's toothbrush (designed to be soft and small) so that they become familiar with it – they will naturally take it

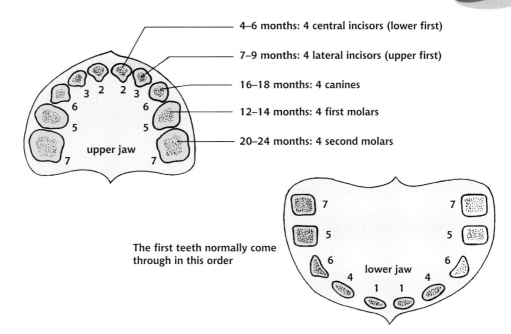

4–6 months: 4 central incisors (lower first)

7–9 months: 4 lateral incisors (upper first)

16–18 months: 4 canines

12–14 months: 4 first molars

20–24 months: 4 second molars

The first teeth normally come through in this order

Tooth development

to their mouth to explore it. Very gently clean the first tooth with the brush, morning and evening, so that the habit is formed. Children should be encouraged to:

- Begin brushing their own teeth as soon as they are able
- Brush at least twice a day: after breakfast and after the last time they eat or drink before bedtime
- Brush after all meals if possible. Some settings facilitate this and minimise cross-infection from toothbrushes by providing safe individual storage for each child's own brush
- Visit the dentist regularly. It is a good idea to read stories about going to the dentist to familiarise children with this process. Role play can also be helpful.

Cleaning teeth should be a daily habit

Families are generally encouraged to take a child along to an adult's appointment initially before they have an appointment of their own. Do your best to ensure children do not become aware of any adult fears of the dentist's surgery

- Eat a healthy diet that is high in calcium (which is good for teeth) and low in sugar (which encourages decay). Avoid giving children sugary snacks between meals. Sugary drinks should also be avoided. Never give sweet drinks from a bottle as this helps to coat the teeth with sugar. Sugar can even pass through the gums and cause decay in teeth that have yet to come through

- Eat foods that are hard and crunchy to chew as they are good for teeth and gums – apples, raw carrot and celery are good options.

Basic food hygiene

It is extremely important for all practitioners to be aware of basic food hygiene regimes and to observe them closely. Children can become seriously ill if food becomes contaminated. It is good practice for all practitioners handling and preparing food to take a course in Basic Food Hygiene. The principles of basic food hygiene are included in Unit CCLD 302 Develop and maintain a healthy, safe and secure environment for children.

A separate rubbish bin with a lid should be used for the disposal of food, and this should be emptied daily so that perishing food items do not cause cross-contamination. The bin should not be accessible to children.

 Link   **Unit CCLD 302** Develop and maintain a healthy, safe and secure environment for children

Element 307.2

Are you ready for assessment?

Plan and provide food and drink to meet the nutritional needs of children

You need to show that you can competently plan and provide food and drink to meet the nutritional needs of children. To do this you will need to be directly observed by your assessor and present other types of evidence. The amount and type of evidence you need to present will vary. You should plan this with your assessor.

Direct observation by your assessor

Observation and/or expert witness testimony is the required assessment method to be used to evidence some of each element in this unit. If your assessor is unable to observe you,

s/he will identify an expert in your workplace who will provide testimony of your work-based performance. Usually your assessor or expert witness will observe you in real work activities and this should provide most of the evidence for the performance criteria for the elements in this unit.

Preparing to be observed

You must show your assessor that you can plan menus that meet the dietary and nutritional needs of children in line with relevant guidelines, involving children in planning and preparation where appropriate. You must also show that you can provide interesting food and encourage healthy choices and independence. You must show that you can ensure high standards of hygiene, document dietary requirements and share this information with the relevant people.

You will need to arrange to be assessed at a time when you will be preparing and providing food and drink.

Other types of evidence

You will need to present different types of evidence in order to:

- Cover criteria not observed by your assessor
- Show that you have the required knowledge, understanding and skills.

Such evidence could include:

- Work products such as menus and food-preparation activity plans
- Case studies, projects, assignments and reflective accounts of your work
- Confidential records such as individual children's dietary requirements. These should not be placed in your portfolio – they must remain in their usual location and be referred to in the assessor records in your portfolio.

Element 307.3

Promote children's healthy physical development

Raising children's awareness of their own bodies

K3H303
K3H304
K3H305

Children need to develop an awareness of their own bodies in order to learn how to care for themselves and keep themselves healthy and safe. This is an ongoing process for children because their bodies are changing and developing all the time. They will find they can do things they could not do before, such as reach a shelf, but that they can no longer do other things, such as sitting in a high chair or fitting into a favourite hiding spot. These changes continue until children become adolescents – and that brings even more change. Children will benefit from understanding that in order to grow and develop their body needs healthy food, water, exercise, rest and to be cared for in a hygienic way.

In addition, all children will experience times when they feel unwell. For some children with chronic illnesses, there may be frequent instances of this. Children need to learn to recognise how their bodies are feeling and what their bodies might need. That begins with simple awareness. Ensure you provide activities in accordance with children's age, gender, needs and abilities. The following activities can be helpful:

- Themes such as 'All About Me'

    To encourage children to focus on themselves and their bodies

- Creating a photographic time line or height chart

  To show the growth and development of children visibly (Obtain parental permission before taking photographs of children)
- Role plays

  To act out feelings, both emotional and physical. This can be extended by developing the imaginary area into a hospital and so on
- Feeling charades

  Children act out feeling tired, thirsty and so on, and their peers attempt to guess the feeling
- Providing puppets and dolls with expressions

  For recognising feelings and using them in play
- Masks

  To allow children to 'try on' feelings
- Stories

  That show positive images of children who sometimes feel unwell or have physical difficulties. Stories about feelings and about children growing up and developing
- Linking up events and changes in children's minds

  'You were very hot and bothered, but you're feeling better now you've had a drink', or 'You were a bit breathless, but you took your inhaler, had a sit down, and now you're ready to play again', or 'You've got your energy back now because you had a good rest when you were tired'.

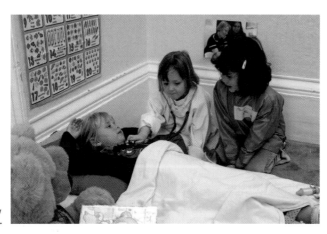

Imaginary play

Discussing healthy development

It is helpful to promote discussion about healthy development with children. This can be planned, and many of the activities listed above create a good, natural starting point. But it is also important to make the most of spontaneous opportunities to discuss development. Listen out for cues when children are talking to you. Answer their questions and ask them open questions to prompt their thinking. Discussions should be pitched and conducted appropriately, according to the children's age, needs and abilities.

Making positive health decisions

It is a practitioner's role to give children accurate information about health and the health decisions they have to make, in line with current best practice and government guidelines. However, thinking and policy change regularly, and it is up to practitioners to keep themselves fully up to date and informed. Professional early years journals are a good way of achieving this as they report changes within the industry when they occur.

A good understanding of the body and what it needs can help children to make positive health decisions.

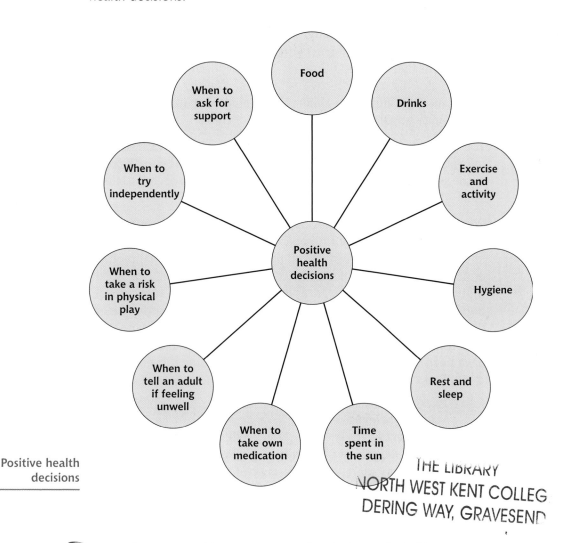

Positive health
decisions

Chronic illnesses and physical difficulties

Children who have chronic illnesses and physical difficulties must be given opportunities to join in fully with all discussions and activities. Discussions about health, development and their well-being are particularly important. Monitor sensitively to see if children need support in doing this – children might be aware that their own experiences are different to those of their peers, particularly as they mature, so they may feel self-conscious. However, you should be led by what the child feels comfortable discussing and doing at that time.

All children need to be given equal opportunities to participate in all activities. Children with chronic illnesses may miss sessions due to feeling unwell or due to frequent health-related appointments at places such as hospitals. Practitioners can keep track of children's participation, so they can identify key activities to make available to that child when they are in attendance. Children with chronic illnesses may have good days and bad days in terms of how they feel – although there may be no reason why they should not attend the setting. Practitioners should be sensitive to this.

Children with chronic illness may tire quickly and so miss out on activities, even when they are present at the setting. Do not be tempted to encourage them to participate when they are tired and don't under-estimate how bad a child with a chronic illness can feel when they are tired. When a child is tired, their body and mind needs to rest, so reschedule activities accordingly. If there is a pattern to a child's energy levels, try to make the most of it, doing activities that require good concentration first thing in the morning, if that is a good time for them. Work in partnership with children and their families to discover effective strategies. Missing out on activities and sporadic attendance can impact on children's development and progress because they have less opportunity to participate.

The physical development of children with chronic illnesses and physical difficulties may also be affected in other ways. Children may not be expected to develop and grow in the same way as their peers, or they may not be expected to develop certain physical skills. Strength and stamina may also be affected.

Practitioners can seek further support and information about particular conditions. The child's family will be the first point of contact. Parents and carers are often very well informed about their child's condition, and are usually happy that you are seeking to understand their child better by asking for their assistance, so they will pass on all the information they can. In addition, libraries keep a record of contact details for organisations that support people who have chronic conditions or who are caring for those with chronic conditions. For instance, there are organisations supporting those with asthma, heart conditions, childhood cancers, ME and epilepsy. The organisations have been set up to help people, and they welcome those who use their services.

Cassius monitors progress

Practitioner Cassius knows that Heidi, one of his key children, is not expected to develop in the same way as her peers. She generally uses a wheelchair although she walks very short distances using crutches. Little development or change is expected in terms of her physical locomotive skills. Cassius talks with Heidi's parents and finds out what alternative skills she is likely to learn so that he can encourage her progress and look out for achievements. She is currently learning how to manoeuvre her wheelchair up and down a single step.

There are no steps at the setting, so Cassius was previously unaware of this. Cassius asks Heidi's parents to let him know how she gets on. This allows him to monitor Heidi's progress. When she has successfully learnt the skill, Cassius will be able to record it and celebrate Heidi's achievement with her.

➤ *Why was it important for Cassius to talk with Heidi's parents?*
K3H305, K3D292, K3D289

Health surveillance

The term 'health surveillance' can be explained as close supervision or observations that are primarily carried out to detect any problems with a child or young person's development, with the aim of getting them the appropriate support and/or treatment early on. Health visitors and the primary health-care team have local responsibilities to manage limited resources, including the caseloads of workers. To help them, they may identify target groups of people who are likely to benefit most from health surveillance. This may include:

- Families living in bed and breakfast accommodation
- Families living in poor housing
- Families living in poverty
- Families dealing with a bereavement
- Families within which a previous child died from Sudden Infant Death Syndrome (SIDS)
- Very young parents
- Parents who are isolated – they may have little or no support from other adults, have emotional difficulties (mental health difficulties), or experience cultural, linguistic or environmental barriers (if they are disabled)
- Parents having difficulty relating to their child or understanding their needs, particularly with their first child
- Parents with low self-esteem and/or confidence, particularly with their first child
- Where there are concerns that abuse may take place within a family.

The role of immunisation

The role of immunisation is to protect children from serious diseases that may result in death or impairment. The word 'immunisation' comes from the word 'immunity'. Immunity is when the body is able to resist the infections that it comes into contact with. The infections are caused by pathogens.

People build up a certain amount of immunity naturally after having had illnesses. They also gain immunity through immunisations. These two methods of building up immunity are known as 'active immunity'. Via the placenta, unborn babies gain immunity to illnesses that their mother is immune to. When they are born their mother's breast milk continues to provide some immunity. This is known as 'passive immunity'.

The NHS routine immunisation programme, at the time of writing, is shown in the table.

The immunisation programme

When to immunise	Diseases protected against	Vaccine given
Two months old	Diphtheria, tetanus, pertussis (whooping cough), polio and Haemophilus influenzae type b (Hib) Pneumococcal infection	DTaP/IPV/Hib + Pneumococcal conjugate vaccine (PCV)

When to immunise	Diseases protected against	Vaccine given
Three months old	Diphtheria, tetanus, pertussis, polio and Hib Meningitis C (MenC)	DTaP/IPV/Hib + MenC
Four months old	Diphtheria, tetanus, pertussis, polio and Hib MenC, Pneumococcal infection	DTaP/IPV/Hib + MenC + PCV
Around 12 months	Hib, MenC	Hib/MenC
Around 13 months old	Measles, mumps and rubella Pneumococcal infection	MMR + PCV
Three years and four months or soon after	Diphtheria, tetanus, pertussis and polio Measles, mumps and rubella	DTaP/IPV or dTaP/IPV +MMR
Girls aged 12 to 13 years	Cervical cancer caused by human papillomavirus types 16 and 18	HPV
13 to 18 years old	Diphtheria, tetanus, polio	Td/IPV

You can visit www.immunisation.nhs.uk/Immunisation_Schedule to find out more about immunisations, including those that are offered non-routinely: for example, the Hep B immunisation is offered at birth to babies whose mothers are Hepatitis B positive. Updates to the present schedule will also be posted on the site.

There has been controversy over the immunisation of children and recently about the MMR vaccine. If families ask your advice, you should refer them to their GP who is qualified to talk over their concerns with them and to help them make a decision.

Element 307.3

Are you ready for assessment?

Promote children's healthy physical development

You need to show that you can competently promote children's healthy physical development. To do this you will need to be directly observed by your assessor and present other types of evidence. The amount and type of evidence you need to present will vary. You should plan this with your assessor.

Direct observation by your assessor

Observation and/or expert witness testimony is the required assessment method to be used to

evidence some of each element in this unit. If your assessor is unable to observe you, s/he will identify an expert in your workplace who will provide testimony of your work-based performance. Usually your assessor or expert witness will observe you in real work activities and this should provide most of the evidence for the performance criteria for the elements in this unit.

Preparing to be observed

You must show your assessor that you can provide opportunities for children to learn about their bodies and their health needs, and for discussion about healthy physical development. You must also show that you can support children in making health decisions, and that you can ensure that those with chronic illness or physical difficulties can positively participate in discussions and activities.

Other types of evidence

You will need to present different types of evidence in order to:

- Cover criteria not observed by your assessor
- Show that you have the required knowledge, understanding and skills.

Such evidence could include:

- Work products such as activity plans and discussion notes
- Case studies, projects, assignments and reflective accounts of your work
- Confidential records such as children's individual participation plans. These should not be placed in your portfolio – they must remain in their usual location and be referred to in the assessor records in your portfolio.

Check your knowledge

- Name five activities that will encourage children's fine motor skills.   **K3D288**
- Name five activities that will encourage children's gross motor skills.   **K3D288**
- Explain what it means to balance challenge and risk.   **K3D291, K3H294**
- Why should you provide opportunities for children to rest and recover after physical activity?   **K3D293**
- Why must you ensure you understand and communicate children's dietary requirements?   **K3H297, K3S298**
- How can you encourage good oral hygiene?   **K3H300**
- What is health surveillance?   **K3H304**
- How may chronic illness affect development?   **K3H305**

Reflective practice

Choose to reflect on your provision of either gross motor skills activities or fine motor skills activities. Then think about the opportunities you have provided in that area over the last two weeks. Have the activities been sufficiently varied? Are there new opportunities you could introduce? (You may get some ideas from pages 195–9.)

UNIT 309

Plan and implement curriculum frameworks for early education

*T*his unit includes planning and implementing curriculum frameworks for early education within the four home countries – England, Ireland, Scotland and Wales. It includes the development of curriculum plans according to the framework being followed, the implementation of plans, and the monitoring and evaluation following implementation. The unit relates to work with younger children in the early stages of education.

The unit contains three elements:

⌒ **CCLD 309.1** *Prepare curriculum plans according to requirements*

⌒ **CCLD 309.2** *Implement curriculum plans*

⌒ **CCLD 309.3** *Monitor and reflect on implementation of curriculum frameworks*

Key Terms

Monitoring process/strategies

Methods, planning and approaches to monitoring. *(National Occupational Standards)*

Introduction

When it comes to offering high-quality provision, the way in which practitioners plan, implement and monitor curriculum frameworks for early education is at the heart of the matter. Good planning must be in place to ensure high-quality implementation, and plans are informed by the findings of the monitoring process. This ensures continual evolution and consistent high standards.

Element 309.1

Prepare curriculum plans according to requirements

K3D319
K3P320
K3D321
K3D322
K3D323
K3D324
K3D325
K3D326
K3D327
K3D328
K3D329
K3D330
K3D331
K3D332

⌒ ### Early education curriculum requirements

Most settings will plan how they will promote learning and development through the activities and care that they offer. Planning and the implementation of plans must be carried out in accordance with any statutory curriculum that applies to the setting. Some settings may choose to follow a non-statutory framework. Structured frameworks vary across the four home countries, although there are many similarities, including a focus on learning through play in the early years. Each country has its own inspectorate:

- In England, this is Ofsted (www.ofsted.gov.uk).
- In Scotland, this is Her Majesty's Inspectorate of Education (www.hime.gov.uk).

- In Wales, this is Estyn (www.estyn.gov.uk).
- In Northern Ireland, this is the Department of Education (www.deni.gov.uk).

Key Terms

Relevant inspection regime

Inspectorates in your home country that register and inspect your setting. *(National Occupational Standards)*

Early education framework

Frameworks that are discretionary or statutory, currently in use in the home country. *(National Occupational Standards)*

Inspectors working for the government visit settings and schools to inspect and judge the quality of their provision.

Curriculum frameworks in the home counties

The curriculum frameworks in England are the Early Years Foundation Stage and the National Curriculum. These are outlined on the following pages. In Scotland, there is the Excellence for All 3–18 Framework, which is currently being developed. You can find full, up-to-date information at www.ltscotland.org.uk/curriculumforexcellence/. A key Scottish document is *Birth to Three: Supporting Relationships, Responsive Care and Respect* (visit www.ltscotland.org.uk/Images/birthtthreeleaflet_tcm4-161670.pdf to read a guide to Birth to Three).

In Wales, children may be instructed in Welsh or English. There is a 10-year strategy in place, known as Learning Country. A new curriculum, the Framework for Children's Learning, is being introduced following a trial in some schools. There is a Foundation Phase for children aged three to seven years, which will be implemented in stages between 2008 and 2011. The National Curriculum has also recently been revised. You can find full, up-to-date information about both of these at wales.gov.uk/topics/educationandskills/?lang=en (select 'Curriculum and Assessment' from the menu).

In Northern Ireland, there is the *Curricular Guidance for Pre-School Education* (you can view this at www.deni.gov.uk/preschool_curricular-2.pdf). A Revised National Curriculum is being phased in between 2008 and 2010 (you can find full, up-to-date information at www.deni.gov.uk/index/80-curriculum-and-assessment.htm).

The Early Years Foundation Stage

Since September 2008, the Early Years Foundation Stage (EYFS) has been mandatory for:

- All schools
- All early years providers in Ofsted-registered settings.

It applies to children from birth to the end of the academic year in which the child has their fifth birthday.

In the *Statutory Framework for the Early Years Foundation Stage* the Department for Education and Skills tells us that:

'Every child deserves the best possible start in life and support to fulfil their potential. A child's experience in the early years has a major impact on their future life chances. A secure, safe and happy childhood is important in its own right, and it provides the foundation for children to make the most of their abilities and talents as they grow up. When parents choose to use early years services they want to know that provision will keep their children safe and help them to thrive. The Early Years Foundation Stage (EYFS) is the framework that provides that assurance. The overarching aim of the EYFS is to help young children achieve the five *Every Child Matters* outcomes …'

Every Child Matters is the government agenda that focuses on bringing together services to support children and families. It sets out five major outcomes for children:

- Being healthy
- Staying safe
- Enjoying and achieving
- Making a positive contribution
- Economic well-being.

The EYFS aims to meet the *Every Child Matters* outcomes by:

- **Setting standards** for the learning, development and care young children should experience when they attend a setting outside their family home – every child should make progress, with no children left behind
- **Providing equality of opportunity and anti-discriminatory practice**, ensuring that every child is included and not disadvantaged because of ethnicity, culture, religion, home language, family background, learning difficulties or disabilities, gender or ability
- **Creating a framework for partnership working between parents and professionals**, and between all the settings that the child attends
- **Improving quality and consistency in the early years** through standards that apply to all settings – this provides the basis for the inspection and regulation regime carried out by Ofsted
- **Laying a secure foundation for future learning** through learning and development that is planned around the individual needs and interests of the child –this is informed by the use of ongoing observational assessment.

Note: the EYFS replaces *The Curriculum Guidance for the Foundation Stage*, the Birth to Three Matters Framework and *The National Standards for Under 8s Daycare and Childminding*, which are now defunct.

Themes, Principles and Commitments

The EYFS is based around four Themes. Each theme is linked to a Principle. Each Principle is supported by four Commitments. The Commitments describe how their Principle can be put into action. The Themes, Principles and Commitments are shown in the table below.

Themes, Principles and Commitments

Theme	Principle	Commitments
1 A Unique Child	Every child is a competent learner from birth who can be resilient, capable, confident and self-assured	1.1 Child development 1.2 Inclusive practice 1.3 Keeping safe 1.4 Health and well-being

Theme	Principle	Commitments
2 Positive Relationships	Children learn to be strong and independent from a base of loving and secure relationships with parents and/or a key person	2.1 Respecting each other 2.2 Parents as partners 2.3 Supporting learning 2.4 Key person
3 Enabling Environments	The environment plays a key role in supporting and extending children's development and learning	3.1 Observation, assessment and planning 3.2 Supporting every child 3.3 The learning environment 3.4 The wider context
4 Learning and Development	Children develop and learn in different ways and at different rates. All areas of learning and development are equally important and interconnected	4.1 Play and exploration 4.2 Active learning 4.3 Creativity and critical thinking 4.4 Areas of learning and development

Additional statements are provided within the EYFS to explain each Commitment in more detail. You can see these on the Department for Education and Skills' 'Principles into Practice' poster, an extract from which is reproduced below.

'Principles into Practice'

Areas of Learning and Development

Theme 4, Learning and Development, contains six Areas of Learning and Development. These are shown in the diagram below.

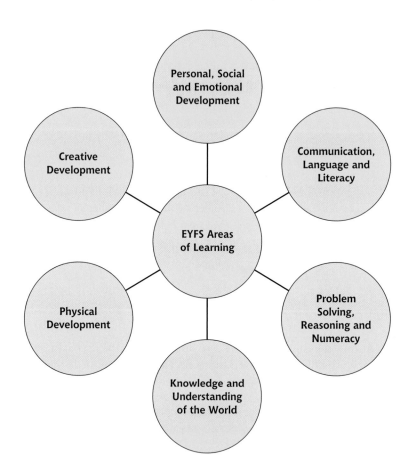

The Areas of Learning and Development

Each Area of Learning and Development is divided into Aspects. You can see these on the Department for Education and Skill's Learning and Development card, reproduced below. Together, the six Areas of Learning and Development make up the skills, knowledge and experiences appropriate for babies and children as they grow, learn and develop. Although these are presented as separate areas, it is important to remember that for children everything links and nothing is compartmentalised. All Areas of Learning and Development are connected to one another and are equally important. They are underpinned by the principles of the EYFS.

As you'll read below, there is a set of EYFS resource cards for practitioners. The set includes a card for each Area of Learning, which provides guidance on what practitioners must do to promote children's development and outlines what this means to children. You can find examples and further information in Unit CCLD 312. You are advised to read these pages in conjunction with this unit.

 **Link** **Unit CCLD 312** Plan and implement positive environments for babies and children under three years

Extract from a Department for Education and Skill's Learning and Development card

Welfare requirements

Settings must also meet the EYFS welfare requirements, which relate to:

- Safeguarding and promoting children's welfare
- Suitable people
- Suitable premises, environment and equipment
- Organisation
- Documentation.

These are in addition to the learning and development requirements.

 Link **Unit CCLD 306** Plan and organise environments for children and families

So what does all this mean?

Childcarers working in settings following the EYFS need to meet the standards for learning, development and care. Their responsibilities include:

- Planning a range of play and learning experiences that promote all of the Aspects within all of the Areas of Learning
- Assessing and monitoring individual children's progress through observational assessments
- Using the findings of observational assessments to inform the planning of play and learning experiences
- Ensuring that children's individual interests and abilities are promoted within the play and learning experiences.

In its *Key Elements of Effective Practice* (KEEP), the Department for Education and Skills tells us that:

> 'Effective practice in the early years requires committed, enthusiastic and reflective practitioners with a breadth and depth of knowledge, skills and understanding. Effective practitioners use their own learning to improve their work with young children and their families in ways which are sensitive, positive and non-judgemental.
>
> 'Therefore through initial and on-going training and development practitioners need to develop, demonstrate and continuously improve their:
>
> - relationships with both children and adults;
> - understanding of the individual and diverse ways that children learn and develop;
> - knowledge and understanding in order to actively support and extend children's learning in and across all areas and aspects of Learning and Development;
> - practice in meeting all children's needs, learning styles and interests;
> - work with parents, carers and the wider community;
> - work with other professionals within and beyond the setting.'

EYFS resources for childcarers

The EYFS pack of resources for providers includes the following elements.

The Statutory Framework for the Early Years Foundation Stage

This booklet sets out:

- The welfare requirements

  These set out providers' duties to ensure children's welfare and well-being within the setting
- The learning and development requirements

  These set out providers' duties under each of the six Areas of Learning and Development.

Practice Guidance for the Early Years Foundation Stage

This booklet provides further guidance on:

- Legal requirements
- The Areas of Learning and Development
- The EYFS principles
- Assessment.

Twenty-four cards

These give the Principles and Commitments at a glance, with guidance on putting the principles into practice; they include an overview of child development.

CD-ROM

This contains all the information from the booklets and cards. It includes information on effective practice, research and resources. This can also be accessed via the EYFS website (www.standards.dcsf.gov.uk/eyfs/).

It is a good idea to take the overview tour to familiarise yourself with the site on your first visit. You can then follow the links to the Areas of Learning, and read more about the Aspects, then follow the links to 'Principles in practice' for examples of how practitioners following the EYFS work with children within their settings.

The National Curriculum

The English National Curriculum (National Curriculum) sets out the minimum curriculum requirements for all maintained schools, including:

- The subjects taught
- The knowledge, skills and understanding required in each subject
- Attainment targets in each subject
- How children's progress is assessed and reported.

Within the framework of the National Curriculum, schools are free to plan and organise teaching and learning themselves. Many schools choose to use schemes of work from the Qualifications and Curriculum Authority. These help to translate the National Curriculum's objectives into teaching and learning activities for children.

Key stages

The National Curriculum is divided into four key stages that children pass through as they move up through the school system. These stages are in addition to the Early Years Foundation Stage described earlier:

- Year 1 and Year 2 of primary school are known as Key Stage 1.
- Years 3 to 6 of primary school are known as Key Stage 2.
- Years 7 to 9 of secondary school are known as Key Stage 3.
- Years 10 to 11 of secondary school are known as Key Stage 4.

Subjects at Key Stages 1 and 2

The compulsory National Curriculum subjects for Key Stages 1 and 2 are:

- English
- Maths
- Science
- Design and technology
- Information and communication technology (ICT)
- History
- Geography
- Art and design
- Music
- Physical education

Schools also have to teach:

- Religious education.

    Parents have the right to withdraw children from the religious education curriculum if they choose.

Schools are advised to teach:

- Personal, social and health education (PSHE)
- Citizenship
- One or more modern foreign language.

There are attainment targets and a programme of study for each subject. Programmes of study describe the subject knowledge, skills and understanding that pupils are expected to develop during each key stage. It is acceptable for schools to use different names for the subjects, as long as they're covering the National Curriculum.

Levels and formal teacher assessments

Attainment targets are split into levels. Teachers carry out regular checks on children's progress in each subject. There will also be formal teacher assessment at the end of Key Stages 1–3. This indicates which National Curriculum level best describes individual children's performance in each subject. Schools send parents a report telling them what National Curriculum levels their child has reached in formal assessments. (Pupils will usually take GCSE/equivalent exams at the end of Key Stage 4.)

Subjects at Key Stages 3 and 4

Key Stage 3 compulsory National Curriculum subjects are:

- English
- Maths
- Science
- Design and technology
- Information and communication technology (ICT)
- History
- Geography
- Modern foreign languages
- Art and design
- Music
- Citizenship
- Physical education.

Schools also have to provide:

- Careers education and guidance (during Year 9)
- Sex and relationship education (SRE)
- Religious education

   Parents can choose to withdraw their child from religious education curriculum.

In Year 9, children do national tests and choose what to study at Key Stage 4, when they will study both compulsory and optional subjects. Most pupils work towards national qualifications. Pupils are advised to choose a balance of options to give them more choice when deciding on courses and jobs later on. Pupils may also choose from a growing range of vocational qualifications. The compulsory Key Stage 4 subjects are:

- English
- Maths
- Science
- Information and communication technology (ICT)
- Physical education
- Citizenship.

Schools must also provide:

- Careers education
- Work-related learning
- Religious education

    Parents can choose to withdraw their child from religious education curriculum

- Sex and relationship education (SRE)

One subject from each of the four 'entitlement' areas, which are:

- Arts subjects
- Design and technology
- Humanities
- Modern foreign languages.

Review of the curriculum

A new secondary curriculum was published in September 2007. Its aims include cutting back on compulsory subject content and developing pupil's personal attributes and practical life skills. The Department for Education and skills tells us that:

> 'The new Key Stage 3 curriculum will be brought in over a three year period. It becomes compulsory for Year 7 pupils in September 2008. From September 2009, it will apply to all Year 7 and Year 8 pupils, and from September 2010 it will apply across Years 7, 8 and 9. Changes to the Key Stage 4 curriculum will be brought in from September 2009.
>
> As part of changes to the curriculum for 14 to 19 year olds, from September 2008 a new Diploma qualification will be introduced alongside GCSEs and A levels in selected schools and colleges.'

For more information about the National Curriculum, follow the links at www.direct.gov.uk. For more information about the new secondary curriculum, visit the Qualifications and Curriculum Authority website at www.qca.org.uk.

The Children's Plan

In 2007, the Government published the *Children's Plan* which sets out ambitious new goals for 2020. The Plan is intended to:

- Strengthen support for all families during the formative early years of their children's lives
- Take the next steps in achieving world-class schools and an excellent education for every child
- Involve parents fully in their children's learning
- Help to make sure that young people have interesting and exciting things to do outside of school
- Provide more places for children to play safely.

The Government says that the Children's Plan:

'... also means a new leadership role for Children's Trusts in every area, a new role for schools as the centre of their communities, and more effective links between schools, the NHS and other children's services so that together they can engage parents and tackle all the barriers to the learning, health and happiness of every child.'

There will be regular reports on the progress the Government is making. For more information, visit www.dfes.gov.uk/publications/childrensplan/.

Many practitioners use shorthand to identify particular aspects of learning within an area of learning, particularly in plans and assessments. For instance, they may write 'KUS 2' to mean 'Designing and making skills' in 'Knowledge and understanding of the world'.

Helpful Stepping Stones show the way that children are likely to progress towards the ELGs. They identify what children need to develop if they are to reach the ELGs by the end of the Foundation Stage in terms of:

- Knowledge
- Skills
- Understanding
- Attitudes.

The Stepping Stones have three levels that are identified in the curriculum documents by bands of colour. The ELGs are also indicated by colour:

Yellow = Early Stepping Stones (that are most likely to be relevant to three-year-olds)

Blue = Mid Stepping Stones

Green = Late Stepping Stones

Grey = Early Learning Goal at the end of the Foundation Stage.

The Curriculum Guidance for the Foundation Stage (published by the Qualification Curriculum Authority) is a document that helps practitioners to plan the setting's curriculum. It identifies principles for good practice in early education. They are 'drawn from and evident in good and effective practice in early years settings' and they are 'the basis on which every part of the guidance has been developed, and are reflected throughout'. The principles state that:

- Effective education requires both a relevant curriculum and practitioners who understand and are able to implement the curriculum requirements
- Effective education requires practitioners who understand that children develop rapidly during the early years – physically, intellectually, emotionally and socially
- Practitioners should ensure that all children feel included, secure and valued
- Early years experience should build on what children already know and can do
- No child should be excluded or disadvantaged
- Parents and practitioners should work together
- To be effective, an early years curriculum should be carefully structured
- There should be opportunities for children to engage in activities planned by adults and also those that they plan or initiate themselves
- Practitioners must be able to observe and respond appropriately to children
- Well-planned, purposeful activities and appropriate intervention by practitioners will engage children in their learning process
- For children to have rich and stimulating experiences, the learning environment should be well planned and organised
- Above all, effective learning and development for young children requires high-quality care and education by practitioners.

Under the Ofsted regime, all settings that receive Nursery Education Grant Funding are required to offer high-quality provision. To ensure this, Ofsted inspectors visit settings periodically to conduct Ofsted inspections. They make judgements about the quality of the provision, and these are made public in an Ofsted report.

Learning and stages of development

Children's learning is affected by their stage of development, in all areas of their learning, and this will have informed the curriculum documents drawn up for your home country. (See Unit CCLD 303 Promote children's development.) Consider these examples:

- Children who are just beginning to walk alone cannot yet learn to jump – they have not reached the right stage in their physical development
- Children who currently only play in parallel (alongside others but with little interest in their activities) cannot yet learn to play co-operatively (taking turns, sharing) – they have not reached the right stage in their social and emotional development.

Link **Unit CCLD 303** Promote children's development

Concentration span

One of the key factors that affects children's learning is the development of their concentration span – that is the period of time that they are able to focus completely on one activity or task. Children's concentration span (or attention span) typically lengthens as they get older and develop. Three-year-olds can generally concentrate for a short period. By the time they are five this period has generally lengthened considerably. However, children's concentration spans vary considerably from child to child and even from activity to activity. It is the job of practitioners to provide interesting, engaging activities for children, which will capture their attention and encourage them to concentrate. It also helps to minimise distractions – for instance, ensuring adults cannot be heard talking at story time when you want children to listen, or keeping noisy and quiet activities separate as far as possible. However, practitioners should have realistic expectations of children's concentration.

Key Terms

Concentration span
The period of time that an individual child is able to focus completely on one activity or task.

Individual children's development

Practitioners need to have a good understanding of the stage of development of the individual children they are working with. This is established through observation and assessment (see Unit CCLD 310 Assess children's progress according to curriculum frameworks for early education and Unit 303 Promote children's development). Planning should be informed by assessment, since it identifies the developmental and learning progress of individual children. This will indicate if children need support in any area. It also allows the practitioner to anticipate what children are likely to learn next. They can then plan to meet the child's needs accordingly, with inclusion in mind

Link Unit CCLD 310 Assess children's progress according to curriculum frameworks for early education
Unit CCLD 303 Promote children's development

It is generally accepted that children need a variety of activities and experiences appropriate to their stage of development that will allow them to:

- Consolidate

  Consolidation is when children have opportunities to repeat activities and experiences, confirming their previous learning, practising skills and perhaps developing a deeper understanding. Children are naturally drawn to consolidating in their play, e.g. a child may frequently build the same house or aeroplane from small interlocking bricks

- Extend

  Extension occurs when children's existing learning is moved forward in a new way, perhaps by applying consolidated learning and skills to a new situation. For example, a child who has learnt to thread cotton reels learns to do the same with threading buttons. Practitioners can link activities to encourage such learning (see practical example below). Extension activities are particularly helpful when you are working with groups of children with different levels of development. For instance, you can plan a core activity for all of the children and follow this up with an extension activity for the children who are ready for it

● Challenge

Children are challenged when they are introduced to new activities and experiences that are just beyond their current competence, e.g. a child who has learnt to jump is introduced to the skill of hopping on one leg.

These strategies promote learning and development.

Antonio plans extension activities

Practitioner Antonio has planned to read a story about a bird that drops pebbles into a bottle of water to make the water level rise. Afterwards, one group of children goes outside with another practitioner to play with pebbles in the water tray. Antonio stays with a group of children who are ready for an extension activity he has planned. The children retell the story themselves using props – a bird puppet, pebbles, water and a bottle. They measure the water level and record how much it rises.

➤ *Why was it important for Antonio to plan two different activities for after story time?* **K3D329**

➤ *How did the extension activity extend the children's learning?* **K3D329**

Theories about how children learn and develop

Practitioners should understand theories about how children learn and develop. This allows them to support children effectively when planning to meet their needs and when working with them in practice. Some key theories about this are outlined here, but there are many books dedicated to the subject of learning, development and play theories. You may find it interesting to learn about additional theories and the research and experiments that underpin them. Psychologists and other theorists have been making observations on this subject for hundreds of years.

Piaget

Jean Piaget was born in 1896. He developed 'constructivist' theories that have been influential, although they have been challenged over the years. Piaget was the first to say that when children play they can make discoveries for themselves without being taught. He observed that children generally shared the same sequential pattern of learning, and he noted that children of the same age often made the same mistakes. This led him to believe that children's cognitive development (their ability to think, reason and understand) developed through a series of sequential stages of development. He believed that children should not be hurried through these stages as that would be detrimental – he said they should be allowed to pass through them naturally.

Piaget focused on children's cognitive development in isolation – he did not consider other areas, such as children's social and emotional development. He referred to children as 'lone scientists' believing that adults should seek to provide environments where children could make their own discoveries. The idea that adults should intervene only sensitively in children's play stemmed from Piaget.

Piaget referred to children at play as 'active participants in their own learning'. He believed that children use their first-hand and previous experiences to learn. He thought children made assumptions based on experiences – he called these 'schemas'. Piaget called the process of applying one schema to another circumstance 'assimilation'. For example, imagine a child had only ever poured water through a funnel. They then discover that dry sand will also pass through the funnel. They have assimilated a new concept into their existing schema – sand and water can both pass through funnels.

Piaget believed that when children cannot fit a new experience into an existing schema, they create a new schema that will fit. He called this process 'accommodation'. For example, a child who has only ever eaten one type of biscuit may believe that all biscuits taste the same. When they find out this is not the case, they accommodate a new schema – different biscuits have different tastes.

To take our first example, accommodation may take place if a child discovers that wet sand will not pass easily through a funnel in the same way as dry sand or water.

Piaget believed that children pass through four stages of cognitive development. He did not believe that everyone would attain every stage, particularly stage four:

Piaget's stages of cognitive development

Stage One: Sensory-motor. Child's Age: 0–2yrs
Key Aspects: Babies use their sense to learn. They can only see things from their own point of view – they are 'egocentric'. They do not know that something they cannot see still exists, e.g. if a ball rolls out of view, they will not look for it. At about 18 months this changes. They have then achieved 'object permanence'

Stage Two: Pre-operational. Child's Age: 2–7yrs
Key Aspects: Children are still 'egocentric'. They believe animals and inanimate objects have the same feelings as people – they are 'animalistic'. They use language to express their thoughts, and use symbols in their play, e.g. they pretend a length of string is a snake

Stage Three: Concrete Operations. Child's Age: 7–11yrs
Key Aspects: Now children 'decentre' – they can see other points of view and understand that inanimate objects do not have feelings. They are establishing complex reasoning skills, and they can use writing and other symbols, e.g. mathematical symbols – this is called 'conservation'

Stage Four: Formal Operations. Child's Age: 11–adulthood
Key Aspects: Children can use logic and work methodically. They can think 'in abstract' – doing mental arithmetic and thinking things through internally. They can problem solve thoughtfully

---

How Piaget's theory may influence your practice today:

It is generally agreed that while adults can enhance children's play experiences, they should only intervene sensitively, particularly during imaginative play when they should take their cues from children, only joining in when invited, when play is flagging or when children are about to do something inappropriate or unsafe.

Piaget's theory

Vygotsky

Lev Vygotsky, born in 1896, was one of the first academics to disagree with Piaget. He died when in his thirties, so his career was short, but he has had a major impact on current thinking. He believed that children learn through social interaction and relationships, through the social tool of language. His theory is called the 'social constructivist theory'.

Interested in children's play, he was of the opinion that all play contains an imaginative element, and that this is freeing for children. He agreed with Piaget that children at play are 'active participants in their own learning'. However, he felt that the emotional aspect of play was as important as the learning aspect. He believed that play was a good way to learn, but he did not think it was the only way.

He developed a concept known as 'the zone of proximal development' which centres around the idea that adults can help children learn, and that children can also help one another. This idea has become known as the 'Vygotsky tutorial'. The Russian word 'proximal' translates to the word 'nearby'. He used the term 'the zone of actual development' to describe the things that children can do without any help at all, and the term 'zone of proximal development' to describe the things that children could potentially do with assistance – the learning that was next or 'nearby'.

He believed that children should always be challenged by some activities that are just beyond them and in their current zone of proximal development, as this would motivate them and move their learning forward. The process of offering activities that will slightly stretch children in this way is referred to as 'scaffolding learning'. In summary, through scaffolding learning with some challenging activities just beyond what a child can do, children can move from the actual zone of development to the proximal zone of development. This contrasts with Piaget's view that children should be allowed to pass through the stages of development naturally with little intervention.

How Vygotsky's theory may influence your practice today:

You may group children of different skill levels together for an activity, and encourage children to help one another – this is the 'Vygotsky tutorial' in action. He believed that all children would benefit – the 'learner' by learning the new skill or concept and the 'teacher' by developing a deeper understanding of their existing skill or concept.

Vygotsky's theory

Burrus Skinner

Burrus Skinner was born in 1904. He discovered a theory known as 'operant conditioning'. He demonstrated how this worked in experiments conducted with rats. He gave rats food as a reward when they displayed behaviour he wanted, in this case pressing a lever. He did not feed them otherwise. The rats learnt to repeat the rewarded behaviour. They would systematically press the lever and then wait at the position in the cage where the food was dispensed. He called this 'positive reinforcement'. He also taught them not to display behaviour he did not want – he gave them electric shocks when they entered a specific area of a maze he created. They learnt to avoid the area.

Skinner's theory

How Skinner's theory may influence your practice today:

Skinner's theory of positive reinforcement is still widely used today in the behaviour management of children. We reward children with praise, attention and sometimes tangible items such as stickers when they behave well, to encourage them to repeat the desirable behaviour

Jerome Bruner

Jerome Bruner was born in 1915. He extended Vygotsky's theories, and called his new theory the 'spiral curriculum'. This makes reference to his belief that children learn through discovery with the direct assistance of adults who should provide opportunities for them to return to the same activities (in terms of materials and ideas) again and again. He believed that by doing this children would extend and deepen their learning of the concepts and ideas that adults introduce to them.

He observed how children like to return to activities over a period of some years, and felt they are motivated to learn through the spiral curriculum. You may have noticed children who enjoy building the same model time and again, or drawing the same pictures. Resources like interlocking bricks can be a favourite of children for some years.

Bruner's theory

How Bruner's theory may influence your practice:

It is generally accepted that children should have plenty of opportunities for free-play and child-initiated activities. This allows them to revisit previous experiences or ideas if they would like to. In addition, it is widely believed that children should be provided with activities to consolidate existing learning and new opportunities to challenge and motivate them.

Neuro-scientists

New theories about the way in which human beings think, remember and learn are being developed in light of new technology that has emerged in recent years. Using advanced imaging techniques, neuro-scientists (brain scientists) can now look right inside living, functioning brains. They can actually watch what happens when people are thinking, remembering and learning. Interesting new research is being carried out around the world. Practitioners are advised to keep themselves up to date with developments. Professional journals are a good source of new information as it is released.

Curriculum planning

Practitioners must plan how they will provide activities and experiences that will promote children's learning and development and help them to progress, in line with any learning frameworks that apply to the setting. Planning allows practitioners to ensure that the learning environment is:

- Purposeful

  Play and activities should benefit children in terms of learning and experience. (Don't forget that having fun is an experience!)

- Supportive

  Activities and play are planned with regard to the support that individual children may need. They are also devised with children's sense of confidence, self-esteem and general well-being in mind

- Challenging

  Opportunities that challenge children are offered as well as those that consolidate learning. This encourages motivation and progression in terms of learning

- Varied

  There should be both planned adult-led activities as well as free-play and child-initiated activities. Learning should take place both indoors and outside. A range of physically active pursuits should be offered as well as those that require quiet concentration

- Balanced

  Opportunities should be provided to stimulate children's learning in all areas of their development and learning, and they should appeal to different styles of learner

- Vibrant and exciting

  Interesting, exciting activities motivate children, helping to foster a love of learning and discovery.

Practitioners make plans to show how learning will take place in the:

- Short term
- Medium term
- Long term.

Most practitioners approach this by planning for the long term first, then the medium term and lastly the short term.

Making and recording plans

There are many good ways to make and record plans. Examples are given here, but it is important that you follow your setting's requirements when drawing up your own plans.

Long-term planning

▶ Long-term planning

	SEPT	OCT	NOV	DEC	JAN	FEB	MARCH	APRIL	MAY	JUNE	JULY	AUG
Theme	Autumn	Animals	Light	Patterns	Winter	Storytime	Health	Spring in the garden	Carnival	Summer holidays	Sport	Our homes
Special events and activities	Trip to country park	Visits to children's farm	Diwali visit to Hindu temple	Visit by artist Christmas	Parents' evening	Visit from an African story teller	Visits from a dentist and a doctor	Trip to garden centre	Fancy dress party	Picnic by the sea	Sports open day	Family barbecue
PSED												
CLL												
PRN												
KUW												
PD												
CD												

The aspects of Learning and Development to be promoted are entered here. Settings often number the bullet points of the aspects so that they can be identified easily on the plans, e.g. if ICT is being promoted, practitioners may enter 'KUW 3'.

Short-term planning

▶ Short-term planning

THEME: 'All About Me'   DATE: 10–14 September

WHAT DO WE WANT THE CHILDREN TO LEARN?		HOW WILL WE ENABLE THIS LEARNING TO TAKE PLACE?	HOW WILL WE KNOW WHO HAS LEARNED WHAT?	WHAT NEXT?
LEARNING INTENTIONS BASED ON THE ASPECTS OF LEARNING AND DEVELOPMENT	VOCABULARY	ACTIVITIES/ ROUTINES	ASSESSMENT	NOTES ON HOW ASSESSMENTS MADE WILL INFORM FUTURE PLANS
Personal, social and emotional development	Separate from family with support	Greetings in various languages	Self-registration Selecting activities Changing books	Note which children are finding it hard to separate	[This column will be filled as assessments are made.]
Communication, language and literacy	Talk about home/ community. Listen to others Enjoy rhymes Show awareness of rhymes Use talk to connect ideas Listen with enjoyment and respond to stories, songs and other music, rhymes and poems and make up their own stories, rhymes and poems	Names of body parts Names for family Alliteration in rhymes	Circle time focus Make a class book about the children Sing and recite favourite nursery rhymes	Collect examples of stages in drawing and mark making Record significant comments made by the children	

The short-term planning example shows that a theme has been selected. While it is generally agreed that themes are not beneficial for younger children, i.e. those under two and a half years, many settings do find them effective for older children. They can

THEME: 'All About Me'   DATE: 10–14 September

	WHAT DO WE WANT THE CHILDREN TO LEARN?		HOW WILL WE ENABLE THIS LEARNING TO TAKE PLACE?	HOW WILL WE KNOW WHO HAS LEARNED WHAT?	WHAT NEXT?
	LEARNING INTENTIONS BASED ON THE ASPECTS OF LEARNING AND DEVELOPMENT	VOCABULARY	ACTIVITIES/ ROUTINES	ASSESSMENT	NOTES ON HOW ASSESSMENTS MADE WILL INFORM FUTURE PLANS
Problem solving, reasoning and numeracy	Numbers connected with home Numbers in games Show an interest in numbers and counting Use number names Begin to understand and use numbers	Counting numbers more/less	Workshop – making house fronts Counting games in garden	List children who know and can use numbers 1–5 List children who are aware of larger numbers	
Knowledge and understanding of the world	The 'Now' and 'Me' in the past Show interest in the lives of people familiar to them Begin to understand past	Family name Home Work Body parts	Circle time focus Collect baby photos Take photos Class book (graphic)	Checklist of the names of the parts of the body	
Physical development	Use space safely Show increasing control in using equipment Use tools appropriately Understand equipment and tools have to be used safely	Climb, jump, scramble swing Cut, stick	Garden – climbing equipment, etc. Workshop and graphics	Record children who use/do not use equipment Note on their ability to cut with scissors Record right- and left-handed children	
Creative development	Use bodies to investigate colours and textures	Feel hard, soft, rough smooth	Creative area Finger painting Materials for collages	Keep selection of items for 'me' booklet	

be a good way to link activities and play experiences, making them purposeful and progressive. The following table shows how a group of practitioners may plan a theme together for a setting following the Early Years Foundation Stage.

Theme-planning process

STEP ONE
Take a theme and set a timescale, e.g. Gardening, two weeks
(This may be informed by the long-term plan.) Let parents and carers know the theme and encourage them to become involved – with planning ideas, or collecting resources perhaps
STEP TWO
Divide the theme into subcategories, identifying a logical order for progressive learning, e.g. Planting, Growing, etc.
STEP THREE
Referring to the Aspects within the Area of learning, plan activities and play for children's learning, related to the theme. Take account of individual children's needs, play plans and individual learning styles. Plan a balance of activities and play across the curriculum, for all areas of learning
STEP FOUR
Take the activities and play opportunities identified, and fit them into a timetable for each week, around the normal routines such as circle time and snack time. Ensure variation between the types of activities to keep children interested and to give time for being active as well as time for them to rest and recharge their batteries, taking children's attendance patterns into consideration
STEP FIVE
Identify the roles of adults. Who will do what, and how should children be generally supported? What resources/equipment are needed, and who will organise them?
STEP SIX
Identify opportunities for assessment/observation and plan for them
STEP SEVEN
Identify how the plan will be monitored/evaluated
It is important to note that everything does not need to be themed, and that a theme need not cover all aspects of learning – in fact, this could be rather overwhelming. Routine activities such as news time or pouring out drinks should still be recognised as learning opportunities although they are not theme related. Free-play and child-initiated activities should not be replaced with themed activities

Consultation, roles and responsibilities

It is good practice to involve parents, carers and families in the planning of provision, regardless of whether a theme is used. Familiarity with the setting's plans can help parents and carers to understand how the EYFS works and how their children are learning. You may have parents and carers who would like to join in and suggest ideas, which is to be encouraged. However, many parents and carers may be willing to participate in other ways. For instance, they can help to collect resources (such as yoghurt pots to plant seeds in), or they might like to volunteer practical help during a session. A parent or carer may be able to visit the group to share something with the children – perhaps to show them their family's new pet kitten, or to demonstrate a skill they use in their job.

In addition it is important that colleagues plan together where possible, or make another arrangement for consultation on planning matters. This allows for a melting pot of ideas, and it also shares the workload. It is an effective way to make sure that everyone understands their roles and responsibilities during a session (that includes volunteer helpers and students) so that the children can be supported effectively, and the activities led as intended. If roles and responsibilities are not clearly defined, the implementation of the plan may well be adversely affected.

Outside professionals may also contribute to plans when appropriate: for instance, a speech and language therapist may suggest ideas for the support of a child with communication difficulties.

It is also important to consult children when supporting their learning, as appropriate to their abilities. This promotes 'active learning'. It also helps you to plan activities that meet children's needs, and to work with children in the ways that suit them best. Babies and very young children won't be able to tell you what they want verbally. But by being a responsive carer, you can notice what they want and how they want to do things. Think of it as a kind of 'silent consultation'.

Adequate resources

Organisation is behind successfully managing resources. It is very frustrating when activity plans cannot be fulfilled because of a lack of resources, and it is ultimately detrimental to the children's experience, so it is well worth the effort required to maintain adequate stock levels.

Consumable items such as paper, paint, glue, crayons and so on will need replenishing. Settings often order their resources from catalogues, and it is not uncommon for items to take three or four weeks to arrive. There should be systems in place to monitor the stock levels so that these essential items can be ordered in plenty of time. This requires team effort. The person ordering may monitor levels occasionally, but they will need to be informed if you notice you will be short of an item after you have taken what you need, and they will need to know ahead of time if you will be using a lot of a resource – card at Christmas time, for example. Equipment that becomes damaged or worn will also need to be replaced.

If you are the person responsible for ordering, scanning the future activities planned will help you to anticipate the setting's resource requirements. Many settings identify the resources that will be needed directly on their plans, which can be a useful way of ensuring they are available and organised in advance. If special resources are to be brought in by children and/or staff (favourite soft toys, for example), it is important that the appropriate adults are clear about what to bring in and when.

Depending on your organisational procedures, you may need superiors to approve your resource requirements. This may need to be done well ahead of time, to allow first for the approval and then the subsequent purchasing. You should also allow time to acquire books and other support materials from the library if necessary.

You may need to check the availability of equipment. For example, in a day nursery some pieces may be shared between units, so it will be necessary for staff to consult on its use. You should consider if any special resources or equipment are necessary to support children's individual learning needs.

Appropriate resources

It takes a wide range of equipment and materials to support a diverse range of activities and experiences. The list is extensive; the table shows a few examples for each area of learning in the Early Years Foundation Stage.

Resources

AREA OF LEARNING	RESOURCES/EQUIPMENT	ACTIVITIES
Personal, social and emotional development	Puppets, dolls and soft toys (with expressions for exploring feelings), table-top games, dressing-up clothes, cultural artefacts, a range of dolls showing a representation of people in the world (in terms of ethnicity, age, gender, ability), well-resourced imaginary areas including a home corner, comfortable quiet areas for resting and talking	New activities to build confidence, excitement, motivation to learn: leaves in the water tray, or earth to dig instead of sand, games for rules and turn taking, celebrating festivals for awareness and respect of the wider world, handling living things for sensitivity, pouring drinks for independence, circle time for talking about home
Communication, language and literacy	Varied range of mark-making materials and paper, letter frieze, letter cards/tiles/magnetic letters, comfortable book area/corner, books, pictures, poetry, fiction and non-fiction, story tapes, talking books, word processor, musical recordings, communication boards, signs, notices, labels, lists, sequencing cards/pictures	Story time, children retelling stories with props for understanding elements of stories, feely bags to promote descriptive language, role play for negotiation, mark-making opportunities in role-play area for writing with purpose, participating in and making up stories, rhymes, songs and poems, opportunities to write alongside adults
Problem solving, reasoning and numeracy	Counting beads, sorting trays, diverse objects to sort, scales, weights, rulers, measures, height chart, number cards/tiles/magnetic numbers, number and shape friezes/posters, number line, number signs/notices/symbols and labels, shape sorters, shape puzzles, different shaped construction resources, clocks, cash till, money	Counting how many we need (cups, for example), sharing out for calculating, singing number songs/rhymes for number operations (e.g. 'How many speckled frogs are left now?'), tidying up for sorting objects/positioning (e.g. 'That goes on the shelf'), finding numbers on our doors for number recognition, weighing cooking ingredients

AREA OF LEARNING	RESOURCES/EQUIPMENT	ACTIVITIES
Knowledge and understanding of the world	ICT resources (e.g. computers, programmable toys, tape recorders), magnifying glasses, binoculars, money, books and CD-ROMs, water and sand tray/water and sand resources (e.g. funnels, wheels, rakes) living plants, manufactured construction materials (e.g. interlocking bricks), natural resources (e.g. fir cones, wooden logs)	Bark rubbings for observing closely, looking up information for asking questions and investigation, growing plants from seeds for observing change, patterns, similarities and differences, going for a walk and discussing ICT, e.g. traffic lights to identify technology, making recycled models from junk for building and joining
Physical development	Tools – scissors, brushes, rolling pins, cutters, computer mouse, etc. – threading beads, play dough/cornflour paste/jelly, different sized balls, hoops and quoits, large wheeled toys (ride-on toys), tunnels, carts to push and pull, low stilts, skittles, hoopla, bats, parachutes, slide, climbing frame, balance beam, swing, stepping stones	Playground games, e.g. 'What's the time Mr Wolf?' for movement – creeping, running etc., negotiating a chalk-drawn 'road' on wheeled toys for awareness of space (themselves and others), obstacle courses for travelling around, under, over and through, pretending to go 'on a bear hunt' for moving with confidence/imagination
Creative development	Diverse range of art and craft resources including different colours and textures, e.g. paper, card, tissue, cellophane, paint, glue, felt tips, crayons, craft feathers, lollipop sticks, sequins, buttons, pipe cleaners, etc., musical recordings, musical instruments, equipped role-play areas, dolls	Painting anywhere outside with water and large brushes for expression and imagination, making tactile collages for responding to what they see, touch and feel, music and movement for using imagination in movement and dance, singing time with musical instruments for play with expression

Remember: children's learning is not compartmentalised – all of these activities and resources can be used in many ways to promote different aspects/areas of learning, even at the same time

Learning styles

People (adults and children) have different preferred styles of learning, that is, ways of learning that are particularly effective for them. The styles are known as:

- Visual
- Auditory
- Kinaesthetic.

There are some differing theories about these, but essentially styles of learning are about the way people:

- Perceive information

  The way they learn information
- Process information

  The way they think and interpret
- Organise and present information

  How they retain and pass on information.

People generally employ all of their senses to perceive, process, organise and present information, but they tend to employ one of the senses more than the others.

Visual learners prefer to learn by seeing. They may:

- Often prefer an orderly environment
- Become distracted by untidiness or movement
- Be good at imagining
- Be good at reading (may have good early literacy skills, such as letter recognition)
- Particularly enjoy looking at pictures.

Auditory learners prefer to learn by hearing. They may:

- Learn things well through discussion
- Think things through well when asked questions
- Enjoy listening to stories
- Like reciting information
- Be good at remembering what they are told.

Kinaesthetic learners learn through doing, movement and action. They may:

- Learn well when they are moving around
- Learn best when they have the opportunity to do a task rather than listen to theory
- Be good at constructing things
- Use expressive movements
- Become distracted by activities around them
- Prefer to jump right in rather than being shown what to do
- Prefer action stories.

Key Terms

Learning styles
Styles people prefer to use when learning and that help them to learn best, such as focus on seeing, hearing or doing. *(National Occupational Standards)*

When you are planning you should take the different learning styles into consideration so that you provide a balance of activities that are likely to be beneficial for the different styles of learner. However, you should remember that young children are only just establishing their styles, and you should be wary of labelling them as solely a particular type of learner. Even if you recognise yourself as a particular type of learner, you probably have several traits that will fit into the other styles.

Starting points

When establishing plans, you also need to consider the starting point of all the children – what do they already know and understand? What do they have experience of? This allows you to pitch the activity to the right level for the children. The starting points will differ within any group of children, even those of the same age, so this will require knowledge of the children and some careful thinking. Consider the best way to group children for activities, and what the role of adults will be in terms of supporting children's learning. For instance, through effective deployment of adults and thoughtful grouping of children, practitioners can plan activities that operate on more than one level, meeting the needs of different children working on the same activity.

Lisa's planning

Practitioner Lisa is planning some tabletop games for her group. She decides to split the group into three sub-groups for the activity. One group of mainly four-years-olds will play a game of sound lotto. An adult will be on hand, but they will be encouraged to manage the game themselves, and to operate the tape recorder. A group of mainly three-year-olds are going to play a sequencing lotto game. An adult will work with them, encouraging them to talk about what is happening in the pictures, and the order the pictures should go in. A third group of mainly two-and-a-half-year-olds will play a game of picture lotto with two adults. They will focus on sharing out the cards, taking turns, naming the pictures and matching.

➤ *Why has Lisa decided to split the group?*   **K3D325, K3D326**
➤ *Why is she planning three groups in total?*   **K3D325, K3D326**
➤ *Why is the focus of the game different, despite the fact all groups are playing lotto games?*   **K3D325, K3D326, K3D329**

Inclusion and anti-discriminatory practice

You must always promote anti-discriminatory practice when you are planning. You must ensure that you provide inclusive activities that are suitable for all of the children in the group, regardless of their age, gender, culture and ethnicity, needs, abilities and learning styles.

When children need additional support or have particular learning needs or disabilities, practitioners should focus on removing barriers where they exist and on preventing them from developing, so that children can fully participate within the setting.

It is good practice to note on your plans any special support, adaptation, resources or equipment that may be required to facilitate a child's participation. You must make the necessary arrangements as part of your preparation. Where children have Individual Education Plans (IEPs) or play plans, you should incorporate the goals contained within them into the overall planning, indicating them on your plan. For instance, a child who lacks confidence when speaking within the group may be identified within the plan as in need of support during circle time, when they may feel under pressure. See Unit CCLD 321 for more information about IEPs.

It is important to promote positive images of people and include cultural activities within the programme. See Unit CCLD 305 for further details.

Link **Unit CCLD 305** Protect and promote children's rights

Multilingual and bilingual settings

Linguistic diversity should be valued within settings, and practitioners should be aware of the ways in which children who are multilingual, bilingual or learning through an additional language tend to learn and develop, as this will impact on the planning and implementation of activities.

Children who are learning two or more languages may start to talk later than their peers. This is thought to be because they are absorbing different language systems – or twice as much. They may listen for a long time before they speak the setting's home language, although they may understand what other people say. Children learning more than two languages may sometimes mix up whole sentences or words from different languages.

With support overall language development need not be affected. (See Unit CCLD 301 Develop and promote positive relationships.) Assessments are helpful for pinpointing the support that individual multilingual and bilingual children may need – this will inform your planning. (See Unit CCLD 310 Assess children's progress according to curriculum frameworks for early education, and Unit CCLD 303 Promote children's development.) It will be important to provide good opportunities for a range of speaking and listening activities with adults and peers, and opportunities for children to learn words through games with picture cards such as lotto. You should also ensure that all languages are valued and respected by the children, and arrange for bilingual/ multilingual support, including a translator if necessary.

Link **Unit CCLD 301** Develop and promote positive relationships
Unit CCLD 310 Assess children's progress according to curriculum frameworks for early education
Unit CCLD 303 Promote children's development

Use of ICT

You should ensure that you plan activities that will make effective use of ICT (information and communication technology) to support children's learning and development. Taking our example of the EYFS, there is an Aspect in the area of Knowledge and understanding of the world that directly refers to the use of ICT. It is important to note that this refers to its use across the curriculum, within the integrated approach. ICT resources may include:

- Computers

  Which may be used to find out information, or with CD-ROMs that may support particular areas of learning via activities included (counting programmes, for instance)

- Talking books

  For developing communication, language and literacy skills, and personal, social and emotional development when shared

- Programmable toys such as floor robots, roamers, painters

  For understanding why things happen and how things work, and learning about direction

- Tape records/CD players/dictaphones

  For recording voices, sound games and playing music and story tapes

- Video and television

  For finding things out and recording.

In addition, children can be encouraged to notice ICT and its use in the environment, for instance traffic lights, telephones, cash register scanners and bar-codes, remote controls, street lights, walkie-talkies, satellite navigation systems.

You can also use appropriate ICT language such as on, off, switch, rewind, fast forward, record, eject, play, stop, pause, mouse, screen, keyboard, cursor, cassette, CD, CD-ROM, etc.

The effects of low self-esteem and confidence on learning

If a child has low self-esteem, they may feel that they are incapable of doing all sorts of things well. They may expect to fail, or expect adults and their peers to disapprove of them. When a child feels that way, they may stop trying to achieve, or only attempt tasks half-heartedly. They may withdraw from activities and/or the group. This is a self-fulfilling prophecy: the less a child tries, the more likely they are to fail; this reinforces their belief that they will fail, and they may try even less as a result.

All children lack confidence sometimes, particularly when they find themselves in a new situation. However, some children experience an intense lack of confidence which may persist for long periods or occur in many different situations. This can stop children from participating in activities altogether, limiting their experience and therefore their learning. Or, they may only partially join in. Children cannot become fully absorbed and engaged in an activity if they are unable to relax. Children who feel tense and unsure are therefore less likely to learn as much as their peers.

It is important that practitioners identify children who appear to have low self-esteem and/or a lack of confidence. The two often go hand in hand. Look out for children who:

- Are frequently reluctant to try activities or experiences
- Frequently show little enthusiasm
- Are often reluctant to join in, or only partially join in, hanging around the edges of activities or withdrawing altogether
- Seem tense or worried
- Often say phrases like, 'I can't' or 'I don't know how to' or 'I won't be able to'.

Children with low self-esteem and/or confidence need:

- To have their problem identified
- To have practitioners who understand the implications on their learning
- To have activities and experiences planned sensitively to help them develop their self-esteem and confidence – a practitioner may participate alongside them for instance
- Gentle encouragement – but they should not be pushed into things
- Lots of praise when they do try or participate.

Supporting future learning and development skills

What children learn during their early years underpins all of their future learning. You should have high expectations of children and commitment to supporting the development of their skills. Some studies within schools have found that the attitudes of teachers can influence how well children actually achieve. In one study, teachers were told completely at random that certain children were high achievers. With their teachers believing in them, many of the children actually performed better than they had before.

You should base your expectations on a realistic appraisal of what children's current capabilities are, and what they might achieve next. But always aim to let children know that you believe that they are good at learning, and remember to praise them for both achieving and trying their best. Key skills that help children to become effective learners are shown in the diagram below.

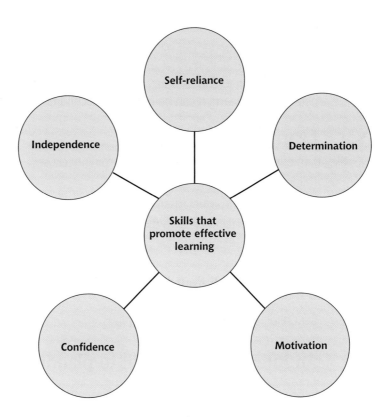

Skills that
promote effective
learning

You can encourage these skills in a range of ways:

- Determination and motivation

  Encourage children to persevere when they can't get something right at first. Motivation and determination are linked, because a child who is motivated to achieve a goal grows in determination. You can motivate children by celebrating their achievements and praising them for trying. A small reward to look forward to often helps to motivate older children, even if it is as simple as saying to them, 'When you've finished your assignment, why don't we hire that film you wanted to see?' But the best motivation of all is the desire to learn. That's why it is so important to foster a love of learning and an interest and curiosity about the world when children are young.

- Confidence

  A child who feels nurtured (cared for) and respected for who they are as an individual is likely to develop confidence. Children also develop confidence when they take emotional risks successfully. Experiencing physical risk and taking on challenges in a supporting environment also helps . Teamwork activities can give confidence a boost too.

- Independence

  Confidence breeds independence. Children experience a desire to do things for themselves and in their own way from an early age. Most of us will have experienced being with a frustrated two-year-old who can't quite manage a task, such as putting on shoes by themselves but who definitely doesn't want our help! From early on, it is important to encourage independence as appropriate to children's age and abilities. This helps children to become increasingly independent as they grow up. Adults won't always be with children in the older age range, so independence is a very important life skill.

- Self-reliance

  Independence breeds self-reliance. Self-reliant learners trust themselves to pick up the knowledge and skills they need. This helps children to feel relaxed, which makes it easier for them to concentrate and participate in activities and experiences. In turn, this helps them to learn. It can help to remind children of their past learning successes.

Learning through play

Play is an effective vehicle for children's learning because:

- Children enjoy playing
- Children are intrinsically motivated to play (they are internally driven)
- Children can make their own discoveries through play
- Children can initiate their own activities and explore their own thoughts and ideas through play
- Children can actively learn through play – the learning is a real, vivid experience
- Play is necessary for children's well-being – under the UN Convention on the Rights of the Child, children have a right to play.

An integrated approach to planning

Key Terms

Integrated approach
Pulling together different areas of learning into activities and experiences.
(National Occupational Standards)

It is important to develop an integrated approach to planning. To do this you must recognise that the activities and experiences you provide for children will generally promote more than one area of their development, since children's learning is not compartmentalised. For instance, children playing with ride-on toys in the playground could simultaneously be learning and consolidating in many ways. They could be:

- Co-operating and taking turns (Personal, social and emotional development)
- Using peddles, steering, changing direction (Physical development)
- Pretending they are going to the garage for petrol (Creative development).

By pulling together different areas of learning into activities and experiences when you are planning, you can maximise the potential learning opportunity for children. It is not necessary to mould every activity to fit every area – this would probably make your activity so broad that it would lack purpose – but it is effective to integrate those that are a natural fit.

For example, if you were planning to plant sunflower seeds with the children, you could cover the following:

- Reading about seeds and how they grow, and discussing things already growing in the environment (Communication, language and literacy)
- Handling seeds, looking at them closely (Knowledge and understanding of the world)
- Counting the seeds and sharing them out (Problem solving, reasoning and numeracy)
- Planting the seeds gently, thinking about how to care for them (Physical development, Knowledge and understanding of the world)
- Pretending to be seeds unfurling and growing to music (Creative development).

Consider the best way to group children for activities, and what the role of adults will be in terms of supporting children's learning. For instance, through effective deployment of adults and thoughtful grouping of children, it is possible to plan activities that operate on more than one level. This meets the needs of different children working on the same activity.

Sources of planning support

You can access sources of support in planning and development to help you to draw on best practice. Curriculum documents relevant to your home country will provide helpful guidance, supporting and underpinning your work. Extra support is also available online. The EYFS website (www.standards.dcsf.gov.uk/eyfs/) holds very useful information. You can also visit www.direct.gov.uk and follow the links to online National Curriculum support.

Training on curriculum frameworks may be offered in your region. You can also access support from relevant membership organisations, such the National Day Nurseries Association (www.ndna.org.uk) and the Pre-School Learning Alliance (www.pre-school.org.uk), and from statutory organisations such as Sure Start (www.surestart.gov.uk).

Element 309.1

Are you ready for assessment?

Prepare curriculum plans according to requirements

You need to show that you can competently prepare curriculum plans according to requirements. To do this you will need to be directly observed by your assessor and present other types of evidence. The amount and type of evidence you need to present will vary. You should plan this with your assessor.

Direct observation by your assessor

Observation and/or expert witness testimony is the required assessment method to be used to evidence some of each element in this unit. If your assessor is unable to observe you, s/he will identify an expert in your workplace who will provide testimony of your work-based performance. Usually your assessor or expert witness will observe you in real work activities and this should provide most of the evidence for the performance criteria for the elements in this unit.

Preparing to be observed

You must show your assessor that you can research and extract relevant information from curriculum documents and base short-, medium- and long-term planning on this, consulting appropriately and considering resources, attendance and the need for a balanced programme. You must show that you can cover each area of the curriculum, developing plans that reflect inclusion, include use of ICT to support learning, and define the roles and responsibilities of adults. You must also show that you can involve appropriate people in the planning process.

Other types of evidence

You will need to present different types of evidence in order to:

- Cover criteria not observed by your assessor
- Show that you have the required knowledge, understanding and skills.

Such evidence could include:

- Work products such as curriculum plans
- Case studies, projects, assignments and reflective accounts of your work
- Confidential records such as children's individual play plans These should not be placed in your portfolio – they must remain in their usual location and be referred to in the assessor records in your portfolio.

Implement curriculum plans

K3D319
K3D322
K3D326
K3D328
K3D329

Communicating plans

Once your planning is complete, you must communicate your plans to all relevant people within the setting. Make sure you discuss the roles and responsibilities of other adults – the plan cannot be implemented well if people are unsure what is required of them. Some settings display a copy of the plan in a communal area for all to see, while others distribute a copy of plans to those concerned – this is handy for practitioners to refer to when they may be bringing in resources from home or perhaps working from home during non-contact time. However, it is still advisable to verbally check that everyone has looked at, and is happy with, the plan and their role within it. Relevant people will include colleagues, parents, carers and perhaps outside professionals.

Regularly referring to the available curriculum documents will assist with the implementation of plans. It is useful to refresh your own memory in this way (a period of time may have elapsed between the planning and the implementation of a plan), and it is also helpful for colleagues to see clearly what children should learn from activities and experiences. You should check that other relevant adults involved in the delivery of the curriculum understand it and their role in delivery. It is worth noting that adults may sometimes say they are clear because they *think* they understand – sometimes we do not know that we do not know! If you are concerned about someone's understanding, try asking them to explain to you the purpose of an activity or experience – you can then offer clarification if necessary. Some adults may benefit from early years education training – most regions have courses and workshops that run periodically. Your local EYDCP or Sure Start will have information on learning opportunities.

Flexibility and adaptations

It is important to remember that plans should be regarded as guidance. They should be flexible, a work in progress. You should be prepared to adapt them when appropriate – some practitioners find this difficult to accept after they have spent time on the planning stage. However, it is necessary to remain flexible so that your plan fits changing circumstances, meets the needs of the children and makes the most of opportunities that arise unexpectedly. For instance, you may need to adapt your plan if:

- You were unaware which children you would have in when the plan was designed. It may need to be altered to reflect individual children's needs, abilities and stages of development
- You did not know how many adults would be available to support activities – perhaps no volunteers are available, so an activity that required extra adult support will have to be adapted or postponed
- A natural event such as snow or hail occurs, and you decide to make the most of the experience and postpone other planned activities
- A key piece of equipment is broken or unexpectedly unavailable
- An activity does not interest or engage the children as expected, and you decide to cut it short
- Children are so interested or engaged in an activity or experience that you decide to extend it.

Providing a stimulating environment

By carefully planning the environment, practitioners can make effective use of space both indoors and outdoors, and create a stimulating and enjoyable place to be. When planning the layout of both indoor and outdoor areas, there are some important considerations.

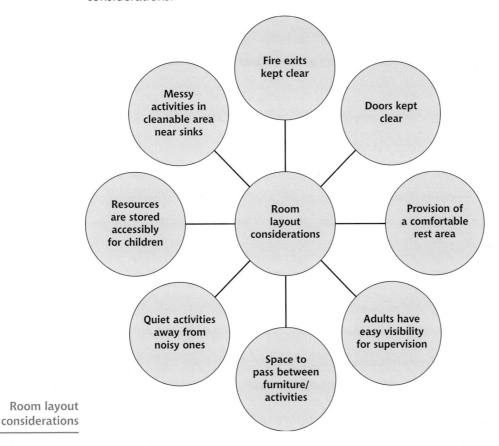

Room layout considerations

Room layout can affect:

- Atmosphere
- Mood of children and adults
- How children participate in activities
- How children play
- What children learn
- Whether children rest
- Whether children play indoors and/or outdoors.

Changing the environment

Most settings change the layout of the environment as the day progresses. For instance, they may begin with free-play toys available, set out across the space. They may then pack everything away and perhaps push back tables and chairs to allow space for dancing. This is practical and makes good use of the space available. However, it can also be valuable to periodically change the layout of the room in terms of large pieces of furniture, such as bookcases, and established areas such as the book corner or imaginary area. This can be refreshing and exciting for children. It encourages them to interact with resources in different ways, and to explore areas that they may not have visited in their play for a while. Thoughtful wall displays and interest tables and can be stimulating too. They should also be changed regularly.

When presenting resources and activities, try to vary things. It is easy to always put the same things out in the same way without thinking about it, so you may find it helpful to record how an activity will be presented on your plans. Think about the following:

- Use the outside area as an additional 'room'. Outside should not be just for letting off steam or large physical play, although they are important. Lots of activities that can be set up inside can also go outside. This may give children a fresh experience. For instance, when the tea set goes out, children may role play having a picnic. When magnifying glasses go out, children may spontaneously look closely at plants. Some children seem drawn to activities outside that do not hold so much appeal for them inside – mark making for instance
- If extreme weather prevents you from taking children out (if the playground is icy, for instance), move furniture back and give children opportunities to be physically active inside. Exercise is good for children
- Combine resources that do not usually go out together. Put interlocking bricks out with cars, and children may create garages; put cars out with long lengths of paper and they may draw roads
- Change the position of items. Try a trainset on the table and move the chairs away instead of setting it up on the floor. Take craft resources such as paper, cellophane, fabric, tissue, etc. and put them on the floor instead of the table
- Set activities up attractively, so they look welcoming, interesting and inviting. When setting up the home corner, set the table and sit a teddy there ready for play, for instance. Start off an activity as a play cue for children – set out the blocks with a partially built tower, or begin a puzzle. Do activities look flat? When resources are just placed on a table, they often look static and uninspiring. A table of pipe cleaners that has two or three bright pipe-cleaner structures standing upright is far more interesting than just the raw materials lying flat.

Meeting children's needs

All children need environments that are safe and secure, and you must keep this as your primary consideration when thinking about layout. Be particularly careful outside to ensure that there is appropriate matting or other safety surface under physical play resources such as slides, climbing frames and swings – especially after you have moved things around. Check nothing is likely to fall on children. Ensure that children do not have access to anything unsuitable, such as poisonous plants or outdoor dustbins, and ensure that any gates to the play area are shut before allowing children outside. Ask parents and carers to supply sun protection (hats and high-factor lotion or sunblock), and keep children inside during the hottest part of the day (11 a.m.–3 p.m.) on very sunny days if the play area is exposed to the sun and cannot be adequately shaded.

Maintaining the environment and resources

It is also important to keep the environment and resources clean, hygienic and in good order. Many settings have a checklist of jobs to complete after activities or daily, weekly and monthly to ensure everything is done. This may include washing paint pots, sterilising toys, washing soft toys and cushion covers in a washing machine, sweeping up sand, sieving dirt out of the sand pit, wiping off the doll's house, rinsing and drying water toys and so on. Broken or worn equipment should be removed and the appropriate person should be informed.

Environments that meet children's needs

You should also ensure that the environment meets the needs of individual children and adults, making adaptations where necessary – the Disability Discrimination Act 1995 has made this not just good practice but a legal necessity. Depending on the needs of the children and adults, you may need to consider some of the following:

- Using bright lighting/diffused lighting in some areas
- Using colour to indicate certain areas
- Using scents to indicate areas or activities
- Having tactile wall borders or floor runners
- Changing the height of tables
- Increasing the space between activities
- Taking some activities to children instead of children going to them, e.g. having individual trays of sand or bowls of water to play with
- Installing hearing loops
- Making the environment quieter by having carpet and rubber cushioning under furniture
- Having non-slip rubber matting on meal tables so that plates and bowls do not move around.

Selecting resources and equipment

When selecting resources and equipment, consider the following.

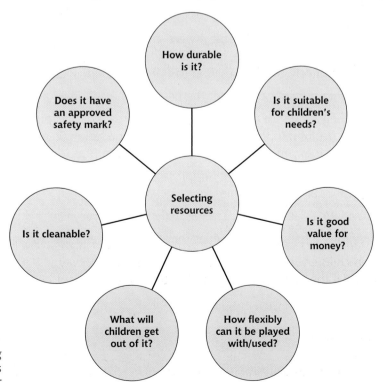

Selecting resources

For information about safety marks see page 158 of Unit CCLD 306 Plan and organise environments for children and families.

Everyday routines

Everyday routines are essential to the care of children, and they also provide them with a sense of security and structure to their day. However, they should not be overlooked as learning experiences. Plan to enhance learning through everyday routines. Consider the following:

- Promoting children's understanding of healthy foods through discussion at snack times and mealtimes
- Promoting good manners at the table
- Making sets when setting the table (i.e. putting in order the things that belong together), and talking about position, e.g., 'The fork goes opposite the knife'
- Counting out how many cups and plates are needed
- Encouraging children to pour their own drinks
- Encouraging children to put on and fasten their own outdoor clothes
- Talking about hygiene with children when washing hands and toileting
- Discussing respect for the environment when tidying up
- Name-recognition opportunities when marking the register
- Allowing children to see you writing when you make notes.

Encouraging participation

Children need to engage with activities and experiences in order to learn effectively. Practitioners sometimes make the mistake of thinking that children have experienced or learnt all of the things that they were offered that day, or that week or month. However, children may have benefited little or not at all if they have not actually participated actively themselves. You can promote participation by:

- Providing activities that meet the needs of the children
- Providing a balance of activities across all areas of children's development, and the curriculum. In the case of Early Years Foundation Stage, this means providing activities to promote each area of Learning and Development
- Providing activities that are fun/playful, and present them to children in a playful or engaging manner
- Providing a balance of structured activities and free-play
- Providing a balance of activities for all styles of learning
- Providing a balance of indoor and outdoor activities
- Grouping children appropriately
- Providing appropriate adult support
- Initiating an activity by participating yourself (try going into the dressing-up corner alone and trying on hats – you are likely to have company very soon)
- Participating alongside children.

Expectations of children

You should have high expectations of children, and commitment to raising their achievement – practitioners' attitudes are believed by many to be an important part of how well children actually achieve. An old saying goes, 'If you think you can or if you think you can't, you're probably right' – it is important to think you can help children to do well.

However, you should base your expectations on a realistic appraisal of what children's current capabilities are, and what they might achieve within a given timescale in light of this. (This is another example of assessment informing the planning and implementation – see Unit CCLD 310 Assess children's progress according to curriculum frameworks for early education).

Link   **Unit CCLD 310** Assess children's progress according to curriculum frameworks for early education

Supporting and extending learning

Element 309.1 explains how to plan for the support and extension of learning, drawing on your knowledge of individual children. It is also important to look out for spontaneous opportunities to support and extend during the implementation of a session. It may be appropriate to offer your support if children:

- Could be encouraged to think or discuss further if they were asked a question
- Need a suggestion to initiate an activity or experience
- Show signs that their play is flagging, and new input is needed
- Are becoming frustrated or struggling
- Seem nervous, reluctant or unsure
- Need a demonstration of a skill, e.g. how to hold scissors
- Are not understanding something – a story perhaps
- Are beginning to behave inappropriately.

Checking progress

Assessments and observations of children's learning and development should be regularly undertaken. (See Unit CCLD 310 Assess children's progress according to curriculum frameworks for early education.) Practitioners should regularly monitor the findings to check on the progress made by individual children and the group as a whole. The progress made is an indication of how effective the teaching and learning is. This in turn reflects on the planning and implementation of activities and experiences. In order to be objective, it is helpful to consult widely on this issue with relevant adults including parents, carers, colleagues and outside professionals (whilst maintaining confidentiality with regard to information about individual children).

If improvements need to be made, an action plan should be drawn up – this will inform future planning and implementation. It is important to try to identify where specific changes are needed – is there a lack of challenge, or equipment, or adult support? Any changes made should be monitored to ensure that they are effective. If individual children are not progressing as expected, you should seek additional support (see Unit CCLD 310 Assess children's progress according to curriculum frameworks for early education).

 Link   **Unit CCLD 310** Assess children's progress according to curriculum frameworks for early education

Children's achievements

When children have made achievements you should sensitively acknowledge, praise and celebrate them. If you involve children in the assessment of their progress, milestones can be recorded together. It is important to look out for such achievements not only in order to mark them, but in order to recognise when children are ready to move on in terms of what they are ready to learn and experience next. When you decide what children should learn from activities, consider how you will know when they have learnt it – this will help you to notice new learning.

Moving on in this way keeps children motivated and keen to learn and participate. Children will not thrive in terms of their learning if they are made to carry out activities they have already mastered. However, children should be given sufficient opportunity to consolidate their learning (see Element 309.1) and to choose their own direction via free-play and child-initiated activities.

Records

You must keep appropriate records regarding the implementation of plans in line with your organisational procedures and the requirements of your relevant home inspectorate. Your records may include:

- Details of any changes or adaptations made to the curriculum plan
- Which activities children participated in
- Observations/assessments made
- Progress made by children
- New learning achieved by children
- Evaluation of session
- Evaluation of own performance.

Records should be:

- Dated
- Stored carefully with regard to confidentiality if appropriate.

Are you ready for assessment?

Implement curriculum plans

You need to show that you can competently implement curriculum plans. To do this you will need to be directly observed by your assessor and present other types of evidence. The amount and type of evidence you need to present will vary. You should plan this with your assessor.

Direct observation by your assessor

Observation and/or expert witness testimony is the required assessment method to be used to evidence some of each element in this unit. If your assessor is unable to observe you, s/he will identify an expert in your workplace who will provide testimony of your work-based performance. Usually your assessor or expert witness will observe you in real work activities and this should provide most of the evidence for the performance criteria for the elements in this unit.

Preparing to be observed

You must show your assessor that you can regularly refer to curriculum documents and ensure that relevant people have an awareness and understanding of the plans and the delivery of the curriculum. You must also show that you can provide a stimulating environment and plan activities to meet children's needs, using routines to enhance learning and supporting and extending play effectively. You must show that you can

encourage children's participation and have high expectations, being sensitive to children's achievements. You must show that you can seek additional support if children are not progressing as expected, and that you can keep appropriate records.

Other types of evidence

You will need to present different types of evidence in order to:

- Cover criteria not observed by your assessor
- Show that you have the required knowledge, understanding and skills.

Such evidence could include:

- Work products such as curriculum plans
- Case studies, projects, assignments and reflective accounts of your work
- Confidential records such as referral information. These should not be placed in your portfolio – they must remain in their usual location and be referred to in the assessor records in your portfolio.

Monitor and reflect on implementation of curriculum frameworks

Element 309.3

Monitoring strategies and documentation

K3D322
K3D323
K3D236
K3D329
K3D330
K3D331
K3D332

It is good practice for settings to regularly monitor how well they are delivering their relevant curriculum. You will need to do this and record your findings in line with your organisational procedures and the requirements of your relevant home inspectorate. To monitor effectively you will need to work in partnership with families, colleagues and outside professionals to consider evidence including:

- The formative and summative assessments of children's progress (see Unit CCLD 310 Assess children's progress according to curriculum frameworks for early education)

  The amount of progress that children make reveals how good the planning and implementation is

- Colleagues'/outside professionals' comments, opinions, evaluations and reflective practice notes (see Unit CCLD 304 Reflect on and develop practice)

  Do they feel plans are specific enough? Do they generally understand their roles and responsibilities in the delivery of the curriculum? Do they feel organised and well prepared? Do they feel children are engaged and interested?

- Your own evaluations and reflective practice notes

  See 'Reflect on your planning and implementation of curriculum frameworks' opposite

- Families' comments, opinions, evaluations (including children)

  Do children enjoy activities? Are they motivated, keen to attend and to participate? Do they talk about things they like/dislike about the setting? Do the families feel that the children's needs are met? Have they noticed the children's progression? Are they aware of opportunities to work in partnership with the setting?

- Inspectorate findings and reports

  Written reports and verbal feedback

- Quality Assurance scheme findings and reports

  Written reports and verbal feedback.

Link

Unit CCLD 304 Reflect on and develop practice
Unit CCLD 310 Assess children's progress according to curriculum frameworks for early education

You must ensure that all areas of the curriculum are monitored. You should check that all areas are implemented to a consistently high quality. For example, personal, social and emotional development may be delivered very well when the theme is 'All about me', but is it still promoted to a high standard when the theme is 'Shapes'?

There are various methods of recording monitoring. For instance, some settings may hold monitoring meetings, recorded in the style of minutes. Others may complete forms they have designed for the purpose. Whatever method is used, it is important that records are dated and stored appropriately.

Monitoring children's participation

This can be effectively achieved in a number of ways. Some settings keep a checklist of activities and indicate via initials which children have participated that day. Other settings make a note of participants directly on the plan as it is implemented.

Reflect on your planning and implementation of curriculum frameworks

Reflecting on how you do things, what you do and what you achieve, effectively helps you to see how well you are working in practice. To reflect effectively on your planning and implementation of curriculum frameworks consider:

- How effectively do you plan?

  Is it clear what children should learn and how? Are all children's needs met? Are activities varied and balanced appropriately? Do adults know their roles?
- Are you sufficiently organised?

  Are the resources and equipment available when you need them? Are activities set up and ready at the right time? Is the environment set out attractively?
- Analyse your actions in implementing

  Do you support children effectively when support is planned for, and when it is needed spontaneously?

  Do you group children effectively to maximise their learning and experiences? Do you look out for children's achievements and signs indicating they are ready to move on? Do you follow plans flexibly? Do you gently encourage children to participate?

It is helpful for practitioners to:

- Record their reflections, perhaps in a journal
- Discuss their reflections with others
- Use feedback from others to improve their own evaluations.

Make sure that you actively use your reflections to inform your future practice. It is only then that they are worthwhile and practice develops and evolves.

Are you ready for assessment?

Monitor and reflect on implementation of curriculum plans

You need to show that you can competently monitor and reflect on implementation of curriculum frameworks. To do this you will need to be directly observed by your assessor and present other types of evidence. The amount and type of evidence you need to present will vary. You should plan this with your assessor.

Direct observation by your assessor

Observation and/or expert witness testimony is the required assessment method to be used to evidence some of each element in this unit. If your assessor is unable to observe you, s/he will identify an expert in your workplace who will provide testimony of your work-based performance. Usually your assessor or expert witness will observe you in real work activities and this should provide most of the evidence for the performance criteria for the elements in this unit.

Preparing to be observed

You must show your assessor that you can develop appropriate monitoring strategies and documentation, and that you can communicate regularly with the appropriate people for monitoring purposes. You must show that you can check each area of the curriculum is implemented to consistent quantities, and monitor the participation and learning of children. You must also show that you can reflect on your relevant practice.

Other types of evidence

You will need to present different types of evidence in order to:

- Cover criteria not observed by your assessor
- Show that you have the required knowledge, understanding and skills.

Such evidence could include:

- Work products such as evaluations, monitoring documents and reflective journal entries
- Case studies, projects, assignments and reflective accounts of your work.

Check your knowledge

- Name three ways in which you could use ICT to support the curriculum **K3D323**
- How is children's learning affected by their stage of development? **K3D325**
- What are three key benefits of children learning through play? **K3D328**
- What are styles of learning, and how do they impact on the planning of activities? **K3D330**
- What does 'extending children's learning' mean? **K3D329**

Reflective practice

If you are new to monitoring the effectiveness of planning and implementation of frameworks for early education, you may initially find it a little overwhelming to monitor progress over a period of time. Try the following first to introduce yourself gently.

Take ONE plan that you have devised and already implemented. Ask yourself the questions in the section 'Reflect on your planning and implementation of curriculum frameworks' on page 267, consulting appropriately. Note your answers in your reflective journal.

UNIT 310

Assess children's progress according to curriculum frameworks for early education

This unit includes assessing children's progress within curriculum frameworks for early education within the four home countries – England, Wales, Scotland and Ireland. It includes the identification and planning of assessment requirements and assessing and recording progress. Both formative and summative assessments are covered within the unit.

The unit contains two elements:

- **CCLD 310.1** *Identify and plan assessment requirements of curriculum frameworks*
- **CCLD 310.2** *Assess and record children's progress in consultation with others*

Key Terms

Formative assessment

Initial and on-going assessment. *(National Occupational Standards)*

Summative assessment

Assessment that summarises findings and may draw overall conclusions. *(National Occupational Standards)*

Introduction

Through initial and ongoing assessment (formative assessment) of children's learning and development, practitioners can monitor children's progress. By summarising findings and drawing overall conclusions (summative assessment), practitioners can see what children should be learning next, and they can provide the appropriate learning opportunities. Assessment also helps practitioners to identify areas where children need specific support.

Effective practitioners plan assessment in accordance with local or national requirements. They make and record their assessments with care, and use them to inform their planning. With regard to confidentiality, they share their findings with those who need the information.

Element 310.1
Identify and plan assessment requirements of curriculum frameworks

K3D325
K3D335
K3D336
K3M337
K3M338

Learning and stages of development

Children's learning is generally accepted to be strongly linked to their stage of development. Part of understanding child development is studying key theories of learning. Secure knowledge of the stages of child development enables practitioners to assess a child's capabilities. This is explained in more detail in Unit 303 Promote children's development.

Link   Unit 303 Promote children's development

⌒ The assessment process

There are various methods of assessment which we will go into below, but essentially, practitioners make observations of the children they work with, noticing the things they can do. Some of the observations:

- Will be mental notes, part of what the practitioner knows about individual children
- Are likely to be written down because they have been made at a planned time that the practitioner dedicated to observing that child's behaviour.

In addition some knowledge may have been gained from seeing children's work, or through conversation with parents, carers, colleagues or other professionals.

All of these things provide evidence of a child's achievements, and knowledge of them is collected over time.

When practitioners carry out assessment in relation to a curriculum framework, they generally use an assessment form which prompts them to make judgements about children's achievements. Now all the accumulated knowledge is used formally, and the judgements based on it are recorded. Assessment forms are helpful because they ensure practitioners remember to consider every aspect of development. They also ensure that over time the picture of progress built is based on assessment in the same areas – otherwise progress could not be accurately tracked. Formats used for assessment purposes differ – see 'Assessing within curriculum frameworks'.

It is important to remember that each assessment is only a snapshot of the child's learning and development at that time since young children are constantly mastering new skills, learning new concepts and making new discoveries. The initial formative assessment gives practitioners information about the child's current abilities. After that, ongoing assess-

Children are
constantly
learning

ments will track (monitor) the progress that children are making. The findings will be summarised and conclusions will be drawn from them during summative assessment. Staff will share the information with parents, carers, colleagues and possibly outside professionals.

There is further information on observation and assessment in Unit CCLD 303 Promote children's development.

Link   **Unit CCLD 303** Promote children's development

Theories of how children learn and develop

Practitioners should understand theories of how children learn and develop. This allows them to effectively support children when planning to meet their needs and when working with them in practice. Some key theories are outlined in Unit CCLD 309 Plan and implement curriculum frameworks for early education, and in Unit CCLD 303 Promote children's development.

Assessing within curriculum frameworks

Most settings plan how they will promote children's learning and development through the activities and care that they offer. The planning is likely to be carried out in accordance with a structured early education curriculum framework, such as the Early Years Foundation Stage. Structured frameworks vary locally and nationally across the four home countries, and may be discretionary or statutory. See Unit CCLD 309 Plan and implement curriculum frameworks for early education.

It is good practice for all early years settings to assess the learning and development of children of all ages. When an early education curriculum framework is followed, practitioners will assess the progress that children make towards the goals or objectives for learning and development. This requires practitioners to research the appropriate national or local curriculum documents so that assessments can be based upon them.

Link   **Unit CCLD 309** Plan and implement curriculum frameworks for early education
Unit CCLD 303 Promote children's development

Requirements of relevant inspectorates

Settings across the four home countries are subject to the requirements of the relevant inspectorate for their area. Settings must comply with all requirements, including those concerned with the way assessments are planned, conducted, recorded, shared, acted upon and stored. The timing and frequency of assessments must also meet the requirements of the relevant inspectorate. We will take as an example the requirements for assessment in the Early Years Foundation Stage (EYFS) that apply in England. A brief outline of the assessment process for the English National Curriculum is given on page 232.

Key Terms

Relevant inspectorates
Inspectorates in your home country that register or inspect your setting.
(National
Occupational
Standards)

Link   **Unit 309** Plan and implement curriculum frameworks for early education

The assessment requirements of Ofsted

Within the EYFS, ongoing assessment is an integral part of the learning and development process. The Department for Children, Schools and Families says that assessment should be underpinned by the principles shown in the table.

Assessment principles

Assessment must have a purpose
Observation of children participating in everyday activities is the most reliable way to build up an accurate picture of what children know, feel, are interested in and can do
Observation should be planned. However, practitioners should also be ready to capture spontaneous but important moments
Judgement of children's development and learning should be based on skills, knowledge, understanding and behaviour that they demonstrate consistently and independently
An effective assessment will take into account all aspects of a child's development and learning
Accurate assessment will also take into account contributions from a range of perspectives
Parents and other primary carers should be actively engaged in the assessment process
Children should be fully involved in their own assessment

Children doing finger rhymes

Assessment at the end of the EYFS

The EYFS profile is an assessment document. All registered early years providers are required to complete an EYFS profile for each child at the end of the academic year in which the child reaches the age of five.

The Department for Children, Schools and Families tells us that:

> 'The primary purpose of the EYFS profile is to provide year 1 teachers and parents with reliable and accurate information about each child's level of development as they reach the end of the EYFS. This will enable the teacher to plan an effective, responsive and appropriate curriculum that will meet all children's needs, to support their continued achievement more fully.'

A practitioner will use their observations to make judgements and to record each child's development against the profile's 13 assessment scales. These are based on the Early Learning Goals and are divided between the six Areas of Learning and Development.

By following links on the National Assessment Agency website (www.naa.org.uk/eyfsp), you can view the EYFS profile, the EYFS profile handbook, the assessment scales guidance sheet and other support materials. An extract from the EYFS profile is provided here with notes to help you understand how practitioners use the profile in practice. You can also visit www.naa.org.uk/naa_19379.aspx to watch video clips that show children displaying behaviours that link with the assessment scales.

Whether routinely tracking a child's progress or completing an EYFS profile, practitioners are advised to use their knowledge of each child to make judgements of their learning in relation to the scales. So following our example, if a practitioner already knows from experience that the child they are assessing joins in with songs and rhymes, they can make a judgement based on that knowledge. They need not produce extra evidence.

Where practitioners feel they need further information to support judgements they can carry out additional observations of the child's behaviour in different contexts – these should be planned for but integrated into the normal curriculum provision. Special assessment activities do not have to be provided. If a practitioner did not know about a child's singing and rhyming activity, they could plan to observe the child during some appropriate everyday activities.

In addition, practitioners may consider when appropriate records from previous settings that a child has attended. The practitioner may be able to gain some insight into singing and rhyming capacity from previous records completed at another setting – but these will only be a snapshot of the child's ability at the time the records were made.

24 Early years foundation stage profile handbook

07 Using the assessment scales

There are 13 scales, based on the early learning goals and divided between the six areas of development and learning. The scales are:

Dispositions and attitudes (DA)
Social development (SD)
Emotional development (ED)
Personal, social and emotional development

Language for communication and thinking (LCT)
Linking sounds and letters (LSL)
Reading (R)
Writing (W)
Communication, language and literacy

Numbers as labels and for counting (NLC)
Calculating (C)
Shape, space and measures (SSM)
Problem solving, reasoning and numeracy

Knowledge and understanding of the world (KUW)
Physical development (PD)
Creative development (CD)

Each scale has nine assessment points. A summary listing of all scale points can be found on the separate Assessment scales reference sheet, published by NAA and available either as a hard copy or as a download from naa.org.uk/eyfsp.

EYFS profile scale points and accumulative scale point scores are statutory assessments in their own right. They are not equivalent to any national curriculum levels or sub-levels and no such equation should be made.

Scale points 1–3	describe the attainment of a child who is still progressing towards the early learning goals.
Scale points 4–8	describe the attainment of a child in the context of the early learning goals. They are not hierarchical or linear, indeed some scale points require ongoing assessment over time and a child may achieve them in any order.
Scale point 9	describes the attainment of a child who has achieved scale points 1–8 and developed further, working consistently beyond early learning goals. This will be attained by children who have significant abilities in an area of learning. Its purpose is to identify these abilities to year 1 teachers and ensure that these children's specific development and learning needs will be met.

Using the
assessment scales

The practitioner may be able to gather contributions from:

- The child

  The practitioner could ask the child if they like to sing and join in with rhymes

- Parents and carers

  Parents and carers can tell the practitioner if their child enjoys singing or rhyming – some children are reluctant to sing in a group but are comfortable to do so at home

- Colleagues

  The practitioner's colleagues may have had experience of singing or rhyming with the child

- Other professionals

  For example, a speech therapist may already have made observations about a child's singing, rhyming and general use of language, which could inform the assessment.

Observations

There are many different ways of carrying out observations, as you learnt in Unit CCLD 303. You should always work in line with the guidelines of your setting and the requirements of the inspectorates within your home country. However, many settings have decided to record ongoing formative assessments in a narrative that reflects the style shown in the example 'Linking sounds and letters'.

 Link   **Unit 303** Promote children's development

Consultation

Whatever assessment system you use, you should plan assessments in consultation with relevant adults. The following table explains the people who are likely to be involved in assessment and their roles.

People involved in assessment and their roles

People involved in assessment	Role in assessment process
Key worker	Usually the key worker is selected (as the practitioner who knows the most about an individual child) to plan and implement assessment. They must ensure there are adequate resources to carry out assessment, i.e. sufficient human and material resources to assess children's progress. (Ensuring there are enough observation forms available for instance.) They must ensure those involved are confident, well informed, clear about assessment methods, requirements and the importance of making judgements based on a variety of sources
Other practitioners within setting	Colleagues of the key worker who work with the child are likely be required to contribute evidence and assist with making a summative assessment. All those who plan and support the child's learning and development will need to know the findings so that planning and practical work is informed. Anyone present at the time of assessment should be informed of the setting's process, and if appropriate their role
The child themselves	The child can be involved in talking about and celebrating their achievements, as well as expressing their opinions, preferences, knowledge and feelings
Parents, carers (and the wider family)	As the people who know the most about their child, parents and carers should be asked to contribute to the formative and summative assessment. They should also receive information about their child's progress and the learning and development planned for the future
Outside professionals	Any outside professional who will be asked to contribute to the assessment through the provision or consideration of evidence

 Link Unit 309 Plan and implement curriculum frameworks for early education

Safeguards and objectivity

There are many advantages to knowing a child well when it comes to assessment. But when assessing children's learning and development, it is important to remain objective, and the better you know a child the harder this can be. You should record facts based on evidence rather than your opinion or what you believe to be true. Because they acknowledge this is difficult, practitioners often build safeguards into the assessment process to ensure accuracy.

The following strategies are safeguards:

- Drawing on evidence from a variety of sources, including everyday observation, assessment and knowledge of individual children and information given by the child concerned
- Consulting with colleagues who have also worked with individual children, and their parents and carers, and outside agencies or professionals so that evidence comes from different people

● Asking colleagues who do not know individual children very well to contribute to the process of gathering evidence for formative and summative assessment, as they are likely to have the most objective view.

Planning for assessment

Assessment methods must be in line with your setting's procedures. However, whatever method is used, organisation is important. You can ensure you have prepared thoroughly for assessment by checking that the following considerations have been addressed.

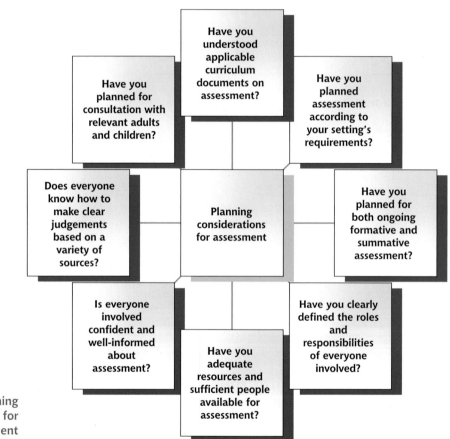

Have you understood applicable curriculum documents on assessment?

Have you planned for consultation with relevant adults and children?

Have you planned assessment according to your setting's requirements?

Does everyone know how to make clear judgements based on a variety of sources?

Planning considerations for assessment

Have you planned for both ongoing formative and summative assessment?

Is everyone involved confident and well-informed about assessment?

Have you adequate resources and sufficient people available for assessment?

Have you clearly defined the roles and responsibilities of everyone involved?

Planning considerations for assessment

Element 310.1

Are you ready for assessment?

Identify and plan assessment requirements of curriculum frameworks

You need to show that you can competently identify and plan assessment requirements of curriculum frameworks. To do this you will need to be directly observed by your assessor and present other types of evidence. The amount and type of evidence you need to present will vary. You should plan this with your assessor.

Direct observation by your assessor

Observation and/or expert witness testimony is the required assessment method to be used to evidence some of each element in this unit. If your assessor is unable to observe you, s/he will identify an expert in your workplace who will provide testimony of your work-based performance. Usually your assessor or expert witness will observe you in real work activities and this should provide most of the evidence for the performance criteria for the elements in this unit.

Preparing to be observed

You must show your assessor that you can research and extract information from curriculum documents on which to base assessments, and that you can plan assessments according to relevant requirements and in consultation with relevant adults and children. You must also show that you can plan for formative and summative assessment, defining the roles of those involved, ensuring that they are clear about the assessment procedures and that required resources are available.

Other types of evidence

You will need to present different types of evidence in order to:

- Cover criteria not observed by your assessor
- Show that you have the required knowledge, understanding and skills.

Such evidence could include:

- Work products such as assessment plans and information on the assessment process compiled for families and/or colleagues
- Case studies, projects, assignments and reflective accounts of your work
- Confidential records such as individual children's assessment records. These should not be placed in your portfolio – they must remain in their usual location and be referred to in the assessor records in your portfolio.

Assess and record children's progress in consultation with others

The planning cycle

K3M339
K3D331
K3D340
K3D341
K3P342

Assessment is part of a constant cycle of planning for learning and development, implementing opportunities for learning and development, and reviewing learning and development. Many practitioners call this the plan, do, review cycle, as this is easy to remember. You must ensure that all relevant people involved in the setting are informed about their roles and responsibilities at each stage of the cycle, and that the agreed methods are working and are followed.

Once a summative assessment has been made, practitioners should use the information they have gathered about a child's progress to inform their planning. This is achieved by analysing the summative assessment. Practitioners should ask themselves, 'In light of the conclusions drawn, what should I plan to do to support this child's future progress and learning?'

Key Terms

Planning cycle
Constant cycle of planning, implementing, reviewing/evaluating. *(National Occupational Standards)*

Review
Assessment of progress is made, revealing support needed and what children should learn next

Plan
Practitioners plan activities to help children reach learning/development goals or objectives

Do (implement)
Children take part in the planned activities

Plan, do, review cycle

For example:

- If children are having difficulties learning a particular skill and/or understanding a certain concept, extra support or learning opportunities may be planned to help them

  For instance, a child may need more opportunities to use scissors because they are having difficulties mastering this skill. Or they may find it difficult to follow stories and have little idea of how to handle books – they would benefit from opportunities to share books on a one-to-one basis with an adult

- If children have particular, persistent difficulties in one or more areas of their learning or development, further consideration is needed to plan the next step

  Sometimes difficulties are expected, for example when a child has a special educational need, when they have missed learning opportunities due to a period of illness, or because they are bilingual or multilingual and learning the home language of the setting. In these cases practitioners may already be receiving support from outside professionals and agencies, and an Individual Education Plan (IEP) may already be in place. If so, practitioners should consider the child's progress towards curriculum requirements and their IEP since the last assessment. If progress is being made, practitioners should consider what children should learn next in light of their current development. If sufficient progress is not being made, practitioners can, in consultation with families, refer back to outside professionals and agencies for advice and support.

  If those difficulties are unexpected, practitioners should work in consultation with colleagues, families and, where appropriate, children to try to identify the cause. Then children can be given the right support. Outside professionals and external agencies should be contacted if necessary (again in consultation) if practitioners suspect that a child has an impairment or special educational need

- Where children are progressing well, practitioners should plan for continued progress

  Practitioners should consider what the child should learn next. What is the next step of their development? What opportunities should be provided for them? What support may they need to continue their progress?

You should refer to curriculum guidance to assist you. In consultation with parents, carers and children (where appropriate), specialist support and advice can be sought from many professionals who focus on particular areas including:

- Educational psychologists

  Focusing on behaviour and learning

- Child psychiatrists

  Focusing on thoughts and emotions

- Play therapists

  Focusing on dealing with emotions through play

- Paediatricians

  Focusing on health and development

- Health visitors

  Focusing on development of under-fives

- Physiotherapists

  Focusing on the function of the body

- Speech therapists

  Focusing on speech and language

- Advisory teachers

  Focusing on learning and progress towards national or local curriculum

● SENCO adviser

Focusing on supporting SENCOs (Special Educational Needs Co-ordinators) in settings.

The support available can vary between regions. Your local Early Years Childcare and Development Partnership or Sure Start will have details. There is much more information in Unit CCLD 321, Support children with disabilities or special educational needs and their families, which you should need in conjunction with this Unit.

Link   **Unit CCLD 321** Support children with disabilities or special educational needs and their families

Sharing assessment findings

Practitioners should share the findings of their assessments with parents and carers. Informing them about their child's progress is a crucial part of working in partnership. Many settings do this effectively by arranging a time for parents and carers to meet privately with their child's key worker. At the meeting, the key worker talks about the assessment methods that were used and the outcome of the assessment. They will summarise the progress that has been made and establish what children are expected to learn next, drawing attention to any areas that may need particular attention. Parents and carers are often keen to know how they can support their child's learning at home, so practitioners are advised to think this through before the meeting. For instance, the practitioner may suggest that the parents or carers give their child plenty of opportunities to mark make at home by providing pencils, crayons and paper perhaps.

The key worker should summarise carefully. If a child has not been progressing as expected this will of course need to be discussed. The matter should be handled openly but sensitively. The practitioner should ensure that they focus on what children *can* do and the achievements they *have* made too, as this will give parents and carers a balanced report. Practitioners will want to work in partnership with parents and carers with regard to what should happen next, and to decide if outside support is needed. However, parents and carers may not know about the options open to them.

An effective team should value the contributions of all team members

Practitioners should be ready with information about the support available and should have strategies in mind to help the child progress, so that they can end the meeting looking ahead positively. Families may want to think about what has been said and to meet again for further discussion on the way ahead.

Practitioners should share their assessment findings with appropriate colleagues. This ensures that everyone working with a group of children understands how individual children are progressing, what the child is expected to learn next, and how this will be achieved. This informs practitioners' practical work with the children – they know how to support them effectively to encourage and extend their learning and developmental progress. Many settings share the planning of activities. It is essential that those involved in planning are clear about the summative findings of individuals' assessments – only then can the assessment inform the planning, ensuring that appropriate activities are planned to meet the needs of all the children in the group.

When liaising with outside specialists and other professionals supporting a particular child, it is often appropriate to share assessment information to inform the planning for the child concerned.

Representatives of visiting local or national inspectorates (Ofsted, for example) will also require access to assessments.

Confidentiality and data protection

Any personal information about children or families should be treated as confidential.

This includes information about children's individual development, learning and individual needs. You must not disclose details about this to anyone who does not need to know. There is important information about confidentiality and data protection in Unit 301 Develop and promote positive relationships.

 Link   **Unit 301** Develop and promote positive relationships

Improvement of provision and staff development

Summative assessments can reveal not just how well an individual child is learning and progressing, but also how well the provision is meeting children's learning and development needs.

Looking at a number of summative assessments allows practitioners to evaluate the bigger picture. If children are generally not progressing well in one or more particular areas, it may be necessary to improve the way the setting works in that area. Practitioners should discuss this to pinpoint what action can be taken. In some regions an Advisory Teacher may be able to offer support. For instance, it may be that more activities are needed to promote the learning of certain concepts that have not been given due attention. Or perhaps there is a lack of equipment to support specific types of play and learning.

Sometimes staff lack confidence in a certain area or have gaps in their knowledge, which impacts on children's progress. In this case, staff development or training is needed. Identifying these issues is a positive step – once the issues are identified they can be addressed and rectified.

Justine's review

Justine has been reviewing summative assessments at her setting. She has noticed that several three- and four-year-olds are not making good progress with their mark making and early (or emergent) writing skills. She raises this in a staff meeting so that she can discuss the possible implications with her colleagues.

The practitioners conclude that while they have mark-making activities available on the table tops at every session, not all of the children choose to participate in them. So some children actually have very little experience of making marks and practising early writing. They decide to provide children with opportunities to write and mark make in many different areas of the setting. They introduce several new strategies, including the provision of paper and pencils to the role-play area – children can now make shopping lists and so on. They also take chalk outside so that children can make marks on the ground. They plan to purchase some new and interesting mark-making materials, as supplies are old and have started to dwindle.

➤ *How can Justine and her colleagues monitor the impact of their new strategies over time?* **K3P342**

➤ *If introducing new activities and resources does not impact on children's progress in this area, what else may need to be considered?* **K3P342**

Factors that may negatively affect learning

There are some factors that may negatively affect children's learning:

- Low self-esteem

  If a child has low self-esteem, they may feel that they are incapable of doing all sorts of things well. They may expect to fail, or expect adults and their peers to disapprove of them. When a child feels that way, they may stop trying to achieve or only attempt tasks half-heartedly. They may withdraw from activities and/or the group. This is a self-fulfilling prophecy – the less a child tries, the more likely they are to fail. This reinforces their belief that they will fail, and they may try even less as a result

- A lack of confidence

  All children lack confidence sometimes, particularly when they find themselves in a new situation. However, some children experience an intense lack of confidence, which may persist for long periods or occur in many different situations. This can stop children from participating in activities altogether, limiting their experience and therefore their learning. Or they may only partially join in. Children cannot become fully absorbed and engaged in an activity if they are unable to relax. Children who feel tense and unsure are therefore less likely to learn as much as their peers

- Being the subject of discrimination

  If a child is the subject of discrimination, they may have low self-esteem and/or a lack of confidence as a result. But there are also additional issues that may impact on their learning. Children who are discriminated against are not given equal opportunities in comparison to their peers. This can limit children's experiences and relationships, which in turn affects their learning.

If children are not given equal opportunities to attend settings, participate fully in activities and have their needs met, they are unlikely to learn as effectively as children who do not experience discrimination and are therefore treated superiorly. Sadly, children can be discriminated against in many ways, for a range of different reasons. Here are some examples:

- A practitioner will not allow boys to play with dolls and the home corner because she thinks they are girls' toys
- A practitioner tells the parent of a disabled child that the setting is full when it is not, because he thinks meeting the child's needs will involve too much extra work
- A child from a family learning English as an additional language misses events including a Christmas party, a trip and an open day. Her parents could not read the notices written in English. No one told them about the events
- A key worker avoids spending time with a child who lives in a caravan because she thinks living on a traveller's site is dirty
- A wheelchair user is encouraged to read a book inside while the other children go outside to play because the practitioner thinks they will not be able to join in with the physical activities.

Whenever practitioners identify that a child may have an issue that is impacting negatively on their learning, they should seek ways to overcome the problem. (See the planning cycle on page 280.)

 Link **Unit 321** Support children with disabilities or special educational needs and their families
Unit 305 Protect and promote children's rights

Multilingual and bilingual settings

If a setting has children who are multilingual or bilingual, it is important for practitioners to understand that this may impact on the assessment process and the findings. For instance, children may have difficulties carrying out instructions or following a game not because they do not have the ability to do so, but because they have not fully understood the language used to explain what to do. In this case, working closely with parents and carers will help practitioners to build up a true picture of a child's learning and development.

Children who are learning two or more languages may start to talk later than their peers. This is thought to be because they are absorbing different language systems – or twice as much. With support, overall language development need not be affected. See Unit 301 Develop and promote positive relationships. Children learning more than two languages may also mix up whole sentences or words from different languages at times. Assessments are helpful for pinpointing the support that individual multilingual and bilingual children may need. (See the planning cycle on page 280.)

Link **Unit 301** Develop and promote positive relationships

Element 310.2

Are you ready for assessment?

Assess and record children's progress in consultation with others

You need to show that you can competently assess and record children's progress in consultation with others. To do this you will need to be directly observed by your assessor and present other types of evidence. The amount and type of evidence you need to present will vary. You should plan this with your assessor.

Direct observation by your assessor

Observation and/or expert witness testimony is the required assessment method to be used to evidence some of each element in this unit. If your assessor is unable to observe you, s/he will identify an expert in your workplace who will provide testimony of your work-based performance. Usually your assessor or expert witness will observe you in real work activities and this should provide most of the evidence for the performance criteria for the elements in this unit.

Preparing to be observed

You must show your assessor that you can refer to available guidance to assist with assessment, and that you can communicate requirements to relevant people. You must also show that you can undertake formative and summative assessment appropriately, drawing on everyday observations and assessments, and that you can liaise with and involve others as required. You must show that you can record assessments appropriately and use assessments to identify areas for improving practice.

Other types of evidence

You will need to present different types of evidence in order to:

- Cover criteria not observed by your assessor
- Show that you have the required knowledge, understanding and skills.

Such evidence could include:

- Work products such as assessment plans and information on the assessment process compiled for families and/or colleagues
- Case studies, projects, assignments and reflective accounts of your work
- Confidential records such as individual children's assessment records. These should not be placed in your portfolio – they must remain in their usual location and be referred to in the assessor records in your portfolio.

Check your knowledge

- Why is it important to remain objective when carrying out assessment? **K3M338**
- What impact does the Data Protection Act 1998 have on assessment records? **K3M339**
- What part does assessment of children's progress play in the planning cycle? **K3D341**
- How should assessment of children's progress inform staff development? **K3P342**

Reflective practice

You will have used assessments of children's progress to inform staff development and improve provision. Keep a note of staff development undertaken. When assessments are next recorded, evaluate the progress that has been made in staff practice by considering any changes that may have occurred.

UNIT 312

Plan and implement positive environments for babies and children under three years

*T*his unit is about the process of observing babies and children under three years, assessing and recording the results of observations and using them to plan environments, routines and activities that will enhance development. It includes methods of observation and assessment, strategies and planning.

This unit contains four elements:

- **CCLD 312.1** *Observe, assess and record developmental progress of babies and children under three years*
- **CCLD 312.2** *Communicate with babies and children under three years to develop positive relationships*
- **CCLD 312.3** *Plan and implement activities to enhance development*
- **CCLD 312.4** *Exchange information and respond to parents' needs and preferences for their babies and children under three years*

Introduction

The observation and assessment of babies and children is essential. It tells us about the stage of children's development, and informs the way in which we work with children to meet their care and developmental needs.

Element 312.1

Observe, assess and record developmental progress of babies and children under three years

K3D386
K3D387
K3D388
K3D389
K3D390
K3D391
K3D392
K3D393
K3D394
K3M396
K3M397

The purpose of observing babies and young children

Observation is a tool used by practitioners to distance themselves from the children they work with so that they can be objective about their behaviour and development. Through observation, practitioners can evaluate the progress and development made by babies and young children in all areas of their development. Unit CCLD 303, Promote children's development, explains how to carry out observations, analyse the information gathered, and use it to inform planning. Details about how to share information gathered while respecting confidentiality are also included.

Link **Unit CCLD 303** Promote children's development

Patterns of development

In order to make meaningful observations, practitioners must know and understand the accepted usual patterns of development of children aged 0–3 years. It is only then that practitioners can draw conclusions about how well children are progressing and what support they may need.

It is important to understand that the accepted developmental norms, which can be found in Unit CCLD 303 Promote children's development, are approximate guides to when babies and children are likely to achieve certain milestones. This is explained in detail in the unit.

Link **Unit CCLD 303** Promote children's development

Theories of child development and frameworks

Theories of child development inform the way in which we work with babies and young children. You can read more about the key theories of learning and development in Unit CCLD 309 Plan and implement curriculum frameworks for early education, Unit CCLD 303 Promote children's development and Unit CCLD 318 Plan for and support self-directed play. Further information about the Early Years Foundation Stage (EYFS) is outlined in Element CCLD 312.3.

Link **Unit CCLD 309** Plan and implement curriculum frameworks for early education
Unit CCLD 303 Promote children's development
Unit CCLD 318 Plan for and support self-directed play

Element 312.1

Are you ready for assessment?

Observe, assess and record developmental progress of babies and children under three years

You need to show that you can competently observe, assess and record the developmental progress of babies and children under three years. To do this you will need to be directly observed by your assessor and present other types of evidence. The amount and type of evidence you will need to present will vary. You should plan this with your assessor.

➤

Direct observation by your assessor

Observation and/or expert witness testimony is the required assessment method to be used to evidence some of each element in this unit. If your assessor is unable to observe you, s/he will identify an expert in your workplace who will provide testimony of your work-based performance. Usually your assessor or expert witness will observe you in real work activities and this should provide most of the evidence for the performance criteria for the elements in this unit.

Preparing to be observed

You will need to show your assessor that you can observe, assess and record developmental progress of babies and children under three, using appropriate observation techniques. You must also show that you can provide information on the progress of babies and children to parents, and refer any concerns

appropriately. You must follow your setting's organisational policies and procedures.

Other types of evidence

You will need to present different types of evidence in order to:

• Cover criteria not observed by your assessor

• Show that you have the required knowledge and understanding and skills.

Such evidence could include:

• Work products such as information leaflets for parents and carers

• Confidential records such as child observations. These should not be placed in your portfolio – they must remain in their usual location and be referred to in the assessor records in your portfolio

• Case studies, projects, assignments and reflective accounts of your work.

Communicate with babies and children under three years to develop positive relationships

Element **312.2**

Communication methods

K3C395
K3D398
K3C399
K3C400
K3C401
K3D402
K3C404
K3C405

Language is generally thought of as the main way in which we:

● Communicate with one another

● Express ourselves.

Learning how to use language is vital to the social development of babies and young children. We use language in our social interactions in many ways, including to:

● Share information

Children learn (and teach) through listening and talking. They can also demonstrate what they know and put forward their own ideas

- Share our feelings and experiences

    Children develop emotionally when they can use language to express themselves. For example, rather than simply crying they can explain to a carer what is wrong. They can share their interests, achievements and news, and receive feedback

- Ask questions

    Children become more independent and self-reliant as they ask questions and ask for desired objects for themselves

- Negotiate

    Children's social relationships with peers develop as they are able to negotiate with language – they can agree to share toys and take turns

- Organise and plan

    Children's independence and self-reliance grows, along with their confidence and self-esteem as they are able to plan and organise for themselves – 'I'll meet you on the bench in the playground at lunchtime.'

- Get to know each other

    Conversations are often the starting point for friendships.

Language is also a tool for thinking. Most of us think in words when we mentally direct ourselves. For example, you may think, 'I need to buy a birthday card on my way home'. People sometimes say their thoughts aloud to themselves without even realising they are doing it – you may have had experience of this. It happens because thinking in words comes so naturally.

Words can also help us to bring to mind information we have stored in our brains. If someone mentions the word 'beach', a visual image of the seaside may come to you, or perhaps you will think back to your last holiday. So we have learnt that language is important to social and emotional skills, and also to intellectual (or cognitive) development.

But communication is not just about language. There are a range of communication methods you can use with babies and young children. They are not all verbal. For example, think how easy it is to let someone know whether you approve or disapprove of something they are doing, just by the expression on your face. A range of communication methods is shown on the diagram below.

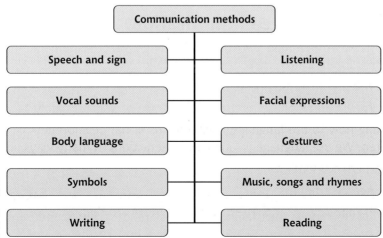

Organisational chart of communication methods

Practitioners need to select methods of communication that are appropriate to the babies and young children they are working with, and the situation or activity at hand. To do this, practitioners need to have good knowledge and understanding of:

- How babies and children learn to communicate
- How to communicate effectively with babies and children
- Individual children's developmental stages
- Individual children's communication needs.

It is important to be aware of the pattern of communication development outlined below because it helps practitioners to know how to interact with children in the right ways at the right time. By doing this, practitioners can engage babies and children and encourage their skills.

Talking with others is essential for children to adjust and refine their language skills

Patterns of communication

Experts have identified two phases of language development, in which babies and children listen, watch, make sounds and talk:

- The pre-linguistic phase, occurring at the age of approximately 0–12 months
- The linguistic phase, occurring at the age of approximately 1–5 years.

The pre-linguistic phase can be divided into three typical age categories, given below. Methods to engage the attention and interest of babies at each age category are suggested.

- Age 0–3 months

  Babies express their feelings (such as tiredness, hunger and emotional distress) by crying. They learn to recognise the sound of their parents' and carers' voices through listening. They can be soothed with gentle tones from a well-known adult. They will smile. They are interested in faces – they watch them and respond to them.

Methods to engage and interest: spend plenty of time talking to babies in a lively tone when they are content, and soothe them reassuringly with gentle tones when they are distressed. Ensure babies can see your face – make eye-contact with babies when communicating with them. An ideal time to communicate is when attending to babies' care needs. The baby and carer can look into each other's eyes during nappy changing and bottle feeding, for example.

Making eye contact is very important

● Age 3–6 months

Babies start to make a range of playful, short sounds – they babble and coo. They experiment with sounds, rhymes and volume. They enjoy vocal exchanges with adults in the style of conversation. They laugh and squeal to express delight, and cry to express distress.

Methods to engage and interest babies: join in with babies' playful babbles, repeating sounds back to them. Continue to talk to babies frequently and engage them in 'conversation' – talk to them, then pause to allow the baby to 'reply', then 'answer' them once again. Respond with delight with your facial expressions, body language and your speech when babies communicate their delight to you. Show sympathy in your facial expressions, body language and your speech when babies communicate their distress to you. Remember to talk WITH babies, not TO them.

● Age 6–12 months

Babies learn to use sound deliberately – to imitate and to get attention. They may make sounds whilst gesturing to show adults what they want. Babbling begins to sound tuneful. Babies play around with sound, joining vowel sounds and consonant sounds together. Most of the sounds needed for language can now be made. By 12 months most babies understand the meaning of around 15–20 words.

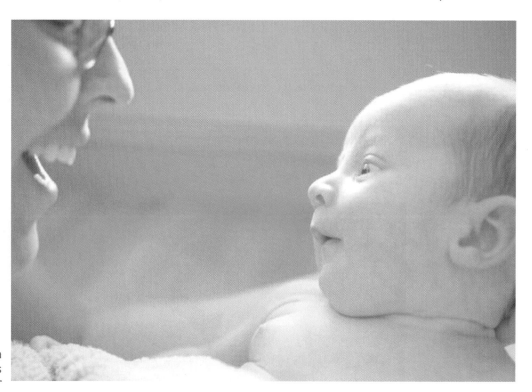

Talking with babies

Methods to engage and interest: continue talking with babies. Look out for signs that they are using sounds for deliberate communication – respond to this to encourage babies to repeat their efforts. Simple songs and rhymes are often appreciated – babies enjoy getting to know them and like to anticipate the fun endings to old favourites such as 'Round and Round the Garden' (that ends in a tickle), or 'Horsey, Horsey' (that ends with the child being softly bounced up and down on the carer's knee). As babies learn to clap, they can join in with 'pat-a-cake' rhymes.

The linguistic phase can also be divided into three typical age categories, given below. Methods to engage the attention and interest of children at each age category are once again suggested.

- Age 12–18 months

  Babies begin to say single words at around 12 months, although these may only be understood by their parents/carers. The vocabulary expands to about 15 words within the next three months. Babies become more aware of other people's body language – for instance, they may follow someone else's gaze.

  Methods to engage and interest: make sure that you respond encouragingly to babies' first words, so that they will be motivated to keep talking to you. Babies enjoy sharing first picture books with adults. They enjoy learning the names of objects they see in the pictures. They also enjoy learning the sounds that familiar animals make. As they become aware of body language, children enjoy simple songs with actions they can copy.

- Age 18–24 months

  Children start to use two words together first, and then begin to say simple phrases. Most children can communicate their meaning to parents/carers by two years or shortly after. They have a vocabulary of about 200 words – they are saying up to 20 new words each month.

Methods to engage and interest: show lots of interest in what children have to say. Ensure that you reply to children whenever they talk to you. Take what they say seriously, even if words are missing, or you are not sure what is meant. Take note of children's gestures – they often use them to fill in the gaps in their vocabularies. It is important that children feel their efforts at communicating meaning are worthwhile. Give them plenty of opportunities to interact with their peers and slightly older children if possible. Read children short, simple stories, and sing familiar songs slowly so they can join in with words or phrases they know.

- Age 2–3 years

Children speak in simple sentences. They begin to ask simple questions (what/where). They pick up new words easily, and their vocabulary continues to expand. They make mistakes such as saying, 'I goed' rather than 'I went', or 'I sleeped' rather than 'I slept'. Children now use plurals and negatives, e.g. 'dolls' and 'No drink left'. Children may need time to stop and think during speech, which can be mistaken for stammering.

Methods to engage and interest: make sure children are in an environment rich with exciting language – conversation, songs, rhymes and stories will be absorbed and used as inspiration for communication. Children's questions should be answered, even if they are repetitive. Introduce children to expressive words for feelings and describing, e.g. happy, sad, excited, angry, wet, dry, soft, hard. Demonstrate language for thinking by using it aloud yourself, 'I wonder what will happen if I pour this water into the sand . . . oh look, it's all wet now!'

Language continues to develop – most children talk fluently by the age of five.

The diagrams below and on page 296 show the main characteristics of the phases of language development:

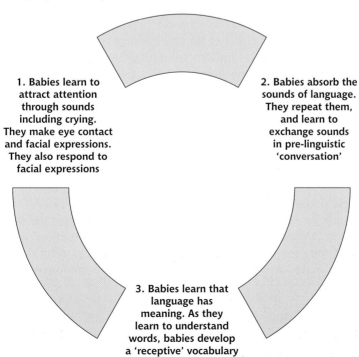

1. Babies learn to attract attention through sounds including crying. They make eye contact and facial expressions. They also respond to facial expressions

2. Babies absorb the sounds of language. They repeat them, and learn to exchange sounds in pre-linguistic 'conversation'

3. Babies learn that language has meaning. As they learn to understand words, babies develop a 'receptive' vocabulary

The pre-linguistic phase

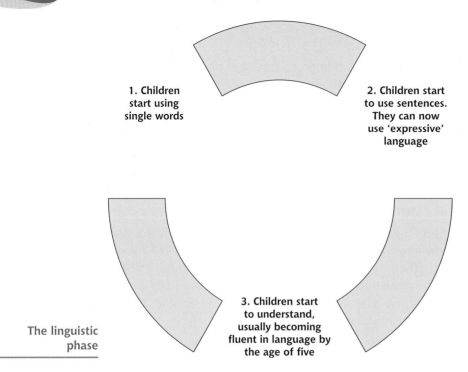

1. Children start using single words

2. Children start to use sentences. They can now use 'expressive' language

3. Children start to understand, usually becoming fluent in language by the age of five

The linguistic phase

Reading and writing

As we have identified, reading and writing are forms of communication. Children are not expected to read and write in the under-three age range. However, children under three can be encouraged to develop an interest in books – this will provide motivation to learn to read later on. Children under three can also be encouraged to make marks. In time children learn to make finer marks, and eventually they are able to write letters and words.

It is never too early to read to babies and young children. Even the youngest infants will enjoy hearing the rise and fall of an expressive voice reading aloud, even if the words cannot yet be understood. Children will enjoy stories long before they can read words – but a desire to read is the first step, and a love of stories fuels the desire. Just as children learn that spoken words carry meaning, they will learn that the words on the page are meaningful too. Children often learn this before the age of three – think how often a two-year-old will bring you a book to read to them. Most children will learn to recognise letters and odd words that are familiar to them by the time they leave nursery education, but most will not read until they start school.

Mark-making is the term we use to describe any activity in which children can deliberately make a mark. The obvious activities are art based – children make marks when they draw, crayon, paint, print, stamp and so on. But there are also more subtle alternatives – children can draw with a twig in the sand, or trace patterns on the ground with water.

Whenever children deliberately make such marks they are practising the skills they will need to write. They are learning the techniques for pencil control, and learning how to make their marks stop, start, flow and join. They are discovering how to move their arms and hands to make big shapes, small ones, thick ones and thin ones. They are feeling the satisfaction of leaving their mark, and feeling proud of their achievements.

At around three years, children will start emergent writing

It is not until their third or fourth year that most children make the small symbols in a row that we recognise as 'emergent writing', which is often mingled with real letters children have learnt from their own name. This emergent writing, which eventually evolves into writing, has its roots in those important early mark-making opportunities.

Sign language

Other forms of non-verbal communication include sign language, as we have mentioned. Sign language is generally used with children who have a hearing impairment. Makaton, a basic form of sign language, is frequently used with children who have learning difficulties which affect their ability to communicate through speech. There has recently been some interest in using signs with hearing babies. Some experts believe that teaching babies simple signs can help them to communicate before they have the ability to express themselves with words. They believe that this reduces frustration in babies, and that it does not delay verbal communication.

Allowing children to initiation conversation

There is a debate between experts about how and why children learn to communicate. Some believe that babies are born with an inbuilt desire to communicate, thanks to nature. Others believe that children develop a desire to communicate because they are brought up in a world of communication – in other words, it is down to nurture. Whether nature or nurture (or perhaps a mixture of both), babies and children do want to communicate with other people.

Practitioners should allow children to act on the motivation they feel by allowing them to initiate (start) communications themselves. Young babies may do this by cooing or babbling whilst looking at the carer changing their nappy perhaps. An older child may tap a carer on the arm and then gesture towards something that they want. Practitioners can take these things as 'conversational cues' – signs that the baby or child wants to communicate and is looking for a response. It is the response of the adult that shows the child that their communication was not only received and understood, it was valued.

We are all familiar with the desire to communicate. We are also familiar with wanting to end a conversation, and times when we do not want to communicate at all. Sometimes we do not want to communicate because we are concentrating, or thinking about something. Perhaps we are tired or just feeling quiet. Babies and young children are just the same. Practitioners should be aware of signs that the children in their care are ready to disengage from communication (ready to end it), or signals that reveal that they do not wish to communicate at all. Signs include children:

- Showing a lack of eye-contact, or disengaging from eye-contact
- Physically starting to move away
- Ignoring communications made to them
- Appearing distracted or more interested in something else that is going on.

Tone and expression

Aim to show the warmth and affection that you have for children by your tone of voice when you are communicating with them. This certainly makes communication more enjoyable for children, and it is likely to motivate them to communicate with you. Expression is also important. The way in which your voice rises and falls engages babies and young children. Your tone and expression also lets them know that you are being friendly or playful – even before they can understand the actual words that you are saying to them. Babies and children learn to trust people who frequently interact with them sensitively. This is at the heart of building a good relationship with babies and children.

Remember that your face and your body 'speak' for you even when you are not deliberately communicating. Be aware of this – try to ensure that your facial expressions and body language are appropriate to each situation. It is an essential part of communicating with babies and children. For example, leaning slightly forward with an open posture (not crossed arms) and looking at someone with your head tilted a little to the side, shows that you are receptive to communication. Crossed arms, hunched shoulders and leaning away all indicate that you are not interested in communicating. There are many specialised books that explain body language in detail.

As a matter of respect you should give your attention to individual children when you are talking with them. This can be difficult in group situations. Children are sometimes demanding, and they will interrupt one another with their communications. Children under three may have little concept of the need to wait. You can deal with this effectively by acknowledging children, so that they know you have noticed them, but asking them to wait. You could say for instance, 'Were you starting to tell me something Jack? I'll just finish listening to Sadie, and then I'll listen to you'. Make sure you always remember to listen to the child as you promised.

Speak with children at a level they can understand and a pace that suits them. Your knowledge of child development and individual children will once again be called upon. Respect the methods of communication chosen by babies and children, and respond to them. You should not force conversation or make children feel self-conscious about the way they communicate, or they may become reluctant to communicate in the future.

Using appropriate language when talking with or in front of children is a matter of professional conduct. Practitioners should ensure that adults do not carry on conversations between themselves that are not relevant to the job of work at hand. Discussions about individual children's progress or issues should not be carried out in earshot of the children. The language used should be positive and appropriate to the age and stage of development of the children. Remember that you are a role model for children – you must always model behaviour that shows respect for others. You should encourage children to communicate respectfully with adults and each other – being a good role model is essential to achieving this.

Language that labels children or makes them feel bad about themselves should never be used. For instance, a child may need to be told that an aspect of his behaviour is inappropriate, but he should never be told he is a 'naughty boy' or a 'troublemaker'. A child may need to be told to keep the noise down and to listen at story time, but she should never be told to 'shut up'. Using language in this way is hostile, unnecessary and unprofessional.

Encouraging communication through play

Many activities can be used to successfully encourage communication through play. Some encourage talking, others listening, and some encourage non-verbal communication. Touch, mark-making and pretend play are all valuable ways to encourage children to communicate through different media. The list of possible activities is extensive, but some ideas are listed here:

- Role play with dressing-up clothes, a home corner and other props
- Play opportunities with dolls, puppets and soft toys
- Small world play with resources such as a farmyard and animals, or a garage and vehicles

Allowing children to explore and practise a wide range of activities will help to develop their language skills

- Basic playground games such as 'Ring-a-ring-o-roses'
- Use of toy telephones
- Art activities featuring mark making, such as painting and colouring
- Playing side by side at the water tray, sharing resources
- Interesting objects to explore, such as items that scrunch, squelch, rattle or jingle
- Ball games between two or more players (rolling, kicking, throwing, etc.).

You can find further play activities to encourage communication in Element 312.3. They are identified as promoting Communication, language and literacy (CLL).

Providing a good range of activities to stimulate all areas of development allows children to explore a range of interests. Practitioners can share these with children, using them as a topic of conversation. Joining in alongside babies and children and talking with them about their activities helps to develop relationships as well as communication skills. With experience it becomes a very natural, intuitive part of a practitioner's role.

 ## Communication differences and difficulties

Some children learn more than one language. When this is the case, there may be noticeable differences in the way in which children's patterns of communication develop.

Some children will experience communication difficulties, which may be long or short term. Relevant information about communication differences and difficulties is given on pages 8–12 of Unit CCLD 301 Develop and promote positive relationships, and on pages 392–4 of Unit CCLD 321 Support children with disabilities or special educational needs and their families.

 **Link**   **Unit CCLD 301** Develop and promote positive relationships
Unit CCLD 321 Support children with disabilities or special educational needs and their families

Element 312.2

Are you ready for assessment?

Communicate with babies and children under three years to develop positive relationships

You need to show that you can competently communicate with babies and children under three years to develop positive relationships. To do this you will need to be directly observed by your assessor and present other types of evidence. The amount and type of evidence you will need to present will vary. You should plan this with your assessor.

Direct observation by your assessor

Observation and/or expert witness testimony is the required assessment method to be used to evidence some of each element in this unit. If your assessor is unable to observe you, s/he will identify an expert in your workplace who will provide testimony of your work-based performance. Usually your assessor or expert witness will observe you in real work activities and this should provide most of the evidence for the performance criteria for the elements in this unit.

Preparing to be observed

You will need to show your assessor that you can use a range of appropriate communication methods to communicate and interact with babies and children under three years, and in doing so promote positive relationships. You must show that you can encourage babies and children under three to communicate respectfully with each other

and adults, and that you effectively manage children's responses when communication differences are experienced.

Other types of evidence

You will need to present different types of evidence in order to:

- Cover criteria not observed by your assessor
- Show that you have the required knowledge, understanding and skills.

Such evidence could include:

- Work products such as resources or materials made or selected to enhance communication
- Case studies, projects, assignments and reflective accounts of your work
- Original certificates/attendance records and other evidence of prior experience and learning that matches the requirements of the standards.

Element 312.3 *Plan and implement activities to enhance development*

⌒ Curriculum frameworks

K3D403
K3C404
K3D406
K3H407
K3D408
K3H409

Practitioners must always plan activities with reference to any curriculum frameworks for children under three that apply to their home country, and they should seek to work in line with best practice.

We will take the EYFS, which applies in England, as our example in this unit. Turn to Unit 309 for details of the curriculums that apply in the other home countries.

You learnt about the EYFS in Unit CCLD 309. It will be helpful to re-read pages 225–232 now before returning to this chapter.

Link **Unit CCLD 309** Plan and implement curriculum frameworks for early education

Early Years Foundation Stage

The EYFS was introduced in 2008. It applies to all children from birth to the end of the academic year in which they have their fifth birthday. Prior to this, there was a curriculum known as the Foundation Stage, which applied to children aged three to five years, and a separate framework (the Birth to Three Matters Framework) for younger children. So when learners are first introduced to the EYFS, they sometimes become a little confused.

Most can see how the Themes, Principles and Commitments apply to children of all ages. But they cannot always see immediately how the Areas of Learning and the Aspects they are broken into can apply to such a broad age range. However, for each Area of Learning, there is an individual, double-sided resource card, which provides important information.

Personal, social and emotional development

The card for personal, social and emotional development has been reproduced below. On side one, you'll find the requirements for personal, social and emotional development. This concisely tells providers what they must do to promote this Area of Learning. You'll see that each Aspect of personal, social and emotional development has been expressed in more detail, and there's also a section which explains what personal, social and emotional development means for children. Take some time to study side one of the resource card now, remembering that babies and children will progressively work towards the aspirations that are listed for their development throughout their first five years.

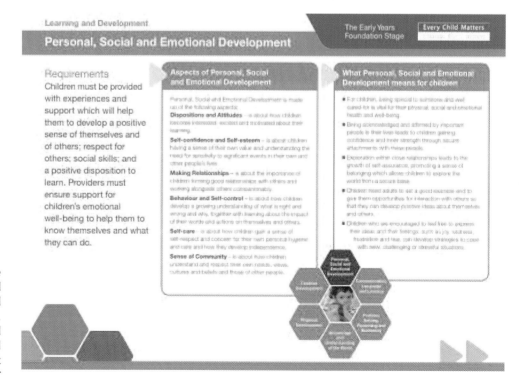

Side one of the EYFS Learning and Development card for Personal, Social and Emotional Development

We'll now consider examples of how some of the information given on side one of the card relates to children of all ages:

- You've already learnt about bonding and the importance of babies' forming key relationships with carers, so you'll know that being special to someone is as important to young babies as it is to older children. (You'll learn more about this is Unit CCLD 314.)
- Growth of self-assurance should ideally begin when a child is very young and carry on throughout their life, although self-assurance will be displayed in different ways at different ages, as highlighted in the practical example below.

 Link **Unit CCLD 314** Provide physical care that promotes the health and development of babies and children under three years

Elliot's self assurance grows

Elliot attends a day nursery. When he was 11 months old, Carolina was his baby-room key worker. She often sat on the carpet and played with Elliot. He would eventually crawl off to explore the room and resources available, but he would frequently return to the security of being by Carolina's side.

When he was two, Elliot moved to the toddler room. Carolina accompanied him on visits at first to help him to settle in and get to know his new key worker, Mo. Mo supported Elliot as he got to know the other children. Before long, Mo and Elliot's family helped him to become toilet trained.

Now Elliot is three and he's starting to think of things to tell the whole group at circle time. He sometimes gets frustrated when he needs to wait for his turn, particularly when another child has a toy that he'd like. But with support Elliot is learning about feelings and how to cope with them.

➤ *Was Carolina effectively promoting Elliot's development in the area of personal, social and emotional development? Give reasons for your answer.*

➤ *Is Elliot's personal, social and emotional development being promoted effectively now? Give reasons for your answer.*

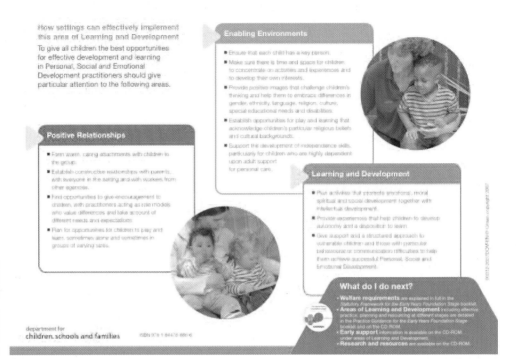

Side two of the
EYFS Learning and
Development card
for Personal,
social and
emotional
development

Side two of the resource card tells practitioners which areas they should focus on particularly, in order to give all children the best opportunities for effective personal, social and emotional development. These are presented in the form of the EYFS Themes and Principles. Read them carefully now.

Returning to the practical example, which of the principles do you think Carolina and Mo were promoting in their work with Elliot? Hopefully, you've spotted several. Obviously, the practitioners would be doing much more than is described in the brief example of practice given here. Spend a few minutes thinking of other ways in which the staff would be likely to promote Elliot's personal, social and emotional development during his years at nursery.

Problem solving, reasoning and numeracy

Study the resource card for problem solving, reasoning and numeracy, which is reproduced below.

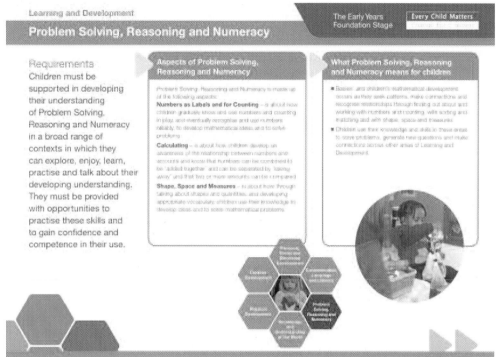

Side one of the EYFS Learning and Development card for Problem solving, reasoning and numeracy

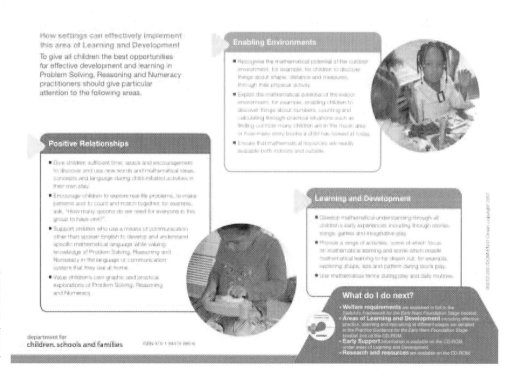

Side two of the EYFS Learning and Development card for Problem solving, reasoning and numeracy

Hopefully, you are beginning to see how problem solving, reasoning and numeracy can be promoted for babies and young children, as well as for older children. It is all a matter of providing activities and experiences that are appropriate to the child's level. So a toddler may play with a shape sorter, while a four-year-old may draw shapes in the sand with her finger. The older child may independently count out how many knives and forks are needed at lunchtime, while the toddler may follow a request to 'give one to everyone'.

You can view all the learning and development resource cards online at www.standards. dcsf.gov.uk/eyfs/site/resource/pdfs.htm.

Activities to support learning and development

When planning activities for babies and young children, practitioners should:

- Include a good range of activities to support all areas of children's learning and development
- Provide activities that are sufficiently challenging
- Consider the interests and needs of individual children (this will be informed by observations)
- Ensure that activities are in line with the overall plan for the setting
- Plan to use the play space effectively

It is important to develop an integrated approach to planning. To do this you must recognise that the activities you provide for babies and young children will generally promote more than one area of their learning development. Children's learning is not compartmentalised, even though we may talk about the different areas of learning and development separately.

For instance, when a young child talks with an adult whilst they are watering the setting's houseplants together, the child could be simultaneously learning and developing in all of the following areas:

- Learning to pour – Physical development (PD)
- Listening and talking – Communication, language and literacy (CLL)
- Counting the plants – Problem solving, reasoning and numeracy (PRN)
- Learning how to care for plants – Knowledge and understanding of the world (KUW)
- Taking turns – Personal, social and emotional development (PSE).

By pulling together different areas of learning into activities when you are planning, you can maximise the potential learning opportunity for babies and young children. It is not necessary to mould every activity to fit every area – this would probably make your activity so broad that it would lack purpose – but it is effective to integrate those that are a natural fit.

Here are some examples of activities for babies and children across the 0–3 age range. The abbreviations in brackets show which of the Areas of Learning the activities are likely to promote.

0–6 months

- Playing with rattles (PD)
- Lying underneath a baby gym, reaching up to play with the resources suspended (PD)
- Interacting with carer in early conversational style – the adult will talk, wait for the baby's response of a babble or coo, then talk again (CLL, PSE)
- Game of 'Round and Round the Garden' and enjoying other rhymes (CLL, PSE, CD)
- Splashing in the bath or pool (PD, KUW).

6–12 months

- Sitting up at the table with peers at mealtimes, helping to feed oneself (PSE, CLL, PD)
- Crawling or walking after pull-along toys (PD, KUW)
- Plenty of conversation with time to respond, as first words are spoken and babbling becomes expressive (PSE, CLL)
- Playing with stacking cups (PRN, PD)
- Finger painting (CD, PD).

1–2 years

- Playing with sand and water (PD, KUW, PRN)
- Pushing and pulling large wheeled toys, such as baby walkers and prams (PD, KUW)
- Sharing number rhymes and baby songs with actions (CLL, PSE, CD, PD, PRN)
- Colouring with chunky crayons (PD, CLL, CD)
- Playing with dolls, puppets and soft toys (PSE, CD, CLL).

Playing in the sand

2–3 years

- Using large wheeled ride-on toys (PD, KUW)
- Throwing and catching large soft balls (PD, PSE)
- Learning and sharing songs, rhymes and stories with peers (PSE, CLL, CD)
- Playing first lotto matching games (PSE, CLL, PRN)
- Making simple collages with natural materials, paste and a brush (PD, CD, KUW)
- Counting out 'how many' (PRN).

Challenging activities

Lev Vygotsky developed a theory about how children learn from challenging activities, known as the 'zone of proximal development'. You can read about it in Unit CCLD 309 Plan and implement curriculum frameworks for early education. The theory still influences the activities we provide for babies and young children today. There is also further information about the provision and implementation of activities in the Unit.

Many experts now agree that providing babies and young children with challenging activities helps to:

- Encourage their developmental progress
- Stimulate their interest and curiosity
- Keep them motivated to participate
- Foster a love of learning.

It is important that you have a good understanding of the patterns of child development. This enables you to provide activities that are challenging enough to stretch the abilities of babies and young children, without causing the frustration that comes when activities are *too* challenging and difficult. There is information about the benefit of linking activities to extend skill and understanding in Unit CCLD 314 Provide physical care that promotes the health and development of babies and children under three years. Child development information is included in Unit CCLD 303 Promote children's development.

Link **Unit CCLD 309** Plan and implement curriculum frameworks for early education
Unit CCLD 314 Provide physical care that promotes the health and development of babies and children under three years
Unit CCLD 303 Promote children's development

Asher works in a crèche. He is planning some art and craft activities for a group of one- and two-year-olds.

He plans finger painting, a new experience for some of the youngest children. He also plans painting with brushes of varying thickness, which will be a challenge for several children of 15 months and over who are learning how to manipulate tools. He plans a simple collage-sticking activity for the two-year-olds. This will be challenging and it will build on the children's existing ability to use a paintbrush. They will use similar skills in a new way to paste pictures onto paper.

➤ *Why has Asher planned different activities for different age ranges?*
K3D408

➤ *Why has he chosen activities that link with children's existing skills and understanding?*   **K3D408**

Interests and needs

As human beings, what we are interested in and what like to do is part of our personality and identity. Personal interests are important and should be respected. All children, even babies, have their own interests. Practitioners can find out about these through:

- Conversations with families
- Own observations of babies and children
- Discussions with colleagues.

The interests of the children in your care can be incorporated into the activities that are offered. This fuels the motivation of individual children to participate and helps to foster a love of learning early on in childhood.

The provision of activities should also take into account the individual development capabilities of babies and young children. This will be informed by discussions with families and observations made by key workers and colleagues. It may also be necessary to adapt some activities to meet individual children's needs.

You must check that any activities that you plan fit in with the overall plans for the setting. You must also ensure that the resources you need will be available at the time of the activity. There is further information about this on pages in Unit CCLD 309 Plan and implement curriculum frameworks for early education.

Link **Unit CCLD 309** Plan and implement curriculum frameworks for early education

Rewards

Babies and young children respond well when they are rewarded for something they have done. They are encouraged to repeat the rewarded behaviour. Praise is the most effective (and most practical) reward. Show that you are pleased when babies and young children make an effort during activities as well as when they achieve. It will motivate them to try again and it will build up their confidence to try something new. It also helps to foster a love of learning. Basic but effective forms of praise appropriate for use with babies and young children include giving a big smile, saying well done and clapping.

There is more information about giving rewards to encourage repetition of behaviour on page 413 of Unit CCLD 337 Create environments that promote positive behaviour.

Link **Unit CCLD 337** Create environments that promote positive behaviour

Use space effectively

All children need space to exercise their whole bodies and to develop their physical skills. This is particularly important for children in the 0–3 age range since it is during the development phases of the first three years that children master key physical skills – rolling, sitting, crawling, standing, walking and running. Children become naturally very physically active from about 15–18 months, and they need plenty of opportunities to move and exercise their bodies.

You should take this into consideration when planning the layout of the environment, so that space can be used effectively. There is more about this on page 307 of Unit CCLD 314 Provide physical care that promotes the health and development of babies and children under three years, and also on pages 161–3 of Unit CCLD 306 Plan and organise environments for children and families.

A toddler using a small slide

Link Unit CCLD 306 Plan and organise environments for children and families
Unit CCLD 314 Provide physical care that promotes the health and development of babies and children under three years

Changing and adapting activities or routines

Sometimes it is necessary to change or adapt activities that have been planned. Reasons for this can be found in Unit CCLD 309 Plan and implement curriculum frameworks for early education. Information about how to adapt activities to suit the individual needs of babies and children can be found in Unit CCLD 321 Support children with disabilities or special educational needs and their families.

Practitioners may need to adapt a child's routine in response to changes of circumstance. For instance, a baby who has had a poor night's sleep may refuse breakfast because she is over tired. She may need to go to sleep instead, and have her breakfast when she wakes up. Consequently, the rest of the day's usual meal and sleep times will need to be adjusted. Other circumstances that may affect a baby's or child's routine include illness, teething, weaning, adjusting to new environments and going on an outing. It is also necessary it change routines in response to children's development – as time goes on babies and children will need less daytime sleep for example, and new routines will be introduced as toilet training begins.

Link Unit CCLD 309 Plan and implement curriculum frameworks for early education
Unit CCLD 321 Support children with disabilities or special educational needs and their families

Risk assessment and safety

You must follow the health and safety policy of your setting. This will explain how to carry out essential risk assessments. You must also know what to do if equipment or aspects of the environment do not meet the safety standards. The relevant information can be found in Unit CCLD 302 Develop and maintain a healthy, safe and secure environment for children and in Unit CCLD 306 Plan and organise environments for children and families. There are details about ensuring that risk assessment does not limit opportunities for babies and children on page 316 of Unit CCLD 314 Provide physical care that promotes the health and development of babies and children under three years.

Link Unit CCLD 302 Develop and maintain a healthy, safe and secure environment for children
Unit CCLD 306 Plan and organise environments for children and families
Unit CCLD 314 Provide physical care that promotes the health and development of babies and children under three years

Element 312.3

Are you ready for assessment?

Plan and implement activities to enhance development

You need to show that you can competently plan and implement activities for babies and children under three years. To do this you will need to be directly observed by your assessor and present other types of evidence. The amount and type of evidence you will need to present will vary. You should plan this with your assessor.

Direct observation by your assessor

Observation and/or expert witness testimony is the required assessment method to be used to evidence some of each element in this unit. If your assessor is unable to observe you, s/he will identify an expert in your workplace who will provide testimony of your work-based performance. Usually your assessor or expert witness will observe you in real work activities and this should provide most of the evidence for the performance criteria for the elements in this unit.

Preparing to be observed

You will need to show your assessor that you can plan and implement a variety of activities to stimulate the development of babies and children under three years. The activities must be appropriate for the children with whom you are working. You must show that you can link activities and encourage babies and children to extend their range and levels of skill and understanding. You must also assess risk and plan activities with reference to curriculum frameworks.

Other types of evidence

You will need to present different types of evidence in order to:

- Cover criteria not observed by your assessor
- Show that you have the required knowledge, understanding and skills.

Such evidence could include:

- Work products such as activity plans
- Case studies, projects, assignments and reflective accounts of your work
- Confidential records such as notes from meetings. These should not be placed in your portfolio – they must remain in their usual location and be referred to in the assessor records in your portfolio.

Element 312.4

Exchange information and respond to parents' needs and preferences for their babies and children under three years

Sharing information with parents and carers

K3M410
K3D411
K3P412

Practitioners must share with parents and carers information that can affect the care and well-being of young children. Details of day-to-day information to be shared are given on page 312 of Unit CCLD 314 Provide physical care that promotes the health and development of babies and children under three years. Families should also be informed periodically about the developmental progress of babies and young children. Information about this is included in Element 312.1.

Practitioners should also encourage families to share information they have about their baby or child which may affect their care and well-being. This information may include details about and changes to:

- Medical conditions including allergies and details of any medication or treatment
- Medical history
- Dietary requirements
- Likes and dislikes
- General routine – including details of eating and sleeping patterns
- Events in the child's life that may impact on their emotions.

The information should be documented, usually on the registration form, in line with the setting's organisational policies and procedures. Some information, about feeding or allergies for example, may also be displayed in food preparation areas.

Practitioners must pass on relevant information to colleagues – such as a child's sleeping pattern. However, information of a confidential nature must only be shared on a need-to-know basis. Parents should be reassured of this fact.

How to encourage families to share information is outlined in Unit CCLD 314 Provide physical care that promotes the health and development of babies and children under three years. Information about confidentiality is given in Unit CCLD 301 Develop and promote positive relationships.

Link

Unit CCLD 314 Provide physical care that promotes the health and development of babies and children under three years
Unit CCLD 301 Develop and promote positive relationships

Parents' preferred care routines

Practitioners must always respect parents as the primary carers of their children. As such, the views and preferences of parents must also be respected. Families will have preferences concerning the care routines of their babies and young children – how and when they are fed and put down for a sleep for example.

It is good practice for practitioners to meet with parents or carers to discuss their child's care routines before the child starts attending the setting. The meeting is usually conducted by the child's key worker. At this meeting, the key worker should ensure that he or she fully understands the child's needs and the parent's preferences. These should be documented as described above.

Where possible, practitioners should accommodate parental preferences if they are in line with current best practice. It is best for babies and young children to have similar routines at home and in the setting. Consistency makes for smooth transitions and continuity of care. Disturbed routines can affect children's well-being, leaving them unsettled and out of sorts.

Care routines need to be monitored, adapted and changed from time to time to ensure that they meet the needs of babies and children. These changes should be discussed and agreed with parents and carers. There is more information about this in Element 312.3.

Best practice

Sometimes the wishes of parents and carers do not reflect the current accepted best practice. In this case, it is important to discuss and resolve the issue in a harmonious way, with the best interests of the child in mind. Further information about this can be found in Unit CCLD 314 Provide physical care that promotes the health and development of babies and children under three years.

Families can be referred to other sources of advice both nationally and locally, including:

- Health visitors
- GPs
- Government websites
- Local parenting groups/classes
- Up-to-date books and leaflets.

Some families may need assistance from a language or sign interpreter when accessing sources of advice. Health visitors and GPs will have access to a range of leaflets and booklets in different languages and in large print and these are available on request. A directory of government websites can be found online at www.open.gov.uk.

Element 312.4

Are you ready for assessment?

Exchange information and respond to parents' needs and preferences for their babies and children under three years

You need to show that you can competently exchange information and respond to parents' needs and preferences for their babies and children under three years. To do this you will need to be directly observed by your assessor and present other types of evidence. The amount and type of evidence you will need to present will vary. You should plan this with your assessor.

Direct observation by your assessor

Observation and/or expert witness testimony is the required assessment method to be used to evidence some of each element in this unit. If your assessor is unable to observe you, s/he will identify an expert in your workplace who will provide testimony of your work-based performance. Usually your assessor or expert witness will observe you in real work activities and this should provide most of the evidence for the performance criteria for the elements in this unit.

Preparing to be observed

You will need to show your assessor that you can exchange information and respond to parents' needs and preferences for their babies and children under three years. You must show that you can exchange and discuss information that may affect children's welfare and routines, both with parents and within the setting. You must show that you can discuss and resolve issues when parents' preferences are not in line with best practice, and that you can monitor and adapt routines and relationships when necessary.

Other types of evidence

You will need to present different types of evidence in order to:

- Cover criteria not observed by your assessor
- Show that you have the required knowledge, understanding and skills.

Such evidence could include:

- Case studies, projects, assignments and reflective accounts of your work
- Confidential records such as notes from meetings or children's records. These should not be placed in your portfolio – they must remain in their usual location and be referred to in the assessor records in your portfolio.

Check your knowledge

- What is meant by baseline assessment?   **K3D389**
- What methods of observation might you use for babies and why?   **K3D386**
- Explain three ways to encourage children to communicate through play.   **K3C405**
- Explain what is meant by the term 'challenging activities' for individual babies and young children.   **K3D408**
- Why should you respect parents' preferences concerning the care routines of their babies and young children?   **K3M410**
- What sources of childcare advice are available to parents and carers?   **K3P412**

Reflective practice

What do your non-verbal communications say about you?

Try setting an alarm on a watch to go off at three occasions during one day. Each time it goes off, stop and consider your body language. What is it communicating at that exact moment? Is it sending children signs that you are open to communication? Make a note and reflect on your findings later. Do you need to re-train yourself to adopt more positive postures?

Provide physical care that promotes the health and development of babies and children under three years

*T*his unit is about providing care for babies and children in partnership with their parents.

The unit contains five elements:

- **CCLD 314.1** *Provide a safe and secure environment for babies and children under three*

- **CCLD 314.2** *Provide for the nutritional needs of babies and children under three years*

- **CCLD 314.3** *Supervise and use physical care routines to promote development*

- **CCLD 314.4** *Provide an emotionally secure and consistent environment in partnership with parents and carers*

- **CCLD 314.5** *Recognise and respond to illness in babies and children under three years*

Introduction

Babies and children under the age of three have specific physical care requirements. Practitioners must learn to recognise these and to meet them sensitively and with confidence, so that babies and young children can thrive in terms of their health and development. In this unit the term 'young children' refers to children under the age of three.

Element
314.1

Provide a safe and secure environment for babies and children under three years

K3H413
K3H414
K3H442
K3D415
K2H294

Legislation and regulations

Settings caring for babies and young children must comply with the relevant laws and regulations. The key ones are outlined in Unit CCLD 306 Plan and organise environments for children and families. The relationship between the safety and security requirements of the setting and the relationship between these and legislation/

regulations is also explained. There is further information in Unit CCLD 302 Develop and maintain a healthy, safe and secure environment for children.

 Link   **Unit CCLD 306** Plan and organise environments for children and families
Unit CCLD 302 Develop and maintain a healthy, safe and secure environment for children

Organisational issues

In order to ensure the health and safety of babies and young children, practitioners need to give careful consideration to the following.

Room arrangement

Babies and young children need to have plenty of clear floor space. Very young babies will need room to lie out comfortably on baby mats placed on the floor and there should be sufficient space to roll around. They will also spend some time in their baby chairs. As babies start to crawl they need plenty of room to manoeuvre and explore. When babies first start to walk they frequently fall over – when they are moving around in an open area there is less chance of them injuring themselves on furniture.

As they grow into busy toddlers, children often enjoy moving around a room quite quickly, making the most of the space they have to play in. They have not yet developed the concentration span necessary to spend very long in one place doing one activity.

Practitioners need to ensure that the layout of the setting accommodates plenty of clear floor space. It makes sense to keep furniture to the minimum. The stability of the furniture chosen is important as babies will use it to pull themselves to standing position and will hold onto it for support when they first start to walk.

Floor space must also be allocated to the equipment that is needed by this age group – high chairs and cots take up quite a lot of space in group settings.

Staffing levels and supervision

Babies and young children need constant and close supervision. They must not be left unsupervised at any time. In addition, much adult time is spent attending to their physical care needs. Practitioners will be making up feeds, feeding, changing nappies and so on. Babies and young children also need to have the time and attention of adults to meet their emotional needs (there is more about this in Element 314.4).

To allow for this, regulations stipulate that there must be a higher ratio of adults to young children than is required for older age ranges. The required ratios in England are:

- Children under two years: one adult to three children
- Children aged two years: one adult to four children.

These ratios are the accepted minimum standards. Many settings exceed them. There is more information about levels of supervision in Unit CCLD 302 Develop and maintain a healthy, safe and secure environment for children.

 Link   **Unit CCLD 302** Develop and maintain a healthy, safe and secure environment for children

Assessment of hazards and risks

Risk assessments are a vital part of keeping babies and children safe. There is information about how and why you should conduct risk assessment in Unit CCLD 302 Develop and maintain a healthy, safe and secure environment for children. A good understanding of children's development informs the assessment process – this is also explained in that Unit.

Practitioners should take all reasonable precautions to ensure that babies and children are safe. However, it is important that opportunities for development are not restricted. Practitioners have to accept that all children will incur minor injuries as they play and develop. As long as children run around and use equipment they will occasionally have minor accidents leading to grazes, bumps and bruises. But to deny children the opportunity to run and play would be wrong – it would limit their experiences and ultimately affect their development.

Health and safety policies held by settings will explain how the organisation manages risk assessment. Practitioners can take the opportunity to explain in the policy that risk assessment should ensure that all reasonable precautions are taken without restricting opportunities for development.

Give children the opportunity to play outside

⟍ Responsive care

It is important to have responsive, reflective and knowledgeable adults caring for babies and young children. 'Responsive care' is the term used to describe how practitioners identify and respond to the care needs of children. This is extremely important with this age group as they do not generally have the language to explain to adults what they need – practitioners must interpret this for themselves. This is a skill based on practitioners' knowledge of:

- The development pattern of babies and children
- The individual baby or child.

For instance, a baby may cry for a number of reasons. The practitioner needs to find out what is wrong so that they can attend to the child. The practitioner will look for signs accompanying the crying in order to work out what the baby needs. They will consider what they know about babies and young children in general, as well as what they know about the specific child. They will want to find out if the baby is:

- Tired

    Are they rubbing their eyes or yawning? Are they blinking heavily and slowly? When did they last sleep? Do they often sleep around this time?

- Hungry

    When did they last have a feed? Did they take all of their feed? Are they ready to start weaning – perhaps they seem to be hungry again a short time after feeding, and are they right age to begin weaning?

- Lonely

    Are they alone? Do they need a cuddle or someone to play with? In the case of a baby who cannot crawl yet, do they need to be repositioned nearer other children for company?

- Bored

    Have they been in the same position or playing with the same toy for some time? Have they got access to resources or activities likely to stimulate them at their stage of development?

- Unwell

    Is the child displaying any signs or symptoms of illness? Is the child the right age to be teething, and are they showing any signs of this (dribbling, red cheek, inflamed gums)?

- In need of a nappy change

    A quick check will reveal if the child is wet or dirty.

- Frightened

    Has the baby been startled by a sudden or loud noise? Have they seen a stranger? Do older, mobile children scare particular younger babies when their play becomes boisterous or too close to them?

- Frustrated

    Is the child experiencing difficulty with a task? Are they frustrated because they cannot reach a toy they have dropped? Or are they hungry but struggling to feed themselves effectively – has most of the food ended up on the floor?

Effective practitioners are constantly using their responsive caring skills. These skills are informed by experience – the more time you spend with babies and young children, the more 'tuned in' you will become to recognising their care needs. It is eventually a very natural, intuitive part of a practitioner's role.

One of the most effective ways to learn from experience is be a reflective practitioner. Reflective practitioners think about their practice, notice areas for development and plan how to improve their knowledge, understanding and skills. Unit CCLD 304, Reflect on and develop practice, gives relevant information throughout. Reflection is a key part of developing the skills of responsive caring. Since responsive caring is at the heart of providing high-quality care for babies and young children, it is important to have reflective and knowledgeable practitioners working with this age group.

 Link   **Unit CCLD 304** Reflect on and develop practice

Safety equipment

There are many pieces of equipment that help adults to keep babies and young children safe and secure. While it is essential to use safety equipment when it is required, practitioners must ensure that they do not restrict the movement of babies and young children unnecessarily. For instance, while reins may be used to take two-year-olds on a short walk, such walks should not be used to replace time spent running around and exploring freely outside.

The following diagram shows the safety equipment that may be used.

Safety equipment
for 0–3 years

Toys and equipment

Care must be taken when choosing toys and equipment for all children. See Unit CCLD 306, Plan and organise environments for children and families, for information on how to choose equipment safely. You will see the safety marks you should look for before purchasing any toys or equipment. Many children's products are not suitable for children under three – you must always read the safety labels closely. The Unit also covers the importance of maintaining equipment and toys to keep them safe and hygienic.

To prevent cross-infection, toys used by young babies should be sterilised between each use as infants will put everything into their mouths. Highchairs and changing mats must also be cleaned thoroughly after each use. As children grow, toys can be cleaned at the end of each day. (Once children are over the age of three cleaning can be less frequent, as explained in Unit CCLD 306 Plan and organise environments for children and families.)

Strap babies safely into highchairs

To keep their clothes in a clean and hygienic condition, babies and young children need to wear protective garments when they are engaged in activities that could be messy. This may include:

- Bibs worn at feeding and meal times
- Aprons worn during activities such painting or playing with sand/water/play dough and so on.

Link **Unit CCLD 306** Plan and organise environments for children and families

Handling waste

It is essential that all kinds of waste are disposed of hygienically to prevent cross-infection. There is information about this on pages 54–5 of Unit CCLD 302 Develop and maintain a healthy, safe and secure environment for children.

Link **Unit CCLD 302** Develop and maintain a healthy, safe and secure environment for children

Handing back to parents and carers

As with all children, great care must be taken to ensure that those under three are handed back only to the people authorised on the registration form to collect them from the setting. This person must be capable of looking after the child. Sometimes parents may want to send a young person to collect their child – an older sibling perhaps, or a babysitter. It is very difficult for practitioners to tell from a brief meeting whether someone is suitably experienced to look after a young child alone. Depending on the type of setting and the home country, it may be mandatory for someone over the age of 16 to collect children. Excluded settings may have also adopted this as their policy. You should follow your setting's guidelines on this issue.

It is important that the person collecting a child under three is given the appropriate information that they need in order to continue with the child's care. The information they need includes:

- Whether the child has taken a milk feed or eaten a meal. If so, how much was consumed and when. If not, when they were last offered food
- When the child last had a drink
- Whether the child has slept, when, and for how long
- Whether the child has been generally happy and well throughout the session – if not, further details should be supplied
- Brief information about an activity the child has done today or a toy they enjoyed. (Remember that many children in the age range will not have the language to tell parents and carers about their day.)

Many settings provide this information in a short, written daily report.

Element 314.1 — Are you ready for assessment?

Provide a safe and secure environment for babies and children under three years

You need to show that you can competently provide a safe and secure environment for babies and children under three years. To do this you will need to be directly observed by your assessor and present other types of evidence. The amount and type of evidence that you need to present will vary. You should plan this with your assessor.

Direct observation by your assessor

Observation and/or expert witness testimony is the required assessment method to be used to evidence some of each element in this unit. If your assessor is unable to observe you, s/he will identify an expert in your workplace who will provide testimony of your work-based performance. Usually your assessor or expert witness will observe you in real work activities and this should provide most of the evidence for the performance criteria for the elements in this unit.

Preparing to be observed

You will need to show your assessor that you can ensure the environment is safe and secure for babies and children under three years by using safe and hygienic toys and equipment, checking that appropriate safety equipment it is properly installed and checking that the environment is free from hazards. You must show that you can ensure babies and children are supervised at all times, and that you can take necessary steps to safeguard them from harm. You must show that you can hand babies and children back to families appropriately and dispose of waste products safely.

Other types of evidence

You will need to present different types of evidence in order to:

- Cover criteria not observed by your assessor
- Show that you have the required knowledge, understanding and skills.

Such evidence could include:

- Work products such as plans of room layouts and risk assessments
- Case studies, projects, assignments and reflective accounts of your work.

Element 314.2 *Provide for the nutritional needs of babies and children under three years*

K3C424
K3D426
K3H276
K3H297
K3H416
K3H417
K3H418
K3H419
K3H421
K3H422
K3H423
K3H425

Regulations for food handling

The Food Safety Act 1990 and the Food Hygiene Regulations were introduced to protect people from food poisoning. Under the Act:

- All staff who handle or serve food must have a Basic Food Hygiene Certificate
- The person in charge has responsibility for ensuring safety
- It is illegal to cause illness to people through contamination of food if the contamination was avoidable
- It is illegal to contaminate food on purpose or knowingly.

General food preparation and storage guidelines are given on pages 54–5 of Unit CCLD 302 Develop and maintain a healthy, safe and secure environment for children.

 Link Unit CCLD 302 Develop and maintain a healthy, safe and secure environment for children

Policies on nutritional needs of babies and children

In order to have a balanced diet, children should receive the recommended nutrients each day. Promote the health and physical development of children, for more information about the nutrients needed by the human body.

The nutritional needs of babies and children vary according to their age, height and weight. Until the age of four to six months, babies will be fed exclusively on either breast milk or formula milk.

Link   **Unit CCLD 307** Promote the health and physical development of children

Supporting breast-feeding

Breast milk naturally contains all the nutrients that babies need in the correct proportions at the right stage. It is also convenient – there is no need to prepare bottles, the milk is already the right temperature and it is free of charge.

Colostrum is the name given to the first milk that is produced. This contains maternal antibodies produced within the mother's body. They are passed on to the baby through the milk and can protect them against some infections. There is less risk of infection occurring in the feeding process when babies are breast-fed. The milk itself does not contain germs.

Some mothers want to continue breast-feeding their baby when they start attending a setting. Practitioners should discuss the mother's needs with them, following their setting's guidelines. The mother may wish to express her breast milk and supply it in a feeding bottle so that practitioners can bottle feed the baby with breast milk. In this case:

- All equipment must be sterilised as described below
- Bottles should be clearly labelled with the date and the baby's name
- Expressed breast milk must be stored in the fridge and used within 24 hours
- Expressed breast milk may be kept in the freezer for up to three months by parents and carers at home. It must be thoroughly defrosted before use.

At a workplace crèche, a mother may be able to come and breast-feed her baby when necessary. Settings can provide a comfortable, private area where mothers can breast-feed or express milk.

Preparing formula feeds

There are two stages to preparing a formula feed for babies – the cleaning and sterilising of equipment, and making up the formula.

Sterilising equipment

When making up formula for babies under one year old, all of the equipment that will be used must be thoroughly cleaned and sterilised. This is to kill germs that may still remain after the usual washing and drying of dishes. The same applies to all feeding equipment (such as bowls and spoons) used for this age group. The equipment used will be:

- Bottles
- Teats
- Bottle caps

- Measuring spoons
- Plastic knife
- Plastic jug
- Bottle brush
- Teat cleaner
- Sterilising unit with sterilising tablets or liquid OR
  a steam sterilising unit.

Before sterilising, the equipment must be cleaned. It must be rinsed, washed and rinsed again (see the diagram below). A bottle brush must be used to clean the bottles. A much smaller version of this, know as a teat cleaner, should be used on the teat. At one time salt was used to clean teats, but this is no longer considered good practice as there is a risk of increasing the salt intake of a baby if residue remains in the teat. Never use this method.

The equipment can now be sterilised. There are different methods of sterilising. The traditional method is to make up a sterile solution by mixing either sterilising tablets or sterilising solution with water, according to the manufacturer's instructions. The equipment is then submerged in a sterilising unit for a specified time (see below). However, steam sterilising units are also now available. They come with manufacturers' instructions for use.

Cleaning and sterilising feeding equipment

Making up formula

It is very important to make up formula correctly otherwise babies could become ill.

The diagram on page 326 shows the procedure that should be followed. There are some important things to remember:

- Use the brand of formula milk agreed upon with the parents unless a doctor or health visitor advises otherwise
- Only use boiled water to make up feeds
- Always measure the formula powder out carefully. Formula that is too strong is dangerous to babies' health. Formula that is too weak means that babies will not get the nutrients they need. Never use more powder than necessary. Do not pack the powder down into the scoop, do not use heaped scoops and do not add extra scoops of powder. You must level the scoop off with a sterilised knife, as shown in the diagram.

1 Check that the formula has not passed its sell-by date. Read the instructions on the tin. Ensure the tin has been kept in a cool, dry cupboard.

2 Boil some fresh water and allow to cool.

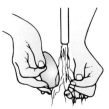

3 Wash hands and nails thoroughly.

4 Take required equipment from sterilising tank and rinse with cool, boiled water.

5 Fill bottle, or a jug if making a large quantity, to the required level with water.

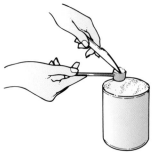

6 Measure the <u>exact</u> amount of powder using the scoop provided. Level with a knife. Do not pack down.

7 Add the powder to the measured water in the bottle or jug.

8 Screw cap on bottle and shake, or mix well in the jug and pour into sterilised bottles.

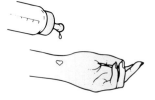

9 If not using immediately, cool quickly and store in the fridge. If using immediately, test temperature on the inside of your wrist.

Preparing a feed

10 Babies will take cold milk but they prefer warm food (as from the breast). If you wish to warm the milk, place bottle in a jug of hot water. <u>Never keep feeds warm for longer than 45 minutes</u>, to reduce the chance of bacteria breeding.

Note: whenever the bottle is left for short periods, or stored in the fridge, cover with the cap provided.

Once a feed is made:

- It should either be used immediately or cooled and stored in the fridge
- Once taken from the fridge and warmed in preparation for a feed, formula must be used within 45 minutes. Otherwise it must be thrown away
- After 24 hours any unused feeds must be taken from the fridge and thrown away.

To warm a feed:

- Shake the bottle well as some of the powder may have settled in the bottom
- Place the bottle in a jug of hot water to heat it through. This will take a few minutes
- Shake the bottle again to make sure that the formula is heated through evenly. (When microwaves are used to heat milk there can be 'hot spots' caused by uneven heating)
- Test the temperature of the milk by putting a few drops on the inside of your wrist (this is a sensitive area). It should feel just warm.

Bottle feeding babies

The amount of milk that should be offered to babies depends on their weight. The formula will have directions which you should follow. As a general guide, over each 24 hour period, babies need 150 ml of milk for each kg of their weight.

At first, babies who are bottle-fed should be fed when they are hungry. This is known as 'feeding on demand'. However, babies should soon settle into a routine where they are fed at regular intervals. The routine will vary from baby to baby, but generally, new babies need about eight feeds a day, given at approximately four hour intervals.

Adults can calculate how much milk babies need at each feed by:

- Dividing the amount of food needed in 24 hours (see above) by the number of feeds per day

Practitioners should bottle feed babies in accordance with current best practice and the wishes of parents and carers.

How to bottle feed

Bottle feeding is a time for bonding and closeness, and so ideally a baby's key worker should feed her as often as possible. It is important to establish a comfortable and calm environment in which to feed a baby. You must not rush the feeding process. Use the time to talk to the baby, and to hold her gaze with eye contact.

1. Gather together everything you will need – bottle, bib, and muslin cloth – and wash your hands thoroughly.

2. Before feeding, CHECK THAT YOU HAVE THE RIGHT BOTTLE FOR THE RIGHT BABY – a child with an allergy could become seriously ill or even die if they are given the wrong bottle. YOU MUST ALWAYS BE ABSOLUTELY SURE THAT YOU HAVE THE RIGHT FEED. Babies can experience wind if the flow of the teat is too slow, as they will take air into the stomach as they are forced to suck too hard. However, if the flow of the teat is too fast, a baby may choke. Check the flow of the teat by tilting the bottle – the milk should steadily fall from the teat in drops. It is the size of the hole in the teat that controls the flow. Teats with holes of differing sizes are available to suit the needs of differing babies. As a general rule, young babies need a slower flow of milk than older babies.

3. Warm and test the temperature of the milk as described above.

4. Put a soft bib on the baby, and sit together somewhere comfortable. Some settings may have suitable soft furniture to sit on, or you may sit on the carpet.

5. Hold the baby in a semi-reclining position with one arm, so that her head is resting in the crook of your arm. The baby's head should be higher than the rest of her body.

6. Hold the bottle at an angle with your opposite hand so that the teat fills with milk, and allow the baby to latch on to the teat (take the teat into her mouth). Babies often curl their hand around your fingers as you hold the bottle. Continue to tilt the bottle further as the baby drinks the milk.

7. Go at the baby's pace. Some babies like a break or two during their feed. Wind a baby during this time (as well as at the end of their feed). After a short break, offer the baby the bottle again. Younger babies generally require breaks more frequently than older babies.

8. Wind can be uncomfortable for babies, and since a baby's mobility is limited, it can be difficult for a baby to pass wind in order to release the air in her stomach. You should always wind a baby after feeding. To do this, hold the baby on your lap in a sitting position, her body leaning slightly forwards. Gently rub her back. Sometimes babies will bring up a little of their feed. You can anticipate this by having a muslin cloth (or other suitable material) to hand to clear up with. The bib helps to protect the baby's clothes. Some babies tend to bring up more feed than others. Some may have been prescribed drops to take in advance of their feed to help them keep their milk down.

9. After feeding, gently clean the baby's face and settle her in a new position. You should not clear away until the baby is settled. However, do not leave bottles unattended within the reach of other children – they may put the teat in their mouth and perhaps even drink left over milk that is not for them.

10. In line with the procedures at your setting, record the relevant details of the feed, as parents will need this information when they collect the child. It is usual to record the date and time of the feed, how much milk was taken and any difficulties – if the baby was more than a little sick afterwards, for instance.

Babies sometimes need specialised feeding equipment, such as teats with a fast or slow flow, or with a special angle. These should be used in consultation with parents, carers and if necessary, medical professionals. Information about the requirements should be documented and shared with all those who feed babies within the setting.

The importance of weaning

Weaning is the term used to describe the process by which babies are introduced to solid foods. Weaning is usually introduced when babies are taking plenty of fluids but are no longer satisfied by breast milk or formula milk alone. In a report in 1994 The Committee on Medical Aspects of Food and Nutrition Policy (known as COMA) recommended that weaning should not begin before a baby is four months of age, but should start by the time they reach six months. The Scientific Advisory Committee on

Nutrition (SACN) has since replaced COMA, but the recommendations still stand. The advice is to begin weaning between four and six months because:

- Babies' kidneys are sufficiently mature to handle natural salt in weaning foods by four months
- The digestive system and bowel are developed enough to handle solid foods by four months
- By four months a baby can hold up their head, move food to the back of their mouth and swallow it. If solids are not introduced by six months, this developmental stage may be missed, and babies may subsequently refuse food or have difficulties chewing.

It is dangerous to introduce babies to solids before the age of four months.

The main aims of weaning are:

- To gradually decrease nutritional dependence on milk, and to introduce sufficient nutrients to meet the health needs of growing babies (such as iron)
- To introduce new textures and flavours
- To introduce bowls and spoons, allowing babies to join in socially at mealtimes
- To establish acceptance of healthy eating patterns and habits.

Practitioners should discuss weaning with parents and carers and agree a joint approach. Families are sometimes anxious about weaning, but they can be reassured that in the early days children will still be getting most of their nutrients from milk as solids will be introduced gradually. At this stage the main priority is to get children used to flavours and textures, and to remain relaxed about feeding so that mealtimes do not become battlegrounds.

The process of weaning

The following recommendations are made for weaning:

- Establish a relaxed atmosphere. Make sure babies are not too tired or too hungry before introducing solids. Some babies respond well to having some milk to settle them before they are offered solids
- Sterilise all feeding equipment, including bowls and spoons. A broad, flat plastic spoon is best with most babies
- At first babies should be offered a small amount of bland, warm food of a loose or sloppy consistency. The food should be free from salt, gluten and sugar. Baby rice and banana are both ideal, and they can be mixed with warm milk from the baby's bottle. Half to a full teaspoon of food is enough to start with
- Babies may refuse the food at first because the experience is new. But the same food can be offered again the following day. It is good practice to give babies the opportunity to get used to one taste over two or three days before a new taste is introduced. This also means that adults can easily identify a food that may upset a baby's stomach
- Pureed fruits, vegetables and bland baby cereals are all good foods for early weaning. (Give cereals only once per day.) Gradually babies will begin to take

more spoonfuls of food. As the amount of solids taken increases, the amount of milk given should decrease. By about the fifth week of weaning, one of the baby's milk feeds should be replaced entirely by solid food. Cooled boiled water can be offered to drink at this mealtime

- Babies gradually learn to manage lumps, and by seven months they can be offered harder foods such as peeled apple cubes and bread crusts. Babies can chew these with their hard back gums. They are ideal 'finger foods' for babies to feed to themselves

- As babies become interested in their feeding spoon, have an extra one for them to hold at feeding times, and allow them to help. This is the first step towards independence at mealtimes. Protect clothing and flooring well so that you can relax about this as learning to feed is generally a messy affair!

- Remember that mealtimes should be a positive social experience. Always supervise young children's eating in case of choking, and be particularly aware when new textures and lumps are introduced.

Younger children need to practise feeding themselves

Opposite is a suggested weaning plan of foods that are considered suitable for most babies and that represent a healthy balanced diet.

Weaning plan

Age/months	4 months	4½ months	5–6 months	6–7 months	7–8 months	9–12 months
On waking	Breast or bottle feed	Breast or bottle feed	Breast or bottle feed	Breast or bottle feed	Breast or bottle feed	Breast or bottle feed/cup
Breakfast	1–2 teaspoons baby rice mixed with milk from feed or with water; breast or bottle-feed	2 teaspoon puréed or sieved vegetables, or vegetables and chicken; breast or bottle-feed	Baby rice or cereal mixed with milk from feed or with water or puréed banana; breast or bottle-feed	Cereal mixed with milk from feed or water; fruit, toast fingers spread with unsalted butter	Cereal, fish or fruit; toast fingers; milk	Ceral and milk, fish, yoghurt or fruit; toast and milk
Lunch	Breast or bottle-feed	1–2 teaspoon puréed or sieved vegetables, or vegetables and chicken; breast or bottle-feed	Puréed or sieved meat or fish and vegetables, or proprietary food; followed by 2 teaspoons puréed fruit or prepared baby dessert; drink of cooled, boiled water or well-diluted juice (from a cup)	Finely minced meat or mashed fish, with mashed vegetables; mashed banana or stewed fruit or milk pudding; drink of cooled boiled water or well-diluted juice in a cup	Mashed fish, minced meat or cheese with vegetables; milk pudding or stewed fruit; drink	Well-chopped meat, liver or fish or cheese with mashed vegetables; milk pudding or fruit fingers; drink
Tea	Breast or bottle-feed	Breast or bottle-feed	Puréed fruit or baby desert; breast or bottle-feed	Toast with cheese or savoury spread; breast or bottle feed	Bread and butter sandwiches with savoury spread or seedless jam; sponge finger or biscuit; milk drink	Fish, cheese or pasta; sandwiches; fruit; milk drink
Late evening	Breast or bottle-feed	Breast or bottle-feed	Breast or bottle - feed, if necessary			

Unsuitable foods

The following table explains which foods are unsuitable for babies and children at different ages, and the reason for this.

Unsuitable foods

Details of food	Details of age restriction	Reason
Salt Must not be added to babies' food. It is not allowed to be added to baby foods on sale in the UK. Limit the intake of food high in salt, such as cheese, bacon, sausages. Do not give processed foods not intended for babies (such as breakfast cereals) as these may be high in salt	Up to six months babies should have less that 1g of salt. From seven months to one year they should have no more than 1g. (Formula and breast milks contain the right amount of salt)	A baby's immature kidneys cannot cope with more than the recommended amount of salt
Sugar Do not add it to food or drinks. Sour fruit such as rhubarb can be sweetened with alternatives such as mashed banana or formula/breast milk	This is advisable for all babies and young children	Sugar can encourage an unhealthy sweet tooth and cause tooth decay as teeth come through
Honey	Do not give honey until babies are at least one year old	Honey can contain a bacteria that produces toxins in immature intestines, causing serious illness
1. Wheat-based foods and other foods containing gluten, including bread, wheat flour, breakfast cereals and rusks 2. Nut and seeds 3. Eggs 4. Fish and shellfish 5. Citrus fruit and citrus fruit juice	Avoid these five foods until a baby is six months old. Only ground or flaked nuts should be given to children under five. Many settings have a no nut policy due to the commonality of nut allergies among children. Egg white and yolk must always be cooked to a solid consistency to prevent food poisoning	These foods can cause allergic reactions, so it is advised that they are not introduced before the age of six months. GPs may advise introducing certain foods even later if food allergies run in the family
Full-fat cow's milk Goat's and sheep's milk	Avoid until the baby is one year old. (All milk must be pasteurised)	It does not contain enough iron and nutrients to meet the needs of younger babies
Semi-skimmed milk	Avoid until the age of two years	Can be introduced then if a child is a good eater with a varied diet
Skimmed milk	Unsuitable for children under five	It does not contain sufficient nutrients
Squash, fizzy drinks, flavoured milk, herbal drinks, diet drinks, tea and coffee	These are unsuitable for babies and toddlers	These are not recommended for one or more of the following reasons: they may contain sugar or caffeine, they may cause tooth decay or fill babies up, leading to a poor appetite and poor weight gain

Further information about suitable and unsuitable foods for weaning and general weaning guidance can be found on the Food Standards Agency website: www.eatwell. gov.uk/agesandstages/baby/weaning/

Special dietary requirements and information

Some babies and children have specific dietary and/or food preparation requirements. These can relate to the milk a baby drinks as well as the food taken – some babies may have soya milk, for example. The special requirements may be due to allergies or medical conditions or they may be related to culture, ethnicity or religious beliefs. So it is essential that all dietary requirements are fully understood. They must be documented and the information must be shared with appropriate colleagues.

Encouraging healthy eating

Encouraging healthy eating in under threes means offering healthy food options. Children under three are only introduced to the foods that adults give them. Strategies for encouraging healthy eating are outlined on page 209 of Unit CCLD 307 Promote the health and physical development of children.

Link   **Unit CCLD 307** Promote the health and physical development of children

Best practice and parental wishes

Parents can be influenced by many things when it comes to making decisions about the way their child is brought up. For example, they may plan to care for their baby or child in the same way as they were cared for themselves. Family members may be advising them, and they may have come across information in the media – on television, in newspapers and magazines, and also in books.

Sometimes the wishes of parents and carers do not reflect the current accepted best practice. In this case, it is important to resolve the issue amicably (in a harmonious way), with the best interests of the child in mind. Practitioners should explain what the current best practice is as the parent or carer may not be aware of it. The practitioner and the carer can then talk this through – it is important to explain the reasoning behind the current practice.

If necessary, the practitioner should direct the parent or carer to other sources of information about the issue. The health visitor can offer parents and carers advice on caring for young babies and young children, and they have access to many leaflets and booklets explaining current practice. Websites (such as the Government's nutritional site www.www.eatwell.gov.uk) can also be useful. The setting may have some relevant books that could be lent to the parent or carer if appropriate.

Practical Example

Alana discusses current best practice

Nursery key worker Alana meets with the parents of one-year-old Josiah who will soon be attending the setting. When talking about his routine, his mum says that she puts him to bed with his bottle in the afternoon. He falls asleep drinking it.

Alana explains that a danger of choking is associated with babies taking bottles of milk to bed. Although at one time it was common practice, it is not recommended now. Josiah's mum says she had no idea – an older family member had suggested it because she had difficulties settling Josiah in his cot. Alana and Josiah's mum talk through alternative strategies for settling him down to sleep. They agree to try a different method. Josiah will no longer take a bottle to bed at the nursery or at home.

➤ *Why did Alana talk the issue through with Josiah's mum?*   **K3C424**

Element 314.2

Are you ready for assessment?

Provide for the nutritional needs of babies and children under three years

You need to show that you can competently provide for the nutritional needs of babies and children under three years. To do this you will need to be directly observed by your assessor and present other types of evidence. The amount and type of evidence you will need to present will vary. You should plan this with your assessor.

Direct observation by your assessor

Observation and/or expert witness testimony is the required assessment method to be used to evidence some of each element in this unit. If your assessor is unable to observe you, s/he will identify an expert in your workplace who will provide testimony of your work-based performance. Usually your assessor or expert witness will observe you in real work activities and this should provide most of the evidence for the performance criteria for the elements in this unit.

Preparing to be observed

You will need to show your assessor that you can competently provide for the nutritional needs of babies and children under three years. You must show that you can prepare formula and bottle feed appropriately, and provide support for breast-feeding mothers. You must also show that you can ensure that the setting's nutritional policies are in line with best practice and government guidelines, and that you can provide a varied diet to meet nutritional needs. You must show that you can agree, confirm and document dietary requirements, and agree feeding and weaning schedules with parents appropriately.

Supervise and use physical care routines to promote development

Element 314.3

Care routines

K3D426
K3D427
K3H428
K3H429
K3D430
K3D431
K3D432
K3D433
K3D438
K3D439

When practitioners care for young babies and children repetitive tasks are carried out, such as:

- Washing
- Dressing
- Feeding
- Changing nappies.

The ways in which children's care needs are met are part of children's daily routines. Because these routines are repeated so frequently when children are young, they are an important part of their overall experience of life and their knowledge of interacting with adults. Practitioners must remember this and ensure that they attend to children's care needs sensitively.

For children to have a positive experience, it is important that practitioners do not rush when attending to care needs. Sometimes you may need to remind yourself of this. Practitioners working in busy group settings with several babies to attend to must remember to take their time with each child, avoiding the 'treadmill approach' of simply dealing with one task after another without engaging with the individual babies or children concerned. Every child must be and must feel respected during care routines. This is achieved through affectionate and appropriate touch, speech and gesture.

During care routines adults can:

- Make the most of one-to-one time

    Care routines are a great time to bond and play with babies and children on a one-to-one basis. Approaching care routines playfully also helps children to enjoy them. While babies are changed or fed, they are lying or sitting in front of their carer. It is an ideal time to make eye contact and to talk

- Let children know they are cared for and respected

  By attending to care needs at a child's pace, and by using respectful, affectionate touch, speech and gesture

- Use the experience as a learning opportunity

  For instance, it is never too soon to talk with babies and children about care routines. While washing a child's hands for instance, you can say, 'We'll rub some soap in to make your hands nice and clean'

- Encourage independence

  Children will eventually take responsibility for all of their own care needs. It is the job of practitioners to encourage this.

A one-to-one
experience

⸂ Self care

As we have mentioned, most children will eventually take care of their bodies independently. The skills required to do this are learnt gradually. There is further information about this in Unit CCLD 306 Plan and organise environments for children and families. When attending to a child's care needs, practitioners can:

- Show children how to carry out tasks such as washing, dressing and cleaning their teeth
- Encourage children to help the adult as the child is washed, dressed and so on. The extent of help will depend on the child's age and ability
- Encourage children to take care of the environment as they care for themselves by keeping areas tidy and safe (for example, by avoiding or cleaning up spillages of water in the bathroom)
- Praise children for their attempts at self care
- Have high expectations of what babies and children can achieve whilst ensuring they are properly supported.

Practitioners should appreciate which aspects of self care children are comfortable with and respect their wishes when it comes to the level and type of assistance they require. However, sometimes practitioners may need to step in. For example, in preparation for lunch, a child may have washed their own hands after painting, but they may still be covered in paint. In this situation the practitioner should gently point out the missed paint and direct the child back to the sink, offering help if it is needed. This must be done sensitively so that the child's confidence in hand washing is not undermined. It is part of having high expectations whilst ensuring that proper support is available.

Link Unit CCLD 306 Plan and organise environments for children and families

Practical Example

Gail adjusts her approach

Practitioner Gail adjusts her approach when washing the hands of different children. She knows that one-year-old Daniel still needs lots of help from her, but he will hold out his hand ready for some liquid soap. Eighteen-month-old May will press the nozzle on the soap bottle herself, and rub her hands together – but she still needs Gail's help to rinse and dry her hands. Two-and-a-half-year-old Kayleigh can manage everything but turning the tap on and off. Gail assists her with this.

➤ *Why is it important for Gail to adjust the level of help she offers to these children?* **K3D427**

Procedures and processes that protect children and adults

When attending to children's care needs, practitioners must follow their setting's procedures and processes for promoting good hygiene. This protects both adults and children from cross-infection. Procedures and processes that promote hygiene include:

- Washing your hands before and after changing, washing and toileting
- Wearing disposable gloves for changing (and toileting if necessary)
- Wiping the changing mat thoroughly with disinfectant spray
- Keeping soiled laundry away from clean clothes and washing it thoroughly
- Keeping the bathroom area clean and well stocked with soap, toilet paper and paper towels.

There is further information in Unit CCLD 302 Develop and maintain a healthy, safe and secure environment for children.

Link Unit CCLD 302 Develop and maintain a healthy, safe and secure environment for children

Children are vulnerable when their care needs are attended to – see Unit CCLD 305 Protect and promote children's rights, for information about how to protect children from abuse and how to protect practitioners from allegations of abuse.

Unit CCLD 305 Protect and promote children's rights

Caring for skin, hair and teeth

It is essential that practitioners know how to care for babies' and children's skin, hair and teeth. Details of how to care for skin and hair and how to bathe babies can be found in Unit CCLD 306 Plan and organise environments for children and families. Information about toiletries and sun awareness in included. Details of how to care for children's teeth are on pages 212–15 of Unit CCLD 307 Promote the health and physical development of children.

Unit CCLD 306 Plan and organise environments for children and families
Unit CCLD 307 Promote the health and physical development of children

Bath time fun

Nappies

Wet and dirty nappies are uncomfortable for babies and they can cause a baby's skin to become sore and inflamed. To avoid this, practitioners should change a baby's nappy as often as necessary. It is usual to change nappies every three to four hours to coincide with mealtimes and in between if the baby is awake and uncomfortable. Babies should always be settled down to sleep in a clean nappy. Many settings establish a routine of changing nappies at regular times to ensure that no child is left feeling uncomfortable. In addition, practitioners will change babies should they become aware that they have a wet or dirty nappy.

It is good practice for key workers to change their key babies' nappies as much as possible, as changing is a time for closeness, talking and play. The key worker will also be more likely to notice any changes that may be cause for concern (see page 330). Many settings require practitioners to make a note of the times that children are changed and whether they have been wet or dirty. This also helps key workers to spot patterns revealing cause for concern, and ensures that all children are changed at appropriate times. In addition, a written record allows practitioners to accurately inform parents and carers about the changes their baby has received. It is essential for key workers to talk with parents and carers about their child's individual nappy changing requirements, and the families' preferences.

Baby changing areas must:

- Be located in a separate area, right away from food preparation and eating areas
- Be warm and draught free
- Be stocked with the necessary equipment/toiletries (these may be provided by the setting or brought in by parents and carers), and a changing mat. Settings often have a mat on top of a changing unit. However, the mat can be placed on another suitable flat surface, or on the floor
- Have hygienic facilities for the safe disposal of dirty nappies (the content of which is referred to as 'stools') and wet nappies. There must also be a container for the storage of soiled clothes ready to be laundered. There must be facilities for the thorough cleansing of surfaces and changing mats after each baby has been changed.

There are two types of nappies, both listed below.

- Reusable nappies

  Although shaped nappies are available, reusable nappies are generally made from a rectangle of absorbent terry towelling. Such nappies are folded to fit individual babies and fastened with nappy pins (these have been designed with a safety feature to ensure they do not come undone). There is a range of nappy folding techniques to suit babies of different sizes, and some methods are more suited to boys or girls. It is best to learn how to fold nappies from an experienced practitioner who can demonstrate on one nappy whilst you follow along using another. A disposable nappy liner may be used inside of the nappy. These help to keep babies comfortable since they remain dry (keeping wetness away from a baby's skin) but let wetness through to the nappy. Disposable liners can be flushed down the toilet along with stools. Whether or not a liner is used, plastic pants are placed over the nappy – these are available in various sizes. For reuse, terry nappies must be thoroughly rinsed out. They should then be placed in a nappy pail (a bucket with a close fitting lid) filled with sterilising solution, and be left to soak. They can then be fully laundered.

- Disposable nappies

  These days, disposable nappies are not only available in a range of sizes, but also especially shaped to be suitable for boys or girls, although unisex nappies are still available. Used nappies must always be hygienically disposed of. Some settings have a nappy unit that automatically seals a nappy into a plastic wrapping as it is placed inside. In other settings, practitioners will place soiled nappies in plastic bag and tie the bag closed. The bag will then be disposed of in the appropriate bin, and the bin lid will be replaced.

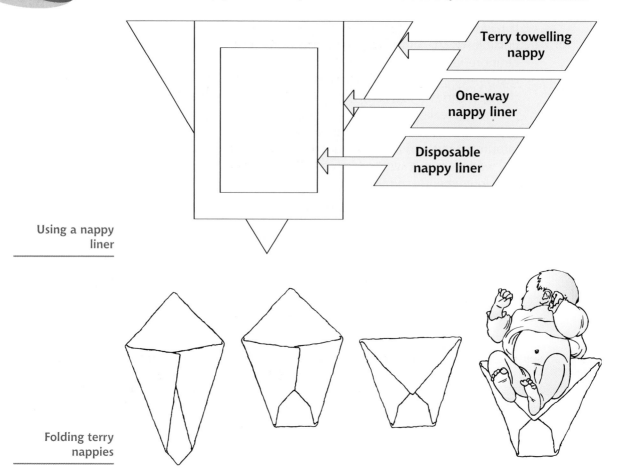

Using a nappy liner

Folding terry nappies

Parent's preferences of nappy should be discussed and followed. In some cultures a cloth may be placed under young babies in place of a nappy.

Cause for concern

Changing nappies gives practitioners the opportunity to detect any cause for concern in the nappy area of a baby's body. Details of some such concerns, along with concerns about infection and irregular bowel movements or urination, are given in the table opposite.

Changing nappies

The changing area should be suitable as previously described. It is important that all the necessary equipment is at hand so that you will not need to leave the nappy area. In the interests of safety, you must NEVER LEAVE A BABY UNATTENDED ON A CHANGING MAT. You MUST NOT LOOK AWAY, EVEN FOR A MOMENT. If you do need to leave the area for any reason, YOU MUST TAKE THE BABY WITH YOU.

1. Wash your hands and put on protective clothing – latex gloves and an apron.
2. Place the baby on the changing surface. If the changing mat is not on the floor, it is safest to keep one hand on the baby throughout the changing process. If the baby is happy, talk to her playfully and make eye contact. Soothe the baby with your voice if she is unhappy.

Cause for concern	Possible explanation and what to do
Baby passing stools very frequently. Stools are loose in consistency, and may be watery.	The baby may have diarrhoea caused by infection. In a group setting, a child with diarrhoea should be sent home as soon as possible. Parents and carers will need to seek medical advice if diarrhoea persists.
Baby passing hard stools which may be green in colour, or failing to pass stools regularly.	The baby may be constipated. It is important to make parents and carers aware of this. Initially, giving a weaned baby fruit may be sufficient to solve the problem.
Blood can be seen in stools or streaks of blood are on the nappy.	The baby may have an injury. Or, sometimes a small amount of blood is passed with hard stools when a baby is constipated. This information should be passed on to parents and carers who can seek medical advice.
Bruising or other marks on the skin of the nappy area.	The baby may have been injured in an accident, or they may have been injured intentionally. If you do not know how the marks occurred, you may need to ask parents or carers, and/or log the incident. See Unit CCLD 305, Protect and promote children's rights, for further information.
Soreness/redness, a rash, blisters. This is very painful, and a baby may cry when her nappy is changed. Untreated soreness can quickly progress to a rash/ blistering.	The baby may have nappy rash or an allergy to the nappy/nappy liner, or in the case of reusable nappies, the detergent used for laundering. Or, the baby may have an infection such as thrush. Report to parents and carers, and ensure nappies are changed frequently – at least every two hours and when necessary in between. Make sure the baby's bottom is thoroughly dried after cleaning. Creams should be used sparingly (if appropriate). Sometimes special creams are prescribed by a doctor.
Failure to urinate regularly.	The baby may not be drinking enough liquid. Offer frequent drinks and report to parents and carers.
Strong smelling urine, which may be dark in colour.	The baby may have a urine infection. Offer plenty of fluids, and report to parents and carers who will need to seek medical advice.

3. Undress the bottom half of the baby, gently pulling her clothes well out of the way before you remove the nappy. Sometimes a nappy leaks a little, so check that clothes have not become wet or dirty. If they have, remove them.

4. Clean the nappy area thoroughly but gently. The method chosen for this will depend on the baby's requirements – you may use wet wipes or other lotions, or water and cotton wool. Ensure that the area you have cleaned is left dry to prevent soreness. Then apply any lotions in line with parents or carer's wishes.

5. Give the baby time to move her legs around while the nappy is off, sometimes called 'kicking free'. This helps to make nappy changing an enjoyable experience. However if the baby is distressed, you should finish the changing process so that you can comfort her.

6. Put a clean nappy on the baby and redress her, using fresh clothing if necessary. Settle the baby safely elsewhere before clearing away.

7. Dispose of the nappy correctly, according to your setting's facilities. Place any soiled clothes into the correct container ready for laundering.

8. Do not remove your gloves yet. Wash your hands.

9. Clean the changing area, including the mat, following your setting's procedures.

10. Dispose of your protective clothing (including gloves) in the correct bin, then wash your hands again.

11. Make a record of the nappy change if required, in line with your setting's procedures.

Changing a nappy is an opportunity for playing and talking to the baby

Toilet training

It is important for practitioners to recognise the signs that indicate a young child is ready to learn how to use the toilet or potty. The approach to toilet training should be planned with parent and carers. Details of this are given in Unit CCLD 306 Plan and organise environments for children and families.

Link   **Unit CCLD 306** Plan and organise environments for children and families

Key attachments

Babies begin to emotionally bond with their parents after birth. It is thought that this gives them a sense of safety, security and love. Most experts agree that babies and young children also need to make emotional attachments with other adults that care for them in order to feel settled and secure.

Key attachments are made when familiar adults spend time with babies and children, interacting with them frequently and sensitively. The attachment felt by the child is strengthened when a familiar adult attends to their care needs. A young child will come to trust and depend on the adult to support them, both emotionally and in a practical sense. Good care routines help children to feel cared for.

We will take the intimate way that babies are fed a bottle as an example. The infant will be held securely against the body of the adult feeding them. They will receive undivided time and attention. The adult and baby will often gaze into one another's eyes. The infant may hold the fingers of the adult around the warm bottle. This is a time of closeness shared by the adult and the baby.

To allow such attachments to form and thrive between babies, young children and adults, it is good practice for group settings to appoint a key worker for each child. The role of a key worker is to take special interest in the well-being of their key children, and to form attachments with them. Attending to children's care needs is an important part of forming such an attachment. There is further information about the role of key workers in Unit CCLD 312 Plan and implement positive environments for babies and children under three years.

 Link   **Unit CCLD 312** Plan and implement positive environments for babies and children under three years

Routines provide opportunities for learning and development

Everyday routines such as eating, drinking, personal hygiene, washing and dressing give opportunities for children to learn about independent self care, as we have discussed. But there are also many opportunities for children to learn and develop in other areas. The list is extensive, but here are some examples of learning opportunities:

- Babies and young children can communicate with their carers, practising their early language. Adults and children may also share rhymes or songs
- When dressing, children can practise the fine motor skills required to fasten buttons, Velcro, toggles and zips
- Children can help each other with putting on outside clothes, developing their social skills
- When eating, children can practise the hand/eye co-ordination needed to pick up food with cutlery
- When pouring out their own drinks from a jug children can learn about capacity and volume
- While sitting at the table at mealtimes, children can learn about manners and social skills as they interact with one another
- Children can count out the right number of cups or plates at snack time, learning about numbers.

There is more information about this in Unit CCLD 309 Plan and implement curriculum frameworks for early education.

Link **Unit CCLD 309** Plan and implement curriculum frameworks for early education

---

Activities that promote development

The list of activities that can be used to promote the development of babies and young children is also extensive. However, the table below gives three examples relating each area of development. It is important that practitioners provide babies and children with a balance of activities so that all areas of their development are stimulated regularly.

It is possible for practitioners to theme and link activities for under threes to extend their skills, knowledge and understanding. For instance, during a water theme/linked activities children may have opportunities to:

- Dip their hands in water
- Play at a water tray
- 'Paint' outside with water and paintbrushes
- Pour out water to drink at snack time
- Water the plants.

Activities that promote development

Area of development	Example of activities
Gross motor skills	Pushing baby-walkers or trolleys Chasing after rolling balls Riding on first ride-on wheeled toys
Fine motor skills	Connecting large interlocking bricks (such as Duplo) Turning the pages of a board book Colouring with chunky crayons
Hand/eye co-ordination	Playing with hammer and peg toys Playing with stacking cups Operating pop-up toys
Intellectual and thinking skills	Completing play-trays and simple jigsaws Posting shapes into a shape sorter Identifying pictures in a book
Social and emotional skills	Sitting up to the table in a social situation at mealtimes Play with imaginary toys (such as dolls, puppets and soft toys) Opportunities for expression through music and dance
Language development	Rhymes and songs Stories Conversations and interaction with adults and peers

Action rhymes such as 'Pat-a-cake' encourage listening and responding

Experiencing these activities within a short period of time may help young children to link their experiences in their mind, enabling them to extend their skills, knowledge and understanding in terms of water.

However, practitioners need to be careful to ensure that any themed activities offered are relevant to younger children. For instance, whilst a 'tropical island' theme may excite older children who have a concept of islands, it is not likely to be meaningful to most children under three. The theme would be beyond their direct experience, and at this age children find it difficult to understand abstract ideas. A sand-and-water theme would be much more relevant. Practitioners must not exclude core activities that are important for learning and development in favour of themed or linked pastimes. The two should be offered alongside.

Sensory exploration

Babies use their senses to explore the world by:

- Seeing
- Hearing
- Touching
- Tasting
- Smelling.

Babies rely on their senses to tell them about the world, so sensory exploration is an important part of a baby's development. Babies can use their senses to find out about the world long before they can crawl or walk to explore their physical environment.

Practitioners can promote sensory opportunities in many ways including:

- Introducing babies to a range of textures

  There are many good textured toys on the market, such as baby mats or soft toys made from several different materials, some that are furry, others that are silky and so on. This allows the baby to make comparisons as they play

- Introducing babies to music and songs
- Having a good range of toys that make sounds
- A range of coloured and contrasting resources to explore
- Providing interesting features in the environment to see and hear

  Such as mobiles and wind chimes

- Taking babies out

  To experience the sights and sounds of the wider world

- Introducing babies to a range of safe food and drink when they are ready.

Ty stimulates babies' senses

Practitioner Ty works in the baby room of a day nursery. He has been looking for a way to stimulate babies' senses during care routines. He decides to hang a brightly coloured mobile that incorporates wind chimes above the changing mat.

➤ *How will this help to stimulate babies' senses?* **K3D432**

Using space effectively

Babies and young children need plenty of floor space to move around in. They must have space:

- For exercise
- To develop mobility
- To explore their environment safely.

They need more clear floor space than older children because of the way that they play and learn. Practitioners need to give this special consideration when planning the layout of the setting, as explained in more detail in Element 314.1.

In addition to providing appropriate space, practitioners can encourage babies and young children to exercise, develop mobility and explore their surroundings by:

- Providing appropriate resources, equipment and experiences for the developmental stage of babies and children
- Joining in play with babies and young children
- Praising babies and young children when they exercise, explore or engage in activities that develop mobility
- Helping babies yet to crawl to explore their environment by moving them periodically and changing the resources within their grasp.

There is more information in Unit CCLD 306 Plan and organise environments for children and families. There is also important information about ensuring the safety of the environment.

Link   **Unit CCLD 306** Plan and organise environments for children and families

Communicating with parents

Part of the role of practitioners is to observe, assess and record the developmental progress and achievements made by children under the age of three. The information gathered should be used to update parents and carers. There is more information about this in Unit CCLD 312 Plan and implement positive environments for babies and children under three years.

Practitioners should let parents and carers know about the progress babies and children make in the area of self care within the setting. This is particularly important as parents and carers will be using and supervising the same care routines at home. A consistent approach to the care routines will help babies and children to learn effectively and to feel secure.

Link   **Unit CCLD 312** Plan and implement positive environments for babies and children under three years

Element 314.3

Are you ready for assessment?

Supervise and use physical care routines to promote development

You need to show that you can competently supervise and use physical care routines to promote the development of babies and children under three years. To do this you will need to be directly observed by your assessor and present other types of evidence. The amount and type of evidence you will need to present will vary. You should plan this with your assessor.

Direct observation by your assessor

Observation and/or expert witness testimony is the required assessment method to be used to evidence some of each element in this unit. If your assessor is unable to observe you,

s/he will identify an expert in your workplace who will provide testimony of your work-based performance. Usually your assessor or expert witness will observe you in real work activities and this should provide most of the evidence for the performance criteria for the elements in this unit.

➤

Preparing to be observed

You will need to show your assessor that you can competently use appropriate and respectful techniques when attending to and supervising a variety of care needs of babies and children, including nappy changing, care of the skin and toileting. You must show that you can provide opportunities for learning, sensory development, exercise, mobility development and safe exploration of surroundings. You must also show that you can update parents on their child's development and progress.

Other types of evidence

You will need to present different types of evidence in order to:

- Cover criteria not observed by your assessor
- Show that you have the required knowledge, understanding and skills.

Such evidence could include:

- Confidential records such as child development records. These should not be placed in your portfolio – they must remain in their usual location and be referred to in the assessor records in your portfolio
- Case studies, projects, assignments and reflective accounts of your work.

Element
314.4

Provide an emotionally secure and consistent environment in partnership with parents and carers

Feelings

K3D434
K3D435
K3D436
KM437

Young children's feelings can be confusing, both for the children themselves and for adults. Practitioners must understand that while adults will moderate and control their feelings, most young children will not. That is why young children may be happy and laughing one minute and very upset moments later. Children can experience a range of feelings each day. The diagram opposite gives examples.

Practitioners can help children to understand their feelings, and they can encourage children to express them in an emotionally safe and secure environment. Children of all ages should be encouraged to express negative feelings as well as positive ones. This is important, as repressing feelings can lead to pent-up aggression, tension and anger.

In Element 314.3 we have discussed the value of the attachments that babies and children form with familiar carers.

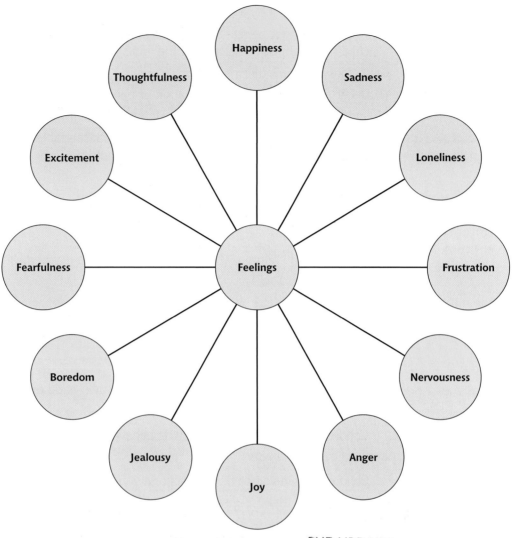

Feelings

Expressing emotional distress

Practitioners should respond to the feelings of babies and young children in a way that lets them know that their feelings are important. Babies and young children will have little or no language to express their feelings, and so it is up to the practitioner to identify signs that reveal how a child may be feeling. Children may demonstrate emotional distress in several ways including:

- Crying
- Having an emotional outburst/temper tantrum
- Becoming quiet and/or withdrawn
- Clinging to an adult
- Comfort-seeking behaviour, e.g. thumb sucking, asking for a favourite soft toy/comforter or a bottle
- Reluctance to play or participate in activities.

Distress can be caused by a number of everyday events including:

- Frustration at not being able to do something – either because of the limits of the child's own ability or because of the limits set by adults
- Jealousy over another child's toy
- Uncertainty of a new place, situation or person
- Sudden noises or movements that frighten them
- Finding that they are alone – at an activity or at the table for example, or on waking in the sleep area (young children should never be left unsupervised, but sometimes children can still *feel* alone).

If emotional distress is ongoing over time, babies and children may respond to their feelings in additional ways including:

- Wetting or soiling

  In the case of children who have previously been dry and clean during the night and/or day
- Changes to the appetite

  Babies and children may be less or more hungry
- Sleeping difficulties
- Self harm

  Hurting themselves, for example biting their own hand or pulling their own hair
- Difficulties getting along with other children

  Children may show signs of bullying behaviour
- Regression behaviour

  Children may revert to behaviours of a younger child – for example, a two-and-a-half-year-old may want to be fed by a carer.

This could be in response to many events, including:

- A new sibling
- Moving house
- Change of carers
- Transitions within settings – starting a setting or moving groups (from the baby room to the toddler room, for example)
- A stay in hospital
- Bereavement (deep sadness after a death)
- Tension/illness within the family.

In such cases, practitioners should speak with their supervisor to discuss the way forward. In line with the setting's policies (including the confidentiality policy), practitioners will need to discuss the issue with parents and carers. Some children may need to be referred to outside professionals, such as social workers or psychologists, for assistance. See Unit CCLD 305, Protect and promote children's rights, for emotional and physical signs and symptoms of abuse.

 Link   **Unit CCLD 305** Protect and promote children's rights

Sharing information with families

Ideally, practitioners should establish a good partnership with parents and carers so that families feel confident in approaching staff to discuss issues that may affect their child's emotional well-being. This allows practitioners to be aware and understanding of children's feelings. It gives them the opportunity to plan how they can best offer appropriate support. This is important not only when big life events occur, but on a day-to-day basis. For instance, a baby or young child may be in an irritable mood if they are tired following a night of disturbed sleep at home. Or they may feel cross about an argument with a sibling, or perhaps because they have been told off by a parent before coming to the setting.

You can encourage families to share such information by:

- Explaining the benefits of working in partnership when families first visit the setting
- Making families aware of the setting's confidentiality policy

  It is very important to reassure parents and carers that information will only be passed along on a need-to-know basis
- Making a private area available for confidential conversations
- Ensuring that key workers are accessible to parents who wish to talk
- Sharing information about the child's feelings within the setting as sharing is a two-way process.

There is more information about confidentiality on pages 4–6 of Unit CCLD 301 Develop and promote positive relationships.

 Link | **Unit CCLD 301** Develop and promote positive relationships

Techniques for calming and comforting

There are various techniques for calming and comforting children. Practitioners must use techniques that suit individual babies and children, taking their age, needs, levels of understanding and preferences into account. Whatever technique is used, it is important to remember that sensitivity is at the heart of helping children to deal with their feelings. Practitioners must:

- Be respectful of children's feelings

  Never belittle children's emotions or dismiss them. For instance, do not tell children they are 'being silly' or 'getting upset over nothing'
- Use only respectful and appropriate physical contact

  Children should only be touched or held with respect. For instance, a cuddle from a well-known carer can comfort a baby or young child – but carers must respect times when children would prefer their own space.

Acknowledging and talking about feelings

It is possible for practitioners to calm, comfort and reassure babies and children in ways that also encourage them to express their feelings. If you notice a child showing signs of unhappiness, you can begin by acknowledging the child's emotions, then talking about them. You can do this by using a soothing, gentle tone to enquire about a child's feelings. For instance, you may say, 'Are you feeling a bit sad?' You can demonstrate empathy by showing your concern in your facial expression and your body language. It is helpful to get down to the child's level. This can be effective with babies and children of all ages – as an adult you will know that sometimes all you need is someone else to understand you.

However, if the child has a suitable level of understanding, practitioners can also talk with them about their feelings. By doing this a practitioner can:

- Show that the child's feelings are important
- Show that the child is understood
- Demonstrate language for expressing feelings
- Encourage children to share their feelings in the future
- Offer comfort where appropriate, and perhaps a solution to an upsetting situation.

Children may need further support, such as physical comfort (see opposite). Be aware that young children may use basic language to describe how they are feeling – the word 'sad' may cover a range of negative feelings such as frustration, jealousy and anger, for instance.

Comforting a child

Play activities

Children can also learn to recognise, explore and deal with their feelings through play. The following activities can be helpful for young children:

- Imaginary play with dolls, puppets and so on – children can act out and work through their own feelings
- Expressive art, such as painting or crayoning – children can use colour, shapes and images to express their feelings
- Gross motor activities such as running freely outside – children can experience physical release of emotion, including stress, which may be pent up
- Playing with malleable materials such as dough – children can experience physical release of emotion through the pounding of the material (which is not generally permitted with other types of resources).

Physical comfort

Sometimes children need physical comfort or reassurance from well-known carers. This is particularly true of babies and young children because they have less understanding of the language we use to comfort and reassure (although a soft and gentle tone may still have some effect). Babies and children may gain comfort and/or reassurance from:

- Being picked up and held
- Having an adult's arm around their shoulders
- Holding hands with an adult
- Having an adult's hand on their back
- Having a cuddle
- Sitting with an adult or being close by.

These techniques should only be used when children want them, and always with respect.

Distraction

Babies and young children should be given opportunities to express their feelings as we have discussed. However, it is in the interests of children to move on positively after they have experienced emotional distress. Once a child has been comforted, finding a way to distract them can help them to move on. Introducing favourite toys or a new activity, a look out of the window or an adult joining in with play can all be effective distraction techniques. A change of environment (such as going outside) can also be very helpful.

Boundaries for behaviour

It is important that practitioners let babies and young children know what behaviour is acceptable and unacceptable. The boundaries and limits of acceptable behaviour must be communicated clearly and consistently, in a way that young children can understand. The theory of how to encourage positive behaviour through reward applies to this age range in the same way as it does to older children. However, practitioners must always take the level of children's understanding into consideration when responding to both acceptable and unacceptable behaviour.

When managing the unacceptable behaviour of children under three, a simple, firm 'no' can be communicated clearly. It is important that even babies learn to understand the meaning of the word. The desired effect is for the child to stop in their tracks when they hear it. This can prevent them from getting hurt or from hurting someone else. For this to work, the word must not be over used. As soon as a baby or child complies, they should be rewarded with praise – a smile and a positive comment go a long way, even with the youngest children.

It is unfair to expect children to behave in ways that are inconsistent with their development. Make sure you have realistic expectations for the children in your care. For instance, between the age one and two years children generally start to understand that they cannot have someone else's toy or food – before this they will not have had any concept of ownership. They may repeat behaviour that attracts the attention of adults.

Children between the age of two and three years often show jealousy when attention is given to other children and they often do not understand the concept of waiting for things. They may understand sharing but still find it difficult to do. They may be very active and become frustrated when they cannot do things for or by themselves.

There is more information about behaviour in Unit CCLD 337 Create environments that promote positive behaviour. Details can also be found in Unit CCLD 301 Develop and promote positive relationships. This includes information about dealing with emotional outbursts/tantrums, which tend to occur when young children are overwhelmed by negative feelings.

 Link   **Unit CCLD 337** Create environments that develop and promote positive behaviour
Unit CCLD 301 Develop and promote positive relationships

 **Element 314.4**

Are you ready for assessment?

Provide an emotionally secure and consistent environment in partnership with parents and carers

You need to show that you can competently provide an emotionally secure and consistent environment in partnership with parents. To do this you will need to be directly observed by your assessor and present other types of evidence. The amount and type of evidence you will need to present will vary. You should plan this with your assessor.

Direct observation by your assessor

Observation and/or expert witness testimony is the required assessment method to be used to evidence some of each element in this unit.
If your assessor is unable to observe you,

s/he will identify an expert in your workplace who will provide testimony of your work-based performance. Usually your assessor or expert witness will observe you in real work activities and this should provide most of the evidence for the performance criteria for the elements in this unit.

Preparing to be observed

You will need to show your assessor that you can competently provide an emotionally secure and consistent environment in partnership with parents by using a range of techniques to recognise and respond to emotional distress, showing respect for the feelings of children, and encouraging children to express and manage their emotions appropriately. You must also show that you can provide routines that promote the value of attachments, and encourage parents to share information that may affect children's emotional well-being.

Other types of evidence

You will need to present different types of evidence in order to:

- Cover criteria not observed by your assessor
- Show that you have the required knowledge, understanding and skills.

Such evidence could include:

- Confidential records such as notes of discussions with parents. These should not be placed in your portfolio – they must remain in their usual location and be referred to in the assessor records in your portfolio
- Case studies, projects, assignments and reflective accounts of your work.

Element 314.5

Recognise and respond to illness in babies and children under three years

Signs and symptoms of illness

K3H441
K3H442
K3H443
K3H444
K3H445
K3H446
K3H447
K3H448

It is particularly important that practitioners learn to recognise the signs and symptoms of illness in babies and young children who will have little or no language to explain how they are feeling.

Young children sometimes misuse words they have in their vocabulary in an effort to explain how they feel when they are ill. For example, a child may say they are 'sad' or perhaps 'tired'. If they have learnt the terms 'headache' or 'tummy ache', children may use these to describe pains in other parts of their body, not just their head or stomach. Practitioners should listen carefully to children in addition to observing signs and symptoms. 'Where does it hurt?' is a useful question as children may point to the relevant area of their body. But remember, children may have a general feeling of being unwell without a specific pain to speak of.

Managing illness

It is a legal requirement that all registered settings have written guidelines for the management of illness within the setting. You must ensure that you know and understand your own setting's policy in relation to the care and treatment of sick babies and children. Not implementing policy correctly may endanger a child's health and well-being and that of others within the setting. It could also cause your professional conduct to be questioned and may lead to disciplinary procedures being taken.

When a baby or child becomes ill it is the job of practitioners to:

- Manage signs and symptoms of illness, taking any appropriate measures such as cooling a child down (see further details below)
- Contact the child's parents or carers at the earliest opportunity to inform them of their child's condition and to arrange for the child to be collected
- Get medical advice or attention for the child if necessary (see opposite)
- Monitor the child's condition until they are collected by parents/carers or cared for by a medical professional.

When informing parents and carers of a child's illness, practitioners must take a sensitive approach. There is more information about this on page 43 of Unit CCLD 302 Develop and maintain a healthy, safe and secure environment for children. When parents or carers collect a child they must be given full information about the any care and treatment their child may have received. This is crucial to the ongoing care of the child. For instance, if a parent did not know that a child's emergency medicine had been given they may also give the medicine, resulting in an overdose.

Link   **Unit CCLD 302** Develop and maintain a healthy, safe and secure environment for children

Temperature

A high or low temperature can indicate that a child is unwell. Practitioners should learn how to take a child's temperature so that they can monitor suspected illness. It is good practice to record the temperature taken in writing according to the procedures of the setting. Some settings write this in the incident book – initially the child's name, date and the reason for taking the temperature is entered, along with the name of the practitioner taking the child's temperature. Then, if it is appropriate to monitor the child's temperature, the subsequent times and temperatures continue to be recorded. This information can then be accurately passed on to parents or carers, or medical professionals as necessary. See Unit CCLD 302, Develop and maintain a healthy, safe and secure environment for children, which gives further information about temperature.

It is not the role of practitioners to diagnose illnesses – that is the role of medical professionals. However, practitioners should recognise and know how to respond to the signs and symptoms that indicate illness in babies and young children. Common signs and symptoms are given in Unit CCLD 302 Develop and maintain a healthy, safe and secure environment for children. It is important to note that some signs and symptoms are physical (such as a cough) while others involve changes in behaviour, such as irritability or fretfulness. In addition, the table in the unit gives information about common childhood infections.

Link   **Unit CCLD 302** Develop and maintain a healthy, safe and secure environment for children

Seeking medical advice or attention

Some signs and symptoms presented by babies and young children need to be acted on right away, and practitioners may need to seek medical advice or attention urgently. Information about this is given in Unit CCLD 302 Develop and maintain a healthy, safe and secure environment for children.

Link   **Unit CCLD 302** Develop and maintain a healthy, safe and secure environment for children

Managing symptoms of illness

The symptoms of babies and young children will need to be managed whilst they are in your care. Feeling ill can be particularly frightening for children under three as they may have had little or no previous experience of illness, or they may not be able to recall times when they have been unwell. Being sick can be particularly alarming.

Whatever the symptoms, it is important to calm, comfort and reassure children. To do this effectively practitioners must stay calm themselves and take charge of the situation firmly but gently. Practitioners must follow the procedures of their setting as mentioned previously, but as a general rule children who are ill should stay in the close company of a familiar carer until they are collected. They should be amused with quiet activities, such as sharing books with their carer, away from other children.

Children who are unwell may appreciate a cuddle, but remember that this will not help a child with a temperature to cool down – in this case it would be better to sit alongside a child, perhaps holding their hand if they are in need of physical comfort. Information about cooling down children with a fever is given in Unit CCLD 302 Develop and maintain a healthy, safe and secure environment for children. It is particularly important to cool down babies and young children gradually, so that they are not shocked by a sudden change of temperature. If water is used to cool the body, it must be tepid not cold.

When a baby or child has diarrhoea, they are likely to lose control of their bowels, even if they are generally clean through the night and/or day. Practitioners should reassure children who are upset about soiling themselves, and deal with any accidents quickly and without fuss, settling children into clean, comfortable clothes as many times as necessary. Children should be taken to sit on the toilet or potty as they ask to do so. Babies will need their nappy changed each time they soil.

Babies and children with diarrhoea can easily become dehydrated, so it is good practice to offer sips of water to drink (boiled water in the case of babies). Soiled clothes or linens will need to be sluiced then washed separately on a hot wash in the washing machine. Any soiled areas or equipment must be cleaned thoroughly with disinfectant.

As we have mentioned, being sick can alarm babies and young children. Practitioners should be aware of this and should be prepared for the fact that babies and children under three can sometimes be violently sick. When children are being sick, practitioners should ensure that the child leans forwards so that they will not choke on their vomit. Practitioners can gently hold long hair back out of the way. Babies can be held forwards. Practitioners can offer physical comfort by gently rubbing the child's back. It is best for a child to be given or taken to something suitable to be sick into – but often sickness catches children and practitioners unawares as there may be little or no warning – babies and young children may not recognise the feeling of sickness before vomiting occurs. If a baby or child has been put to bed and you hear them being sick, you should go to them urgently as children lying down are at the greatest risk of choking on their vomit.

Once a child has been sick, they should be cleaned up gently, and their clothes should be changed if necessary. The practitioner should be prepared for the baby or child to be sick again, and should have ready something suitable for the child to be sick into. It is sensible to place a bib on a young baby and have a muslin cloth to hand, as you would when winding a baby who tends be sick after feeding. The area in which children have been sick will need to be cleaned thoroughly with disinfectant. Clothes or linens will need to be sluiced then washed separately on a hot wash in the washing machine.

Information about dealing with other signs and symptoms of illness and accident, including meningitis, is given in Unit CCLD 302 Develop and maintain a healthy, safe and secure environment for children. Information about handling bodily waste hygienically is also given in that unit.

Link   **Unit CCLD 302** Develop and maintain a healthy, safe and secure environment for children

Hygiene and cross-infection requirements

It is very important to ensure good hygiene procedures to protect babies and young children from the risks of cross-infection. Practitioners must ensure that:

- Food and drink are handled and stored safely

  See Unit CCLD 302 Develop and maintain a healthy, safe and secure environment for children

- Feeding equipment is sterilised effectively

  See Element 314.1

- Appropriate procedures are followed when handling all waste materials, including body fluids

  See Unit CCLD 302 Develop and maintain a healthy, safe and secure environment for children

- The environment, equipment and resources are kept in a clean and hygienic state

  See Unit CCLD 306 Plan and organise environments for children and families

- Children who are ill are treated according to the setting's procedures

  See Unit CCLD 302 Develop and maintain a healthy, safe and secure environment for children.

Link   **Unit CCLD 302** Develop and maintain a healthy, safe and secure environment for children
Unit CCLD 306 Plan and organise environments for children and families

Sudden infant death syndrome

Sudden infant death syndrome (SIDS) is the term used to describe the sudden and unexpected death of an infant that is initially unexplained. Some deaths are later explained at a post-mortem examination. Deaths that cannot be explained at post-mortem are generally registered as sudden infant death syndrome. A specific cause is identified in less than half of sudden infant deaths. The babies usually die peacefully and without distress in their cots during the day or night time, but sudden infant deaths can occur during any period of sleep – when babies are in their prams or in the arms of a parent or carer for instance.

SIDS can affect any babies, but those which are premature and have low birth weight are more at risk, as are boys and babies born to mothers who are still young. SIDS is most common in babies' second month and the risk reduces as babies grow. Almost 90% of sudden infant deaths occur by six months. SIDS is uncommon in babies under one month and in babies over one year. SIDS is more common in families who smoke heavily or live in difficult circumstances. It is uncommon in Asian families although the reason for this is not yet known.

On average seven babies currently die from SIDS every week in the UK. This figure is an improvement on the death rates before a 'reduce the risk' campaign in 1991. This shows how important it is to follow the guidelines issued by the Foundation for the Study of Sudden Infant Death Syndrome (FSIDS) for reducing the risk of SIDS. The guidelines are as follows:

- Parents should stop smoking in pregnancy (fathers as well as mothers)
- No one should be permitted to smoke in the same room as a baby
- Babies should be placed on their backs to sleep
- Babies should not be allowed to get too hot
- Babies' heads should be kept uncovered. They should be placed to sleep with their feet at the bottom of the cot to prevent them from wriggling down under the covers
- Medical advice should be sought promptly if a baby is unwell

Babies should be placed to sleep on their backs with their feet at the bottom of the cot

- It is safest for babies to sleep in a cot in their parent's bedroom for the first six months
- It can be dangerous to share a bed with a baby
- It is very dangerous to sleep together with the baby on a sofa, armchair or settee.

Sleeping babies must be checked on frequently and, in daycare settings, a record of these checks must be kept. Many nurseries keep a log somewhere near the sleep-room door. When they put a baby to bed, the practitioner records the time. They then check the baby every 10 minutes and log the time of the check on the form. They also record what time the baby gets up. Additional information can also be recorded, such as when the baby actually fell asleep and whether they slept soundly. It is also sensible to have a baby-room thermometer on the wall of play and sleep areas.

Are you ready for assessment?

Recognise and respond to illness in babies and children under three years

You need to show that you can competently recognise and respond to illness in babies and children under three years. To do this you will need to be directly observed by your assessor and present other types of evidence. The amount and type of evidence you will need to present will vary. You should plan this with your assessor.

Direct observation by your assessor

Observation and/or expert witness testimony is the required assessment method to be used to evidence some of each element in this unit. If your assessor is unable to observe you, s/he will identify an expert in your workplace who will provide testimony of your work-based performance. Usually your assessor or expert witness will observe you in real work activities and this should provide most of the evidence for the performance criteria for the elements in this unit.

Preparing to be observed

You will need to show your assessor that you can competently recognise and respond to illness in babies and children under three years by recognising and managing the physical and behavioural signs and symptoms of illness calmly and effectively. You must also show that you can apply the relevant policy of the setting, informing parents of their child's illness appropriately and seeking medical assistance when necessary.

> **Other types of evidence**
>
> You will need to present different types of evidence in order to:
>
> - Cover criteria not observed by your assessor
> - Show that you have the required knowledge, understanding and skills.
>
> Such evidence could include:
>
> - Case studies, projects, assignments and reflective accounts of your work
> - Questioning/professional discussion – questions may be oral or written. In each case the question and answer will need to be recorded.

Check your knowledge

- What is the required ratio of adults to children within your setting for children aged under three? **K3H414**
- How can you support mothers who wish to continue breast-feeding when their baby attends the setting? **K3H417**
- Why is it important that care routines are not hurried? **K3D426**
- Why is sensory exploration important for babies? **K3D432**
- How can activities be linked to extend the learning and understanding of babies and young children? **K3D439**
- How should you put babies to bed to reduce the risk of sudden infant death syndrome? **K3H448**

Reflective practice

Think about the way in which you currently respond to babies and children who are showing signs of distress. Do you let them know that their feelings are important, and encourage them to express their feelings before attempting to distract them? Make notes, and if necessary plan strategies you can use in the future to improve your practice. Refresh your memory by looking back at pages 341–2.

UNIT 318

Plan for and support self-directed play

*T*his unit is about identifying the play needs and preferences of children and young people, developing play spaces that will meet these needs, and supporting children and young people during play.

This unit contains four elements:

- **CCLD 318.1** *Collect and analyse information on play needs and preferences*
- **CCLD 318.2** *Plan and prepare play spaces*
- **CCLD 318.3** *Support self-directed play*
- **CCLD 318.4** *Help children and young people to manage risk during play*

Introduction

This unit is not only an optional unit of the qualification NVQ Level 3 in Children's Care, Learning and Development, it is also a unit of the NVQ Level 3 in Playwork. It is suitable for practitioners working in a play setting with school aged children and young people. This will be during children's leisure time – typically before or after school, weekends and during school holidays. Practitioners who choose this optional unit may work in various settings, including out-of-school clubs and adventure playgrounds.

If you are working with a broad age range of children (which is likely if you have chosen this optional unit), it is important that you learn how to adjust the way in which you work to suit the needs of older children and young people. To do this effectively you need a good understanding of the values of playwork.

The Playwork Principles explain the values playwork is based on. You should always promote them in your work with older children in play settings. The Principles themselves appear below. They are rather wordy. You should know that the information given in this unit reflects and promotes the Principles, so you will be learning and understanding more about them as you work your way through this part of the book.

Note: the Playwork Principles were endorsed by SkillsActive. They replace the old Playwork Assumptions and Values.

Playwork Principles

These Principles establish the professional and ethical framework for playwork and as such must be regarded as a whole.

They describe what is unique about play and playwork, and provide the playwork perspective for working with children and young people.

They are based on the recognition that if children and young people are given access to the broadest range of environments and play opportunities their capacity for positive development will be enhanced.

1   All children and young people need to play. The impulse to play is innate (built in). Play is a biological, psychological and social necessity and is fundamental to the healthy development and well-being of individuals and communities.

2   Play is a process that is freely chosen, personally directed and intrinsically motivated. That is, children and young people determine and control the content and intent of their play, by following their own instincts, ideas and interests, in their own way for their own reasons.

3   The prime focus and essence of playwork is to support and facilitate the play process and this should inform the development of play policy, strategy, training and education.

4   For playworkers, the play process takes precedence and playworkers act as advocates for play when engaging with adult-led agendas.

5   The role of the playworker is to support all children and young people in the creation of a space in which they can play.

6   The playworker's response to children and young people playing is based on a sound up-to-date knowledge of the play process and reflective practice.

7   Playworkers recognise their own impact on the play space and also the impact of children and young people's play on the playworker.

Playworkers choose an intervention style that enables children and young people to extend their play. All playworker intervention must balance risk with the developmental benefit and well-being of children.

Collect and analyse information on play needs and preferences

Throughout this element reference is made to the publication *Best Play: What play provision should do for children* (abbreviated to *Best Play* in this unit). This publication is the result of a partnership between the National Playing Fields Association, PLAYLINK and the Children's Play Council. It is about how children benefit from play and how play services and spaces can provide the benefits. It was published by the National Playing Fields Association in 2000 and can be viewed online at www.playlink.org.uk/publications/.

Benefits of play

Play has many benefits for children and young people, as outlined in *Best Play*. These

318K01
318K02
318K03
318K04
318K05
318K06
318K07
318K08
318K09
318K10
318K11
318K12
318K13

can be divided into two categories:

- Short term: benefits that are experienced at the time children/young people are actually playing
- Long term: benefits that develop over a period of time.

Short-term benefits of play to children/young people include:

- Opportunities to enjoy freedom
- Opportunities to test boundaries
- Opportunities to explore risk
- Opportunities exercise choice and control in terms of their own actions.

Long-term benefits of play to children/young people include:

- Fostering of independence
- Fostering of self-esteem
- The support of well-being, healthy growth and development
- An increase in knowledge and understanding
- The promotion of creativity
- The promotion of the capacity to learn.

Supporting play

It is the role of the practitioner to:

- Support children/young people's play
- Enrich children/young people's play
- Effectively manage risk involved in play.

Because of the benefits of free play (including the enjoyment it gives), it is good practice for practitioners to intervene in or interfere with children and young people's play as little as possible, as long as their play remains safe and their behaviour is acceptable. The emphasis is more on supporting children and less on directing them. This approach is sometimes called 'low intervention, high response'. Practitioners remain on hand to join in with play if they are invited to do so. Information about acceptable behaviour and encouraging children to resolve their own conflicts is given throughout Unit CCLD 337 Create environments that promote positive behaviour.

Link   **Unit CCLD 337** Create environments that promote positive behaviour

It is up to practitioners to enrich play by providing children and young people with suitable, stimulating environments that give rich opportunities for play of different types. This means the provision of appropriate play spaces and a wide variety of resources. There is more about play spaces and resources in Element 318.2. Practitioners must foster positive attitudes within the setting. Attitudes are a key element of the environments that children experience, and they form the very culture of a setting.

Practitioners must manage risk by balancing the benefits of activities and experiences with levels of risk during risk assessments. There is further information about this in Element 318.4.

In addition, practitioners may become important 'significant adults' in children's lives. They may be valuable role models who introduce children to new and different ideas. Practitioners may be someone for children and young people to talk to and confide in if they are unhappy. Practitioners may also become 'advocates' for children and young people and their play – that is, people who stand up for children's rights to play in public places such as parks, since play can sometimes be misinterpreted as antisocial behaviour. Practitioners can also be 'custodians' of the play space – the people responsible for securing its use for play.

Practitioners can supplement the play opportunities that families can offer children through the provision of play environments (such as large spaces or adventure play-grounds) and diverse resources. Practitioners are trained, in a way that most parents or carers are not, to promote opportunities for risk taking that will not endanger children and young people. The low-level supervision that practitioners are trained to offer is also important to children – this can help families to give children and young people the opportunity to feel safe playing in public spaces without being accompanied by family members.

Playing in a safe environment

Using objectives to evaluate play provision

The effectiveness of play provision can be evaluated by considering seven 'play objectives' that have been identified in the *Best Play* publication. These are broad statements that practitioners can use as indicators of good practice. By comparing the setting's practice against the objectives, practitioners can identify how well the setting is doing in terms of supporting play. Practitioners should consider what evidence they have of the setting's work against each objective. Once complete, the evaluation can be used to develop and improve the setting's practice as areas for development will have been highlighted.

The objectives identified in *Best Play* are as follows. The provision:

- Extends the choice and control that children have over their play, the freedom they enjoy and the satisfaction they gain from it
- Recognises the child's need to test boundaries and responds positively to that need
- Manages the balance between the need to offer risk and the need to keep children safe from harm
- Maximises the range of play opportunities
- Fosters independence and self-esteem
- Fosters children's respect for others and offers opportunities for social interaction
- Fosters the child's well-being, healthy growth and development, knowledge and understanding, creativity and capacity to learn.

Behaviour modes associated with play

The table below gives information about the behavioural modes associated with play.

Behavioural modes associated with play

Behavioural modes associated with play	Features
Personally directed	Occurs when children and young people make a choice about their activities. They decide for themselves what they will do and how they will do it
Intrinsically motivated	Occurs because children and young people have an inner drive to play – to run around, for example
In secure context	Occurs when children and young people play in a certain way in a particular circumstance. For instance, they may dance at their holiday club but be reluctant to do so in another environment, such as on the stage at school
Spontaneous	Occurs when children and young people play spontaneously. For instance they may, without forethought, start to join in another child's game that they come across, or jump off a moving swing
Goalless	Occurs when children are playing just for the fun of it, not for the sake of an end product or an achievement

Play types

Play expert Bob Hughes studied children and young people's play extensively. He identified different types of play. He gave each type of play a name and defined the characteristics of each, explaining the role he believed each type of play had in children's development. He called his research findings the 'taxonomy of play types'. This is referred to in *Best Play*. It is now widely accepted within the playwork field that practitioners should support children's development within each type of play and provide good opportunities for children and young people to experience them. The information is adapted from Hughe's *Taxonomy of Play Types and Best Play* (1996, PLAYLINK, London).

Bob Hughes has identified criteria which will enrich the play environment and provide opportunities for play of all types. This is also reported in *Best Play*. The criteria are outlined below.

- A varied and interesting physical environment

   Including different play spaces of various sizes; places that inspire imagination, create mystery and allow children to hide; manmade features and natural forms such as bushes and trees

- Playing with identity

Opportunities to take responsibility and to role play, dress up, enact or perform

Play types

Play type	Characteristics of play type	Examples of how this play type can be provided for by practitioners
Communication play	This is play that uses words, gestures or nuances, including conversation, debate, jokes, singing, poetry, play acting	Through musical activities, group circle time/debate time, consultation activities, drama games and performances
Creative play	This occurs when children play in a way that allows them to transfer information, respond in new ways and develop an awareness of new connections with an element of surprise. An example of this would be to create a sculpture from clay or to paint a picture, for the sake of creation	Through art and craft activities such drawing, painting, collage, chalking, sculpture with malleable materials and tools. Access to a broad range of materials both natural and man-made including wool, fabrics, cellophane, tissue paper
Deep play	This play occurs when children participate in experiences that are risky, perhaps even potentially life threatening. It allows children to conquer fear and to develop survival skills. Examples of this play include balancing on a high beam and skateboarding along a wall	Through exhilarating play within adventure setting – using zip wires, climbing trees, caving, mountain biking. Participating in sports/physical activities such as skateboarding, rollerblading or sledging. (As always, practitioners must carry out a risk assessment before these activities)
Dramatic play	This occurs when children dramatise events which they do not participate in directly. This includes playing TV shows or games based on cartoons or super-heroes, or the enactment of a religious/festive event, perhaps even a funeral	Through time and space for children to develop their own such games and activities. Practitioners can support this play by not interrupting unless play becomes dangerous, and allowing children to use resources and materials freely to develop 'sets' and so on
Exploratory play	This occurs when children gain factual information through manipulation or movement. This can include handling objects in a range of ways, such as throwing, banging or mouthing – this allows children to assess the properties of the object and to assess its possibilities. An example of this is the way in which children manipulate recycled objects to make a model	Provide interesting resources for children, and regularly introduce new objects, both man-made and natural. This could include autumn leaves for example. Allow children to find their own way of using tools and objects as long as this is safe – do not insist on showing them the 'right' or 'proper' way unless children ask for help
Fantasy play	This takes place when children rearrange the world in a way that is unlikely to occur, but that appeals to them. For instance, they may play at owning a zoo, or an expensive car, or play at being a pop star or a pilot	Through allowing children the time and space to develop fantasy play and worlds themselves. Practitioners can support this play by not interrupting unless play becomes dangerous, or they are invited to participate. In this case practitioners should follow the child's lead, and not impose their own ideas on the child's fantasy world
Imaginative play	This occurs when the conventional rules that govern our real physical world have no meaning or do not apply to the world of children's play. For example, children may pretend to be a plant, scarecrow or an aeroplane. Or they may act out pumping petrol from an invisible pump	Through allowing children the time and space to develop their imaginary play. Practitioners can support this play by not interrupting unless play becomes dangerous, or they are invited to participate. In this case practitioners should follow the child's lead, and not impose their own ideas or rules on the child's play. Practitioners should accept without question the rules children have devised

Locomotor play	This occurs when children move around in any and every direction for the sake of doing so. Examples of this include playing playground games such as tag and climbing apparatus and trees	Through allowing plenty of free-play time in large areas, so that children can develop their own games and travel around the play space spontaneously. Practitioners can also organise and join in with playground games such as Sticky Glue (also known as Stuck-in-the-Mud)
Mastery play	This occurs when children's play controls the physical and affective ingredients of the environment. Examples include making fires, building dams, digging holes and creating shelters	Through activities that involve the elements, such as building a camp fire and cooking on it or making and flying windsocks or kites. If necessary (depending on the nature of the play space) practitioners can arrange visits/trips so that children can experience making shelters in the woods or digging trenches in the sand
Object play	This occurs when children handle an object using an interesting sequence of manipulations and movements. This includes examining properties of objects closely, or using items in a new or novel way – using a ruler as a twirling baton for instance	Through providing interesting resources for children and regularly introducing new objects likely to stimulate curiosity and imagination (both man-made and natural). Allowing children to find their own way of using objects as long as this is safe
Rough and tumble	This occurs when all children involved are obviously unhurt and enjoying themselves while they play chasing, wrestling or playful 'fighting' games. This 'close encounter play' is about discovering physical flexibility, gauging relative strength and the exhilaration of display. It involves safe touching	By not stepping in too soon if children are enjoying rough-and-tumble play – monitoring the play enables practitioners to step in if rough and tumble escalates to play which is outside safe or acceptable limits. Resources such as soft play equipment and soft play zones are helpful for facilitating this type of play in otherwise 'formal' areas – within a classroom used for an after-school club for instance
Social play	This occurs when children play together. Rules and criteria for social engagement and interaction between the children can be revealed, explored and amended (changed during play). Examples are activities where children involved are expected to stick to rules or protocols such as in games or conversations	Through allowing children plenty of time and space to develop rules and protocols for themselves. Practitioners should support children when the rules of play and interaction are explored or changed, as long as behaviour does not become unsafe. Team activities and opportunities for children to design their own board games can facilitate this type of play
Socio-dramatic play	This occurs when children act out experiences of an intense personal, social, domestic or interpersonal nature. The experiences acted out may have really happened to children, or they could potentially occur. Examples of this play include playing homes/families, playing shopping and even arguing	Through providing play areas such as home corners and the provision of prop resources such as play money, play telephones and so on. Older child may enjoy role play or moral dilemma games where they act out or describe how they would behave in certain situations – if they missed the last bus home for example
Symbolic play	This occurs when children use an object to symbolise something else, e.g. a piece of wood may become a snake, or a piece of string may be used as a wedding ring. Symbolic play allows control, gradual exploration and increased understanding, without children risking being out of their depth	Through providing interesting resources for children, and regularly introducing new objects likely to stimulate curiosity and imagination (both man-made and natural). Allowing children free access to resources, so they can get out items they want to play with

- Playing with the natural elements (earth, water, fire and air)

  Building campfires, water play, flying kites, digging in earth/sand

- Challenge in relation to the physical environment

  Activities and experiences that allow children to test the limits of their capabilities, e.g. rough-and-tumble games, chasing and running games

- Experiencing a range of emotions

  Opportunities to experience being scared and confident, brave and cowardly, in control and out of control

- Movement (such as running, jumping, balancing, etc.)

  Balancing on beams or stilts, riding bicycles, skateboarding, skipping

- Stimulation of the five senses (sight, hearing, taste, touch and smell)

  Having quiet places and places where noise (such as shouting) is permitted; hearing music; trying a range of food and drinks; variety of colour, shapes, textures and brightness in resources and play spaces

- Experiencing change in the natural and built environment

  Outdoor access that allows children to experience changes in the weather and the seasons, participation in building or transforming the environment

- Manipulating natural and fabricated (manmade) materials

  Art and craft resources, tools, materials for building and creating, a broad range of 'bits and pieces'

- Social interactions

  Opportunities to solve own conflicts, to negotiate, co-operate and compete with others of different ages, abilities, ethnicity, culture and gender. Also, opportunities to choose when to play alone and when to play with other individuals and groups.

Hughes' research and conclusions are explained in the book *Taxonomy of Play Types* (Bob Hughes, PLAYLINK, 1996).

Stages of development

Key Terms

Mood descriptors
Individual behaviours that indicate the mood of a child or young person as he or she plays.

The stages of child development influence children and young people's play needs and behaviours. Practitioners must remember that all children develop at different rates and so their play needs and behaviours will also vary. For example, children tend to have different interests and be drawn to different types of play as they grow up and develop, and the amount of independence that children are comfortable with increases over time. A good knowledge and understanding of children's development is essential to the provision of good, appropriate play opportunities. There is more about this throughout Unit CCLD 303 Promote children's development.

 Link **Unit CCLD 303** Promote children's development

Mood descriptors

The following table explains how mood descriptors can be identified in children's play, and how they are of value.

Mood descriptors

Mood descriptors associated with play	How to recognise mood descriptors
Happy	Children and young people may be smiling, laughing or exhibiting playful behaviour during their play
Independent	Children and young people may be keen to try things for themselves and may be reluctant to be 'shown' how to do new things/operate new tools. They may prefer to find their own solutions than to ask for or receive help. They may prefer to play without adults, and may play alone
Confident	Children and young people are confident enough to take emotional and/or physical risks in their play. They may be keen to try new things and put forward their ideas and opinions. They may be keen to interact with peers and adults.
Altruistic	Children and young people may be willing to help their peers and adults. They may share and encourage others to join in with their games. They may adjust the level of their play to suit younger children
Trusting	Children and young people may show their trust by allowing peers and adults to support them in their play, or by taking an emotional risk with/in front of peers and adults. They may participate in team activities that require a reliance on others
Active or immersed	Children and young people are absorbed in their play. They are actively doing something which requires their attention (such as playing tag), or they are engaged with and focusing on their activity (such as playing a board game)
At ease	Children and young people may seem relaxed and comfortable within their play – they are being themselves. They may seem restful, calm or at home with their activity. They do not perceive there to be an element of challenge or risk

Barriers to access and adaptation of play opportunities

Some children and young people may experience barriers that affect their access to play. Practitioners must take action to identify and remove barriers to ensure that all children are given equal opportunities to play. There is more about this in Unit CCLD 321 Support children with disabilities or special educational needs and their families.

 Link   Unit CCLD 321 Support children with disabilities or special educational needs and their families

Identifying play needs and preferences

It is important for practitioners to identify the play needs and preferences of the children and young people they work with. This enables practitioners to provide play opportunities that will meet the needs of children and young people and promote their development. It also enables practitioners to provide experiences that all will enjoy and will find engaging and interesting. This increases children and young people's motivation to participate in play experiences. Practitioners can collect information on play needs and preferences by using the following methods:

- Researching playwork theory and practice
- Observing children/young people at play
- Interacting with children/young people.

Researching playwork theory and practice

There are several books dedicated to playwork theory and practice. It is advisable for practitioners to read widely about the subject.

However, it is important to note that play theories and current thinking evolves over time. Consequently practitioners must keep themselves up to date and revise their practice as necessary throughout their careers. Further information on theories of play and development are given in Unit CCLD 309 Plan and implement curriculum frameworks for early education, and within Unit CCLD 303 Promote children's development.

Link   **Unit CCLD 309** Plan and implement curriculum frameworks for early education
Unit CCLD 303 Promote children's development

You may be able to arrange a visit to a play setting different from your own, for example an adventure playground. This can be an effective way of broadening your experience of play in practice. There is further information about play spaces and resources in Element 318.2.

Observing children and young people at play

Practitioners will naturally observe things about individual children's play needs and preferences as they interact and play with children and as they stand back and supervise. These naturally occurring observations can be informative. Writing them down in a notebook is a helpful way to gather information.

Planned observations of children are also valuable. Information about methods of observation and how to analyse observations is given in Unit CCLD 303 Promote children's development.

Link   **Unit CCLD 303** Promote children's development

Interacting and consulting with children and young people

Practitioners should consult with children and young people about their play needs and preferences. This becomes increasingly important as children grow up. Through consultation practitioners can interact with children and young people, finding out what they want and need from their play. This enables practitioners to provide play opportunities that children and young people will enjoy participating in. But consultation has other advantages too. It can help children and young people to feel:

- Listened to

  Children and young people spend a lot of time listening to adults at school and perhaps in the home. Some children naturally initiate conversations with practitioners more frequently than others. When practitioners are consulting and actively looking to seek out everyone's opinion, they have the opportunity to encourage everyone to have their say, including those children/young people less likely to put forward their opinion without it being asked for and those children who do not routinely approach adults and/or gain their attention easily

- Valued and worthwhile

  We know as adults how good we feel if our employers ask for our opinions and ideas. It is good to feel that your thoughts are worthwhile and so your opinion is sought out and valued. The same is true for children/young people

- Included

  Consultation enhances participation. If children/young people are involved in devising play opportunities or play spaces, they are keener to participate.

All of the above can lead to increased self-esteem and confidence and help to encourage the development of feelings of empowerment and ownership.

Children and young people can also learn and practise skills during consultation. They will have opportunities to:

- Form and explain ideas and opinions
- Listen to and respect each other
- Discuss and debate
- Adapt and negotiate
- Plan
- Take responsibility
- Evaluate
- Give feedback
- Record information.

Consultation can take place during casual conversation as practitioners interact with children and young people. But planned consultation activities can also take place during:

- Meetings
- Circle time
- Planning sessions
- Evaluations and reviews.

It is important to tailor the methods of consultation utilised to the ages and abilities of the children in the group. Many methods can be used to consult, including the following:

● Discussion

Practitioners can talk with children and young people individually or in groups about their play needs, preferences and ideas about play experiences and play spaces

● Questionnaires

These can be written or pictorial, depending on the ages and abilities of the children

● Interviews

An alternative to questionnaires – an 'interviewer' can verbally ask children/young people questions and record their answers

● Suggestion boxes

Children/young people can write and draw their ideas, thoughts and feelings and put them into a box anonymously. Suggestion video tapes/audio tapes can also work well, although the element of anonymity is lost

● Voting

A good, quick way of consulting with children/young people – children can vote on the layout of the play space at the start of the session for instance. This can be as simple as a show of hands or can involve a ballot (anonymous paper vote)

● Evaluation

Involving children/young people in the evaluation of play sessions reveals what they have enjoyed – this can inform future planning. There are several visual ways of recording evaluations. It is common to ask children to rank, in order of preference, the activities they have participated in. Here are four examples:

–   Drawing out a large bulls-eye target and asking each child to place a cross on it to indicate how they felt about a particular experience. The nearer to the bulls-eye the cross is, the better they enjoyed the experience. See the diagram below

–   Drawing up a list of play experiences. Children are given a gold, silver and bronze sticker. They are asked to place the stickers next to the experiences on the list awarding them first, second or third in terms of their favourites

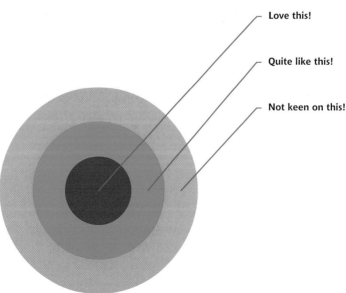

Love this!

Quite like this!

Not keen on this!

The evaluation target

- Drawing a list of numbers, perhaps one to five. Next to the relevant numbers the children write or draw on their top five play experiences of the session

- Four corners of the play space are identified as 'really liked it', 'liked it', 'didn't like it', and 'really didn't like it'. Practitioners call out play experiences, and children run to the relevant corner depending how they felt about the experience

- Thought-storming

    There is a practical example of this on page 14 of Unit CCLD 301 Develop and promote positive relationships.

To encourage children/young people to participate in consultation, practitioners can:

- Be motivational in their approach by making the process fun
- Communicate the purpose of the consultation to the children – let them know that what they have to say influences future play experiences
- Ensure everyone gets their say
- Choose methods to suit the children
- Ring the changes with regard to the consultation methods used
- Acknowledge and accept everyone's contribution
- Ensure all contributions are respected.

There is further related information in Unit CCLD 301 Develop and promote positive relationships.

 Link   **Unit CCLD 301** Develop and promote positive relationships

 **Element 318.1**

Are you ready for assessment?

Collect and analyse information on play needs and preferences

You need to show that you can competently collect and analyse information on play needs and preferences. To do this you will need to be directly observed by your assessor and present other types of evidence. The amount and type of evidence you need to present will vary. You should plan this with your assessor.

Direct observation by your assessor

Observation and/or expert witness testimony is the required assessment method to be used to evidence some of each element in this unit. If your assessor is unable to observe you, s/he will identify an expert in your workplace who will provide testimony of your work-based performance. Usually your assessor or expert witness will observe you in real work activities and this should provide most of the evidence for the performance criteria for the elements in this unit. ➤

Preparing to be observed

You must show your assessor that you can collect and analyse information about children's play by researching playwork theory and practice and observing and interacting with children and young people. You must show that you can take account of those who may experience barriers to participation, and that you can consult with children and young people on their play needs and preferences.

Other types of evidence

You will need to present different types of evidence in order to:

- Cover criteria not observed by your assessor
- Show that you have the required knowledge, understanding and skills.

Such evidence could include:

- Work products such as play plans
- Case studies, projects, assignments and reflective accounts of your work
- Confidential records such as observations. These should not be placed in your portfolio – they must remain in their usual location and be referred to in the assessor records in your portfolio.

Element 318.2 *Plan and prepare play spaces*

Types of play spaces

318K14
318K15
318K16
318K17
318K18
318K19
318K20

A range of different types of play space can meet the play needs of children and young people, including:

- Out-of-school clubs, often run on school premises in a classroom or hall, with the use of the school playground. These may open before school, after school and/or in the school holidays

- Adventure playgrounds, featuring outdoor space for adventurous/exhilarating play such as climbing trees or using zip lines (cables fixed between two high points that children can hang off and slide down). Some may also have indoor facilities for play. These are generally open after school and during the holidays

- Holiday clubs run in sports centres, providing a range of play opportunities and usually featuring a broad range of physical activities and sports

- Play buses or other mobile facilities that visit places that would not otherwise have much in the way of play facilities (for example, in remote locations) – the buses are specially converted inside so that children can get on the bus and play. They generally visit during the holidays and at weekends for older children, and on weekdays during term time for pre-school children

- Residential centres where children stay overnight, for a weekend or perhaps a week during the holidays. A range of activities may be offered off- and on-site, including opportunities for activities such as canoeing, caving and team games

Public parks and fields, where children may go to play without supervision. However, some such public sites may be staffed by a practitioner or a park keeper offering 'low-level' supervision. There may or may not be play equipment installed.

Play spaces are sometimes referred to in four categories. These are play spaces for:

- Physical play
- Affective play
- Transient play
- Permanent play.

The table below explains the characteristics of each.

Play spaces

Example of play spaces	Typical features
Breakfast club	Usually open for 1–2 hours before school. Provides breakfast for children and play activities. Children/young people then go to school from the club. Many clubs run on school premises. If not, then children/young people are escorted to school by practitioners
After-school club	Usually open after school until 6 p.m. or 7 p.m. Many are run on school premises, but if not practitioners collect children/young people from school and escort them to the club. Refreshments are provided, and sometimes a meal. A range of activities are offered both indoors and outdoors, typically including arts and crafts, playground games, sports and play with a range of resources such as construction materials, imaginary play equipment and games
Holiday club	Usually open from 7 a.m. or 8 a.m. until 6–7 p.m. Refreshments are provided (and perhaps meals, although children are likely to bring a packed lunch). The activities offered are similar to an after-school club, but there will often be additional trips out and special events. Holiday clubs sometimes have themed events/activities. They are often held in sports centres, on school premises or in community halls
Adventure playground	Often open after school for three or four hours, and all day at the weekend/during school holidays (during daylight hours in the winter). There are generally wide open spaces for play and fixed equipment to climb on, swing from, etc., as well as the provision of loose pieces. There are generally good opportunities for taking risks, and for physical play. There may be good natural features such as trees. There is sometimes an additional inside area. Children/young people are likely to participate in some activities that are not permitted due to the premises/registration of out-of-school clubs – cooking over an open fire, for instance
Play bus	A bus converted for play. The inside is modified to provide similar activities that may be offered at a holiday club. The bus may park somewhere with access to a good outdoor space too – at a local playing field for instance
Residential centre	Open during weekends and school holidays (unless children are on a school trip), these centres provide somewhere to stay away from home for a short period. There may be activities provided on site or a short distance away. These often include many activities that are offered at holiday clubs, but in addition opportunities to try sports such as mountain biking, canoeing and caving
Parks/ playgrounds	These may not be staffed by practitioners. There may be a park keeper/ranger/warden in attendance. There may be wide open spaces, manufactured play equipment such as slides and climbing frames and areas for sport – football goalposts may be provided for instance.

Planning and creating play spaces

Practitioners must plan play spaces that will meet the play needs and preferences of the children and young people with whom they are working. This planning will be informed by:

- Observations made of children/young people's play needs and preferences
- Consultation with children/young people
- Action plans made in light of evaluations of the play setting made against the play objectives.

There is information on the points above in Element 318.1. In addition, practitioners will want to provide play opportunities that promote all of the play types.

The design and layout of a play space will be greatly influenced by the type of space available – what can be offered within a school hall is clearly different from what can be offered within an adventure playground. There are many ways of planning play spaces, but practitioners must always take their own unique play space into consideration. The diagram below demonstrates one method of planning that practitioners may use.

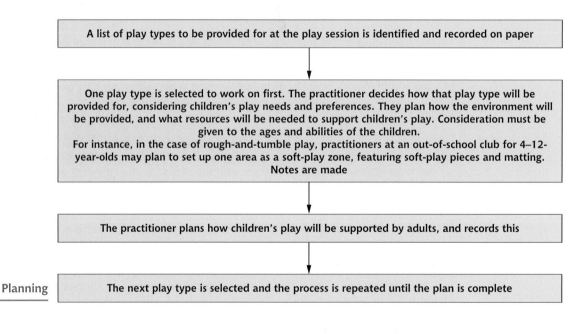

A list of play types to be provided for at the play session is identified and recorded on paper

One play type is selected to work on first. The practitioner decides how that play type will be provided for, considering children's play needs and preferences. They plan how the environment will be provided, and what resources will be needed to support children's play. Consideration must be given to the ages and abilities of the children.
For instance, in the case of rough-and-tumble play, practitioners at an out-of-school club for 4–12-year-olds may plan to set up one area as a soft-play zone, featuring soft-play pieces and matting.
Notes are made

The practitioner plans how children's play will be supported by adults, and records this

Planning

The next play type is selected and the process is repeated until the plan is complete

It is important to create spaces that children/young people can adapt to their own needs according to their age, needs and abilities. This gives them freedom and control within their play and the opportunity to flexibly explore and develop their own play ideas, activities and experiences. Many experts agree that ideally the following types of resources should be incorporated into the design of a play space to facilitate flexibility:

- 'Loose parts' that can be moved around the setting to create new and interesting structures and/or play experiences. Parts may include logs and other pieces of wood, plants, containers, screens, toys, etc. (This idea came from 'The theory of loose parts' developed by Simon Nicholson in 1971). Loose parts can be used in an endless combination of ways and the parts can change over time

Outdoor physical
equipment

- Permanent fixed resources that stay in one place, such as large apparatus or trees
- Physical resources (within a space suitable for physical play) such as climbing frames, ladders, stilts, balls, skateboards, bicycles.

Resources

In addition to toys and equipment, practitioners need to obtain a wide range of resources to effectively support children and young people's self-directed play, such as those described as loose parts. It is essential to always keep within the budget of the setting and to only spend money when authorised to do so by supervisors.

However, many resources can be obtained cheaply or can be adapted with some creativity. For instance, many areas have a scrap stores. Settings can join these, then help themselves to supplies of many scrap resources for a small fee. Items such as wooden planks, tall cardboard tubes from carpet rolls, large sheets of card, paper and cellophane are examples of resources that can be found at scrap stores. You can contact your local council to find out the location of your nearest store.

Involving children

We looked at the importance of consulting with children in Element 318.1. The benefits previously discussed can be extended by involving children in the design and creation of the play space. This builds effectively on consultation activities that gave children opportunities to identify the play experiences they would like.

Children and young people can be involved in a number of ways, including:

- Helping practitioners to draw up plans – this may involve recording details as well as suggesting and discussing ideas
- The gathering of resources
- Setting out the play space and resources, making use of 'loose parts'.

Access for all

Access for all is strongly embedded in the Playwork Principles. It is essential that all children and young people have access to play spaces and resources for play. Practitioners can (and must) make arrangements ahead of time to ensure equality of opportunity in relation to planned activities, experiences and play spaces. However, children and young people will be encouraged to develop their own play, using and changing resources and play spaces as play develops. This means that, to ensure continuing access for all, practitioners must monitor the changing nature of activities, experiences and play spaces, and be ready to make adaptations as it becomes apparent that they are needed.

With this in mind, read through the Playwork Principles again. You will see that each statement links directly to providing access to play for all children. There is further related information in Unit CCLD 321 Support children with disabilities or special educational needs and their families.

Link   **Unit CCLD 321** Support children with disabilities or special educational needs and their families

Health and safety

Information about taking into account the health and safety requirements that apply to play spaces is provided throughout Element 306.1 of Unit CCLD 306 Plan and organise environments for children and families.

Link   **Unit CCLD 306** Plan and organise environments for children and families

---

Element 318.2
Are you ready for assessment?
Plan and prepare play spaces

You need to show that you can competently plan and prepare play spaces. To do this you will need to be directly observed by your assessor and present other types of evidence. The amount and type of evidence you need to present will vary. You should plan this with your assessor.

Direct observation by your assessor

Observation and/or expert witness testimony is the required assessment method to be used to evidence some of each element in this unit. If your assessor is unable to observe you,

s/he will identify an expert in your workplace who will provide testimony of your work-based performance. Usually your assessor or expert witness will observe you in real work activities and this should provide most of the evidence for the performance criteria for the elements in this unit.

Preparing to be observed

You must show your assessor that you can plan appropriate play spaces for physical play, effective play, transient play and permanent play, ensuring that the play spaces provide for a range of play types, and taking account of health and safety requirements. You must also show that you can obtain appropriate resources, working within the available budget. You must show that you can ensure the environments are accessible for all, and that you can create the planned play spaces involving children and young people where possible.

Other types of evidence

You will need to present different types of evidence in order to:

- Cover criteria not observed by your assessor
- Show that you have the required knowledge, understanding and skills.

Such evidence could include:

- Work products such as play plans, resource budgeting documents or consultation notes
- Case studies, projects, assignments and reflective accounts of your work.

Element 318.3 *Support self-directed play*

Choice and exploration

318K21
318K22
318K23
318K24
318K25
318K26
318K27
318K28
319K29

It is important for children and young people to have opportunities to choose and explore play spaces for themselves, according to their age, needs and abilities. This gives children freedom and control within their play and the opportunity to flexibly explore and develop their own play ideas, activities and experiences. In addition, children will respond to and be inspired by the stimulus of their environment in individual ways. They should be empowered to respond and to become inspired in their own time and in their own way. This increases a child's sense of ownership of their play space, which in turn encourages a sense of freedom and flexibility.

Sometimes children and young people may need adult support in choosing and exploring play spaces. For example, when children first arrive at a play setting they may initially show signs of feeling overwhelmed or self-conscious. This can apply whether or not it is the child's first day. Practitioners can help such children or young people to locate friends who have already arrived, provide suggestions of play, e.g., 'Would you like to get the paint out?', or point out a feature of the play space, 'Have you seen that the ball-pool is set up inside today?' A practitioner's knowledge of children, young people and their play preferences can be drawn upon in order to offer support appropriate to their age, needs and abilities.

Content and intent of play

Practitioners must respect that children and young people's play belongs to them. It should be up to the children and young people to decide what they want to do in their play and how they want to do it – this is the 'content' of the play. The 'intent' of the play is its purpose or reason. Sometimes there may be an end product such as a painting or sculpture. But in many cases there is not – play may be driven by many things such as curiosity or exploration. Even when there is an end product, it may be discarded at the end of a 'play frame' – see page 373 for further details.

The exploration of values

Bob Hughes suggests that practitioners enable children to explore their own values. He believes that children will learn that a common value base is important in society if they are allowed to behave in ways that might be considered inappropriate, hurtful or risky. He feels that children will modify and adjust these behaviours naturally as they play if practitioners stand back and allow things to take their course, instead of imposing their own values or codes for behaviour straight away. He suggests this method be applied 'as far as is practicable'. Judging this can be tricky – it becomes easier as practitioners gain in experience. New practitioners can benefit from observing experienced colleagues using this method effectively.

Uninterrupted play

It is important for practitioners to allow children and young people to play uninterrupted whenever possible. When play is interrupted, important benefits of play can be adversely affected. Interruptions can disturb or destroy the play 'world' which children have created and are playing within. A child may not be able to recapture this. In addition, ideas or trains of thought can be lost in an instant when interruptions occur. You will recognise this as an adult – there will be times when you have been interrupted and you have lost track of what you were doing or thinking about – this can be very frustrating.

Practitioners should respect the play of children and young people sufficiently *not* to interrupt it unnecessarily. Sometimes intervention *is* called for – if play becomes unsafe or behaviour inappropriate as discussed in Element 318.1. But unavoidable interruptions are sometimes due to timing. It may be time for a child to go home before they have finished their play, or it may be time to have a meal that is ready. In these cases practitioners can prepare children by giving them a warning such as, 'There's only 15 minutes left before we need to go and have our lunch'. This advance notice gives children the opportunity to wind up their play accordingly. It can also help to leave resources and play spaces as they are, if possible, instead of packing away, so that children can return to their play later if they want to.

Practitioners should not show children or young people what they perceive to be 'better' or 'proper' ways of doing things when they are playing unless they ask to be shown or behaviours are potentially dangerous (the dangerous misuse of a tool for instance). Play is not about the right or wrong way of doing things. It is about exploration, discovery and individual creativity.

The cycle of play cues and play frames

Understanding how the play cycle of 'play cues' and 'play frames' works allows practitioners to respond sensitively to children and young people's invitations to play with them. It also helps them not to intervene in play in ways that would be detrimental.

Play is about
exploration,
discovery and
creativity

A play cue is a signal that a child or young person gives to show that they want to play. They are hoping their cue will get a favourable response. For instance, if a child kicks a ball towards you they are indicating that they want to play – they are hoping you will give them a 'play return'. This is a signal that you are willing to play. In our example, you would kick the ball back as a 'play return'.

Play returns encourage children and young people's play. In some situations the return may come in the form of a positive response from a source other than another person – it could come from things around them. For instance, imagine a child is trying to make a daisy chain. If they manage to find enough daisies before too long (the return) they may keep playing. If not, they may give up.

The process of play cues and returns occurring is known as a 'play frame'. Play frames exist in time and space. In our first example above, the play frame existed in the playground between a child and a practitioner. A practitioner is not involved in a frame unless they are directly playing with a child. In our second example the practitioner was 'outside the frame' – the child was picking daisies alone.

If you observe a play cue you can respond in a number of ways. It may be appropriate to join in with children's play or to make a suggestion, provide resources or offer support and/or encouragement. However, if children are engaged appropriately in an activity and do not give you a play cue, you would not be required to respond, and so you would not intervene.

Play frames end in different ways. There may be a natural end – perhaps a board game has finished or a model has been made. Children tend to get what they want from their play activities and experiences – then they are over. This is sometimes confusing for adults as children may throw away a picture they have spent time and effort working on, or knock down a construction they have built. Whenever possible you should follow children's lead in terms of the end of play frames, participating in the frame (known as 'holding the child's play frame') for as long as the child indicates they want the frame to last. Once a play frame has ended, children initiate a new and different play cue, and so the cycle begins again.

Leana responds to a play cue

Seven-year-old Amy has been playing alone with a balloon. She has been hitting it around the room with her hand. As playworker Leana passes by, Amy hits the balloon towards her. Leana hits it back, then stands still to see how Amy responds. Amy hits the balloon back to Leana again. Leana recognises the play cue and continues to play the game with Amy. After a few turns Amy begins to hit the balloon in the air. She claps her hands before she catches it. The play frame is over, and Leana moves away as Amy carries on alone with her new game.

➤ *Why did Leana respond in this way?*   **318K27, 318K28, 318K29**

Element 318.3
Are you ready for assessment?
Support self-directed play

You need to show that you can competently support self-directed play. To do this you will need to be directly observed by your assessor and present other types of evidence. The amount and type of evidence you need to present will vary. You should plan this with your assessor.

Direct observation by your assessor

Observation and/or expert witness testimony is the required assessment method to be used to evidence some of each element in this unit. If your assessor is unable to observe you,

s/he will identify an expert in your workplace who will provide testimony of your work-based performance. Usually your assessor or expert witness will observe you in real work activities and this should provide most of the evidence for the performance criteria for the elements in this unit.

Preparing to be observed

You must show your assessor that you can encourage and support children and young people to choose and explore play spaces for physical play, effective play, transient and permanent. You must also show that you can leave the content and intent of play to children and young people, enabling them to develop in their own ways and explore their own values. You must show that you can allow play to occur uninterrupted, and hold play frames when necessary, observing and responding to play cues appropriately.

Other types of evidence

You will need to present different types of evidence in order to:

- Cover criteria not observed by your assessor
- Show that you have the required knowledge, understanding and skills.

Such evidence could include:

- Work products such as play plans
- Case studies, projects, assignments and reflective accounts of your work.

Help children and young people to manage risk during play

Element 318.4

Challenge and risk

318K30
318K31
318K32
318K33
318K34
318K35

It is important to give children and young people opportunities for play which is sufficiently challenging. Because of the nature of play, this often incorporates an element of risk. Children and young people should be allowed to experience and explore appropriate risk during their play. There is more about this in Unit CCLD 307 Promote the health and physical development of children.

Offer children challenging activities

There are four types of hazard/risk that should be considered in terms of play. These are:

- Physical
- Environmental
- Emotional
- Behavioural.

Information about risk assessment is given in Unit CCLD 302 Develop and maintain a healthy, safe and secure environment for children. Pages 33–4 explains how to carry out risk assessment and gives examples of physical risks.

Link **Unit CCLD 307** Promote the health and physical development of children
Unit CCLD 302 Develop and maintain a healthy, safe and secure environment for children

Emotional risk

Emotional risk-taking is a life skill. Children and young people (and adults) take emotional risks whenever they pluck up the courage to do something that stretches them emotionally or that risks personal failure or rejection. Examples of emotional risk taking include:

- Speaking in front of a group of peers or adults
- Performing in public (singing, acting, dancing, playing musical instruments)
- Auditioning
- Trying to make a new friend
- Saying no to friends or refusing to give in to peer pressure
- Showing others your own creative work (art or creative writing, for instance)
- Entering a competition
- Suggesting your own ideas to peers/adults
- Telling a joke
- Applying for a college course or a job
- Doing something independently for the first time (e.g. using public transport, living alone).

Activities that feel like a risk to one person may come easily to another. Children and young people are individuals who are comfortable doing different things. The things that children are comfortable with are sometimes referred to as being within their 'comfort zone'. But if children and young people are to continually move on and progress in their development, they need to step out of their comfort zone every so often, and take an emotional risk.

Those with good levels of self-esteem and confidence are generally more willing to take emotional risks. You can help children and young people to feel equipped for emotional risk-taking by providing opportunities for them to participate in activities that foster high levels of confidence and self-esteem, including:

- Team activities
- Trust games
- Games that give all children the opportunity to be the leader
- Consultation
- Displays of art/craft work.

You can also ensure you offer children plenty of praise in general terms, and specifically for having a go or trying hard. This helps to communicate that there is value in being prepared to step out of one's comfort zone, whatever the result of taking the risk.

Behavioural hazards

Behavioural hazards occur when children behave in a ways that could cause harm to themselves or others. For instance, practitioners may provide clay and tools for modelling. Although the tools may be pointed, this would generally be considered a relatively low-risk activity. However, if a child should begin throwing these tools at 'targets' in play, or even deliberately using them as a weapon during a disagreement, the risk is significantly raised to an unacceptable level. Practitioners would need to intervene quickly (step in and take action) to curb the behaviour and therefore the risk.

A child's behaviour can also harm another child or children emotionally. This can happen when teasing or bullying takes place. When necessary, it is important that practitioners intervene sensitively in a way that is appropriate to the nature of the children involved.

Verbal teasing can be very upsetting. If a child is being teased in a nasty way or it is clear that they are upset, practitioners should intervene quickly. The same applies if a child has broken one of the fundamental rules or values of the setting – if they have made a racist remark for instance.

However, young people often relate to each other through light-hearted humour or banter, which could be loosely regarded as teasing. Practitioners must decide when to intervene. Much depends on the nature of what is said and the spirit within which it is

Always judge if and when to intervene

said and received. A young person involved in light-hearted banter may handle the situation quite competently themselves. Often it is best for practitioners to monitor the situation closely and not intervene too soon so that young people have the chance to manage the issue themselves. Remember that one child or young person may find a remark amusing, while another may find the same remark upsetting. Getting to know the children and young people you work with well will help in these situations.

Monitoring risk levels

Although risk assessments will be carried out prior to activities, the level of risk can change during play. This is due to the way in which children and young people decide to play and use the resources. Practitioners must continually monitor the changing levels of risk. There is no need to intervene in children's play unless the level of risk becomes unacceptable. In this case it is the duty of practitioners to intervene and bring the level of risk back to an acceptable level.

An effective technique to keep intervention at a minimum is to encourage children to develop an awareness of hazards and how to manage risk themselves. This is also an important life skill. There is further information about this in Unit CCLD 302 Develop and maintain a healthy, safe and secure environment for children.

 **Link** **Unit CCLD 302** Develop and maintain a healthy, safe and secure environment for children

Element 318.4

Are you ready for assessment?

Help children and young people to manage risk during play

You need to show that you can competently help children and young people to manage risk during play. To do this you will need to be directly observed by your assessor and present other types of evidence. The amount and type of evidence you need to present will vary. You should plan this with your assessor.

Direct observation by your assessor

Observation and/or expert witness testimony is the required assessment method to be used to evidence some of each element in this unit. If your assessor is unable to observe you, s/he will identify an expert in your workplace who will provide testimony of your work-based performance. Usually your assessor or expert witness will observe you in real work activities and this should provide most of the evidence for the performance criteria for the elements in this unit.

Preparing to be observed

You must show your assessor that you can allow children and young people to experience and explore risk during play, identifying and assessing hazards and risks when they occur, and balancing the risks involved with the benefits of challenge and stimulation. You must show that you can raise children and young people's awareness of hazards and risks and how to manage them, only intervening if risk becomes unacceptable.

Other types of evidence

You will need to present different types of evidence in order to:

- Cover criteria not observed by your assessor
- Show that you have the required knowledge, understanding and skills.

Such evidence could include:

- Work products such as play plans and risk assessments, materials/resources made for use with children
- Case studies, projects, assignments and reflective accounts of your work.

Check your knowledge

- What are the short- and long-term benefits of play? **318K01**
- What are the mood descriptors associated with play? **318K07**
- Why is it important to identify children's play needs and preferences? **318K12**
- How can you involve children in the creation of play spaces? **318K18**
- Why should you leave the content and intent of play up to children? **318K23**
- What are play cues and play frames, and how should you respond to them? **318K27, 318K28, 318K29**
- Why is it important to balance risk with the benefits of challenge and stimulation? **318K35**

Reflective practice

In light of what you have learned in this unit, reflect on the last few occasions when you have interrupted children's play. Do you feel your interruptions could have been avoided or perhaps handled in a more supportive way? Make notes in your reflective journal.

UNIT 321

Support children with disabilities or special educational needs and their families

This unit is about supporting disabled children and/or children with special educational needs (or the equivalent terminology used in your home country). It involves establishing the strengths and needs of children in partnership with their families and in collaboration with other agencies. It also includes the identification and provision of resources to enable inclusion and participation.

This unit contains three elements:

- **CCLD 321.1** *Contribute to the inclusion of children with disabilities and special educational needs*

- **CCLD 321.2** *Help children with disabilities and special educational needs to participate in the full range of activities and experiences*

- **CCLD 321.3** *Support families to respond to children's needs*

Introduction

K3D533
K3D534
K3M535
K3D536
K3D537
K3D539
K3D544
K3D548

Practitioners must know how to support children with disabilities and/or special educational needs and their families. Legislation, regulations and codes of practice are in place that effect provision and guide practitioners. You must understand those that apply to your home country. The examples given here apply in England. The assessment and intervention framework outlined here applies to early years settings.

Element 321.1 *Contribute to the inclusion of children with disabilities and special educational needs*

Rights to participation and equality of access

All children have the right to participate in society and to be given equal opportunities regardless of whether they have a disability and/or special educational need. The main laws that safeguard these rights are highlighted below.

The Disability Discrimination Act 1995

The Disability Discrimination Act 1995 (DDA 1995) was devised to support the rights of disabled people (adults and children) to take a full and active part in society, giving them equality of access (the same opportunities to participate as non-disabled people). This important piece of legislation gives disabled people rights regarding the way in which they receive services, facilities or goods. This includes education, care and play services.

The DDA 1995 has been introduced in three stages:

- In 1996 it became illegal for service providers to discriminate against disabled people by treating them less favourably than non-disabled people

- In 1999 service providers became required by law to make reasonable adjustments for disabled people, such as providing extra assistance

- In 2004 service providers became required by law to make reasonable adjustments to their premises so that it is not unreasonably difficult for disabled people to access the services owing to physical barriers such as narrow doorways or steps. If one of a premise's physical features causes a barrier for a disabled person, that feature may be removed or altered. Alternatively, a service may provide a reasonable way of avoiding the feature or may make their service available in a different way.

Under the DDA 1995 practitioners must anticipate the barriers that could be experienced by disabled people within their settings. However, it is acknowledged that it would be unreasonable for services to anticipate every possible barrier. Some problems may not be obvious until the particular need of a disabled person wishing to access the service becomes apparent. In this case, the settings must take reasonable steps to overcome the barrier once they are aware of it. There is more information in Element 321.2.

A disabled person is defined in the DDA 1995 as someone who has a physical or mental impairment that adversely affects their ability to carry out normal day-to-day activities. This will be long-term – it will have lasted for 12 months or be likely to last for more than 12 months.

The UN Convention on the Rights of the Child

The UN Convention on the Rights of the Child was ratified by the UK Government in 1991. All of the 41 Articles of the Act apply to all – disabled and non-disabled – children. Article 23 Disabled Children is of particular note. It states that disabled children must be helped to be as independent as possible. They must be helped to take a full and active part in everyday life.

Every Child Matters

Every Child Matters sets out a government initiative which aims to improve outcomes for all children and young people. As many disabled children's needs are complex and cross traditional service boundaries, they are one of the groups who stand to gain the most from this programme of change. See also Element CCLD 305.01.

 Link   **Unit 305** Protect and promote children's rights

Key Terms

Disability

A physical or mental impairment which has a substantial and long-term adverse effect on the child's ability to carry out normal day-to-day activities.
(National Occupational Standards)

Equality of access

Ensuring that discriminatory barriers to access are removed and that information about provision is accessible to all families in the community.
(National Occupational Standards)

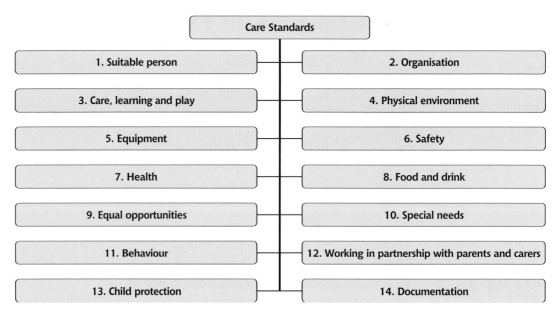

Care Standards

All of the standards apply to practitioners' work with all children. Two of the standards are of particular note here:

- Standard 9 Equal opportunities

  This requires that the registered person and their staff actively promote equality of opportunity and anti-discriminatory practice for all children
- Standard 10 Special needs

  This requires that the registered person is aware that some children may have special educational needs and is proactive in ensuring that appropriate action can be taken when such a child is identified or admitted to the provision. Steps are taken to promote the welfare and development of the child within the setting in partnership with the parents, carers and other relevant parties.

The Special Educational Needs Code of Practice

Key Terms

Special educational needs

Children with special educational needs learn differently from most children of the same age. These children may need extra or different help from that given to other children. (National Occupational Standards)

The Special Educational Needs Code of Practice (SEN Code) was implemented in 1994 and revised in 2002. It applies to schools and early-education settings offering the Early Years Foundation Stage. However, the procedures of Early Years Action/School Action and Early Years Action Plus/School Action Plus can effectively be adopted by early years practitioners working with younger children.

Children with special educational needs are identified as children who learn differently from most children of the same age. They may need extra or different help to learn. The SEN Code sets out procedures to be followed in order to meet the requirements of children with special educational needs.

Under the SEN Code, early years settings (even those in which there are currently no children with special educational needs) must:

- Adopt the recommendations of the SEN Code
- Train staff to identify and manage children with special educational needs

- Devise and implement a Special Educational Needs policy in line with the SEN Code. This must explain how the setting promotes inclusion, which means how it includes children with disabilities and/or special educational needs within the mainstream setting. (You should be familiar with how inclusion works within your setting and your local area, and the reasons for this)
- Appoint a Special Educational Needs Co-ordinator (SENCO), who will have particular responsibility for overseeing the setting's practice with regard to meeting the needs of children and adhering to the SEN Code.

The five fundamental principles of the special educational needs code of practice are:

A child with special educational needs should have their needs met

The special educational needs of children will normally be met in mainstream schools or settings

The views of children should be sought and taken into account

Parents have a vital role to play in supporting their child's education

Children with special educational needs should be offered full access to a broad, balanced and relevant education, including an appropriate curriculum for the Early Years Foundation Stage and the National Curriculum

Assessment and intervention frameworks

Under the SEN Code, two models of graduated action and intervention are recommended to early years settings working with children with special educational needs:

- Early Years Action

  This is the initial stage in which children's special educational needs are identified.

Ensure all children can participate

The setting should then devise interventions (strategies) that are additional to or different from those provided under the setting's normal curriculum

- Early Years Action Plus

    This is the stage in which practitioners feel it is appropriate to involve external specialists/professionals. They can offer more specialist assessment of the child and advise the setting on strategies.

Parents, carers and families are at the heart of provision as they know most about their child. Some parents are 'experts' with wide-ranging and in-depth knowledge of their child and their disability and/or special educational need. This is expanded upon in Element 321.3.

Early Years Action

Practitioners working in the early years are often the first to notice that a child may be experiencing difficulties with their learning and/or development, although sometimes it is a parent or carer who first expresses a concern about their child. When it is suspected that a child is having problems, practitioners need to make focused observations of the child to see if they can identify specific difficulties. These observations should be documented.

The SEN Code explains that practitioners will have cause for concern when, despite receiving appropriate early education experiences, one or a combination of the following criteria applies to a child:

- Makes little or no progress, even when practitioners have used approaches targeted to improve the child's identified area of weakness

- Continues working at levels significantly below those expected for children of a similar age in certain areas

- Presents persistent emotional and/or behavioural difficulties that are not managed by the setting's general behaviour management strategies

- Has sensory or physical problems and continues to make little or no progress despite the provision of personal aids and equipment

- Has communication and/or interaction difficulties, and requires specific individual interventions (one-to-one) to learn.

Once it has been established that a child meets one or more of the above criteria, practitioners should:

- Arrange a time to meet with parents or carers to discuss the concerns and to involve them as partners in supporting the child's learning. The practitioner should explain the role of the setting's SENCO, and discuss the involvement of the SENCO with the parents or carers. The practitioner should ask the parents and carers for their own observations of their child's learning and, if appropriate, for information about health or physical problems, or the previous involvement of any external professionals such as speech therapists. Parents are the prime source of information in many cases

- Meet with the SENCO. Practitioners should make available as much helpful information as possible, i.e. observations, assessments, health details

- The practitioner and SENCO should work together, liaising with the parents and carers to decide on the action needed to help the child progress in light of the observations made. The SEN Code states that action should 'enable the very young child with special educational needs to learn and progress to the maximum possible'. The diagram below gives examples of strategies (actions) that may be used

- An Individual Education Plan (IEP) should be devised for the child. This should concisely record three or four short-term targets set for them, and detail the strategies that will be put in place. The IEP should only record that which is additional to or different from the general curriculum plan of the setting (see Unit 309 Plan and implement curriculum frameworks for early education). The IEP should be discussed with parents, carers and the child concerned

- IEPs should be working documents, kept continually under review. They are primarily for checking the effectiveness of strategies implemented and the progress made towards targets. Reviews should take place as necessary in consultation with parents and carers. But they should occur regularly – at least three times each year. The SEN Code states that reviews need not be 'unduly formal', but a record of them must be kept in the IEP. New targets and strategies decided on at review must also be recorded.

Settings will have adopted a set of documents to complete throughout the stages of Early Years Action and Early Years Action Plus. The blank documents may have been bought or the SENCO may have devised them.

Link   **Unit 309** Plan and implement curriculum frameworks for early education

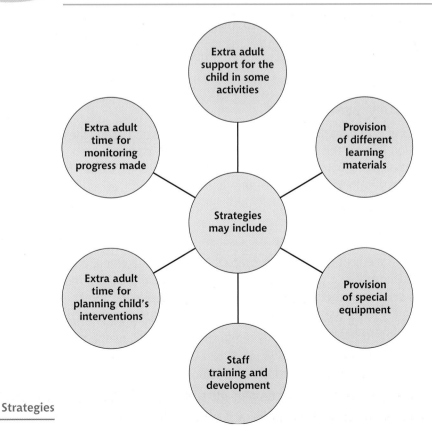

Strategies

Early Years Action Plus

The decision to implement Early Years Action Plus (that is to involve external support services and professionals) is generally taken in consultation with parents or carers at a meeting to review a child's IEP. The SEN Code identifies that the implementation of Early Years Action Plus is likely to be triggered when, despite receiving support tailored to their needs, a child:

- Continues to make little or no progress in specific areas over a long period
- Continues working at a level substantially below that expected of children of a similar age
- Has emotional difficulties which substantially interfere with the child's own learning or that of the group, despite an individual behaviour management programme
- Has sensory or physical needs and requires additional equipment or regular specialist support
- Has ongoing communication or interaction difficulties that are a barrier to learning and social relationships.

The type of support services available to settings under Early Years Action Plus varies according to local policy. You should find out about the provision made in your local area by your Local Education Authority (LEA). Your LEA's support services or local health or medical services may be able to provide support and help in terms of assessment, advice on IEPs, and strategies, activities, equipment and perhaps specialist support for some activities.

At the Early Years Action Plus stage, reviews should continue – external specialists should be consulted as part of the review while they are involved with the child.

School Action and School Action Plus

The same procedures will be followed in schools. The terms 'School Action' and 'School Action Plus' are then used.

Statutory assessment

In some cases, children do not make the expected progress despite the intervention of Early Years Action Plus. At this stage it is appropriate for the parents, carers, practitioner, SENCO and external professionals to meet to discuss if a referral should be made to the LEA requesting a statutory assessment of the child. If it is agreed, an application for assessment is made.

The LEA will require all relevant documentation including observations, IEPs and assessments. These are considered and the LEA decides (within 26 weeks) if the child should be made the subject of a Statement of Special Educational Needs. The statement is legally binding – it sets out a child's needs and outlines what special educational provision must be made to meet them. The LEA concerned is then legally obliged to provide this for the child. This applies to all LEAs in England. The nature of the provision will depend on the child's need, but some examples of provision include:

- A transfer to a specialist setting
- A place at a mainstream setting with additional one-to-one support
- A place at a mainstream setting with additional resources and equipment
- Support of an educational or clinical psychologist

A home-based programme, such as Portage (a programme of activities tailored to suit individual children. Parents and carers carry out the activities with the child at home. A Portage worker will support the family).

Statements for children under the age of five must be reviewed by the LEA every six months. Because of the time it takes to go through the stages of intervention, most children are not referred for statutory assessment until they are over the age of five, by which time they will have started school.

The importance of early recognition and intervention is outlined in Element 321.3.

Critical success factors

The Code of Practice identifies 'critical success factors' by which settings can assess the success of their provision for children with special educational needs. These consider:

- Practice, management and resources deployed to ensure that all children's needs are met
- Early identification
- Children's wishes taken into account
- Practitioners and parents/carers working in partnership
- Multi-disciplinary approach
- Interventions based on best practice and reviewed regularly.

Supporting children through transitions

Transitions (periods of change) can be difficult for children, and so practitioners should take care to support children through them. Strategies can be employed to ease the way, assisting children to cope and helping to maintain continuity of experience, which can be particularly important for children with disabilities and/or special educational needs. See Unit 303 Promote children's development, for further details.

 Link   **Unit 303** Promote children's development

Element 321.1

Are you ready for assessment?

Contribute to the inclusion of children with disabilities and special educational needs

You need to show that you can competently contribute to the inclusion of children with disabilities and special educational needs. To do this you will need to be directly observed by your assessor and present other types of evidence. The amount and type of evidence you need to present will vary. You should plan this with your assessor.

Direct observation by your assessor

Observation and/or expert witness testimony is the required assessment method to be used to evidence some of each element in this unit. If your assessor is unable to observe you, s/he will identify an expert in your workplace who will provide testimony of your work-based performance. Usually your assessor or expert witness will observe you in real work activities and this should provide most of the evidence for the performance criteria for the elements in this unit.

Preparing to be observed

You must show your assessor that you can seek information about children from relevant people to assess children's needs and that you can develop individual plans to meet these, requesting additional resources/statutory assessment where appropriate. You must also show that you can identify and remove barriers to participation in consultation with the relevant people, supporting children's equality of access. You must show that you can support children through transitions and refer concerns about children appropriately.

You will need to arrange to be observed at a time when you will be working with children with disabilities and special educational needs and their families.

Other types of evidence

You will need to present different types of evidence in order to:

- Cover criteria not observed by your assessor
- Show that you have the required knowledge, understanding and skills.

Such evidence could include:

- Work products contributed to by you, such as policies and procedures on inclusion/supporting children through transitions, or information leaflets for families
- Case studies, projects, assignments and reflective accounts of your work
- Confidential records such as information gathered about individual children's needs, discussions with families and children's individual plans. These should not be placed in your portfolio – they must remain in their usual location and be referred to in the assessor records in your portfolio.

Element 321.2

Help children with disabilities and special educational needs to participate in the full range of activities and experiences

Details of the individual children in your care

K3D540
K3D541
K3C542
K3C543
K3C543
K3D545

Practitioners should develop a good knowledge of particular disabilities and/or special educational needs *as they affect the children in their care*. It is important to acknowledge that the same impairment can be experienced by different individuals in very different ways – you need to understand how the children you are working with are affected so that you can meet their needs appropriately. (See Element 321.3.)

Practitioners should also be aware of the expected pattern of development of the children they are responsible for. Children generally (but not always) master skills or achieve learning in a similar sequence, even though they may not do so at the same rate as peers of the same age. However, some children may not be expected to achieve certain milestones 'in order', or to achieve them at all. For instance, some children will not be expected to carry out motor skills such as walking, jumping or running. But it may be appropriate to work with such a child on other ways of travelling, such as rolling across the floor or floating in water. These issues would be discussed at an intervention meeting when devising or reviewing an IEP in consultation with the SENCO, family members, the child and perhaps external professionals (see Element 321.1).

Understanding the needs of the individual children in your care will enable you to feel confident within your roles and responsibilities, empowering you to deliver a high-quality service to children with disabilities and/or special educational needs and their families.

Special educational needs may be due to:

- Physical impairments
- Visual impairments
- Hearing impairments
- Communication/speech difficulties
- Emotional/behavioural difficulties
- General learning difficulties or developmental delay
- Specific learning difficulties (such as dyslexia)
- Medical conditions.

The principles of participation and inclusion

The Disability Discrimination Act 1995 was introduced to give legal rights to disabled people, who have a right to be included in society and to participate within it. But things have not always been that way.

Although disabled people have always been part of society, they have not always been treated equally. Historically, disabled people have been regarded as 'abnormal' or even 'evil'. Some cultures believed that disabled people had mystic powers, while others thought that children were born disabled to punish their parents for a past wrongdoing. There were times when disabled children were drowned at birth or when they spent their lives locked away in institutions, shunned by society and living in fear. The way disabled people lived was dictated by non-disabled people and their attitudes towards disability.

In the more recent past there has been the assumption that disabled people (children and adults) have a problem. Their impairments have been regarded as personal tragedies. It has been seen as the responsibility of non-disabled people to either cure or care for the disabled person, taking steps to fit them into society. Treating disabled people as sick patients in this way is not empowering. This way of thinking is known as the 'Medical Model of Disability'.

There is a worldwide organisation called the Disabled People's Movement. The British Council of Disabled People (BCODP) is a branch of this, formed in 1981. The BCODP believe that disability is not an inevitable consequence of a person's impairment, but that disability arises from the negative way in which disabled people are treated by society. They believe that disabled people are disabled by society's structure, its attitudes and its lack of access, which exclude disabled people from activities that non-disabled people take for granted. It is believed that society should change to meet the needs of disabled people. This gives disabled people rights and choices. This is known as the 'Social Model of Disability'.

The DDA 1995 supports the Social Model of Disability by giving disabled people rights regarding the way they receive services, goods and facilities (see Element 321.1).

Barriers to participation

It is important that practitioners promote inclusive ways of working – ways that are suitable for all children, so that everyone can be included in the group, jointly participating in the activities and experiences offered within the setting.

In order to promote inclusion, practitioners must be aware of features that may cause a barrier to participation. A barrier can be anything that prevents children from participating fully. Barriers fall into three categories:

- Attitudinal

  The belief held by some people that disabled children are incapable, or to be pitied or feared. These barriers may be overcome with training

- Environmental

  Including physical barriers, e.g. premises that are inaccessible due to steps or poor lighting, or other difficulties that occur within the environment such as the use of complex language. The barriers may apply to the provision as a whole or to particular activities or experiences. These barriers may be overcome via changes to the layout of premises or the organisation of activities/experiences – more information is given below

- Institutional

  A lack of anti-discriminatory policies or procedures. These barriers may be overcome with training and subsequent introduction of policies and procedures.

Settings must:

- Examine their provision, identifying existing barriers to participation. Practitioners must be proactive, anticipating features of the setting that are likely to be barriers, regardless of whether those features present a barrier to the children currently attending

- Take action to remove barriers, whenever possible and reasonable, or

- Whenever possible and reasonable, alter the barrier so that it no longer has the same effect, or

- Whenever possible and reasonable, find an alternative way to offer the activity or experience

- Monitor the effects of the action taken, introducing new action if necessary.

Adapting the physical environment

It is likely that your setting will have already identified and overcome some of the barriers to participation that occur within your physical environment. However, it is still necessary for

Key Terms

Barriers to participation
Anything that prevents the child participating fully in activities and experiences offered by the setting or service.
(National Occupational Standards)

The layout of furniture should be carefully considered

practitioners to consider and eliminate any potential barriers that may affect new disabled children or those barriers that become apparent as the needs of existing disabled children change over time.

By considering the layout of a room carefully you can effectively overcome barriers. For instance:

- Furniture of different heights may be used to ensure that wheelchair users can participate in tabletop activities
- Furniture may be positioned and activities set out to allow easy passage for children using wheelchairs, crutches or other aids
- Furniture and equipment may be kept in the same position to assist children with visual impairments to locate and navigate
- Equipment and resources may be stored at a height that makes it accessible to all
- Scent clues or bright colours may be used to mark out certain areas (e.g. lavender in the book corner)
- Adequate task lighting may be employed in activity areas
- Comfortable soft areas may be provided for children who need to rest during play sessions.

Adapting activities and experiences

It is also important that practitioners consider the needs of children in relation to the activities and experiences that the setting offers. This can be done at the short-term planning stage. Once barriers to participation have been identified, practitioners can consider ways of overcoming them. Specialised aids or pieces of equipment may be available to assist children – there is more information about this in Element 321.3. However, simple strategies can often be used effectively. It may be appropriate to:

- Devise your own adaptations
- Change the way an activity is organised
- Offer an alternative.

Barriers and strategies to overcome them

Activity	Barrier	Strategy
Painting with rollers	Child with a physical impairment cannot grip the roller effectively	Practitioners mould thick Plasticine around the handle. The child grips it, altering the shape of Plasticine to suit her grip. The roller has been easily adapted to suit her individual grasp
Game of catch to be played in pairs	Child with a visual impairment has difficulty seeing the ball approaching, and therefore difficulty preparing to catch it accurately	Practitioners attach a tail of bright ribbon to some of the balls, and tie bells (from a textiles shop) securely to the ends. The balls are now more easily located, and they can also be caught by the tail
Game of musical bumps	One child with a hearing impairment cannot hear the music, while a wheelchair user cannot sit on the floor and get up again easily	Practitioners play musical statues instead, and devise two hand signals, one that is used to indicate when children should dance, and another for when they should freeze like statues
Singing songs	A child with communication difficulties has difficult joining in	Practitioners encourage the group to come up with actions they can do as they sing. They also slow the pace of the singing. They allow time to play along with musical instruments too

The table above gives examples of simple strategies that could be implemented to overcome barriers.

It is good practice to consult children about the way in which barriers are tackled if this is appropriate to their age and ability.

Practical Example

Will tackles a barrier to participation

Playworker Will works at a holiday club. Ten-year-old Jade, a wheelchair user, has recently started attending the club. The staff have planned some parachute games and Will needs to ensure that Jade can participate. He thinks that she could join in effectively if the other children played kneeling down instead of standing up. He asks Jade what she thinks of this idea. Jade says her teacher plays parachute games in the same way at school, and that this adaptation works for her.

➤ *Why did Will need to ensure that Jade could participate?*   **K3D534**
➤ *Why did Will include Jade when deciding how to adapt the activity?*
   K3D544, K3D545

Communication difficulties

The SEN Code tells us that 'most children with special educational needs have strengths and difficulties in one, some or all of the areas of speech, language and communication. Their communication needs may be both diverse and complex'.

Communication refers broadly to the process of interacting with others. Children who have difficulties communicating may have difficulties forming relationships as communication is the cornerstone of our relationships with other people. Children may feel isolated, left out or frustrated, or experience a diminishing motivation to communicate. Behaviour and social development may therefore be affected. Children use language to think as well as to speak, and so there may also be an impact on cognitive development.

Key Terms

Barriers to communication

Anything that prevents the child communicating with others or forming relationships, e.g. hearing, speech or visual loss, mental health issues, learning disabilities. *(National Occupational Standards)*

The range of communication difficulties will encompass children with:

- Speech and language delay, impairments and disorders
- Specific learning difficulties such as dyspraxia and dyslexia
- Hearing impairments
- Visual impairments
- Mental health issues.

Communication difficulties also occur in:

- Children who demonstrate features within the autistic spectrum
- Some children with moderate, severe or profound learning difficulties.

The difficulties listed in this section are known as 'barriers to communication'.

Alternative and Augmentive Communication

Key Terms

Alternative and Augmentive Communication (ACC)

This refers to any device, system or special method of communication that helps individuals who have communication difficulties to communicate more easily and effectively. *(National Occupational Standards)*

Alternative and Augmentive Communication (ACC) describes any system or special method of communication that is used to overcome communication barriers. Using ACC can help children with communication difficulties to make the most of their available senses and experiences. Methods of ACC include:

- Symbols

    A child may carry a deck of symbol cards, using them to signify meaning. These can be personalised. For instance, a child may have cards showing pictures of different resources. He may show staff the relevant card to indicate what he would like to play with

- Communication boards

    These generally contain a number of symbols or words. Children express themselves by indicating to them. Some boards are designed to fit onto wheelchairs

Children might use a communication device or system

- Voice output communication aids

  These may be connected to an electronic speaking communication board, or a laptop computer, that enables a child to 'talk'

- Sign language

  Including Makaton – a basic version of British Sign Language which may be taught to younger children or those with learning difficulties. Gestures may also be used

- Facial expressions

  Useful for conveying emotion.

It is important to identify methods of breaking down communication barriers for individual children and to monitor their effectiveness. Sometimes very simple steps can make a real difference. For instance:

- If a child lip reads, adults and peers can be encouraged to face the child when speaking directly to them or to the group they are playing or working within

- If a child has partial hearing, it may help to eliminate all unnecessary background noise when communicating with them. Slowing the pace of conversation and speaking clearly may also help

- Children with learning difficulties may find it easier to understand sentences that are short and simply structured.

Specialist help and advice from external professionals is often needed (see Element 321.1). It is important to note that young children with speech or language delay are most likely to overcome their problems when they receive intervention early on.

Effects of attention deficits

Attention deficit disorders are thought to be caused by a chemical imbalance in the brain that affects the parts of the brain that control attention, concentration and impulsivity. This means that a range of behaviours may be exhibited by children with attention deficits. There are three core symptoms of attention deficits:

- Hyperactivity

  Children may squirm and fidget when seated, or have difficulty remaining seated when this is required of them. They may have a tendency to run about excessively or when it is inappropriate to do so. They may be 'always on the go'. They may talk excessively and have difficulty playing or listening quietly.

  Effect on learning, social relationships and self-esteem: Children may miss out on learning and the development of skills because they are they are not listening, concentrating or participating – they may be busy fidgeting or moving around the room. They may unintentionally distract the rest of the group, or ruin their games or activities. They may play too roughly for their peers. They may be frequently in trouble and this may have an adverse effect on their self-esteem. They may believe they are unable to behave

- Impulsivity

  Children may have difficulty taking turns. They may interrupt other people and intrude in conversations and games. They may not wait for the end of a question before attempting to answer it. They may blurt things out without thinking about them first, making them socially inept. They may have volatile and unpredictable moods. They may lash out when frustrated, and have a short temper.

Effect on learning, social relationships and self-esteem: Being socially inept in these ways can make children unpopular with their peers, which affects their self-esteem and confidence. Some children may be afraid of the impulsive child as unpredictable outbursts can be frightening and they may have been hurt by the child in the past. Some children may enjoy the reaction from a child with a short temper, enjoying winding them up or getting them into trouble

- Inattention

  Children may have difficulty concentrating and may dislike and/or avoid activities which require sustained concentration. They may be easily distracted, finding it difficult to finish tasks. Children may not seem to listen when they are talked to directly, and they may not follow instructions given to them. The child may frequently lose things and be forgetful.

  Effect on learning, social relationships and self-esteem: Children may have difficulties joining in group games and activities as they may forget the rules, lose concentration and not finish what they start. This can deter other children from playing with them, affecting self-esteem. Children may not concentrate in learning situations, and children of school age may avoid study or forget what they should do. This coupled with poor memory may lead to poor performance in tests and exams. Changing rooms or teachers frequently can confuse older children. Children may believe they are stupid or unable to learn.

Attention deficits and associated problems may be treated with a combination of approaches that can include:

- A behavioural management programme
- Behavioural therapy
- Medication
- Educational techniques
- Psychotherapy.

It is essential that practitioners liaise carefully with children, parents, carers, SENCOs and external specialists when working with children with attention deficits. Generally speaking, practitioners will be guided by external specialists regarding how to best support the individual child they are working with depending on their associated difficulties and individual circumstances.

Adapting your practice

It is necessary for practitioners in group settings to adapt their practice as they work to meet the needs of all the children for whom they are responsible. They must take into consideration the children's age, needs, gender and abilities. This is best achieved through careful planning.

When short-term session plans are drawn up, practitioners should consider the individual requirements of the children who will be in attendance. Careful attention should be given to the activities planned – do they suit everyone's needs, or are adaptations or alternatives necessary to ensure participation? Is the provision of specific aids or equipment required? Attention should also be given to the grouping and supervision of children. In addition, might there be a good opportunity to implement a strategy identified within a child's IEP?

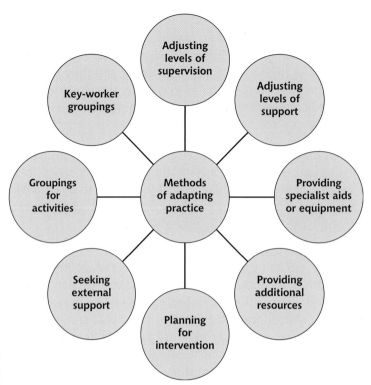

Methods of
adapting practice

In the long term, key worker lists can be carefully managed to ensure practitioners have a manageable level of responsibility across the board in terms of intervention, or extra time available if they are responsible for planning interventions for several children with disabilities and/or special educational needs.

It is important for practitioners to agree boundaries for behaviour with children and families – see Unit 337 Create environments that promote positive behaviour.

 **Link**   **Unit 337** Create environments that promote positive behaviour

Element
321.2   **Are you ready for assessment?**

Help children with disabilities and special educational needs to participate in the full range of activities and experiences

You need to show that you can competently help children with disabilities and special educational needs to participate in the full range of activities and experiences. To do this you will need to be directly observed by your assessor and present other types of evidence. The amount and type of evidence you need to present will vary. You should plan this with your assessor.

Direct observation by your assessor

Observation and/or expert witness testimony is the required assessment method to be used to evidence some of each element in this unit. If your assessor is unable to observe you, s/he will identify an expert in your workplace who will provide testimony of your work-based performance. Usually your assessor or expert witness will observe you in real work activities and this should provide most of the evidence for the performance criteria for the elements in this unit.

Preparing to be observed

You must show your assessor that you can identify and take steps to overcome barriers to communication and participation, offering alternative activities where appropriate. You must also show that you can identify and use specialist aids/equipment where necessary, implement adaptations without use of specialist aids/equipment, and adapt the layout of furniture and accessibility of equipment. You must also show that you can ensure adults are knowledgeable and confident about meeting children's individual needs, and that you can agree boundaries for behaviour with children and families.

You will need to arrange to be observed at a time when you will be working with children with disabilities and special educational needs and their families.

Other types of evidence

You will need to present different types of evidence in order to:

- Cover criteria not observed by your assessor
- Show that you have the required knowledge, understanding and skills.

Such evidence could include:

- Work products such as resources you have developed or adapted to meet children's individual needs policies, or plans of room layouts that you have devised
- Case studies, projects, assignments and reflective accounts of your work
- Confidential records such as information gathered about individual children's needs and minutes of meetings when colleagues have been informed of children's individual needs. These should not be placed in your portfolio – they must remain in their usual location and be referred to in the assessor records in your portfolio.

Support families to respond to children's needs

Element 321.3

Working in partnership with families

K3D531
K3D540
K3D547
K3D550

As we have already established in Element 321.1, families are the primary carers of children – they know their children best. Practitioners should recognise this and form partnerships based upon it.

It is important to respect and value the role of parents and carers. Practitioners working with children who are disabled and/or have special educational needs should be informed by families' knowledge and experience. Remember that having good knowledge about a specific impairment or special educational need is helpful, but it does not tell you much about an individual child.

For example, a practitioner may be very well informed about Down's syndrome. But although there will be some general commonalities (i.e. similarities) between children with Down's syndrome, each child is an individual, just like all other children. Therefore, children with Down's syndrome will develop at different rates and have differing abilities. Some may have additional impairments or special educational needs. They will have different likes and dislikes, different personalities and different learning styles. They will respond differently to activities and experiences. Parents and carers know all of these personal details about their child. When a good partnership is established, this information can be effectively shared and the quality of the practitioner's work with that child will be better as a result.

The impact of having a child with a disability and/or special educational needs

It is important that a child's difficulties are recognised early on. This leads to early intervention, designed to identify and meet a child's current needs whilst preventing further difficulties from developing.

In Element 321.1 we discussed how early years workers are often the first to identify problems with children's learning or development and the first to raise these issues with parents and carers. In other cases, parents or carers may already be aware of a disability or special educational need, but if the child is young they may still be adjusting to this news. It is important for you to understand how having a child with a disability and/or special educational needs can impact on parents, carers, siblings and members of the wider family such as grandparents, aunts and uncles.

It is often a shock for family members to be told that a child has a disability and/or special educational need, and so the matter must be handled with honesty and sensitivity. A traumatic time may follow, and family members may go through a range of emotions similar to those that are experienced by the bereaved (i.e. people who are grieving for a loved one who has died). These emotions may include:

- Disbelief

  For example, a parent may think that the practitioner, doctor or specialist is mistaken
- Denial

  A grandparent may be convinced the child will grow out of it or catch up
- Grief

  A father may grieve for the child he has 'lost' – the one he imagined would be perfect, whose future he had thought about
- Self-blame

  A mother may think it was her fault – she must have done something wrong during pregnancy. Was she too active? Did she eat the wrong things?
- Aggression

  A parent may feel angry, cheated out of the child they imagined. A sibling may feel angry about the extra attention their brother or sister needs.

Practitioners need to be supportive and understanding, even if parents and carers find it hard to accept what they are saying at first. The setting must be a non-judgemental environment where family members can feel safe to express their feelings, whatever they are, and find support.

Families of children with disabilities and/or special educational needs can also feel isolated and ill-informed. Practitioners should liaise closely with SENCOs, who will know about local and national sources of support and information for parents and carers, including organisations, professionals, books and leaflets. These details should be passed on when appropriate.

However, some parents already aware of their child's disability and/or special educational need may feel quite differently. In the case of Down's syndrome for instance, the condition will have been identified at birth (or perhaps during pregnancy) and the family will have had some time to adjust to this. Parents and carers may already be well informed about the syndrome and may have received support from professionals and organisations. They may even be 'expert parents', with wide-ranging knowledge of their child and the disability or special educational need. If so, they may be well-placed to offer support to other parents who find themselves in a similar situation.

The material and personal resources available to families of children with disabilities and/or special educational needs will also vary, and so the experience of the families is likely to differ. We know that free services for children without a statement of special educational needs depend on local policy. Some families may be able to pay for additional specialist support, respite care or equipment for their child, while others will not. Some parents or carers may have a good support network of extended family, while others may be isolated.

In summary, families have differing needs. It is the job of practitioners to be aware of the needs of families and to tailor the support they offer to them accordingly so that needs are effectively met.

Specialist terminology

Practitioners should be aware of, and have the ability to use, the appropriate terminology of inclusion. Impairments, special educational needs, professionals, strategies and equipment all have various terms given to them. You should learn those that are appropriate to the children you work with. You should ensure you use language that is acceptable and not outdated terms that are now considered inappropriate or in some cases offensive. However, you should ensure that terminology does not act as a barrier to communication – it is important that families and other interested parties can understand you.

Participating in observing and identifying needs

Families should be encouraged to participate in the observation of their child and the identification of their needs. Parents and carers can assist practitioners with the observations carried out in the setting (see Element 321.1) and the analysis of these, which leads to the identification of needs. But they can also be encouraged to share the observations that they make outside the setting – as the child's primary carers they will be familiar with the child's experiences at home and in other environments. This helps to give a well-rounded picture of the child. The parents and carers should remain involved as an IEP is drawn up and subsequently reviewed over time.

Participating in activities

It helps all children, including those with disabilities and/or special needs, when their families and their practitioners share a joint approach and a harmonious relationship. It helps children to feel settled and secure. When parents and carers are encouraged to participate in activities with their child, this relationship is demonstrated. In addition, children with special educational needs often benefit from programmes of learning that allow for repetition and consistency.

There are various ways of involving families in activities including:

- Inviting parents and carers into the setting to take part in activities alongside their child

   This helps the family members and the practitioners to establish a consistent approach as they become familiar with each other's ways of working with the child. It is also helpful if families are feeling isolated in their position of caring for a child with a disability and/or special educational need

- Suggesting activities that family members can do with their children at home, following up those done within the setting

   This helps to consolidate and reinforce the work done in the setting, allowing further opportunities for learning and progress. This can be particularly important for children with disabilities and/or special educational needs, who may need extra time to master particular skills or concepts

- Ensuring families know about opportunities to socialise with other children and their families, e.g. the setting's fundraising events, summer trips or festival celebrations

   This encourages wider participation and inclusion, and helps to avoid the isolation of families.

Specialist aids and equipment

You should ensure that you are aware of the relevant specialist aids and pieces of equipment that are available for the children you work with. You must be confident that you know how to use these safely. Liaise closely with your SENCO and external professionals who will be able to advise you.

Some children will already be using aids and equipment at home, in which case parents and carers will be a primary source of information. Educational catalogues and care catalogues are informative – most settings receive new editions regularly, and they are a good way to keep up to date with new innovations and designs.

There are many specialist aids and pieces of equipment available for children. What individuals use will of course depend on their needs, but you may come across:

- Specially angled cutlery designed for children with physical impairments who experience difficulty feeding themselves
- Non-slip matting that has flexible use – it can be placed under plates or bowls at mealtimes to stop them sliding away, or perhaps under pots of paint at the craft table
- Light boxes that can be used to back-light objects so that they may be seen by children with visual impairments

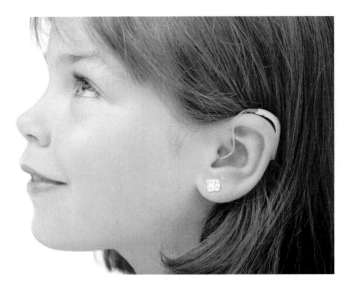

Some children use specialist aids

- Hearing loops that can be installed for those with hearing impairments
- Communication boards that can be used by those with communication difficulties.

Element 321.3

Are you ready for assessment?

Support families to respond to children's needs

You need to show that you can competently support families to respond to children's needs. To do this you will need to be directly observed by your assessor and present other types of evidence. The amount and type of evidence you need to present will vary. You should plan this with your assessor.

Direct observation by your assessor

Observation and/or expert witness testimony is the required assessment method to be used to evidence some of each element in this unit. If your assessor is unable to observe you, s/he will identify an expert in your workplace who will provide testimony of your work-based performance. Usually your assessor or expert witness will observe you in real work activities and this should provide most of the evidence for the performance criteria for the elements in this unit.

Preparing to be observed

You must show your assessor that you can encourage families to participate in observing and identifying the needs of children, and with children's activities. You must also show that you can establish partnerships with families in recognition of their role, tailoring support to meet families' differing needs. You must show that you can encourage families to express their feelings in a non-judgemental environment and adapt your use of specialist language appropriately.

➤

You will need to arrange to be observed at a time when you will be working with the families of children with disabilities and special educational needs.

Other types of evidence

You will need to present different types of evidence in order to:

- Cover criteria not observed by your assessor
- Show that you have the required knowledge, understanding and skills.

Such evidence could include:

- Work products such as information leaflets you have devised for families, or plans for activities where family members will join in with children
- Case studies, projects, assignments and reflective accounts of your work
- Confidential records such as information gathered about the needs if individual families. These should not be placed in your portfolio – they must remain in their usual location and be referred to in the assessor records in your portfolio.

Check your knowledge

- Name three pieces of legislation that affect your setting with regard to equal opportunities for children with disabilities and/or special educational needs. **K3P532**
- Briefly explain Early Years Action.   **K3D533**
- Briefly explain Early Years Action Plus.   **K3D533**
- Identify three of the possible effects of attention deficits.   **K3C542**
- Why is it important to recognise children's difficulties early on?   **K3D548**

Reflective practice

Make a list of all the terminology you currently use in connection with inclusion. Ask yourself:

- Is each term appropriate or outdated?
- Do I know all the current terms relevant to the children I am working with or should I research them?
- When do I use these terms? Do I need to adjust my use of them to avoid creating a barrier when I talk with families who do not use the same terms?

Create environments that promote positive behaviour

This unit is about supporting and implementing behaviour policies for children who challenge.

The unit contains two elements:

- **CCLD 337.1** *Implement behaviour policies, procedures and strategies*
- **CCLD 337.2** *Promote positive aspects of behaviour*

Introduction

Encouraging children to behave appropriately is a key aspect of a practitioner's role. If children do not learn to behave appropriately, they will not be accepted in society as they grow up. This would be detrimental to their welfare. It is in the interests of individual children, and society as a whole, for children to learn how to behave acceptably.

But what is acceptable behaviour? Opinions differ for many reasons – various social and cultural groups often share similar values and beliefs about what is acceptable. In addition, all adults have grown up with individual expectations of their own behaviour, and this can be influential.

There are many ways of encouraging positive behaviour too. But it is generally accepted that children need to be given boundaries to keep to and goals to reach to help them learn how to behave in acceptable ways. A practitioner should encourage children to reach goals, whilst managing inappropriate behaviour (that oversteps the boundaries) when it occurs.

Element 337.1 *Implement behaviour policies, procedures and strategies*

K3C542
K3D691
K3D692
K3D693
K3D694
K3D695
K3D696
K3D699
K3D701

Boundaries and goals

Boundaries set appropriate limits for children's behaviour. In other words, children are not permitted to behave in certain ways because to do so would be unsafe or socially unacceptable. For instance, children are not allowed climb up on tables to play because it would be unsafe. They are not allowed to tease one other because this is socially unacceptable.

Goals for behaviour identify the way children are expected to behave. For instance, children are expected to sit at the table to eat their meals, and to wait their turn when playing a game.

Realistic expectations

The goals set for children's behaviour should be realistic. They should take into consideration children's age, needs and abilities (see Unit CCLD 303 Promote children's development). If expectations are too high and children cannot achieve them, they are likely to be in trouble frequently. This is not good for a child's self-esteem and long term it is not good for their behavioural prospects. Children who are often in trouble may start to feel they are incapable of being good, and they may stop trying to reach behaviour goals. This starts a self-fulfilling cycle – such a child is likely to display more unacceptable behaviour, leading to more disapproval from adults, which reinforces the feeling that they cannot behave well or do the right thing. This is a good example of the clear links between behaviour, self-esteem and children's relationships with others. It is important to always be clear that it is a child's behaviour that is unacceptable not the child themselves. Never label a child as 'naughty' or 'a troublemaker'.

Link   **Unit CCLD 303** Promote children's development

If expectations are not high enough, children will not learn how to behave appropriately, and this is also likely to affect their progress. For instance, a school-aged child that has not learnt how to take turns, share fairly and handle winning and losing is likely to have difficulties with their peers and they may dislike and avoid group activities such as playground games.

Just as a child who is encouraged to reach goals is likely to work towards them and eventually attain them, a child who feels that no one expects them to be able to reach goals is unlikely to achieve. This is also true of children who are not given sufficient goals and boundaries.

Promoting positive behaviour

Practitioners can promote (or encourage) positive behaviour by rewarding children when they behave in acceptable ways. Children enjoy being rewarded, so they are encouraged to behave in the same way again. When children repeat behaviours, over time they become an ingrained, natural part of what the child does. The more a child is given positive attention for behaving appropriately, the less inappropriate behaviour they are likely to display.

Tangible and intangible rewards

The rewards that can be given to children fall into two categories: tangible and intangible. Tangible rewards are real items that physically exist and can be seen. Intangible rewards are not physical items, but something that children can experience. Some examples are shown in the table opposite.

Rewards

Tangible rewards	Intangible rewards
Prizes	Praise
Stickers	Smiles
Certificates	Cuddles
Stars/ink stamps	Round of applause/cheers
Trophies/awards	A thank you
Toys	Public acknowledgement (praise given in front of other people to draw their attention to an achievement)
Money	Pats on the back
Allowed to choose something tangible from a shop	Opportunities to pick a game or story for the group
Work displayed/published (in a newsletter for instance)	Special trips or the provision of favourite activities (e.g. going to the park or baking cakes)

Practitioners use mainly intangible rewards and they are extremely valuable. They show children that they are earning approval from adults and they also demonstrate how to interact positively with other people – how to thank them, for example.

They can be used to encourage children throughout an activity or task, showing them that they are behaving correctly and giving them the confidence to continue. You can give children warm praise, thanks and smiles frequently throughout every day, but it would be impractical to do the same with tangible rewards. However, tangible rewards do have their place.

Tangible items are often used in structured evidence-based behaviour programmes to reward individual children who are working towards specified behaviour goals that have been identified for them (see page 408). They are also effective for rewarding and celebrating occasional achievements that are out of the ordinary and they can be kept as a reminder of that time. Some tangible rewards, such as money, may be given by parents and carers, but in most settings it would be considered inappropriate to use them.

Remember, a reward is only a reward when a child likes it! It is important to reward children in a way that values them as an individual. For instance, some children feel uncomfortable with public acknowledgement or being physically touched – they may not appreciate a pat on the back. Also, while it is natural for a practitioner to cuddle a young child, it is not considered to be appropriate in all environments (such as the classroom) or with all children, particularly as they get older. You must adhere to the accepted policies and procedures of your setting.

Key Terms

Evidence-based programme

Structured approaches and strategies for the development of positive behaviour that research has shown to work. *(National Occupational Standards)*

Certificate of Achievement

Awarded to: ……………………………………………… On: ……………………

For: Helping a friend

Signed…………………………………………………   **Well done!**

A certificate
rewarding
achievement

It is also important to consider how children feel about the rewards being given to others. Tangible rewards in particular may lead to jealousy or a feeling of being treated unfairly if they are not handled carefully. For instance, if one child is given a sticker for sitting quietly at story time because this is one of their individual behaviour goals, children who generally sit quietly at story time and are not rewarded may feel unsettled by this.

Policies and procedures

A clear behaviour policy is beneficial to practitioners, parents, carers and children. The document should be tailored to meet the needs of the setting (even if a ready-designed policy is purchased), and settings will want to ensure that their policy promotes the overall values, ethics and aims of their organisation.

A good policy will set out the goals and boundaries for children's behaviour, expressing what is considered to be acceptable (or desirable) behaviour and what is considered to be unacceptable (or undesirable) behaviour. It will explain the setting's philosophy and strategies for promoting acceptable behaviour and dealing with inappropriate behaviour when it occurs. These must be in line with legislation. PRACTICES THAT PHYSICALLY HURT, FRIGHTEN, THREATEN OR HUMILIATE CHILDREN MUST *NEVER* BE USED. PRACTITIONERS MUST *NEVER* USE PHYSICAL PUNISHMENTS SUCH AS SMACKING. IT IS *ILLEGAL*.

New practitioners should be introduced to the behaviour policy as part of the induction process, and all practitioners must work in accordance with it at all times. You should make sure that you know and fully understand your setting's policy so that you can approach children's behaviour appropriately in your practical work.

Best practice requires all practitioners to share the same structured approach to promoting appropriate behaviour and dealing with inappropriate behaviour. When boundaries are consistently applied children can learn what is expected of them, and knowing this gives children a sense of security. It also helps them to see that they are being treated fairly. Children generally want to have the approval of the people around them, and when they understand what is required of them they have a tendency to behave accordingly.

What children know and understand about boundaries will depend on their age, abilities and experience. Younger children may be just starting to learn about boundaries through repetition – they will need to be reminded of boundaries frequently. Children of school age are likely to have a good understanding of them. Many out-of-school clubs involve the children in establishing a simple set of ground rules that are agreed by everyone. This helps children to accept the boundaries and appreciate their purpose. Displaying the boundaries on the wall helps children to remember and observe them.

Sometimes children can be involved in making the rules

Parents and carers should also have the opportunity to familiarise themselves with the setting's behaviour policy. Many settings explain their policy at the time of children's enrolment. This is beneficial as parents and carers will know what to expect from the setting at the outset and they will have the opportunity to ask questions. When practitioners, parents and carers work in partnership promoting the same behavioural values in similar ways, consistency can be achieved between the setting and the home. This is valuable for the child as it gives an increased sense of security and it is likely to ease the transition between home and the setting.

Some parents and carers may question aspects of a setting's policy. For instance, they may feel that the expectations of behaviour are either too high or too low, or perhaps they would deal with inappropriate behaviour differently themselves at home. They may at times be unhappy with the way a situation has been handled. In these circumstances it is important that issues are discussed openly. Practitioners should explain the

Key Terms

Rationale
Thinking or reasoning that underpins a statement, action, approach or ethos.

rationale behind their policy and their actions. However, it is important for practitioners to listen carefully to what parents and carers have to say, and to monitor and adapt their procedures when appropriate to do so.

Deepak's dilemma

The dad of four-year-old Deepak tells key worker Keirra that his son was upset this morning and that he did not want to come to pre-school. This has stemmed from the fact that he was told off towards the end of the last session, just before he went home, for pushing another child. He has been unduly worried that he is still in trouble with the practitioner.

Although practitioners must be consistent in their approach to dealing with unacceptable behaviour whenever it occurs, Keirra is concerned and wants to make sure that Deepak does not experience these ongoing feelings again.

She tells Deepak's dad that she will explain the situation to her colleagues, so that the adults can ensure that even if Deepak is told off towards the end of a session, he has the opportunity to make restitution (i.e. make up for it) before he goes home. He can then feel that the matter is over with, and end the session on a positive note. Keirra and Deepak's dad agree to talk again to monitor the situation.

When his dad has left reassured, Keirra asks Deepak to help her set out some toys. She is then able to thank him and praise him for his efforts, clearly giving him her approval.

➤ *The new adapted procedure should ensure that Deepak's behaviour is managed in a consistent way that will not be detrimental to his well-being. What may have happened if Keirra had not responded to the parent's concern?* **K3D693**

➤ *Why did Keirra want to create a situation that allowed her to give Deepak praise, indicating her approval?* **K3D699**

Evidence-based individual behaviour programmes

Sometimes it is necessary to plan a behaviour programme for an individual child. This is in line with, but in addition to, the behaviour policy that applies to all (the policy should cover individual behaviour programmes as one of the strategies used for managing children's behaviour). This means that particular behaviour goals are identified to suit an individual child, and strategies are planned to help them achieve the goals.

An example of this is the use of a sticker chart. A child may receive a sticker for reaching behaviour goals throughout the day – for sitting at the table at mealtimes for instance. When a child has earned a set number of stickers, this may lead to a further reward – a small toy or a trip to the park perhaps.

There may also be planned strategies for dealing with inappropriate behaviour from that child, again tailored to suit them.

Individual behaviour programmes may be necessary if:

- A child frequently/persistently displays challenging behaviour
- A child's behaviour is inconsistent with their age
- A child's behaviour has changed recently
- A child has been identified as in need of specialist help and practitioners are asked to work in partnership with parents, carers and specialists. This could be due to an impairment such as a learning difficulty, communication difficulty or attention deficit.

If practitioners suspect an individual behaviour plan may be necessary, it is important that it is based on evidence of the child's behaviour. Practitioners should start to build up a picture of the child's current behaviour patterns. This is done by observing and recording what inappropriate behaviour the child exhibits, when it occurs and the circumstances. It is important to notice how the behaviour is responded to by adults and other children, and what effect this has. Much can also be learned by noting when a child displays positive behaviour.

Days of the week	Morning	Lunch-time	Afternoon
Monday 			
Tuesday 			
Wednesday 			
Thursday 			
Friday			

A sticker chart

Practitioners should work in partnership with parents and carers to gather evidence as they will generally know their child better than anyone else. Talking with them also enables the practitioner to understand the child's behaviour at home.

Reviewing and discussing the record of a child's behaviour will help practitioners to identify the primary goals to address. The best way to support children to reach their goals should be planned, along with the best strategies for managing inappropriate behaviour. Practitioners, parents and carers (and where appropriate other specialists) should discuss the programme to ensure consistency, giving the programme the best chance of success. The details of the agreed programme should be recorded.

Depending on age, needs and abilities, practitioners may be able to discuss the planned approach with the child concerned. It is important to take the opportunity to do this where appropriate. A programme has a better chance of success when a child fully understands what is going to happen and is in agreement with the plan. Listen to children's points of view and negotiate with them where possible, checking their understanding. When they feel a sense of ownership and involvement and they are looking forward to rewards (tangible or intangible), children are generally motivated to work towards their goals.

Once the programme is underway, practitioners should continue to monitor and record children's behaviour patterns as before. Over time practitioners will be able to see the impact of the programme by considering this evidence. If the measures taken seem to be working, they can be persisted with until the child reaches their goal or until their behaviour is effectively managed. If the measures are not successful new strategies may need to be introduced. Once a child has adopted a new behaviour and it has become ingrained it may be appropriate to end the programme or to focus on a new goal.

Communication difficulties, learning difficulties and attention deficits

Communication difficulties, learning difficulties and attention deficits are likely to impact on children's behaviour. All children are different though, and much will depend on the degree of the difficulty or deficit.

Children with communication difficulties, learning difficulties and attention deficits may have an Individual Education Plan (IEP) that has been drawn up as part of their special needs assessment. In this case, behaviour programmes must complement and fit in with the IEP.

Communication difficulties may impact on behaviour because:

- Children may have difficulty understanding the meaning and structure of language and therefore understanding boundaries and instructions
- Children may have difficulty expressing themselves, leading to frustration when other people do not understand their feelings.

In addition, children with learning difficulties may have difficulty understanding and learning to comply with behaviour boundaries and goals.

Children with attention deficits may have a range of traits that make it difficult for them to behave as their peers do (see the diagram opposite). The majority of the traits are either rooted in difficulties with inattention or difficulties with impulsivity (being impulsive). Some children may display only one or two traits, others may have many.

The degree of the traits may also vary. Some children take medication that helps them – some children's behaviour can start to change as their medication wears off. There may be a time gap before the next dose is due to be taken.

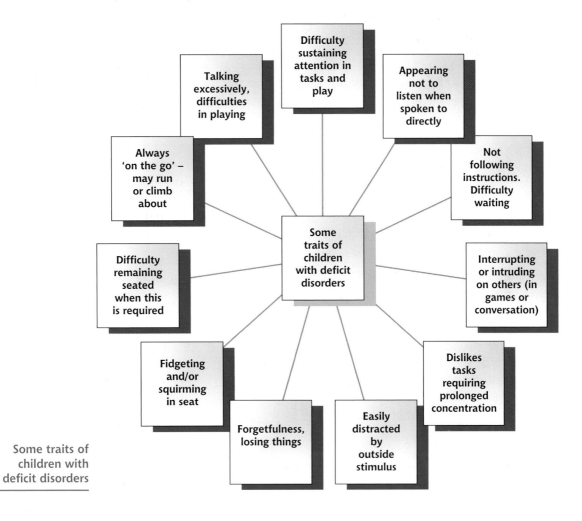

Difficulty sustaining attention in tasks and play

Appearing not to listen when spoken to directly

Talking excessively, difficulties in playing

Not following instructions. Difficulty waiting

Always 'on the go' – may run or climb about

Some traits of children with deficit disorders

Interrupting or intruding on others (in games or conversation)

Difficulty remaining seated when this is required

Dislikes tasks requiring prolonged concentration

Fidgeting and/or squirming in seat

Forgetfulness, losing things

Easily distracted by outside stimulus

Some traits of children with deficit disorders

Are you ready for assessment?

Element 337.1

Implement behaviour policies, procedures and strategies

You need to show that you can competently implement behaviour policies, procedures and strategies. To do this you will need to be directly observed by your assessor and present other types of evidence. The amount and type of evidence you need to present will vary. You should plan this with your assessor.

Direct observation by your assessor

Observation and/or expert witness testimony is the required assessment method to be used to evidence some of each element in this unit. If your assessor is unable to observe you, s/he will identify an expert in your workplace who will provide testimony of your work-based performance. Usually your assessor or expert witness will observe you in real work activities and this should provide most of the evidence for the performance criteria for the elements in this unit.

Preparing to be observed

You must show your assessor that you can identify appropriate policies and procedures for behaviour. You must also show that you can liaise with the appropriate people to plan programmes to respond to challenging behaviour in individual children, and that you can implement the agreed approach, monitoring the effects of strategies and procedures on individuals. You must show that you can adapt the planned approach

appropriately when required, and that you can listen to and negotiate with children.

Other types of evidence

You will need to present different types of evidence in order to:

- Cover criteria not observed by your assessor
- Show that you have the required knowledge, understanding and skills.

Such evidence could include:

- Work products such as consultation plans or records
- Case studies, projects, assignments and reflective accounts of your work
- Confidential records such as documentation relating to individual children's behaviour programmes. These should not be placed in your portfolio – they must remain in their usual location and be referred to in the assessor records in your portfolio.

Promote positive aspects of behaviour

Element **337.2**

⌇ Reasons for inappropriate behaviour

K3D697
K3D698
K3D700
K3D701

Most children want to have the approval of adults, and good practitioners use positive strategies to encourage desirable behaviour (see Element CCLD 337.1). Yet all children display inappropriate or challenging behaviour sometimes. Some children frequently display challenging behaviour over a long or short period. So why does this behaviour occur, and how should practitioners manage it?

Challenging behaviour is often a response to a child's immediate feelings and emotions, or an event in their life. Finding the reason helps practitioners to approach the behaviour in the best way. Sometimes causes are easy to spot. Examples include:

- When a child is tired or unwell, they may feel fractious and irritable. They may fall out with their friends easily as a result

- If children are bored, or if they feel they are not being supervised. Such children may need something different and interesting to do, or to know that an adult is close by

- Jealousy may prompt a child to take a friend's toy away, or to hurt them

- Frustration/anger at not being able to have what they want may cause a child to have a tantrum, for example in the supermarket

- Frustration/anger at not being able to achieve something may prompt a child to behave inappropriately. A child who is 'out' during a game may protest verbally, get cross and cry

- Anxiety/stress at being in unfamiliar circumstances, such as the first day at a new school.

Sometimes reasons for inappropriate behaviour are hidden, unconscious or in the past. This is complicated further by the fact that different children may respond to the same events or the same feelings by behaving in very different ways. For instance, one child who has been abused may become very quiet and withdrawn as a result, whilst another may become aggressive or violent. In these cases, challenging behaviour may be presented over a longer period of time. There is more information about the causes of challenging behaviour in Element 301.3 of Unit CCLD 301, Develop and promote positive relationships. You should read this in conjunction with this unit.

Link   **Unit CCLD 301** Develop and promote positive relationships

A firm and respectful approach

You must always maintain a respectful approach when you are interacting with children, even if they are in trouble. The well-being of children is paramount. You must never seek to control a child by intimidating them, instead you should intervene sensitively. Remember that you are a role model for children. You do not want children to lose their temper with people or to shout at them, so you must not behave like that yourself. You must remain calm and controlled. However, when you are setting boundaries and when you are dealing with instances of inappropriate behaviour you should be firm and clear about the behaviour you want.

Clearly defined boundaries

It is important that the boundaries set are appropriate to the age, needs and abilities of children. They should reflect the setting's behaviour policy, and be agreed in advance with colleagues, families and, when appropriate, with the children concerned and other professionals (see Element 337.1).

Key Terms

Defined boundaries
Clear, firm boundaries for children's behaviour.

It is up to practitioners to help children understand boundaries whilst communicating to them that the boundaries are firm. This is known as defining boundaries. It is done through a consistent approach. When children are about to overstep a boundary, practitioners can take the opportunity to remind them of the boundary and why it exists. For instance, a practitioner may say, 'Remember that we all need to wait our turn. That way the game is fair, and everyone has fun.' Children learn from this, and often it is enough to stop them in their tracks and deter them from inappropriate behaviour.

Sometimes a practitioner can see a source of potential conflict and they can distract a child to avoid problems. This works particularly well with younger children. For instance, if one child is trying to steal a toy away from another, a practitioner may introduce a new toy to play with, successfully distracting them from potential conflict.

Lack of consistency

If consistency is lacking, children will become confused. For instance, if some practitioners let children have extra turns during a board game to keep the peace, a child will learn that it is worth trying to get an extra turn rather than waiting for theirs because sometimes they are rewarded. The same applies if one practitioner varies their approach, sometimes allowing certain behaviour and sometimes not allowing it. This can make children feel insecure – they are not sure what is required of them, and they never know what reaction their behaviour will get.

Implement procedures to manage behaviour

When inappropriate behaviour occurs, adults need to promptly but calmly show that they disapprove of the behaviour. They may also need to apply a sanction – this is a further step which is implemented as a result of the behaviour in order to manage it. The followings strategies to manage behaviour are helpful.

- Facial expressions

  A disapproving look (maintaining a few seconds of eye contact if possible) is an effective way of showing children that they are overstepping a boundary. It can be used in conjunction with other strategies. If a child is already aware of a boundary, a look may be enough on its own to prompt them to think about what they are doing, causing them to alter their behaviour accordingly.

- No

  A firm, simple no is an appropriate way to make even very young children aware of a boundary. It is also useful to quickly halt a child's behaviour – it can stop them from doing something dangerous for instance (the consequences of their action can be discussed once they are safe). If 'no' is to have this effect it should not be used all the time, so that children take notice when they do hear it. Phrase your instructions positively whenever possible. Instead of 'No running in the corridor!' try the more pleasant, 'Please walk in the corridor'. No must also mean no. Do not say no and then give in to children – it teaches them that it is worth not complying because they may get their way if they resist you for long enough. Similarly, never say you will carry out a sanction if an aspect of behaviour reccurs unless you mean it.

- Consequences

  Children need to be aware of the consequences of their actions. This helps them to learn why boundaries are in place and to accept them. Children may not understand why their behaviour is unacceptable unless they are told. A practitioner may say for instance, 'You must not run up the slide because the children coming down will bang into you, and people will get hurt. Please go up the steps instead'. Sometimes it is necessary to point out that if a child continues to behave that way, a sanction (such as time out or limiting children's choices) will have to be applied as a consequence. Children often need to be told why swear words or name-calling is inappropriate and hurtful.

- Time out

   Time out is a sanction, but it should not be used as a punishment. It allows children to clam down and take stock of a situation by removing them from the source of conflict or temptation. Children should feel that this is the purpose of time out – they should not be made to feel that they are being rejected from the group. This strategy is particularly effective with older children and for handling aggression. In the case of aggression, it is preferable to take children somewhere quiet away from others if possible, and to stay with the child until they calm down. You must remain calm and in control yourself – this is particularly important when children have lost control of themselves as this can be frightening for them and for you. After a period of time out, practitioners should talk to children, resolving any remaining issues if necessary and smoothing their transition back into the activities of the group.

- Limiting children's choices

   If a child continues to behave inappropriately it may be necessary to limit the choices available to them by taking away the resource or equipment they are using. Alternatively they may be redirected to another activity (perhaps something calmer). This course of action can be effective and called for, but it should be used sparingly as it does limit the opportunities for play and learning that are available to that child.

   A practitioner might say, 'I have asked you to stop running up the slide. If you carry on doing it you will have to go and play with something else, otherwise someone will get hurt'.

Physical restraint

Rarely, in extreme circumstances, it may be necessary to physically restrain a child to prevent them from hurting themselves or somebody else. If such an event occurs, you must use the minimum force possible. You should record the incident in the setting's incident book and report it to your superiors and the child's parents or carers as soon as possible.

Reins and harnesses must only be used to keep young children safe – when they are in a high chair for instance. Children should NEVER be restrained for punishment, either physically or by reins or harnesses.

When it comes to defining boundaries and dealing with behaviour, you should ensure that you communicate information in a way that children can understand. You must take their age, needs and abilities into consideration (see Unit CCLD 303 Promote children's development).

Key Terms

Sanction
A step that is implemented as a result of inappropriate behaviour, e.g. time out, or taking away equipment.

Unclear (or ambiguous) directions can confuse children. If they do not do what is required of them due a misunderstanding, they may get into further trouble. Rather than saying to a young child, 'You upset Callum so you should go and make friends again', a practitioner could say, 'Callum was upset when you took his toy away. Please go and say sorry to him'. This is a clear instruction, and the child will know what to do.

When children continue to present challenging behaviour, it may be necessary to implement an evidence-based individual behaviour programme (see Element 337.1).

 Link   **Unit CCLD 303** Promote children's development

Rewarding compliance

When a child complies by altering their behaviour, practitioners should respond immediately by demonstrating their approval – a smile, nod or a thank you would all be appropriate. It is important to acknowledge compliance so that a child can see that they are valued as an individual – it was only their behaviour that was disapproved of, and now they have altered it they can feel acceptance once again. This protects children's self-esteem. Children will also be more likely to comply again in the future.

If an adult does not notice or reward positive behaviour, but does take notice of inappropriate behaviour, children may begin to behave inappropriately to seek attention. They may feel that even negative attention is better than no attention at all. If this occurs, practitioners can try rewarding children with plenty of attention when they are behaving appropriately, whilst ignoring inappropriate behaviour as much as possible unless it is dangerous or upsetting for other children.

Key Terms

Compliance
Children co-operating with requests.
(National Occupational Standards)

Problem-solving between children

All children will have problems with other children at some time. Learning to get along and co-operate with other people is an important life skill for everyone. Practitioners can help children to learn how to handle disagreements and disputes positively. The extent to which children are able to this will depend on their age, needs and abilities, and this should be taken into consideration (see Unit CCLD 303 Promote children's development). When working with younger children practitioners can ask questions to prompt them to identify their problems and to come up with their own solutions. This is important as there will not always be adults on hand to step in as children grow and become more independent.

Link   **Unit CCLD 303** Promote children's development

Learning to get along is an important life skill

When working with older children, practitioners need to resist the temptation to intervene in children's problems right away, giving them the opportunity to resolve things for themselves as long their behaviour is not dangerous or so inappropriate that it should be stopped immediately (in the case of bullying for example).

Resolving conflict

Four-year-old Jordon and Toby are playing with the sand. There is only one sieve. Each has hold of it and both children are attempting to pull it away. This is a familiar scene in any setting. By the time they are four, most children will have had plenty of experience of an adult settling this type of dispute for them. These children are likely to know how this is done.

Marcus, a practitioner, intervenes. He asks the children to put down the sieve and to tell him what the matter is. Both say they want to play with the item. Marcus says, 'Oh, and there's only one. What can we do?' Jordon suggests that they take it in turns to play with the sieve. Marcus says, 'That sounds like a good idea. What do you think Toby?' Toby agrees.

➤ *Why is it good for Jordon and Toby to think about how they can solve their dispute for themselves?* **K3D693**

Are you ready for assessment?
Promote positive aspects of behaviour

You need to show that you can competently promote positive aspects of behaviour. To do this you will need to be directly observed by your assessor and present other types of evidence. The amount and type of evidence you need to present will vary. You should plan this with your assessor.

Direct observation by your assessor

Observation and/or expert witness testimony is the required assessment method to be used to evidence some of each element in this unit. If your assessor is unable to observe you, s/he will identify an expert in your workplace who will provide testimony of your work-based performance. Usually your assessor or expert witness will observe you in real work activities and this should provide most of the evidence for the performance criteria for the elements in this unit.

Preparing to be observed

You must show your assessor that you can adopt a firm and respectful approach when promoting positive aspects of behaviour, and that you can set limits and boundaries appropriately. You must show that you can give appropriate directions and choices within the boundaries of acceptable behaviour, and implement agreed procedures when children continue to challenge. You must show that you can encourage co-operation and problem solving and positively reward compliance.

➤

Other types of evidence

You will need to present different types of evidence in order to:

- Cover criteria not observed by your assessor
- Show that you have the required knowledge and understanding and skills.

Such evidence could include:

- Work products such as consultation plans or records

- Case studies, projects, assignments and reflective accounts of your work
- Confidential records such as documentation relating to individual children's behaviour programmes. These should not be placed in your portfolio – they must remain in their usual location and be referred to in the assessor records in your portfolio.

Check your knowledge

- What is the purpose of a behaviour policy?   **K3D692**
- What is meant by a firm and respectful approach to goals and boundaries? **K3D697**
- Why should boundaries be clearly defined?   **K3D698**
- What is the link between behaviour and self-esteem?   **K3D699**
- Identify some possible underlying causes for instances of inappropriate behaviour.   **K3D700**

Reflective practice

Identify an occasion when you have found a child's inappropriate behaviour challenging to handle. Make notes about what happened, how you responded and the impact that had. Would you do anything differently if the incident occurred again? If so, make a note of how you would respond.

Index